Women and Work in Asia and the Pacific

Women and Work in Asia and the Pacific
Experiences, challenges and ways forward

*Edited by Jane Parker, Marian Baird,
Noelle Donnelly and Rae Cooper*

DEDICATION

Lina Cabaero was a woman of valour and a woman for all seasons. She was everywhere, with everyone, with full commitment, power and love. Lina had been the chairperson, and later treasurer, of the Immigrant Women's Speakout Association (IWSA) in Australia. She also held positions as the coordinator of the Asian Women at Work (AWatW) and Philippine Australia Community Services Inc. (PACSI).

Even when Lina was terminally ill, she continued to contribute to campaigns for migrants' rights. In these campaigns, she used her skills in cultural work, singing progressive songs while strumming her guitar. Her talent as a true artist was in depicting the socio-economic and political realities of life. Lina was able to visualise her views by working with deprived sectors in society, especially workers. She had intended to co-author the chapter on Philippine women workers in this book, but passed away on 8 August 2021. We dedicate this work to Lina.

CONTENTS

Foreword 8
Elizabeth Broderick

Introduction: Working women in Asia Pacific 11
Jane Parker, Marian Baird, Noelle Donnelly and Rae Cooper

1. Working women in Aotearoa New Zealand 40
Jane Parker and Noelle Donnelly

2. Working women in Australia 61
Marian Baird, Rae Cooper and Daniel Dinale

3. Working women in Japan 84
Shingou Ikeda and Kazufumi Sakai

**Japan in focus: Working women and men's changing
family responsiblities** 109
Shingou Ikeda and Kazufumi Sakai

4. Working women in China 114
Huiping Xian

5. Working women in Cambodia 133
Kristy Ward and Michele Ford

6. Working women in India 149
Vibhuti Patel

India in focus: Women, technology and the future of work 173
Binitha V. Thampi

7. Working women in Sri Lanka 182
Kasuni Weerasinghe and Thilini Meegaswatta

8. Working women in Fiji 203
Natalia D'Souza

9. Working women in Pakistan 221
Fatima Junaid and Afia Saleem

10. Working women in the Philippines 237
Daisy Arago, Jane Brock and Peter Brock

**The Philippines in focus: Breaking-in — union women
and young leaders** 260
Cedric Bagtas

References 273
About the contributors 347
Acknowledgements 355
Index 357

FOREWORD

Women and girls across the globe are disadvantaged by discriminatory regulation, policy, practices, behaviours and attitudes. Although many countries have made progress in some areas for women at work and beyond, gender equality has not been achieved in any nation, with undertakings to eliminate inequalities being only partially pursued.

In 2010, the United Nations (UN) Human Rights Council established a working group on the issue of discrimination, in law and practice, against women. Renewed in 2019, this mandate was renamed as the Working Group on Discrimination Against Women and Girls (UN Office of the High Commissioner for Human Rights, 2022). That year, the Working Group consulted extensively with national experts around the world on key issues and challenges for working women and their communities. In the Asia Pacific region, the Expert Group Meeting, which was held at the University of Sydney, involved representatives from trade unions, civil society organisations, employer organisations, universities and elsewhere. I would like to thank Marian Baird, Rae Cooper and the team at the Women and Work Research Group for their collaboration in organising this Expert Group Meeting.

This book extends the Working Group's (2020) global thematic report to the UN Human Rights Council, which focused on four themes — demography, globalisation, technological development and sustainability — with deeper analyses of working women in 10 countries in Asia Pacific, as well as a cross-country comparison. It confirms the report's observation that working women's challenges are substantial and require coordinated responses while nuancing our understanding of how the four thematic areas intersect with the lives of working women in different national contexts.

Drawing on a wide range of quantitative and qualitative evidence, *Women and Work in Asia and the Pacific* also provides a much-needed examination of working women's challenges and opportunities during the Covid-19 pandemic and with an eye to the future. The intensification of already-diverse work arrangements, labour forces and contextual dynamics in the region underscores the need for such analysis of the challenges and opportunities faced by working women to inform seamless, multilateral, multilevel and context-sensitive initiatives that will significantly ameliorate gender equality and inclusion.

Elizabeth Broderick AO
Independent Expert
Working Group on Discrimination Against Women and Girls
United Nations Human Rights Council

Introduction: Working women in Asia Pacific

Jane Parker, Marian Baird, Noelle Donnelly and Rae Cooper

For the most part, women's engagement in paid work is a more recent phenomenon than it is for men. However, in many national contexts, women's formal labour force participation (LFP) rate has escalated over the last century, and particularly since the Second World War (Ortiz-Ospina, Tzvetkova & Roser, 2018), with women also forming the mainstay of a large informal workforce in most low- and lower-middle-income countries (International Labour Organization [ILO], 2018). Women have also always engaged in, and often carried out the bulk of, unpaid work in their homes and communities. Across these spheres of work activity, women and men have long perceived and experienced gendered challenges and, sometimes, opportunities. This reflects the existence of environmental dynamics, including institutional arrangements and regulation that impact differentially on different worker groups in their places of work, in their domestic settings and in other gendered 'regimes' (Walby, 2020), and of related factors that emanate from 'within' (e.g. women and men's confidence and capacity to engage in their workplace and challenge biased attitudes and workplace processes).

Much has been written about the nature of the progress made and challenges faced by working women at micro, meso and macro levels in individual countries (e.g. UN Global Compact, 2022), emphasising that gender inequities persist across the globe. This is also broadly evidenced by quantitative and qualitative indicators, ranging from the statistics of international gender equity indexes and the evolution of concern with gender in various national regulatory systems to the enduring resonance of International Women's Day and other cross-national initiatives for change.

In 2019, the United Nations (UN) Working Group on Discrimination Against Women and Girls consulted with national experts on key issues and challenges for working women and their communities. In Asia Pacific, the regional Expert Group Meeting took place in September that year at the University of Sydney in partnership with the university's Women, Work and Leadership Research Network. This consultation involved experts from trade unions and civil society organisations, employers' organisations, academics and other relevant stakeholders.

This pre-Covid-19 event was framed by four connected themes — demography, globalisation, technological development and sustainability — each of which is itself multidimensional. It informed the Working Group's global thematic report on women's human rights in the changing world of work, which was submitted to the UN Human Rights Council in June 2020. The report observed that working women's challenges are significant and require coordinated responses (UN Working Group for Discrimination Against Women and Girls, 2020). However, its high-level findings also emphasised an urgent need for deeper regional and national analysis in terms of how these thematic areas intersect with the lives of working women.

This book draws on the UN's four themes — and their challenges and opportunities — to examine selected countries in Asia Pacific. This region, despite being home to nearly 60 per cent of the world's population (UN Economic and Social Commission for Asia and the Pacific, 2021), and including nations that span considerable gender and other forms of diversity, has a dearth of comparative national studies that centre on the challenge/opportunity areas for working women and their communities. The timing of this work has also enabled our chapter authors to proffer insights on the ramifications of the Covid-19 pandemic for demographic, globalisation, sustainability and technological considerations for working women and their communities.

APPROACH AND STRUCTURE OF THIS BOOK

The situation for working women is examined in 10 countries: Aotearoa New Zealand, Australia, Japan, China, Cambodia, India, Sri Lanka, Fiji, Pakistan and the Philippines. Conjointly, these countries emphasise both Asia Pacific's highly diverse and shared characteristics in terms of their scale, regulatory environment, development stage, economic structure, culture, religion, politics, history, institutions and other terms (e.g. see Zanko, 2003; Hansen, 2021). Drawing on primary and secondary data sources, our contributors highlight the global, regional and specific nature of challenges and opportunities faced by working women and how their effects are mediated by country characteristics. However, they also point out the diversity that is found *among* working women (e.g. with regard to their ethnicity, age, carer and domestic responsibilities, geographical location and workplace role), contributing to their varying experiences of work.

Each chapter opens with a précis of the economic, employment, labour market and other contextual circumstances of a country. These considerations inform subsequent sections on the four areas of challenge and opportunity — globalisation, technological development, sustainability and demographic change — for working women and their communities. Our contributors then either consider each of these dimensions in relation to the influence of the Covid-19 pandemic or address the implications of the pandemic for working women in a separate section. Each chapter concludes with recommendations for improving the situation for working women within a particular national context. For several countries, there are also shorter contributions that elaborate on themes from the preceding chapter. Thus, the analysis of working women in Japan is extended with an account of men's changing family responsibilities; the chapter on working women in India is followed by a shorter contribution that focuses on women's employment, technology and the future of work; and the Philippines chapter is supplemented by an examination of the development of women and youth's engagement in unions, with a view to promoting equality, decent work and social and core labour rights.

Figure 1 depicts the multiple levels of analysis and key thematic areas covered in relation to working women in each country chapter. The analytical levels highlighted on the left-hand side of the figure often interconnect (e.g. the informal economy[1] in some countries can be influenced by transnational factors; global institutional arrangements can permeate country and sub-country institutions and arrangements to produce shared and divergent impacts on women who work).

The four dimensions of thematic challenge/opportunity shown on the right-hand side of Figure 1 are similarly intertwined at country and other levels. The double-ended arrow stresses the influence of contextual features and thematic challenges/opportunities at different analytical levels on working women, *and* working women's individual and collective agency and influence — realised and potential — on their context. Using this schema, in this introduction, we supplement each chapter's country coverage with a comparative assessment of the four thematic areas in relation to working women, and outline cross-national recommendations to encourage working women's progress.

DEMOGRAPHIC CHALLENGES AND OPPORTUNITIES

The demographic characteristics of the Asian and Pacific countries studied here are many and varied. They cover the full spectrum of population size and complexity, and present many challenges and some opportunities for

---

1   An informal economy comprises diverse economic activities and jobs that are not regulated or protected by the state. Along with domestic workers, it includes waged workers who work for and are paid by companies but do not have secure contracts, legal protection or social security.

Figure 1: Analytical and contextual framework for assessing the situation of working women in Asia Pacific nations

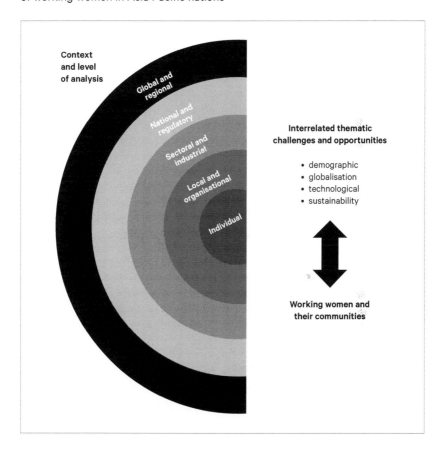

greater equality between women and men. To begin with, their populations vary enormously and thus present quite different issues relating to equality and inequality between the sexes, prosperity and poverty and future sustainability. The two most populous nations are China and India, with around 1.4 billion people each, followed by Pakistan with 220 million people, Japan with a population of 126 million, and the Philippines with 110 million people. The next group includes Australia with 26 million, Sri Lanka with nearly 21 million, Cambodia with almost 17 million and Aotearoa New Zealand with approximately 5 million. The small island nation of Fiji has a population of just under one million.

Population size is not necessarily a demographic challenge on its own, although sustainability issues will likely come to the fore. However, the structure of a population is often a challenge and creates pressure points. For instance, in countries such as Pakistan, China and India, the sex ratio is unequal, with more males than females — a result of gendered beliefs and actions that favour baby boys, creating later pressures on family formation with males unable to find partners. In Aotearoa New Zealand, the multi-racial nature of the population sees different patterns of reproduction and mortality, with Māori and Pasifika having shorter life expectancy and higher birth rates. This has resulted in this country undergoing a restructure or 'demographic transformation' of its population.

Around the globe, the ageing of populations is an increasing concern, and this is represented in many (although not all) of the countries examined in this book. Population ageing occurs as below-replacement fertility rates become normalised and mortality rates decline, the latter a result of medical, nutritional and environmental advances that enable people to live longer. The challenge of ageing populations and declining fertility rates is evident in countries such as China, Japan and Australia, where fertility rates are well below the replacement rate of 2.1.

Population decline leads to reductions in the size of the workforce and therefore a lower tax base, thus putting future economic growth and progress at risk. In response, governments have introduced various policies to stimulate population growth or, to be more explicit about the gendered implications of these policies, to encourage women to have more babies. In Australia, for example, cash incentives were initially used, and a paid parental leave scheme was later introduced, partly in response to declining fertility rates. A universal quality early child education and care system, the most obvious gap in the policy space to enable women to work and reproduce, has not been provided, with parents reliant on a patchy private system of provision subsidised by the government.

In Japan, the country with the oldest population profile in the world (Statista, 2022), the problem of family formation is related to multiple factors, including a growth in single women households eschewing traditional family patterns, which some argue is a result of discriminatory practices against married women in the job market. In an attempt to combat declining fertility, Japan has enacted laws for employers relating to the provision of childcare and anti-discrimination to encourage women to have more children, but to date these policies have not turned the fertility rate around.

By contrast, to limit population growth, China introduced its well-known one-child policy in 1979. This policy was a success, but eventually led to a decline in the overall population, which is now a significant concern to the government. In 2021, the one-child policy was replaced with a two-child policy, and later a maximum of three children per couple was allowed. Again, these changes in policy do not seem to have had the desired outcome of increasing fertility rates in China.

Pakistan represents a different demographic challenge. Rather than a declining population, its population is increasing — a result of high fertility rates, low contraceptive use and people marrying at a younger age, among other causes. But the challenge for this nation concerns how to integrate women more equally into society and the workforce. Women's LFP is increasing slowly, but from a very low base and the majority of people have access only to the informal labour market.

In other countries, the population is younger and the problems and challenges are different. In Cambodia, for example, almost 50 per cent of the population is under 25 years, although the age distribution is becoming more balanced as the country continues to recover from its losses under the Khmer Rouge regime. This has gender implications. Compared to other countries where the sex ratio favours males, in Cambodia there is a prominence of female-headed households, which 'can make them both less wealthy, but also more financially stable and secure' (see Chapter 5).

India is an example of a country that has experienced an increase in the working-age population (15–64 years of age) and demographers estimate that this boost will continue until 2055. At the same time, India is experiencing a decline in fertility rates, with the average number of children born to a woman in her lifetime falling from 3.2 in 2000 to 2.1 in 2020. Paradoxically, there has also been a decline in women's workforce participation. Like Pakistan, India has a very large informal sector, much of which is beyond the reach of government policies that might try to address this imbalance.

There are other gendered patterns in ageing, as in most cases women live longer than men. This problem is highlighted in Fiji, with women comprising a greater proportion of the ageing population and 'more likely to experience economic insecurity, poverty, and vulnerability to illness' (see Chapter 8), a problem that is exacerbated if they live in rural regions. Poverty and homelessness among older women is also increasing in Australia, and is a major concern to many advocates and welfare groups.

Ageing populations may reduce the problem of providing childcare, but they increase the burden and responsibility of eldercare, which is often also borne by women. This is especially notable in China, and also in Australia and Aotearoa New Zealand, where women provide the majority of informal eldercare. In Japan, however, with the decreasing marriage rate, the number of male workers who provide care to an older family member is increasing. This may be an opportunity to increase men's role in care. But it is, in turn, concerning for employers who have traditionally used men as their core workforce and now worry about their departure.

A further consequence of ageing populations and shrinking workforces is the pressure that they put on governments to supplement the workforce through immigration. This is a problem anticipated in Aotearoa New Zealand as the country's workforce ages and shrinks. It is also one that Japan has had to confront for many years. Japan has responded with highly selective immigration measures for certain areas where there are serious workforce shortages, such as nursing, construction, shipbuilding and agriculture, along with a 'technical intern trainee system'. Australia has filled its workforce gaps through targeted immigration schemes of skilled workers. However, this approach was disrupted by the Covid-19 pandemic when the country's borders closed for two years. The pandemic has also induced a further decline in fertility in Australia, as women have both delayed and reduced their intentions to have children. This will have repercussions for years to come.

Demographic changes are intimately interwoven with the issue of gender, culture and workforce patterns. As the chapters in this book illustrate, these are complex and at times confronting challenges — and sometimes opportunities — which are manifesting at times in the same way and at other times in different ways in each of the countries under examination. Fundamentally, the problem is that women are expected to both participate in the paid workforce and provide unpaid care, and to reconcile social reproduction with market production, all without the appropriate structures and cultural supports to enable them to do so. This is becoming an even greater pressure for women, and for governments, as populations age and reconfigure. Demographic changes thus underscore sustainability and wellbeing issues for women workers and their communities.

CHALLENGES AND OPPORTUNITIES AROUND SUSTAINABILITY

Sustainability challenges and opportunities are escalating across the globe, with individual nations' progress on sustainable development varying markedly. For instance, of the 193 UN member states' total progress towards achieving all UN Sustainable Development Goals (SDGs), Aotearoa New Zealand ranks 23rd while Pakistan is 129th (Sachs et al., 2021). This underscores countries' sustainability priorities, impact levels and starting points; regulatory and institutional 'maturity'; resources; political will; and cultural mores.

In Asia and the Pacific, there are regulatory measures concerned with the environment, even in countries that contribute little to climate emissions. Yet it is these countries (e.g. Fiji), and often the women within them, that bear the brunt of these measures due to their geography, sectoral make-up and other factors. However, our contributors identify a relative inattention to, and fledgling efforts around, sustainable development in terms of climate change and working women despite its known gendered consequences. Thus, while there are examples of policies that seek green growth in sectors where women form a significant proportion of employees, short-sighted policies can negatively impact on agricultural and other workers, many of whom are female waged labourers or unpaid family workers.

Furthermore, in countries including Australia and Sri Lanka, men tend to dominate in industries likely to be directly impacted by relevant policy action while women are more economically and socially vulnerable to the impacts of climate mitigation strategies. For example, relocation due to natural disasters can amplify issues for working women due to a gendered division of labour, whereby their care burden and role in preserving food security increase, and they face a greater threat of gender-based violence by shifting away from the protections of communal living and by being in disaster contexts generally (Halton, 2018). Women also experience reduced ownership, disrupted access to resources and work opportunities, and thus greater vulnerability to exploitation and debt traps.

In some nations, including Japan, loss of work due to natural disasters is taken more seriously for men, who are still seen as the main household earner, than for part-time working women, despite such work sustaining the livelihoods of single women and mothers. Deeply embedded thinking around a gendered labour market and societal roles in these nations mutes women's voices, and constrains or does not record their significant, often expanding roles (particularly at the community level) in disaster strategy, prevention and recovery. This reinforces gender-specific difficulties when disasters occur, with rural women particularly vulnerable to climate change impacts.

Sustainability also relates to conflict and terrorist activity, with SDG 16 concerning the promotion of peaceful and inclusive societies. Many countries under review are peaceable or have encountered relatively isolated terrorist incidences (e.g. Aotearoa New Zealand, Australia, Japan). However, the wider region is more familiar with conflict and terrorism, with pervasive forms found in Pakistan, India, the Philippines and Sri Lanka, which rank 10th, 12th, 16th and 25th respectively on the 2022 Global Terrorism Index of terrorism impact (Institute for Economics and Peace, 2022). As our contributors observe, the impacts of conflict and terrorism on workers and wider society are complex and gendered, with implications for women's progress in work and beyond.

During crises or otherwise, the shared and unique aspects of national workscapes also contribute to gendered sustainability challenges. For example, the sizeable informal economy of developing or large nations such as China, Cambodia, Sri Lanka, India, the Philippines and Pakistan provides vital work opportunities for many women, particularly (other than in China) given their relatively low formal LFP rates and attendant gender inequality, poverty and sustainability challenges. However, the precarity of this work reflects an absence of secure contracts or regulatory protection (including personal safety and social security). And while gender-based occupational and industrial segregation occurs across the world, the particularly constrained and narrow labour market of many developing nations drives women and men to neighbouring countries in search of work. As noted in relation to Cambodia, many women in this situation experience physical and sexual assault, lack of social protection, forced labour, wage theft, unpaid overtime and exclusion from institutions and protections, given an ineffective or non-existent legal and regulatory framework. However, as noted above, working women in well- *and* less-regulated countries also continue to shoulder a disproportionately high, and in some cases increasing, share of unpaid work at home despite the need for equality in unpaid work in order to achieve equality in paid work (Elson, 2017), participation in society and wellbeing.

Furthermore, the worst forms of labour, including forced labour, modern slavery, human trafficking and exploitative child labour — often influenced by global transformation processes — vary in scale and longevity in different parts of the region. They are, for example, comparatively recent developments in Aotearoa New Zealand and Australia. Elsewhere, protective legislation and regulation tend to reflect greater familiarity with the gendered and other dimensions of these phenomena, though provisions and enforcement levels vary. The scourge of gender-based violence is also found throughout the region. This suggests that work precarity is only one trigger of such violence, which commonly and directly impacts on the sustainable development of working women and their communities. Some of the authors also show that this challenge is comparatively worse for certain groups of (working) women (e.g. Māori women in Aotearoa New Zealand), stressing the significance of women's intersectionality[2] and context in relation to sustainable development.

Gendered access to education, a portal to decent work, is confirmed in the following chapters to have implications for a country's ability to eradicate poverty and achieve sustainable development. In developing economies, including Cambodia and Pakistan, recent investments and progressive policies, and increased enrolments, particularly of girls, in education are improving women's position in society and labour market opportunities, although dropout levels constrain female literacy rates. However, families with little access to remote learning (e.g. due to a lack

---

2   This refers to women's social, ethnic, sexual, political and other forms of identity.

of ICT infrastructure or devices) face an increased risk of girls and boys engaging in child labour to augment household income.

Sustainable development for working women also encompasses social policy. This is keenly illustrated in China where family ties and support are an important source of reciprocity and trust, particularly since the early 1990s, when welfare supports were reduced. However, the one-child policy of the world's most populated country has been seen to undermine the sustainability of families (see above). Subsequent family policies have sought to increase family development capacity but factors such as high living costs, a low fertility rate, reduced intergenerational childcare and career pressures on women have inhibited couples from having bigger families. Furthermore, some employers' discriminatory perspectives reflect a belief that hiring a woman incurs extra costs, and some deny the promotion of professional women with a child, anticipating that they would avail themselves of the country's two- and now three-child policies[3] designed to stimulate the country's birth rate. However, existing family policies have not provided more targeted support for working women in the family, resulting in gender discrimination and a work–family imbalance, with increased risk for sustainable family development.

Sustainability challenges are thus wide-ranging and their gendered impacts have often been exacerbated by the Covid-19 pandemic. Devastating in its human toll, it has also caused job losses, pay cuts, increased under-employment and a greater need for re- and up-skilling. Reflecting global trends, women in Asia and the Pacific form the rump of those worst affected due to their concentration in 'recession industries', although varying levels of economic and health support reflect national pandemic responses and social security initiatives.

Declining job satisfaction during Covid-19 has also been greater for women, who form a high proportion of non-regular employees in sectors

---

3   Other countries in the region that have previously used a two-child policy include Singapore and Vietnam.

where notable work intensification and mental burdens have occurred. In developing areas, job losses in the informal sector and micro-enterprises, the cessation of remittances and little access to transportation during lockdowns and stay-at-home orders have increased the number of women and men pushed into poverty, and augmented the risk of child labour and wellbeing problems. Escalating domestic violence — the Covid 'shadow pandemic' (UN Women, not dated) — has been further fuelled in nations facing climate change-related disasters.

The pandemic has also curbed travel by migrant workers, their reduced remittances putting further pressure on households, and a lack of work presenting risks to gender gains. Increased access to education, particularly for girls, in some countries is also likely to be undermined, though some forms of study and business have gone online, with requisite re- and up-skilling by women and students who have internet access.

CHALLENGES AND OPPORTUNITIES OF GLOBALISATION

The structural changes taking place in global production and labour markets suggest that globalisation is in the 'midst of a transformation' (McKinsey, 2019). With predictions that Asia Pacific will account for over half of global GDP by 2040, and that China is reorienting itself towards a growing domestic consumer market, analysts note a change in the 'world's centre of gravity, a shift toward regionalisation, and the rise of Asia Pacific as the world's economic growth engine' (McKinsey, 2019; Legge & Lukaszuk, 2021).

The potential of globalisation as a force for greater gender equality has long been promoted (World Bank, 2011). Greater economic integration and interdependence through trade openness, technological diffusion and increased access to information and capital are the primary signifiers of globalisation that contribute to women's advancement through enhanced employment opportunities and economic empowerment, while incentivising governments to remove structural constraints on gender equality. Despite the intention, as the country accounts in this book suggest, globalisation, driven by neoliberal ideology, rarely leads to 'a rising tide' for all working women across the region but rather results in quite varied, complex and unequal outcomes for women, with some stark differences in the experiences of regulated versus unregulated countries.

Globalisation is linked to increases in women's LFP in Asia and the Pacific as the expected economic aspects of globalisation provide employment opportunities and financial resources for women (Gray, Kittilson & Sandholtz, 2006), especially for those in unregulated labour markets. For example, the creation of export processing zones and market extension in Cambodia and Sri Lanka has facilitated the movement of women from unpaid family labour to formal employment in the garment sector, thus providing economic independence for themselves and, in cases where they occupy breadwinner roles, that of their wider family.

Similarly, as a major recipient of foreign direct investment (FDI), China has also benefited from an influx of multinational companies and their 'best practice' human resource practices, many of which are focused on women's equality. Yet, this country case further highlights that globalisation driven by a neoliberal ideology that fails to challenge men's dominance and traditional gender stereotypes contributes little to women's advancement but rather results in additional expectations and burdens on their working lives. Globalisation thus provides employment opportunities for women but requires challenges to traditional gender stereotypes.

Globalisation processes also provide educational opportunities and international sources of casual labour. Greater economic interdependence creates opportunities for women to study overseas (e.g. both Japan and China have seen significant growth in this regard), as women seek to capitalise on their overseas education in the form of enhanced employment opportunities (e.g. foreign language skills are at a premium in the Japanese labour market). However, as Australia, Aotearoa New Zealand and Japan highlight, one country's 'brain drain' is another's (flexible and cheap) labour gain, with international students providing a significant source of casual labour for the hospitality and tourism industries. Yet, as noted in Japan, using women as 'cheap labour' based on economic arguments without associated changes to social mores and values serves to underpin women's position of sustained weakness.

Alongside wider engagement with international markets, increased international competition enables economies (especially less developed ones) to modernise and improve living standards while at the same time challenging gender equality. The Asia Pacific experience described here shows that the benefits of globalisation are not equally shared by all women, as the relocation of labour-intensive industries to developing economies has resulted in significant growth in informal sectors. Women in a number of the less regulated countries work predominantly in the informal sector — a sector that lacks the usual employment and human rights protections of formal employment. For example, in the Philippines, the creation of new employment opportunities in agri-business and mining industries has funnelled women into more specialised and 'dangerous roles' in workplaces that, again, afford little protection or collective voice.

International trade policies also affect labour migration. Declining welfare services and birth rates combined with ageing populations have contributed to rising demand for women workers from southern Asian Pacific countries in medical and care work. Countries including Aotearoa New Zealand, Australia and Japan have adjusted their migration policies (introduced short-term/temporary worker visas) to backfill gaps in labour supply and address skills shortages across selected industries. And in the cases of Australia and Japan, rising globalisation aligned with changing immigration policies has encouraged and channelled gendered migration flows to low-paid care work. Indeed, Japan set up Economic Partnership Agreements (EAPs) to source medical care workers from Indonesia, the Philippines and Vietnam. However, as noted for Australia, the closure of national borders in response to the Covid-19 pandemic and subsequent labour shortages has exposed the fragility of these migration-fed labour markets.

While migration can improve the career and living standards of skilled women, for low-skilled women entering less regulated and protected labour markets, the outcomes are not as positive, with reports that many women fall victim to increasing exploitation and abuse. For example, in Sri Lanka, globalisation has facilitated women's migration to the Middle East in search of domestic work that lacks legal protection and bargaining power, underscoring their vulnerability and the precariousness of their employment. The absence of effective mechanisms to regulate and protect migrants, particularly those that employ the services of labour market intermediaries or visa agents, as is the case with 'foreign technical intern trainees' in Japan, can also underline women's vulnerabilities and result in 'debt workers', where women carry additional financial burden resulting from their entry into a country.

Furthermore, labour mobility and migration affect the international flow of capital. Declining welfare supports in their home countries mean that, for a significant proportion of migrant women from Asia Pacific countries who occupy breadwinner roles, their families are dependent on international remittances — a dependency that, as is shown in Sri Lanka, came under threat with job losses during the recent pandemic. In contrast, men's employment has been prioritised over women's during a period of employment shortages in the cases of Pakistan and Fiji. In both countries, men's migration has resulted in additional burdens on women who are left to fend for themselves and assume solo care of their families.

We also observe that labour market flexibility can lead to greater precarity and employment insecurity, and in some cases labour displacement. Globalisation creates labour demands that favour flexible and temporary employment, with women increasingly meeting that demand. A prevailing pattern throughout many of the chapters concerns women's growing LFP being linked to the deregulation and flexibilisation of labour markets, resulting in the concentration of women in low-paid, low-skilled and part-time roles within industries that are particularly exposed to the negative impacts of global shocks like the pandemic, in which women have borne the brunt of job loss and reduced hours (Foley & Cooper,

2021; Parker, Sayers et al., 2022). For example, in Aotearoa New Zealand, increasing labour market flexibility has negatively impacted Māori, Pacific and migrant women workers, as many work in low-paid, low-skilled casual employment. Likewise, in India, it has contributed to the fragmentation of work and rise in 'gig work' for women — work that again offers little protection and is often underpaid.

Globalisation, premised on free trade, free mobility of trade, services and capital, and the diffusion of ICT and consumer patterns, has been embraced by all of the countries under examination, yet globalisation in a pandemic era is reshaping the nature of global interdependence. Global pandemic impacts are disproportionately borne and absorbed by women in both regulated and less regulated environments. And in countries where welfare supports are declining, women have to work harder in and outside their homes to avoid poverty. In short, women's increasing LFP needs to coincide with greater investment in their capabilities — that is, the associated economic benefits of globalisation need to be shared by all with significant protections for those working in informal sectors (Gray et al., 2006).

TECHNOLOGICAL CHALLENGES AND OPPORTUNITIES

Technological challenges and opportunities also intertwine with sustainability, globalisation and demographic developments, and each chapter in this collection addresses the gendered impact of technology on work and how unfolding technological change is likely to impact on women's working lives.

These discussions counter the narrative in popular discussions of technological change and the future of work that portrays technology as a largely benign force. Instead, the combined contributions suggest that preexisting inequalities and segregations in work and labour markets, coupled with the overwhelmingly male-dominated design and implementation of workplace technologies, can shape and amplify gender gaps at work.

Several common themes emerge. First, women have been employed in sectors and jobs that have been vulnerable to automation, leading to challenges to long-term economic security. Second, men are much more likely to be employed in jobs that shape and control new technologies, thus embedding gendered difference into their operation. And third, the Covid-19 pandemic has presented both technological challenges and opportunities for working women and gender equality that may reverberate into the future.

Some chapters (e.g. on Japan and China) point to the positive impact of technological change on women's working lives, through making new forms of work available to women; in building better access for women-owned businesses to markets and clients in a home country and abroad (e.g. in China and Cambodia); and in potentially offering networking and collectivisation opportunities for women workers, as has been the case in Fiji. In others, such as Chapter 7, on Sri Lanka, the authors argue that if the opportunities presented by technology were better understood by women workers they could capitalise on them as men currently do.

Overwhelmingly, however, the chapters present a more pessimistic picture, with a key theme being that the labour market, industry and occupational segregations shape women's interactions with technology. In India and Aotearoa New Zealand, for instance, industry restructuring and sectoral shifts since the 1990s have impacted women's working lives for the worse, positioning them outside of high-growth, high-skill 'sunrise' sectors and in low-skill and low-paid jobs with vulnerability to automation. Elsewhere, as in Fiji and Pakistan, this is referred to as a process of 'de-feminisation'.

Labour market changes are shown to have been geographically uneven across both the region represented in this collection as well as within individual countries such as Cambodia. Women working in rural and remote areas in countries like Japan and Fiji have even worse experiences due to restructuring, regional 'digital divides' and diasporas in search of better opportunities. The theme of the technologically enabled exploitation of women in the Global South by industry and clients in the North is thus observed in a number of countries, with the term 'digital coolie' used in the India chapter to describe women's role as 'ideal workers' in global supply chains, supplying high-quality output for very low wages.

Another key theme that emerges across the chapters is that as new technologies have been introduced and higher-level skills have been developed, these are captured and hoarded by men. Each chapter outlines how men dominate in the lucrative, secure jobs with career paths in growth areas of the economy, notably in the STEMM (science, technology, engineering, mathematics and medicine) fields.

For some countries, including Australia, it is noted that while 'gig work' and algorithmic management are typically associated with male-dominated jobs and sectors, such as transport, these forms of platform work have encroached into feminised sectors and jobs in the foundational economy (i.e. part of the economy that creates and distributes goods and services used by all because they support everyday life) such as aged and disability care, making already undervalued work even worse. Furthermore, it is observed for Aotearoa New Zealand, China, India, Australia and Pakistan that the imprinting of male biases into the design and roll-out of technologies means that the negative consequences of technological change on women will have long-lasting impacts on their job quality, earnings and career progression.

As with other themes addressed in this book, the Covid-19 pandemic has added to the work intensity and job stress of essential frontline health and care workers, the great majority of whom globally are women. A number of country accounts discuss the ways in which the pandemic period opened up access to remote and technologically enabled working, noting that this allowed sections of the female labour force to retain attachment to employment at a time of crisis, especially in more regulated contexts and for professional and managerial employees, as indicated in Australia and Aotearoa New Zealand. Our contributors, including those writing on Japan, signal hope that the experience of workers and employers of making remote work 'work' through the pandemic may lead to better long-term access to sustainable remote working after the pandemic recedes. They also caution that the 'double burden' of paid and unpaid work — which has intensified significantly during the pandemic — might be made worse by long-term remote working (e.g. China). As well as increasing the gender gaps in unpaid work and the associated exhaustion for women, there is much caution that technology enabled work from home might also lead to missed promotion and development opportunities and the potential further ghettoisation of women into lower-level jobs.

CROSS-NATIONAL RECOMMENDATIONS

The chapters in this book confirm and shed further light on the diverse character of the Asia Pacific region in terms of the various work arrangements in which women engage, and countries' differing conceptions of and progress towards gender equity at work and beyond. However, they also emphasise shared challenges and opportunities for working women and their communities. Framed by our main analytical dimensions and emergent themes, we propose a non-exhaustive series of cross-national, interrelated recommendations for progressing gender equity at work and beyond:

Covid-19 pandemic context

- The pandemic has revealed deep structural problems with work that have impacted in a gendered fashion (e.g. with job displacement), rolling back a number of recent equity gains. Optimistically, it provides a reset opportunity for policy and job redesign, including a reimagining of women's roles in different spheres (UN Women, 2021). For the region, and globally, sustainable recovery strategies will involve the creation of decent work; enhanced opportunities for collective organisation and social dialogue (particularly where the informal economy dominates and is heavily feminised); and increased investments in technological infrastructure and upskilling.

- Part of this change involves a revisioning of what 'gender equity' means in a pandemic/post-pandemic setting, considering diverse worldviews and value sets about women's roles, and whether this reflects equality with men or the equivalence of women's unique roles, knowledge and contributions. Gender lenses thus need to inform recovery strategies to prioritise working women's engagement in decent work, which is the foundation of the ILO's 2030 Agenda for Sustainable Development (ILO, not dated). Concomitantly, for more women to be engaged in decent work or for 'productive work for women and men in conditions of freedom, equity, security and human dignity' (ILO, 2012, v), a transformation of care and responsibilities that reflects a more equitable division of labour between women and men, alongside low-cost, high-quality state or market care, is needed.

Demography
- Within Asia Pacific, connected inequities of many women's work and family roles needs recognition, particularly with government regulations and policies that are seamless, gender equitable and effectively implemented in tandem. Support for employees and employers is needed. For example, women are more underutilised than men in the formal economy, and shoulder the burden of unpaid care, spousal and domestic responsibilities. Women's work and family development could be sustained through extended and paid parental leave; universal childcare; workplace crèches; family tax reductions; flexible working arrangements (FWAs); and social protections for eldercare and sickness. Leave subsidies for employers (e.g. corporate tax reduction) could facilitate these measures.
- Women also work more than men in insecure, lower-paid and non-standard work and in 'dead-end' rural and urban employment. Universal and portable social protection systems will support

workers in precarious jobs in formal and informal sectors to support their health and wellbeing and prevent gendered poverty. Regularisation of fast-developing gig work for women aligns with the ILO's Employment Relationship Recommendation, 2006 (No. 198) on platform work and the employment relationship (de Stefano et al., 2021). Both employer-led and employees-led FWAs (or flexicurity) are particularly important for people to take on family formation responsibilities.

- Across the region, women have long earned less than their male counterparts, despite recent initiatives in some countries to close gender gaps. Regulation and workplace policies thus need to increase women's long-term earnings and pension levels to avoid poverty in later life. More campaigns, regulatory tools and policies are needed to successfully pursue fair pay arrangements, equal value for paid employment and unpaid (care) work, and greater pay transparency. Gender equitable approaches reduce sector and occupational gender biases, augment productivity and lead to better sustainable pay outcomes, particularly for minority and marginalised women workers.
- State and workplace measures need to address labour force shortages arising from demographic shifts and exacerbated by the pandemic, including policies that encourage women's LFP and career development, even when they engage in dependent care.

Sustainability
- For a sustainable future, policies must acknowledge the distinct impacts that climate change and disasters (e.g. natural, human-led) have on women's economic wellbeing and social vulnerabilities. As well as targeted gender-specific indicators for all UN SDGs, SDG 5 (gender equity) and SDG 8 (decent work) in particular need to be meaningfully operationalised to drive sustainable development and equitable economic growth. With or without the

intended achievement of the SDGs by 2030, regional and national development plans must start or continue to fully incorporate gendered analyses.

- Equitable access to resources and opportunities for women prior to, during and in the reconstruction phases of disasters are currently biased against women. Climate change and disaster responses must augment women's voice and role in decision-making, planning, execution and recovery to identify strategic and practical gender needs, particularly given the impact of domestic violence and (sexual) harassment on sustainable work. Women's knowledge and social practices could be used to build community resilience if they are included in efforts to adapt and mitigate against such challenges. Legislation and social dialogue need to be developed or strengthened to counter domestic violence, ensure effective implementation of anti-rape and, in some contexts, anti-honour killing bills, and encourage mass education on women's full citizenship rights.
- As well as changes to employment and other law, especially to facilitate (collective) worker representation and social dialogue mechanisms (Parker, Nemani et al., 2011), exploitative labour practices and unsafe working conditions, particularly for women, need greater monitoring and legislative enforcement (ILO & Asian Development Bank [ADB], 2015).
- Government and others should guide and support women's entrepreneurship, including their ownership of micro- and small businesses that promote social inclusion and combat long-term unemployment. Other measures could include training and business counselling for women; mentoring; positive role-modelling; financial advice and provision of micro-credit finance; networking activities; and greater access to and promotion of employment information, career advancement and training opportunities for rural and urban women. Such measures will

increase women's employment opportunities in non-farm sectors, as well as improve their productivity in and engagement with the agricultural sector. The state could support women's markets with infrastructural facilities (e.g. low-interest-rate loans, transport, storage space, publicity).

- In countries with a large agrarian/primary sector, women need greater ownership of and control over land, irrigated and fishing areas, to undertake sustainable economic activities (e.g. UN Working Group, 2020) and further engagement in entrepreneurial activity (UN Women, 2021).

Technology

- Covid-19 has enlarged future of work debates regarding technological challenges from men working in certain industries to considering women's roles and contributions. Technological advancement has both worsened some gender inequities (e.g. job displacement) and provided new opportunities for women. Their training and upskilling must be redesigned as an investment to promote organisational performance and women's self-development and empowerment through economic, entrepreneurial and social networking opportunities.
- For women to benefit from new technologies, workplace redesign is vital to avoid the ghettoisation of women into work that lacks career paths. Regulatory and policy support, education, training centres, practices and cultures need to break down occupational and industry segregation to build sustainable, gender equitable, well-paid and secure career pathways in STEMM, and traditionally male-dominated sectors.
- Advanced scientific training in core subjects including STEMM (including computer science and enterprise development) needs to be directed towards female students. Cross-agency efforts are needed in particular countries to ensure higher completion rates

for girls and women in secondary and tertiary education.
- To help women balance their work and family life and develop their careers, their accrual of IT skills (e.g. to work remotely, particularly given pandemic conditions) needs to be emphasised. Alongside this, technology that supports all forms of women's work and closes the digital divide in rural and urban areas is needed.

Globalisation
- Women have been impacted disproportionately by globalisation and excluded from some of its potential opportunities, albeit during a period of restricted global trade under Covid-19. For post-pandemic economic recovery, regulation and workplace policy must caution against the 'low road' flexibilisation of labour markets, and be imbued with a gender lens that seeks equitable progress in all sectors (e.g. skills development of women in informal work to help them progress within the sector or build their capacity to transfer across industries (ILO & ADB, 2015).
- For many countries, comprehensive and gender-sensitive foreign worker policy needs to be designed for inward and outward migrant workers to support competitive economic and equitable policies. Awareness of migration policies that are market-driven and result in the segregation of women into feminised and often insecure occupational areas is needed.
- Women's voice, capabilities and participation need to be enhanced in policy and economic governance at all levels, as well as in social practices of equality and non-discrimination to empower women in a globalised world of work (e.g. World Bank, 2020).

Cohesive approaches
- As observed, demographic, sustainability, technology and globalisation challenges are multiple and interlinked. They thus require gender-sensitive, multi-layered and integrative policy

responses in all areas (e.g. the labour market, socio-economic policy, institutional arrangements, health development and social security) to combat structural discrimination for working women. Tripartite approaches are key, although they are often pursued on paper in smaller economies. This all needs to be underpinned by gender-responsive budgeting and resourcing.

- Policy responses need to be multilateral. Employers and employees, their representative bodies, the state, community and women's groups and others need to ensure that responsive and sustainable strategies are implemented to counter gender discrimination and exclusion at work. A bottom-up approach to policy formulation and implementation will ensure greater commitment to change measures.
- In-depth analysis is required to assess when policies have paradoxical, interactive or unanticipated gendered impacts to prevent 'backsliding' in women's workplace progress, as noted during the pandemic. Implementation of progressive legislation and gender-sensitive programmes must be effectively resourced, monitored and enforced to promote gender equity.

Women's diverse characteristics and contexts

- Unless key societal narratives and entrenched gender stereotypes are addressed, the status of women, including those who work, will not change. Socio-cultural, including religious, practices and attitudes that constrain gender roles must be examined. This is particularly important when considering the dynamic ways in which gender, ethnicity, age, disability, geography and migrant status interact to relegate women to the domestic sphere and the 'sharp end' of labour markets.
- Action plans must reflect the diversity of women's circumstances and aim for the inclusion of all. Policy and regulatory support that counters gender discrimination must thus encompass women

engaged in standard and atypical work. Additionally, their own diverse circumstances (e.g. in terms of marital status, household arrangements, mainstreamed or stigmatised communities) and access to social protection measures must be taken into account. Concurrently, issues faced by the most vulnerable groups of women (e.g. migrant, rural, elderly, unpaid domestic labourers, those living with a disability), need to recognise differences in resources needed for self-development.

- Widespread and sustained pursuit of equal employment opportunities (e.g. improvement to women's LFP, representation in local and central government, on public and private sector boards, in the judiciary) is necessary.

- International commitments must be recognised and upheld to recognise the right of women and men workers to join and participate in trade unions, including taking collective action that recognises the meaning of women's diverse circumstances for gender equity progress at work.

Data collection and monitoring

- Our recommendations are premised on the availability of gender data for which Asia Pacific lags behind other regions. This can reflect factors such as hard-to-reach population groups (e.g. refugees, migrants); new/emerging work areas and contextual dynamics (e.g. environmental change); and methodological challenges (e.g. data collection costs at the individual level). Such data gaps inhibit gender-aware policy development, accountability, advocacy and analysis (Duerto Valero, 2019). A greater body of disaggregated data is thus needed, and such data should be publicly available to help organisations and others develop relevant solutions.

- High-level quantitative measures of existing gender equality indexes need to be extended with qualitative, context-sensitive longitudinal and multi-level measures of gender and intersectional trends (Parker, Sayers et al., forthcoming). Furthermore, the scope of gender metrics must be widened (e.g. to include women's productive and reproductive work in the labour force, and women's role in the formal and informal economies).

- Examination of under-researched yet key sectors in particular countries (e.g. the informal economy) where women are heavily engaged is needed. Covid-19 prevented the inclusion of certain countries in this book (e.g. Papua New Guinea) and subsequent analyses of working women could include these nations. Furthermore, future analysis of gender equality policies in regulated and less regulated countries could provide further insights on working women.

These cross-national recommendations can be read in conjunction with those proposed in each chapter. The Asia Pacific countries under examination reflect differing gender equality and equity 'starting points'. Gender equality generally means that individual women's rights, responsibilities and opportunities will not be determined by the sex that they are assigned at birth. Gender equity refers to treatment that might be considered equivalent in terms of rights, benefits, obligations and opportunities, and recognises that women and gender-diverse people are often not in the same 'starting position' as men. However, in both broad senses, all of the nations need to make greater progress for working women and their communities. Related gains must also be safeguarded, particularly in politically unstable environments where women's representation and social dialogue has declined and cultural and other barriers prevail. And the ongoing evolution of equality and equity conceptions raises new gender challenges and emphasises diversity and inclusion aims as a perpetual work-in-progress.

1. Working women in Aotearoa New Zealand

Jane Parker and Noelle Donnelly

Aotearoa New Zealand is a small developed economy in the South Pacific. Since its formal founding with Te Titiri o Waitangi (the Treaty of Waitangi) between the British Crown and Māori rangatira (New Zealand's indigenous chiefs), the nation has developed into one of the more ethnically and culturally diverse populations and workforces in the world. In this chapter, key dimensions of the New Zealand context are examined, followed by an analysis of four major themes — demographic trends, technological phenomena, globalisation and sustainability — in relation to the situation and experience of working women. This discussion focuses on working women in Aotearoa prior to and during the Covid-19 pandemic, and with an eye to the future. It concludes with an assessment of the implications of current macro-policies and initiatives for women in the workplace and outlines potential multilateral responses to key challenges for working women.

Aotearoa New Zealand has a population of 5 million and a total land mass of 268,021 square kilometres. It was first settled by Polynesians around 800 years ago and a distinctively Māori culture ensued. The signing of Te Titiri o Waitangi in 1840 declared British sovereignty over the islands. New Zealand gained full statutory independence in 1947, with the British monarch remaining as its head of state. The majority of the population are of European descent. Indigenous Māori form the largest minority, followed by Asians and Pacific Peoples (StatsNZ, 2020b).

Major economic changes occurred from the mid-1980s, transforming the country from a protectionist to a liberalised free-trade economy. Formerly an agrarian economy, New Zealand's service sector subsequently dominated, followed by the industrial sector, agriculture and international tourism, and expanding New Zealand's network of free-trade agreements remains a top foreign policy priority (Central Intelligence Agency, 2021). Neoliberal thinking has informed changes to the country's labour relations from the late 1980s. The passage of the Employment Contracts Act 1991, which made union membership voluntary, allowed anyone to bargain on behalf of workers, and shifted the locus of regulation to the direct relationship between employees and their employers (Deeks et al., 1994; New Zealand Parliament, 1996). This precipitated a rapid fall in union membership. The country's current cornerstone employment law, the Employment Relations Act 2000, subsequently aims to recalibrate employment relations to strengthen workers' positions and ensure a positive employment relationship by incorporating good faith in every aspect of the employment environment.

New Zealand's comparatively high labour force participation (LFP) rate (68.8 per cent) and low unemployment rate (3.4 per cent) by September 2021 (StatsNZ, 2021b) reflect a comparatively robust job market. Women's rising participation in employment has driven New Zealand's recent strong labour force growth (Hyslop et al., 2019). Today, women form half of New Zealand's population (50.4 per cent) and almost half of its labour force (47.2 per cent), representing their highest employment rate since records began over three decades ago (StatsNZ, 2021b) (see Table 1.1).

While women are joining the labour force at a higher rate than men, they are also staying longer in employment. From 2000–20, women's LFP grew by 13.5 per cent to 65.2 per cent, compared with a 2.4 per cent growth in men's participation rate to 70.6 per cent; and the percentage of employed women aged 65 and over rose from 4.5 per cent to 19.6 per cent, while the percentage of employed men aged 65 and over increased from 11.8 to 30.5 per cent (StatsNZ, 2021b).

Table 1.1: Labour force, unemployment and under-utilisation rates by gender in New Zealand, 2021

	Female (%)	Male (%)	Total (%)
Labour force	47.2	52.8	100
Employment rate	62.8	72.6	67.6
Labour force participation rate	65.6	75.5	70.5
Unemployment rate	4.3	3.8	4.0
Under-utilisation rate	13.0	8.3	10.5
Youth not in employment, education or training (NEET) rate (15–24 years)	12.7	9.1	10.8

Source: StatsNZ (2021b)

Furthermore, women in Aotearoa New Zealand have long been more likely than men to be employed in part-time work, with a significant proportion seeking longer hours of work. In keeping with international trends, gender gaps, including that for labour utilisation, have been exacerbated under pandemic conditions and have become comparatively worse for women who are already facing inequities (Ministry for Women (MfW), 2021) and less secure work.[1] New Zealand's female under-utilisation rate rose from 13 per cent in the June 2019 quarter to 14.9 per cent a year later (an increase of 29,000), while their unemployment rate rose to 4.4 per cent (an increase of 1000). Corresponding statistics for men showed more modest change (StatsNZ, 2020a).

By September 2020, the overall labour under-utilisation rate was 13.2 per cent, with the rate for women reaching 16.2 per cent. For women, this came almost equally from under-employment and unemployment, while

---

1   A significant proportion of part-time workers are parents of dependent children, and some are sole parents; in both cases, most are women. Furthermore, many women were likely to be working part-time for involuntary reasons, with one in six wanting more working hours.

a greater proportion for men came from under-employment. The number of employed men working part-time rose from 10.7 per cent to 11.9 per cent, compared with a smaller increase from an already-high level for women (from 29.1 per cent to 30 per cent) (StatsNZ, 2020a). However, part-time jobs normally cannot provide for a decent living, or for adequate retirement funds, often leading to poverty in old age (e.g. Dale & St John, 2020; also Notz, 1999).

Furthermore, the pandemic has severely impacted on New Zealand's service sectors, with a disproportionate toll on jobs in sectors such as retail, hospitality and tourism, where many women work.[2] In the first six months of the pandemic, 70 per cent of those who lost their jobs (31,000) were women (StatsNZ, 2020a) and women's greater exposure to job loss during this time has been predicted to exacerbate the gender gap in the future (La Croce, 2020; MfW, 2020). Women were also more likely than men to lose their jobs than have their hours reduced during the outbreak, and experienced significant difficulty in securing new employment. Within New Zealand's tourism industry, for instance, where the number of women outnumber men, women's employment dropped by 8.4 per cent — 20.5 per cent of whom were Māori women (StatsNZ, 2020c).

Post-lockdown, the hospitality sector somewhat bounced back, but 'social distancing early on meant it was costly to maintain a full staff rotation', with some firms making their smaller workforces permanent (Vergara, 2020). Furthermore, the Labour government's pandemic wage subsidy may have helped many businesses to survive and retain their workforces, but for others it may have merely delayed the inevitable, with women and migrants over-represented among those who later lost their jobs.

Women also predominate in the healthcare sector and, while Covid-19 cases were initially relatively small in New Zealand compared with many nations, lockdowns have disproportionately impacted on the employment

---

2   In the past, women in New Zealand, especially non-Pākehā women, have been more severely affected by crises and labour market shocks than have men (MfW, 2020).

of workers in care sectors. However, at the time of writing, recovery in women's employment had begun, with their unemployment rate dropping to 3.4 per cent by the September 2021 quarter, converging on the marginally lower male unemployment rate of 3.3 per cent (StatsNZ, 2021d).

New Zealand's labour market is highly gender-segregated. Women are clustered in traditionally female-dominated industries, many of which are lower paid and/or have a high incidence of part-time work (MfW, 2019). Industries with high proportions of women employees include healthcare and social assistance (83.1 per cent) and education and training (72.2 per cent), while those with a low proportion are mining (8.7 per cent) and construction (13.5 per cent) (StatsNZ, 2020f). Furthermore, women not only work in a narrower range of occupations than men do, but also at lower organisational and pay levels, while men are more likely to occupy higher-paid managerial and leadership positions (see Table 1.2).

Women's LFP growth has been concentrated in a small number of traditionally female-occupied jobs, part-time jobs and the lowest-paid sectors, including caregiving, hospitality, cleaning, retail and the food-service sectors, as well as in education and training, where there is a high prevalence of fixed-term and casual employment with generally inferior entitlements (e.g. see Council of Trade Unions [(CTU], 2013). Amid the Covid-19 pandemic, there was also a small but notable increase (17,300) in the number of self-employed women in the year to March 2021, including female entrepreneurs, independent contractors and gig workers. The growth in women-led new businesses appears to reflect the feminised nature of pandemic-triggered redundancies (StatsNZ, 2021c).

The employment experiences of women are also far from uniform. For example, Māori and Pacific women, particularly those aged 15–24, are more likely not to be in employment, education or training; have children at a younger age; receive state benefits; and are both under-employed in general but over-employed as multiple job holders (MfW, 2019). While the country's gender pay gap (GPG) was at a historical low of 9.1 per cent in 2021 (StatsNZ, 2021a), the ethnic pay gaps (EPGs) for Māori, Pacific, Asian

Table 1.2: Employment distribution by occupational category and gender in New Zealand, 2020

Occupation	Male (%)	Female (%)
Managers	15.3	12.0
Professionals	17.1	24.0
Technicians and associate professionals	9.9	15.1
Clerical support workers	4.7	17.4
Service and sales workers	11.5	21.9
Craft and related	16.3	0.9
Plant and machine operators, and assemblers	12.1	2.1
Elementary occupations*	13.0	6.9

*Elementary occupations are mostly routine tasks, often involving the use of simple hand-held tools and, in some cases, requiring a degree of physical effort (e.g. refuse workers, cleaners, labourers, street and related sales and services workers). Source: ILO (2020)

and new immigrant women were also significantly higher than for Pākehā (New Zealand European), even within female-dominated sectors. Even in New Zealand's feminised and highly unionised public sector, where recent government policy and regulation has encouraged an equity drive, women in ethnic minority groupings still experience greater pay gaps than Pākehā women do (Parker, Donnelly et al., in press). Recent employment growth in industries characterised by high levels of part-time work and low pay levels will do little to improve this situation.

Parenthood also negatively impacts on women's pay in Aotearoa, with research showing that the GPG for parents (at 17 per cent) is significantly higher than for non-parents (5 per cent). This indicates a 'motherhood penalty', and this is higher for part-time workers (MfW, 2016). Contributing to this widening GPG is the division between unpaid care and other unpaid work and paid work, with women shouldering responsibility for the former, spending on average twice the time on care work than men (MfW, 2019). This situation is more pronounced for Māori women, who report even higher engagement in unpaid care and community work (StatsNZ, 2020d). The pandemic has, however, disproportionately and negatively impacted on employment in the feminised childcare sector, impacting in turn on working mothers of young children. Insufficient childcare has affected their ability to access work and remain employed, their employment status, working hours, wages and productivity, as they have had to assume an even greater share of unpaid care, household and community responsibilities (Grant Thornton, 2018; Parker, Young-Hauser et al., 2022; Weatherall et al., 2017).

EMPLOYMENT REGULATION

Following economic deregulation in the mid-1980s, New Zealand's labour market was liberalised amid a 'fast track' legislative process (Palmer, 1980). The Employment Contracts Act 1991 replaced a centralised system of bargaining, conciliation and arbitration with enterprise-level and individual contract making. As a result, union membership halved, and union density dropped to 17.1 per cent by 1999 (Ryall & Blumenfeld, 2016).

With a change in government, the Employment Relations Act 2000 superseded the 1991 Act. It was designed to recalibrate the balance of power between employers and workers by emphasising both collective and individual 'good faith' bargaining. Analyses concur that this Act has stemmed rather than reversed union decline (e.g. Carroll, 2020a; Harbridge et al., 2003). Today, most workers are not unionised — in 2020, just 16.4 per cent of the employed labour force in Aotearoa were union members (New Zealand Companies Office, 2022). And while union members are more likely to be women (61.5 per cent in 2020) (New Zealand Companies Office, 2022), and density is higher and more feminised in the public sector (Parker & Donnelly, 2020), many women engage in work where unionisation is low.

Since the 1960s, the New Zealand government has enacted statutes and policies to advance gender equity at work (Parker & Donnelly, 2020). Most recently, the introduction of the Equal Pay Amendment Act 2020 provides a process to address historical and systemic gender pay inequity within a 'good faith' bargaining framework. It also allows bargaining outcomes to be passed on to non-union members, and encompasses roles not previously covered by pay equity claims, thus widening the promise for further gender equality progress. The government introduced equity initiatives to eliminate GPGs in the public sector by addressing equal pay, flexible work by default, non-discriminatory remuneration systems and gender-balanced leadership (Public Service Commission [PSC], 2020). By seeking to remove barriers to gender equality, the government aims to create a catalyst for change across the private sector. The drop in the public-sector GPG to a historical low of 8.6 per cent in 2021 (Thomson, 2021) has been widely attributed to these initiatives, alongside pay equity settlements within female-dominated sectors, campaigning by unions and women's collectives and wider labour market initiatives (Parker & Donnelly, 2020). As noted earlier, however, the EPGs of Māori, Pacific and Asian working women have remained stubbornly higher than for Pākehā women.

More broadly, the government introduced the Public Service Act 2020 to facilitate a cultural shift that builds a unified public service to 'quickly mobilise across the sector to tackle specific issues and deliver better outcomes for New Zealanders' (Public Service Act 2020). This statute has the scope to critique existing (gender) equity notions, initiatives and measurements but research has yet to expose its impact or that of the Covid-19 pandemic on working women in structural terms (Parker, Young-Hauser et al., 2022).

In 2021, the MfW began work to develop a national Women's Employment Action Plan to address structural impediments to gender equality, ensuring that women are protected from labour market shocks such as Covid-19. The first of its kind, this national programme will focus on groups of women who have been further marginalised as a result of the pandemic and will broaden its focus to housing, health, education, social development and violence prevention (MfW, 2021).

KEY CHALLENGES AND OPPORTUNITIES

The following sections align with the four key themes identified in the UN Working Group on Discrimination Against Women and Girls' (2020) global thematic report (see Introduction).

Globalisation

Much discussion of globalisation in Aotearoa has been linked to economic and labour market policy changes of the last decades of the twentieth century, although 'some forms of global interaction have reached unprecedented heights in recent years' (NZ Institute of Economic Research [NZIER], 2017). As a small economy, New Zealand sought to overcome the limitations of its size by opening up the economy in the 1980s and building international trade connections and relationships. The removal of tariffs, import licences and restrictive quotas in the 1980s signalled its intention to access larger markets, primarily through bilateral and multilateral agreements (Treasury, 2017).

New Zealand was less successful in attracting foreign direct investment (FDI), ranking 71st globally on the UN Conference on Trade and Development (UNCTAD) FDI attractiveness index (UNCTAD, 2012). More recently, New Zealand has focused on strengthening international connections through trade, tourism and education (areas that have recently seen contraction due to border restrictions).

Globalisation has impacted on New Zealand in uneven, historically specific and gendered ways. Deregulation and increased flexibilisation of the labour market, alongside policy and social changes, are marked outcomes of the impact of globalisation, which can be linked to steady growth in women's LFP in recent decades. Labour market flexibility, while encouraging flexible working (e.g. just prior to Covid-19, over 50 per cent of employees had flexible work hours, and one-third worked from home — StatsNZ, 2019b), can also lead to a greater amount of insecure work (non-permanent employment, including casual, fixed-term, seasonal, contract and labour hire work). Women and migrants predominate in part-time, casual and low-paid work in industries where new firms can easily enter, and in occupations that are low-skilled or use skills that have been historically undervalued.

Furthermore, globalisation has fuelled interest in flexible work. In 2013, women formed almost seven in every 10 people in fixed-term jobs and six in 10 casual workers, while men constituted six of every 10 workers in temp agency and seasonal work (Ongley et al., 2013). By the June 2019 quarter, those with the highest rates of multiple job holding were women (8.4 per cent) and parents and caregivers of dependent children (8.3 per cent). Combining all job incomes, men with multiple jobs earned a median total weekly income of NZ$1429, while for women, the figure was much lower at NZ$986 (StatsNZ, 2019a). During the time of Covid-19, part-time and casual workers (i.e. predominantly women) have been identified as those most likely to lose their jobs first, as businesses seek to stay viable in a recessionary climate (Carroll, 2020b).

Globalisation has also specifically and often negatively affected worker groups along ethnic and other dimensions (Harawira, 1999). The expansion of multinational corporations in the services sector has essentially defined female employment in New Zealand, with insecure work affecting Māori and Pacific workers, low-paid women, children, young people, migrants and people living with disability. By 2006, more than four in five New Zealand jobs were located in the services sector, and by 2011, 86.1 per cent of the female labour force worked in service-sector employment (Parker & Arrowsmith, 2012). Furthermore, new forms of insecure work have appeared, including zero-hour contracts, although New Zealand sought to stem their occurrence via legislation in 2016.

Focusing on migrants as a dimension of global labour flows, New Zealand's overseas-born population has continued to increase in recent decades, from 19.5 per cent in 2001 (NZIER, 2017) to 27.4 per cent by 2018 (Manch, 2019). While net migration since March 2020 has been a 'trickle' due to pandemic-related border and travel restrictions (StatsNZ, 2020e), in recent years, migrant women who have been in New Zealand for fewer than five years, and migrant men who have been here for fewer than 10 years were over-represented among low paid (National Advisory Council on the Employment of Women, 2010) and personal care jobs.[3] Research indicates that it takes 15 years for migrants' employment rates to become close to those for comparable New Zealand-born citizens, with the income difference halving for men and disappearing for women (Carey, 2019).

Similar patterns were also found for employed immigrants in terms of occupational rank and wage levels (Stillman & Maré, 2009). However, Stillman (2011) points to immigrant status, rather than ethnicity, as driving lower employment rates of Asian and Pacific immigrants, as a result of weaker job networks or higher reservation wages, possibly due to different family obligations, lack of access to informal childcare, or labour market discrimination. Recent reports suggest increasing exploitation of some temporary migrant workers during Covid-19, resulting in the government investing NZ$50 million over the next four years to address this challenge (Employment New Zealand, 2020).

Global transformation processes can challenge the rate of progress of equity interventions adopted by government and private companies to increase organisational competitiveness and lower operating costs. Furthermore, with the pandemic, analysts note that Aotearoa faces new challenges in balancing 'health protection and economic openness', cautioning that 'the burden of the Covid-19 disruption, the economic costs of slow growth and the fiscal costs of government response programmes will fall unevenly' across the population (Bollard, 2020, p. 19).

Restructuring and reduced employment opportunities during and the following Covid-19 pandemic may exacerbate an informal sector in New Zealand in which women predominate in vulnerable jobs. And while world trade and capital flows have slowed as a result of the pandemic, flows of cultural texts, ideas and information continue to accelerate (e.g.

---

3   A proportion of these are qualified nurses or other professionals who are working at a lower level pending their New Zealand registration (Badkar et al., 2008).

NZIER, 2017). For this small, export-dependent nation, the implications of economic and cultural integration remain important, including for underprivileged groups of working women.

Demography

New Zealand's demography reflects its historically high levels of immigration. Following the Second World War, the New Zealand government introduced assisted immigration schemes to encourage the migration of non-British European women and their families, and those displaced by the war. Europe remained the main source of migration until the mid-1960s, when migration from the Pacific began in earnest, with many attracted by employment opportunities. With greater migration in the 1970s and 1980s, the government shifted the focus of immigration policy from race to skills, capital investment and family reunification criteria, resulting in greater diversification of immigration, particularly from China, Hong Kong, India, Japan and Sri Lanka. Immigrants from the Philippines tripled between 1991 and 2006, a high percentage of whom were women marrying New Zealand men (Phillips, 2015).

Migration continues to feed New Zealand's population growth. Prior to pandemic restrictions on border entry, two-thirds of recent population growth — one of the highest in the OECD — came from inward migration. Having such a large migrant population has brought a wide range of ethnicities to Aotearoa. Today, the population is primarily of European descent (70 per cent), with indigenous Māori the largest minority at 16.5 per cent, followed by Asian (15.3 per cent) and Pacific Peoples (9 per cent) (StatsNZ, 2020b). More than a quarter of the New Zealand population was born overseas.

New Zealand is also undergoing an internal 'demographic transformation', involving 'its greatest change since the post-war baby boom' (Spoonley, 2021). Of particular concern are New Zealand's declining birth and death rates. Fertility rates have dropped to 1.6, well below the replacement rate of 2.1 (from a peak of 4.3 in 1961), while life expectancy rates have risen, especially for women (to 83.5 years and to 80 years for men based on 2017–19 death rates). Furthermore, those aged 65 and over outnumber those aged under 15 years, with some forecasts noting that one in four New Zealanders will soon be aged 65 and over.

How people age in Aotearoa differs across ethnicities. The average life expectancy is lower for Māori and Pasifika (in 2013, it was 77.1 years for Māori women and 78.7 years for Pacific women, as compared with a national average of 81.4 years). Pākehā women marry later in life (29.2 years in 2018), have children at a later stage in life (with the highest birth rates among those aged 30–34 years) and live longer than men. By contrast, Māori women marry relatively young, have higher fertility rates, lower life expectancy and higher rates of premature mortality (StatsNZ, 2019c). In addition, health statistics show that Māori women experience poor health and wellbeing, compared with other ethnicities.

With women in New Zealand living longer on average than men, earning less than their male counterparts and spending more time on caring duties, it is estimated that they will enter their retirement with greater care and financial needs and significant gender pension gaps. With the impact of the pandemic more pronounced for women, it is also feared that lower earning power, employment opportunities and higher end-of-life care costs may result in significant 'older female poverty', with calls for greater attention to the gendered perspective of pension policy design (Dale & St John, 2020). Indeed, the Financial Services Council of New Zealand (2018) recently observed that 'women in Aotearoa are less financially well off in retirement, are paid less overall and aren't as financially literate as men'; they are also 'more often the ones juggling money to keep a household running, and shouldering the stress that comes with that'. Furthermore, research indicates that they are more likely to be the victims of financial abuse in relationships (e.g. Scott, 2020).

Aotearoa's ageing population and falling birth rate will also significantly constrict New Zealand workforces in the future and increase pressure on future migration. As a country that has historically relied on international migration for its population growth, the recent closure of borders due to Covid-19 has reversed longstanding migration trends. For the first time on record, in January 2021, the annual net migration of citizens was greater than that of non-citizens, raising concerns of future labour shortages (Yadav, 2021). Basic demographic data indicate that the majority of recent migrant-respondents are female on temporary visas, married and living with their families, and a review by Kanengoni et al. (2018) suggests that women migrants' wellbeing is more likely to be at risk, particularly in the context of Covid-19 (Belong Aotearoa, 2020).

Technology
Economic and labour market reforms in New Zealand in the 1980s and 1990s drove rapid shifts away from manufacturing towards service-sector work and higher-paid and -skilled occupations. However, a recent inquiry suggests that technological change, as measured by productivity growth, business dynamism and labour market change, is static or slowing but that '(e)ven if technological unemployment is highly unlikely, technology adoption can still cause frictional unemployment' (New Zealand Productivity Commission, 2020, p. 31). Furthermore, most new jobs created in recent decades in information- and skill-intensive sectors (e.g. finance, professional and business services) occurred in Auckland, New Zealand's most populous urban area.

The Chartered Accountants of Australia and New Zealand and NZIER (2015) found that 46 per cent of workers faced a high risk of automation, ranging from 75 per cent of labouring jobs to 12 per cent of professional jobs, in which women and men are differently concentrated. A study by McKinsey (Madgavkar et al., 2019) indicates that the earlier automation technologies are adopted, the more jobs will be lost with higher resulting unemployment, while under their late-adoption scenario, net employment increases by 1 million. Employment growth would be concentrated in managerial, technical and associated professional, service and retail jobs, while there would be an overall reduction in administrative, trade and manual jobs.

It is notable that women are under-represented in growing areas of employment that require STEMM (science, technology, engineering, mathematics and medicine) skills and knowledge. Furthermore, the Sustainable Business Council (2019) proffers that, if job losses affect lower-skilled workers, as well as occupations traditionally held by women, such as administration and support services, women could face disproportionately negative consequences. Thus, '(i)n the automation age, women face new challenges overlaid on long-established ones' (Madgavkar et al., 2019, p. vi).

These studies of technological change focus on job gains and losses rather than job modifications, and they predate the pandemic. And while technological job losses have been less widespread than in other sectors, women's under-representation in growing areas of employment involving STEMM re-emphasises why gender equality in this sector is more important than ever.

The impact of technological changes on how women and men work has been thrown into sharper relief during Covid-induced lockdowns and social distancing, which have accelerated a shift towards remote working and virtual businesses. As Aotearoa New Zealand workplaces transition in this way, employers have been forced to re-assess the functionality of their workplace practices and employment relations.

In a recent study of remote work practices during New Zealand's first national lockdown, O'Kane et al. (2020) found that, of the 83 per cent of participants who identified challenges with remote working, 35 per cent reported an inability to switch off from work, 33 per cent found collaboration and communication with co-workers more difficult, 16 per cent encountered distractions and 14 per cent cited challenges with childcare. However, remote working has also protected women's work, with 35 per cent reporting that they maintained their productivity and 38 per cent reporting being more productive while working at home.

Understanding the future nature of work is a long-standing core area of focus for the New Zealand government. In 2019, it commissioned a report to assess the impact of technological disruption on future employment and established four work streams to approach the issue, including a tripartite forum to examine 'just transitions', lifelong learning, technology learning and workplace productivity (Iles, 2019). In response to calls to prioritise the introduction of policies to assist workers to adapt to future technological changes, as noted, the MfW implemented the development of a national Women's Employment Action Plan in 2022 (MfW, 2021).

Widespread adoption of artificial intelligence (AI), machine learning and related tech work upskilling and reskilling will take time to fully impact employment and business processes. The AI Forum of New Zealand (2018, p. 53) reports that 'there is no obvious reason why existing labour market support policies would not be able to cope', but there is potential for shock and radical change (e.g. Healy et al., 2017). Greater understanding of the likely impacts of technology across different sectors and labour market contexts (Halteh et al., 2018) is thus needed in order to strategically address gender inequalities that arise from structural adjustments.

Sustainability

Concerns with sustainability issues are embedded in New Zealand's collective psyche. Just over half (51 per cent) of 500 New Zealand business leaders (particularly young leaders) indicate that business should put sustainability ahead of profit (BMW Group Ltd, 2021), while 86 per cent of New Zealanders surveyed in another study agreed that it was important for them to work for a company that is socially and environmentally responsible (Colmar Brunton, 2019).

To address the impacts of global forces, including Covid-19, climate change and the changing nature of work, in 2018 the New Zealand government established a 'just transitions' strategy and tripartite working group to move Aotearoa to a low carbon emission future. Alongside the working group, the Climate Change Response (Zero Carbon) Amendment Act 2019 was introduced to mitigate and adapt to climate change impacts. For its part, the CTU (2019, p. 1) observes that New Zealand's transition to a climate-resilient, sustainable and low-emissions economy needs to 'ensure that opportunities for decent work in sustainable industries are available for all working people — and that the transition does not repeat existing patterns of inequality', and needs active involvement by Māori. Furthermore, as a signatory to the UN's Sustainable Development agenda, New Zealand has agreed 'to address root causes of inequality in order to make progress toward the eradication of poverty and the sustainable development of a more equitable and just global society' (UN Women Aotearoa New Zealand, 2021).

While few analyses focus on sustainability in relation to working women, women's historical dominance in care and support roles in health, education and public services, and their disproportionate share of unpaid work are critical to New Zealand's wellbeing. While around 60 per cent of men's work is paid, nearly 70 per cent of women's work is unpaid (StatsNZ, 2011). Deloitte's (2021) 2400 survey respondents confirm that women still perform more than their share of unpaid work at home, despite women needing equality in unpaid work in order to achieve equality in paid work (Elson, 2017). Furthermore, young women are playing an increasing role in whānau (family) care, and this can negatively affect their participation in society, mental wellbeing, academic achievement and engagement with paid work. Data also reveal that unpaid care work in Aotearoa (23 per cent of GDP) is comparatively high (OECD, 2019).

The government's 2021 Wellbeing Budget allocations, together with support for vocational education and benefit increases, aim to enable New Zealand businesses 'to benefit from new technologies and lift productivity and wages through innovation and support into employment those most affected by Covid-19, including women and young people' (Thornton, 2021), though the CTU (2019) assesses that more efforts are needed to enable a just transition for all workers.

The eradication of forced labour, modern slavery, human trafficking and the worst forms of child labour has been a relatively recent concern in New Zealand, influenced by global transformation processes. While most victims in Aotearoa, based on prosecutions, have been migrant men who were trafficked for labour exploitation, '(t)his is unlikely to reflect everyone who is trafficked or exploited as the hidden nature of these crimes means that vulnerable people are less likely or able to seek help or report their experience' (Ministry for Business, Innovation and Employment [MBIE], 2021, p. 8). Indeed, submissions to the consultation process on *New Zealand's Plan of Action Against Forced Labour, People Trafficking and Slavery* emphasised the introduction of modern slavery legislation and strengthened responses to trafficking of women, children, Māori and Pacific Peoples, particularly around domestic trafficking for sexual exploitation (MBIE, 2021).

Limited research on child labour shows that child workers are typically found in family businesses in the primary, retail and hospitality sectors; form a significant part of the informal New Zealand labour market; and, accordingly, are not covered by protective employment legislation (Caritas Aotearoa New Zealand, 2003). A survey of young adults reflecting on their work experiences found that a lack of physical safety was particularly prevalent for females (Anderson & Naidu, 2010). Caritas Aotearoa New Zealand (2020), the Catholic Bishops' agency for justice, peace and development, highlighted the risk of child poverty becoming ingrained in New Zealand, with one in five (one in four Māori and nearly one in three Pacific) children living in households facing material hardship, with implications for the unpaid care roles and paid work opportunities for women and girls in particular.

Aotearoa is relatively advanced in regulation that can be applied to promote and enforce non-discrimination on the basis of sex. Its government has sought to address gender inequalities that exist around pay equity, the GPG, family and sexual violence, and economic outcomes for women, particularly Māori and Pacific (New Zealand Government, 2019), though McGregor et al. (2015, p. 85) noted that New Zealand's 'pronounced self-regard that it is a leader in advancing women's progress pegged to historical firsts . . . is partially responsible for the current complacency' (e.g. see

Parker & Donnelly, 2020). For instance, women of Māori, Pacific and Asian ethnicities remain under-represented in the top management tiers and over-represented in lower-paid occupations in workplaces, particularly in the private sector. Such under-representation and lack of empowerment, in turn, impacts on the rate of progress towards and sustenance of gender equity within the work setting and beyond.

Progress has been slow on recognising and valuing unpaid care and domestic work through the promotion of shared household and family responsibilities, public services provision, infrastructure and social protection policies. However, in the government's 2021 Wellbeing Budget, a proposed social unemployment insurance scheme that provides workers with around 80 per cent of their income for a period if they lose their job 'could have transformational results for both the future of work and . . . efforts on delivering just transitions' (CTU, 2021, p. 31). For working women — the rump of those who have lost jobs or been under-employed during the pandemic — such a scheme will be a vital source of sustainability, although it will take some time to implement (Robson, 2021).

Another concern for sustainable development concerns New Zealand's comparatively high incidence of gender-based violence (including in workplaces), with reports of one in three New Zealand women experiencing physical and/or intimate partner violence (IPV) in their lives, and one in two Māori women experiencing IPV (Fanslow & Robinson, 2011). A focus of government action, the interim UN Convention on the Elimination of All Forms of Discrimination Against Women (CEDAW) (2020) report highlights an array of responses, including legislation such as New Zealand's Family Violence Act 2018 and Domestic Violence — Victims' Protection Act 2018, while other responses in relation to the trafficking of women are being formulated. However, while the latter statute has been effective since 1 April 2019 and provides up to 10 days' additional paid leave and short-term flexible work arrangements, just 10 per cent of collective employment agreements concluded by 1 June 2019 included a domestic violence leave clause (Proctor-Thomson et al., 2021).

RECOMMENDATIONS AND CONCLUSIONS

At first sight, Aotearoa New Zealand appears to have made significant inroads into addressing gender inequity at work. Recent pay reforms and the introduction of a series of gender equity initiatives have resulted in notable reductions in the GPG and gender leadership gaps (PSC, 2021). However, closer examination reveals that, not only are such benefits largely confined to the public service, but Māori, Pacific, Asian, migrant and disabled women, in particular, continue to experience significant economic disadvantages and structural barriers to equitable and secure employment. As this chapter highlights, women workers in New Zealand are more likely to be under-utilised, shoulder the burden of unpaid care work and earn less than their male counterparts, resulting in lower long-term earnings, pension gaps and potentially higher levels of poverty among older women (e.g. Dale & St John, 2020).

Furthermore, they are more likely than men to be lower skilled, work non-standard hours and be involved in insecure and 'dead-end' employment, making them more susceptible to job losses and economic shocks. The global pandemic has also had a gendered effect and exacerbated pre-existing gender inequalities, meaning the New Zealand government, social partners and other stakeholders face significant challenges in ensuring women's employment recovery across all industries.

Government commitments seek to redress the disproportionate economic and social impacts of the pandemic on women through a national gender-based employment action plan, but it remains to be seen how the specific needs of marginalised women will be addressed. Linked to demographic shifts, greater understanding of the relationship between women's paid and unpaid work; access to flexible work and funded childcare; providing fair pay and pay transparency; education and training in STEMM; and clearer pathways into and through traditionally male-dominated industries appears to be key, particularly in the mutating context of Covid-19. Current undertakings to counteract the impacts of the pandemic for women provide an important juncture for New Zealand's government to shift direction away from low-paid, low-skilled work towards the provision of more secure, skilled and decent work.

This is increasingly important in a context of lower global trade levels, and cautions against 'low road' flexibilisation of labour markets amid post-pandemic economic recovery. The introduction of a fair pay agreements (FPA) system to drive productivity via more sector- and occupation-level collective bargaining in New Zealand (FPA Working Group, 2018) may lead to the negotiation of more equitable pay outcomes, while the wider introduction of a living wage could have a positive impact on the working and wider lives of Māori, Pacific, migrant and other women in low-paid work (e.g. Parker, Arrowsmith et al., 2022).

Emphasising sustainability challenges, while recent legislative reforms have also gone some way to supporting women who have been subjected to domestic violence and have increased the level of dialogue around gender-based violence in general, more reforms are urgently required to tackle high levels of physical and emotional violence for women in Aotearoa New Zealand, particularly Māori women who experience higher incidence levels. The emulation of successes in New Zealand's public service in its private sector, a greater level and coalition of multi-party and -level responses involving the state, employers, workers, unions and community groups need to be strategically and practically connected to the linked challenges presented by globalisation, technological advancements, demographic change and sustainability.

2. Working women in Australia

Marian Baird, Rae Cooper and Daniel Dinale

In recent years, there has been an increased focus on women and their role in Australian society and workplaces. This interest has been driven by concerns that, despite high levels of investment in education and qualifications, women are not equally represented in leadership positions, and experience persistent employment and entitlement gaps, declining fertility rates, discrimination and harassment in the workplace and rising family and domestic violence. While progress has been made over the past 50 years in many areas of social, economic and reproductive life — and while women are entitled to the same democratic freedoms as men — the challenges posed by demographic shifts, globalisation, the rise in new technologies, climate change and recovery from the Covid-19 pandemic mean that a renewed attention to women and their place in the Australian economy and society is warranted.

In this chapter, we first provide an overview of the Australian country and labour market context and the shape of employment regulation. This is followed by an assessment of the four key themes identified by the United Nations (UN) Working Group on Discrimination Against Women and Girls: demographic shifts, globalisation, technological change and sustainability. We argue that the challenges are multiple and complex, and responses therefore need to adopt a multilayered approach that acknowledges and incorporates the role of government, employers, unions, and women and men themselves.

Australia has a vast land mass, much of it arid but rich in mineral resources, and a population of approximately 26 million. In 2020, women formed 50.2 per cent of the population, an increase from 49.5 per cent in 1960 (Australian Bureau of Statistics [ABS], 2019a). Australia is highly urbanised, with most of the population living in the urban centres on the east coast in the major cities of Sydney, Melbourne and Brisbane, and on the west coast in Perth. Attempts to regionalise Australia's population in the past have not been so successful, but rising city house prices and the opportunity to work from home due to Covid-19 have seen an increase in internal migration to rural and regional centres, as evident in Figure 2.1, which shows an exodus from capital cities.

Figure 2.1: Quarterly net internal migration in Australia, greater capital cities combined

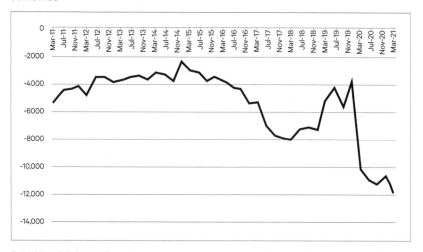

Source: ABS (2021d)

The Australian economy is resource dependent, with iron ore, liquified natural gas production and coal mining being the three major export industries, although employing a very small percentage of the workforce (ABS, 2022). Traditional manufacturing has declined and the service sector has increased to become the major source of employment for Australians. The Australian economy is now one of the more service-sector-oriented economies in the OECD (World Bank, 2021). Employment in the traditionally male-dominated industry sector (mining, manufacturing, construction and utilities),[1] as a percentage of total employment, decreased from 23.5 per cent in 1991 to 19.1 per cent in 2019, while employment in the services sector increased from 71.1 per cent in 1991 to 78.4 per cent in 2019 (World Bank, 2021).

Women are disproportionately represented in service employment in Australia — 90.8 per cent of working-age women compared with 67.5 per cent of working-age men were employed in the service sector in 2019 (World Bank, 2021) — noting that the service sector encompasses health and personal care services through to retail, finance and insurance.[2] The concentration of population and business in the urban areas, coupled with the reliance on income from mining, has had significant implications for the environment, with ongoing debates about the most sustainable population size, industry composition and impact on climate change.

Australian women have steadily increased their participation rate in the labour force from 43.7 per cent in 1978 to 61.2 per cent in 2020, just prior to the onset of Covid-19. By contrast, men's participation rates have fallen from a high of 80 per cent in 1978 to 71.5 per cent in 2019 (ABS, 2022).

---

1   The industry sector consists of mining and quarrying, manufacturing, construction and public utilities (electricity, gas and water), in accordance with divisions 2–5 (ISIC 2) or categories C–F (ISIC 3) or categories B–F (ISIC 4).

2   The services sector consists of wholesale and retail trade and restaurants and hotels; transport, storage and communications; financing, insurance, real estate and business services; and community, social and personal services, in accordance with divisions 6–9 (ISIC 2) or categories G–Q (ISIC 3) or categories G–U (ISIC 4) (World Bank, 2021).

Women's rising participation has been fuelled by two cohorts: women of childbearing age and women over the age of 45. For both groups, providing unpaid care to children, elders and those with disability alongside their labour force contributions is a constant source of pressure and conflict. The subsequent decline in economic activity because of the pandemic in sectors such as hospitality and retail where women predominate, and mandatory work-from-home orders in other sectors, resulted in a sharp rise in women's unemployment and under-employment rates and a decline in participation rates. In seasonally adjusted terms, in October 2021, the participation rate for women fell to 60 per cent and for men to 69.5 per cent (ABS, 2022) with young women among the most profoundly affected groups (Risse & Jackson, 2021).

After the first Covid-19 lockdowns in early 2020, female under-employment reached a peak of 15.0 per cent in April 2020, compared with 12.4 per cent for men. These rates have since dropped, with female under-employment at 8.8 per cent and male under-employment at 6.3 per cent as of November 2021 (ABS, 2022). It is not yet clear what will happen in the post-Covid recovery phase, except that we know from previous research on pandemics and recessions that women's economic security and wellbeing is more negatively affected than men's (see Parker, Young-Hauser et al., 2022), and that full recovery takes from three to seven years (Baird & Hill, 2020). A gender lens on the recovery is therefore urgently needed (Foley & Cooper, 2021).

Women's experiences follow their life course with significant inequality markers occurring at the specific phases of labour market entry, motherhood, mid-career care demands and mature worker eldercare responsibilities, all of which influence women's aggregate labour market outcomes (Baird & Heron, 2020). These markers result in interrupted careers, shorter working hours and fewer leadership opportunities, and together they contribute to a persistent gender pay gap (GPG) and superannuation gap for women (Chomik, 2021). While there have been attempts to address some of these gaps and inequities through legislation, policy changes and ongoing monitoring, persistent differences between men's and women's labour market experiences remain (Baird et al., 2021).

One of the most distinctive differences between women's and men's labour market experiences in Australia, and which also differentiates them from those in many other countries, is in relation to the gender difference in working hours (Anxo et al., 2017), where women work shorter hours than men. However, this is changing and the proportion of women working 35–44 hours is increasing, while the proportion of men working 45 or more hours is decreasing (see Table 2.1) (ABS, 2022).

There has been negligible movement in women's participation in full-time working in the past 40 years, despite the changes in social attitudes, increasing educational attainment and legislation. For women in Australia, work and care responsibilities are typically managed through part-time work and, while the male breadwinner model has declined, it has not been replaced with a shared work/care model but a 'one-plus' household model, where women work part-time and men work full-time, and often long hours. Furthermore, women are more likely to be employed in non-permanent jobs than are men, with 27 per cent of women in casual employment without access to paid schemes such as annual leave, sick leave, carers' leave (ABS, 2022) and employer-provided parental leave.

The labour market in Australia is also highly gendered, with clear horizontal and vertical segmentation. The phenomena of 'concrete walls', 'glass ceilings' and 'sticky floors' are familiar to the gender debates in Australia, referring to occupational segregation and women's limited leadership and promotion opportunities, respectively (Foley & Cooper, 2021). For instance, women are concentrated in the occupations of health and social assistance and education, whereas men are concentrated in construction, mining, transport and utilities, as shown in Table 2.2. In relation to leadership positions where there has been considerable attention paid to women's low representation, women now occupy approximately 38 per cent of managerial positions (ILOSTAT, 2020).

Table 2.1: Proportion of actual hours worked by males and females in Australia, 2015–22

Males						
	0 hours (%)	1–19 hours (%)	20–34 hours (%)	35–44 hours (%)	45–59 hours (%)	60+ hours (%)
Mar 2015	5.1	9.6	16.8	38.1	20.4	9.8
Mar 2016	4.8	10.0	15.7	39.2	20.2	10.2
Mar 2017	5.2	9.9	14.7	40.1	20.5	9.5
Mar 2018	5.1	9.6	18.5	38.6	18.9	9.3
Mar 2019	4.7	10.2	17.4	39.5	19.4	8.9
Mar 2020	5.3	10.4	19.1	39.8	17.8	7.6
Mar 2021	4.5	10.2	18.6	41.5	17.2	8.0
Mar 2022	6.0	10.2	16.6	42.0	17.7	7.5
Females						
	0 hours (%)	1–19 hours (%)	20–34 hours (%)	35–44 hours (%)	45–59 hours (%)	60+ hours (%)
Mar 2015	6.5	21.3	30.3	29.9	9.0	3.0
Mar 2016	5.9	21.4	28.1	32.4	9.0	3.1
Mar 2017	6.2	20.9	28.5	32.3	9.1	3.1
Mar 2018	6.2	21.0	31.2	30.5	8.4	2.8
Mar 2019	6.2	20.2	30.6	31.5	8.9	2.7
Mar 2020	6.8	20.2	30.2	31.9	8.3	2.6
Mar 2021	5.4	19.2	31.2	32.7	8.7	2.8
Mar 2022	6.9	18.2	29.7	33.9	8.6	2.7

Source: ABS (2022)

Table 2.2: Employment by industry and gender in Australia, November 2021

Industry	Male (%)	Female (%)
Healthcare and social assistance	23	77
Education and training	28	72
Accommodation and food services	45	55
Retail trade	46	54
Administrative and support services	49	51
Arts and recreation services	50	50
Public administration and safety	50	50
Financial and insurance services	51	49
Rental, hiring and real estate services	52	48
Other services	54	46
Professional, scientific and technical services	57	43
Information media and telecommunications	58	42
Agriculture, forestry and fishing	65	35
Wholesale trade	66	34
Manufacturing	70	30
Electricity, gas, water and waste services	77	23
Transport, postal and warehousing	79	21
Mining	81	19
Construction	87	13

Source: ABS (2021c)

EMPLOYMENT REGULATION

Australian industrial relations regulation was historically based on a system of compulsory conciliation and arbitration. From 1904 in this system, industry-based 'awards' typically set the terms and conditions of employment across a sector and resulted from disputes between unions and employers and their associations. The national regulator (which has gone by many names since its inception but is now known as the Fair Work Commission) decided outcomes and codified these in 'awards' — documents which set out terms and conditions of employment in a comprehensive way across an industry. Since the early 1990s, this system evolved significantly to include the introduction of enterprise-based collective bargaining, first with unions as central parties but now more sidelined, and the establishment of 'modern awards', where minimum conditions are set by the Commission after review, rather than via a centralised collectively bargained or arbitrated process.

For many decades, feminist scholars have pointed to an uneasy relationship between this regulatory system and workplace outcomes for Australian women. The early history of the system set up and entrenched significant pay inequality and excluded from regulation highly feminised work in areas such as social services, because they were deemed not to be 'industries'. From the late 1960s through to the early 1980s, a series of cases saw changes in these approaches as unions sought to close the gender gaps in pay and other aspects of working life. Yet despite changing principles to make wage discrimination unlawful and to bring women-dominated sectors into the system, significant inequalities remained.

The Fair Work Act 2009 (Cth) is the primary labour legislation in Australia, covering approximately 80 per cent of employees. It substantially renovated the national industrial relations system and included provisions for equal remuneration orders and the introduction of a low-paid bargaining stream, both of which aimed to address historic inequalities in regulation. Regardless, scholars still see the system as falling short of facilitating gender equality, and mechanisms for establishing pay equality seem largely to have failed (Charlesworth & Heron, 2012; Cooper & Baird, 2015; Smith & Whitehouse, 2020).

As well as setting out collective processes, the Fair Work Act also establishes various individual rights for employees. Relevant here is the 'Right to Request' Flexible Working Arrangements. This is a contingent right because there are merely rights to *request* (that is, to ask) rather than rights to *receive* flexible working outcomes. The only compulsion on employers is that they must respond to a request within 21 days, and they may refuse requests on 'reasonable business grounds', a concept which includes increased cost to the business. Additionally, the right to ask for flexibility is limited to workers in specific employment contexts; namely, permanent employees who have completed at least 12 months of continuous service immediately prior to making the request. Requests may be for a range of changes, including shorter working hours, compressed schedules and in relation to remote working (Cooper & Baird, 2015).

There has been a widening of the eligibility criteria for requesting under the Act from the initial need as working parents of pre-schoolers and children under 18 with a disability, to include a broader range of carers, those aged over 55 and those dealing with domestic and family violence-related matters (Pocock & Charlesworth, 2017). Flexibility may also be achieved through the Fair Work Act via an Individual Flexibility Arrangement (IFA), which is a written individual agreement between employees and an employer. IFAs, in the same way as the right to request, include no scope for employees to achieve flexible arrangements as a right. In relation to both the 'right to request' and IFAs, outcomes have been shown to be closely linked to industry and occupational characteristics and the ways in which individual line managers understand, interpret and implement policies (Cooper & Baird, 2015; Pocock & Charlesworth, 2017).

Related employment policy areas include the Paid Parental Leave (PPL) Act 2010 (Cth) and the Workplace Gender Equality Act 2012 (Cth). The PPL Act provides 18 weeks' paid leave for mothers and two weeks for fathers. ABS (2017) analysis shows that mothers use the leave far more than fathers do, which, while financially beneficial for them, also increases their absence from the labour market and reinforces gender roles. Advocates argue for more paid parental leave for men in order to encourage them to be more involved in parenting and to equalise time out of work (Baird et al., 2021). The Workplace Gender Equality Act provides for the collection and monitoring of data on the gender composition, pay and policies in Australia's larger companies (100 or more employees), which is an important source of information and soft regulation, but it has little enforcement capacity.

KEY CHALLENGES AND OPPORTUNITIES

The following section is structured in relation to the four main themes identified by the UN Working Group on Discrimination Against Women and Girls (2020): demographic change, technological change, accelerated globalisation, and environmental degradation and the shift towards sustainable jobs.

Demography

Australia confronts several demographic challenges and phenomena that have implications for working women. Chief among them is the ageing population, which is driven in part by below-replacement fertility rates; that is, below 2.1 births per woman (Heard & Arunachalam, 2015).

The Covid-19 pandemic induced a further decline in fertility, with women both delaying and reducing their intentions to have children. During the earlier stages of the Covid-19 pandemic in 2020, 18 per cent of women who had been trying to conceive prior to Covid-19 ceased trying, at least partly because of the pandemic, with most of these women attributing this to concern over their current (53 per cent) and future (81 per cent) financial situation (Australian Institute of Family Studies, 2021). Younger women (in their late twenties) with less secure jobs were more likely than older women (in their thirties) to report that they would delay having children and they would also have fewer children (Australian Institute of Family Studies, 2021). By the end of 2021, the fertility rate dropped to 1.58 (ABS, 2021a). It is speculated that this was due to the combined effects of Covid-19, increased job insecurity, wage stagflation and rising house prices. McDonald (2020) suggested that the delay in fertility intentions may see a recovery in fertility rates in Australia when the pandemic-induced restrictions imposed since 2020 are lifted.

Australia's future fertility trends suggest a continued decline in fertility rates in the absence of policy change. The long-term educational composition of women in their twenties and thirties is likely to continue, which will overwhelm any increases in the fertility rates of women in their forties as improvements to technology and healthy living extend the age of child-bearing women (ABS, 2019c; McDonald, 2020). The ability to combine female labour force participation (LFP) with care for children is an important theoretical and practical consideration for future fertility trends in Australia (McDonald, 2000a, 2000b, 2013). Hence, future trends may be determined by the willingness of Australian governments to expand support for the affordability of, access to and quality of childcare, as well as paid leave, which would ease the reconciliation of paid employment and childbearing responsibilities for women (Rindfuss & Choe, 2015; Thevenon, 2011).

Like most developed nations, Australia's population is ageing, with direct implications for the age composition of the workforce (ABS, 2019b, 2020b). The median age of the Australian population increased from 35 years at 30 June 2000 to 38 years at 30 June 2020 (ABS, 2020b). As shown in Figure 2.2, slower growth in the working-age population has occurred since 2010. Over the five years to 30 June 2020, the working-age population grew by 6.1 per cent compared with 11.4 per cent for the non-working-age population. The main contributor to that growth was the increase in the population aged 65 and over (ABS, 2020b). However, the rapid declines in Australian international migration due to the Covid-19 pandemic could see the non-working population be more than 1 per cent higher than initially forecast (Chomik, 2021).

By 2050, Australians aged 55 and over are expected to make up about 40 per cent of the adult Australian population (Treasury, 2021). Historic surges in participation rates suggest that increased supply of older workers will

Figure 2.2: Working-age (15–64 years) and non-working-age population (0–14 years and 65+ years) in Australia, annual growth rate comparison (%)

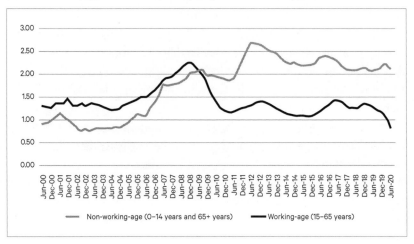

Source: ABS (2020b)

not be sufficient. Instead, the labour market for mature-aged LFP has been driven by a combination of factors, which saw people both re-enter in mid-life and also delay retirement, including the impacts of the global financial crisis (2008–09), which saw reductions in superannuation balances (Baird & Heron, 2020; Chomik, 2021). This was particularly the case for women (Baird & Heron, 2020; McDonald & Moyle, 2020).

Australian women also face more acute care demands. Caring for children, disproportionately carried out by women, is the most common form of care (Australian Institute of Family Studies, 2021). Over 40 per cent of women working part-time over the age of 50 continue to provide care for others (Chomik, 2021), as declines in childcare responsibility in mid-life are partially offset by increased eldercare responsibilities. Delays in childbearing among educated women and ageing parents have increased simultaneous caring responsibilities for many Australians, especially working women (often referred to as the 'sandwich generation' — Gillett &

Crisp, 2017). O'Loughlin et al. (2017) find evidence for the increased growth of grandparental care, mostly provided by women. Hence, concern over low fertility and increased care demands on women is likely to intensify given Australia's demographic trends.

Technology

The 'future of work' discourse assumes a largely homogeneous workforce, uniformly impacted by unfolding disruptions and technological transformations. To date, narratives on workplace change tended to go from 'shop floor to Uber' (Ticona & Mateescu, 2018). The focus has been primarily on *men's* experiences, fears and aspirations in working life. This gender blindness, and bias to men's interests, runs counter to key trends addressed in this chapter, including the rise in women's LFP, ongoing occupational segmentations and segregations, and the inequitable distribution of unpaid work (Foley & Cooper, 2021). In Australia, much of women's participation in the platform labour market, where digital companies broker labour via online applications (also referred to as gig work), has been in care-related fields (Macdonald, 2021), replicating the segmentation in the traditional labour market.

In standard employment settings, the highly feminised occupations in this sector suffer from low pay, high levels of precarity and relatively poor levels of control over working hours (Charlesworth & Heron, 2012; Macdonald & Charlesworth, 2021). There is also evidence that as platforms and algorithmic management have encroached on care work — for example, in areas such as disability support services — it has become even lower-quality work (Macdonald, 2021).

At the other end of the employment spectrum, high-value, high-growth, secure jobs in science, technology, engineering, mathematics and medicine (STEMM) have proven difficult spaces for women to enter and flourish within (McKinnon, 2020; Office of the Chief Scientist, 2020). Recent data make it clear that under-representation of women is severe in sectors like engineering and IT. For example, women make up a mere 13.6 per cent of qualified engineers (Kaspura, 2019) and just 10 per cent of the IT systems and programming workforce (Office of the Chief Scientist, 2020). Women being absent or severely under-represented in these key sectors is not only problematic for gender equality now, as they are missing out on lucrative work, but also means that these inequalities may be imprinted and amplified in the future.

For many years, government, business leaders and gender equality advocate organisations have sought to address these issues by calling for larger numbers of women to train to enter male-dominated sectors, or to get 'women into the pipeline' (Australian Government, 2020; see also Male Champions of Change, 2017). However, this has not radically altered the gendered shape of the student population or the workforce in these sectors (Norton et al., 2018). The challenges for gender equality continue long after women have attained qualifications. Those women who do work in male-dominated occupations experience discrimination, marginalisation and harassment at high rates and with profound personal and professional consequences (Cooper et al., 2021; Foley et al., 2020).

Australian studies have demonstrated that prior to the Covid-19 pandemic there was a strong, unmet demand for high-quality flexible working arrangements, such as forms of technologically enabled remote working, especially among women and parents of young children (Diversity Council of Australia, 2012). Factors including managerial opposition, workplace and industry norms favouring presenteeism, under-development and disjuncture in workplace policies and challenges in job design have limited employees' access to these arrangements (Cooper & Baird, 2015; Cooper et al., 2021).

A large swathe of the Australian workforce, as in most other advanced economies, engaged through 2020 and 2021 with a significant, if forced, experiment in remote working. In 2019, the proportion of people working from home was about 8 per cent but, in line with forced workplace closure and mandated work-from-home measures for 'non-essential' workers, this jumped significantly to 40 per cent in 2020 and 2021 (Australian

Productivity Commission, 2021). Even higher rates of working from home were recorded in states and regions with stronger 'lockdown' arrangements (ABS, 2021b).

Recent survey evidence suggests that as employees plan for post-pandemic working life, they are increasingly interested in maintaining at least partial (or hybrid) work-from-home arrangements and they have an expectation that employers will be in a position to deliver on these demands (Bastion, 2021; Chief Executive Women, 2021). There is a strong gendered element to this demand for remote and hybrid working, with women being significantly more likely to signal interest in these arrangements than men (Ruppaner et al., 2020). Given the longer-run evidence of the penalties that various forms of non-standard work have for career development and earnings and of the strong increase in women's share of unpaid labour in the home during the pandemic (Craig & Churchill, 2021), we must keep an eye on the longer-term gendered implications of remote working post-pandemic (see Priestly, 2021).

Globalisation

Beginning with the British colonisation of Australia in the late eighteenth century, the Australian population has been defined by migration policies, and Australia is commonly referred to as a multicultural society (Department of Social Services, 2020). As of June 2020, 30 per cent of Australia's population was born overseas, with the top four countries of birth being, in order, England, India, China and New Zealand. Most of these immigrants settled in the capital cities where there is employment and infrastructure, and in 2020 they settled mostly in Sydney, Melbourne and Perth.

Original migration policies focused on 'white Australia' and, later, on population growth (with a 'populate or perish' philosophy). Since then, the target of government migration policy has shifted from Europe to Asia and, from the 1990s, has become increasingly focused on workforce growth, addressing employers' skill and labour demands and attracting international students, rather than on family reunions (Wright et al., 2017). The vast majority of Australia's recent migrant intake are on temporary visas, either employer-sponsored migrants, international students or working holiday visa holders.

Of the smaller, permanent migration stream, grouped into skill, family and humanitarian categories, 52 per cent are women, with a higher proportion of women in the family stream (63 per cent) (Dantas et al., 2020). With Covid-19, the federal government suddenly halted immigration and closed Australia's borders (Clibborn & Wright, 2020). Covid-19 has also changed the inflow and outflow of migrants. In the 2020–21 financial year, immigration fell 71 per cent to 145,800 compared with 506,900 arrivals in the 2019–20 financial year, a change of −25 per cent (ABS, 2021d).

Australia's changing immigration policies over the recent past aligned with the rise of globalisation and neoliberalism around the world, with its primary focus on the economy, free trade and international financialisation. The uncritical acceptance of globalisation's benefits for all, however, can be countered by a critical feminist view (Eisenstein, 2010) that globalisation has encouraged migration flows of a particularly gendered character, especially in the Global South (generally referring to nations outside of North America and Europe that are often low-income and politically and culturally marginalised), and enabled the growth in lower-paid jobs that were made available to women. This political-economy realignment was then supported by governments, including in Australia, linking the provision of state-funded benefits increasingly to paid work, and seeing the growth of 'employment citizenship', which directly affects women who, given their care responsibilities, are more likely to receive state welfare (Eisenstein, 2010). As van den Broek and Groutsis (2020, p. 97) argue, migration policy is gendered:

> men have tended to dominate occupational fields such as engineering and information communication technologies, while women have

dominated in fields such as health care, social services and education. Therefore, when governments prioritise the entry of a particular visa category and occupational field, they also unavoidably prioritise the entry of either women or men. These factors reflect how migration policy is inextricably linked to the gendering of work as women and men seek, and are funnelled into, different jobs offered in different parts of the world.

In Australia, the gendered and changing face of migration policy can be illustrated in two key groups: nurses and international students. Both groups provide an important source of labour supply. Internationally and in Australia, migrant women tend to be channelled into 'feminine' jobs, largely in the healthcare and community services sectors, sectors that were highly exposed to and impacted by the Covid-19 pandemic. These female workers, migrating from one country to provide health and care services to often wealthier populations in another country, and sending remittances back to families in their own country, form the global care chain.

Australia plays a part in this global care chain, with many workers in hospital, aged-care and childcare facilities being of migrant origin. Through the stories of six migrant nurses, van den Broek and Groutsis (2020) demonstrate how migration is not only a government strategy monitored in numbers, but also a highly personal process and experience with variable outcomes. For some migrant nurses, migration to Australia was 'to achieve professional and personal opportunity' (p. 97); for others, it was about ensuring their children 'have a better life and education'; and for others, it was about lifestyle, adventure and escape (p. 98).

Another window into the migrant worker experience in Australia is through international students, approximately half of whom are female (Australian Government, 2020). The international student market pre-Covid was the third-highest source of export revenue for the Australian economy. Their visa allows for 20 hours of paid work per fortnight and they provide a significant source of labour for the hospitality workforce.[3] Exploitation and under-payment is widespread (Clibborn, 2021). To overcome this, the Fair Work Ombudsman and others have embarked on inspections, penalties and various education campaigns.

The sudden drop in international student and working holiday visas because of closed borders has impacted on Australia's economic recovery from Covid-19, with many hospitality and agriculture businesses reporting severe shortages in workers. Without a supply of female migrant workers to the country's health sector, there are also serious impending challenges for Australia. The failures of the aged-care sector and the impact of Covid on frontline health workers have further highlighted the need for, and role of, female migrant workers in Australia. Similarly, the earlier reliance on migrant workers and then halting of immigration due to the pandemic have exposed the fault lines in Australia's labour market and training and skill-development policies.

Sustainability

The 2019–20 Australian bushfire season, colloquially known as the 'Black Summer', was a period of unusually intense bushfires in many parts of the country. While climate change does not cause bushfires directly, it has increased the occurrence of extreme fire weather including very low precipitation and high temperature (Commonwealth Scientific and Industrial Research Organisation [CSIRO], 2020). In 2019, Australia experienced its driest year since records began in 1900, and it was also the nation's hottest recorded year (the annual mean temperature being 1.52°C above average) (Bureau of Meteorology, 2019). The intensity of the 2019–20 Australian bushfire season was followed by some of the heaviest rainfall and severe flooding in Australian history (Bureau of

---

3   This was temporarily relaxed during Covid-19 to allow international students to work for more than 40 hours if working in agriculture, supermarkets or tourism/hospitality (Australian Department of Home Affairs, 2021).

Meteorology, 2021). The intensity of climate-change-related natural disasters in Australia has increased the focus of gendered impacts of climate change on women in Australia and brought into sharper relief the voice and role of women in climate change decision-making.

The impacts of climate change on working women in Australia can be divided into two main categories: the damage to women's economic wellbeing and the disruptive impact of natural disasters on women. While men dominate in industries likely to be directly impacted by policy action to combat climate change, such as coal mining, women are likely to be economically vulnerable to cost-of-living impacts of climate mitigation strategies.

The industries at the forefront of political debate in Australia related to climate change, sustainability and environmental management generally tend to be dominated by men: agriculture, forestry and fishing (3.3 per cent of all men in employment, compared with 1.71 per cent of all women in employment in 2019), manufacturing (9.5 per cent of men; 3.9 per cent of women), utilities (1.7 per cent of men; 0.6 per cent of women), and mining and quarrying (3 per cent of men; 0.7 per cent of women) (ABS, 2022). Many of these industries are characterised by lower expected employment growth than more female-dominated employment industries that are less climate-exposed, including healthcare and social assistance, education and training, and administrative and support services (ABS, 2022). Hence, men are more likely to confront the direct burden of shifts away from polluting and unsustainable industries such as fossil fuel mining and coal-fired electricity generation.

Working women in Australia, however, are likely to face greater threats to their economic wellbeing with respect to the associated personal financial costs of climate change mitigation and adaptation. Women are more likely than men to be represented in low economic resource households (defined as belonging in the lowest two quintiles of both equivalised disposable income, including imputed rent, and equivalised household net worth). On average, women earn 14 per cent less than men, and are over-represented in Australia's two lowest income tax brackets ('$0–$18,200' and '$18,201–$45,000') (ABS, 2020a). Hence, working women potentially face higher marginal cost-of-living pressures associated with electricity sector restructuring (Chester & Morris, 2011). In the decade March 2009 to March 2019, the rate of inflation for expenditure classed as 'electricity' saw the second highest increase of 100.9 per cent, second only to 'tobacco' with 'gas and other household fuels' marking the fourth-highest rise (ABS, 2019d).

Food price volatility due to agricultural supply chain disruptions induced by climate change may also emerge as a cost-of-living threat to women's economic wellbeing in Australia (Food and Agricultural Organization of the UN, 2011; UN Development Program, 2020). Single parents are more likely to be renting and so face financial barriers to accessing affordable climate-friendly technologies including solar panels and more energy-efficient household appliances (Infrastructure Australia, 2019). Single- or lone-mother families make up over four-fifths of families (81.8 per cent) led by single parents (ABS, 2016).

The second main category of climate change impacts on working women stems from the social, household and economic disruptions associated with climate-change-exacerbated natural disasters. Analysis of an earlier extreme bushfire event, Australia's Black Saturday bushfire in 2009, indicated that women were more likely to want to flee from properties at immediate exposure to extreme bushfire risk, whereas men wished to stay and defend (Australian Women's Health Network, 2014). Legal centres and domestic violence agencies expressed similar concerns during the 2019–20 Australian bushfire season or 'Black Summer' (Internal Displacement Monitoring Centre, 2020). Post-disaster recoveries are associated with men suffering increased incidences of post-traumatic stress disorder, which increases violence against women (Jewkes, 2002).

The financial stresses associated with a loss of home or other property is especially likely to see financial pressure increase domestic violence against women. The geographical and social dislocation may also lead to a breakdown of broader social supports and structures for women, leading to them being more reliant on the perpetrators of domestic violence for financial survival and/or for access to essential services (VicHealth, 2009). Post-disaster, women are also likely to face a heavy load of unpaid work and care associated with clean-up and subsistence and care for children, elderly and the broader community, often preventing the earning of wages or delaying or creating barriers to returning to paid work (Economic Security4Women, 2020).

Given the gendered dimension to climate change impacts on women, women's voice in climate-change-related decision-making has become more salient in light of climate change mitigation policy increasing in political relevance. However, disaster recovery has often been blind to gender disparity, focusing instead on the heroic roles of men while ignoring the roles and challenges of the women involved (Parkinson et al., 2018). Furthermore, while women make up most volunteering roles, men predominate in paid professional roles in government and organisational involvement in the design and implementation of policies related to climate change and sustainability (Workplace Gender Equality Agency, 2020). This may impede women's voices from being heard as Australia's energy system restructures away from fossil fuels. A total of 66 per cent of women also report having diminished voices in STEMM careers instrumental to innovating new forms of sustainable technologies and practices (Male Champions of Change, 2019).

RECOMMENDATIONS AND CONCLUSIONS

In many respects, Covid-19 and the natural disasters of 2019 and 2020 have been a circuit breaker for Australia and provided an insight into the future. The closure of borders, schools and some workplaces; enforced working from home and the use of new technologies; the importance of the provision of care to the elderly, children, the sick and those with a disability; and the critical role of the state all became more apparent as a result of the pandemic. Prior to this, debates about the future of work, the economy and climate change had focused on men and machines.

As our analyses of the four key areas of change have demonstrated, consideration of women's roles and contributions is central to Australia's future.

We argue that in order to address Australia's fertility and ageing population challenge a reset of government policy in the work and family area that is seamless and more gender equitable is needed. This will require extended parental leave for mothers and fathers, universal childcare and improved eldercare. Changes to workplace regulation are needed to ensure and secure flexible work, which as well as providing economic benefits to society will provide stability for people of childbearing age taking on the responsibilities of family formation.

To enable women to share in the benefits of new technologies — such as the ability to boost their hours, for example through technology-enabled remote working — we need to design carefully for the positive rather than unintended and negative consequences these technologies may bring. We do not want to compound women's disadvantage by ghettoising them into a class of work that lacks a career path, while men enjoy the benefits of progressing within strongly 'presenteeist' workplace cultures. Additionally, while we want women to break down the barriers of occupational and industry segregation to enter into highly paid and secure careers in the STEMM-oriented sectors, sustainable and gender-equitable careers cannot be built for them unless the policies, practices and cultures that make these 'chilly' places for women to work are changed.

To ensure a sustainable future, policies need to to consider the distinct impacts that climate change has on working women in terms of their economic wellbeing and the disruptive effects of natural disasters. Policy responses need to take into consideration women's economic disadvantage in facing greater cost-of-living pressures associated with the electricity sector restructuring and climate change impacts. Responses to natural disasters exacerbated by climate change need to focus on women's social vulnerabilities in the post-disaster recovery phase — including monitoring increases in domestic violence — and to ensure that women's voices in climate change-related decision-making reflect the distinct challenges women face.

The challenges we have noted in the areas of population, globalisation, technology and sustainability are multiple, but they are also interlinked. As women increase their labour market contributions, stresses are placed on the provision of care, both paid and unpaid. As social norms shift, and as industry is restructured and new technologies are introduced, the traditional roles of men and women are challenged and disrupted. As climate change impacts multiply, women's work, family and personal lives are impacted. Therefore, as we have argued, policy responses in all areas, including labour market regulation, work and family, training and skills development and climate change adaptation, need to adopt a gender lens with a multilayered and integrated approach.

3. Working women in Japan

Shingou Ikeda and Kazufumi Sakai

It is often said that Japanese employment practices have been characterised by long-term employment, a seniority age system, and labour unions organised on a company basis that are male dominant (Inagami, 2005; Kawaguchi, 2008; Takeishi, 2006). Employers hire male workers for their core labour force, expecting them to contribute for decades from their graduation to mandatory retirement age (Fujimoto, 2017; Takahashi, 2018). However, female employees are largely treated as a supplementary source of labour and are expected to leave their jobs when they marry or start a family (Imada, 1996; Inagami, 2005). Perhaps unsurprisingly, Japan has a large gender pay gap in comparison with other advanced countries.

Japan's government has made efforts to support women at work, particularly since the Equal Employment Opportunity Act (EEO Act) was passed in 1985, which reformed the Working Women's Welfare Act established in 1972 (e.g. Bishop, 2000; Iwata & Osawa, 2015; Levonian, 2013). The EEO Act regulates gender discriminatory practices and requires that employers support women's job continuation (Imada, 1996; Takeishi, 2006). In the years since the EEO Act was passed, the married women's job continuity rate and the female-to-male ratio of managers in private companies have risen (Gender Equality Bureau Cabinet Office, 2013, 2017). Additionally, Japan's government established the Act on the Promotion of Female

Participation and Career Advancement in the Workplace in 2015.

However, women's work and lives have continued to diversify. Atypical employment, including part-time and fixed-term work, has expanded with post-industrialisation and long-term recession, while policies have continued to be premised on typical (full-time and open-ended contract) ways of working. The number of single women has increased among the labour force population, while public policy has developed support systems for married women (Cabinet Office, 2021; Dalton, 2017; Gordon, 2017). As a result, the scope of such public policies to abolish gender gaps has been limited.

Japan is an island country located in the northwest Pacific Ocean that covers 377,975 square kilometres. It is one of the most densely populated and urbanised countries in the world, with the Greater Tokyo Area's 37.4 million residents constituting the world's most populous metropolitan area. In 1947, two years after its sucrrender at the end of the Second World War, the country adopted a new constitution, under which it maintained a unitary parliamentary constitutional monarchy with a bicameral legislature.

Post-war, Japan experienced record growth. By 1990 it has become the second-largest economy in the world, and has long been known for its leadership in the automotive and electronic industries. In 2021, its economy was ranked third largest globally by nominal GDP. The country is also highly ranked on the UN Human Development Index and has one of the world's longest life expectancies. Japan's population has been declining since 2009 and was 125.8 million in 2020, with women forming 51.2 per cent of this total (World Bank, 2020).

Japan's labour force participation (LFP) rate averaged 64 per cent from 1953 until 2021, peaking at 74 per cent in 1955 and reaching a record low of 59 per cent in 2012. By October 2021, the rate was 62 per cent (Trading Economics, 2021). In contemporary Japan, women, including those who are married and those who have housework and/or childcare duties, commonly engage in the labour market. Around 45 per cent of those employed in Japan are female, and around half of women aged over 15 years are in paid work (see Table 3.1). However, prior to the EEO Act, full-time work was generally only undertaken by unmarried women. It was common practice for women to leave their jobs once they married in order to devote themselves to domestic work. The Act prohibited gender discrimination, and the Child Care Leave Act of 1991 (formally renamed the Child Care and Family Leave Act in 1995) obliges employers to provide long-term leave for childcare to employees with children under one year of age, to facilitate women's job continuity (Imada & Ikeda, 2007).

The M-shaped curve of women's LFP rate by age reveals the decline in women leaving the labour market on account of domestic activity (see Figure 3.1). While the rising bottom of the curve is partly due to the increasing number of unmarried women without family responsibilities who continue to work, the married women's LFP rate is also increasing. Since the 1990s, the ideology of a traditional gender division of labour has been in decline, although it is often reported that a strong gender labour division between paid work and domestic unpaid work still exists in Japan.

The so-called post-industrialisation of the Japanese economy, which means the growth of industries outside of manufacturing, such as service industries, has progressed for decades, expanding the range of vocations (e.g. sales, services, care) deemed suitable for Japanese women. Furthermore, Japan's population is among the most ageing in the world, a feature that is accelerating the expansion of employment in its medical care and welfare sectors. This, and an increasing number of highly educated women, are key reasons behind Japanese employers' use of female labour in white-collar roles, including as managers, professionals and clerical workers, although female managers are still relatively small in number compared to their male equivalents.

While Japan's service sectors have been expanding, they are not as secure in employment wage terms when compared with traditional manufacturing, financial or insurance workplaces. Medical care, welfare services and accommodation, and food and drink services are well-known employers of

Table 3.1: Labour force status in Japan, 2020

	Female (0,000s)	Male (0,000s)	Female ratio (%)	Female (Col. %)*	Male (Col. %)*
Population	64,55	61,56	51.2		
Aged 15 years or over	57,26	53,54	51.7	100	100
Labour force (=A+B)	30,44	38,23	44.3	53.2	71.4
A. Employed persons (=i+ii)	29,68	37,09	44.5	51.8	69.3
i) Total of workers (=a+b+c)	28,15	36,04	43.9	49.2	67.3
a. Engaged mainly in work	20,21	34,41	37.0	35.3	64.3
b. Engaged in work while attending school	86	83	50.9	1.5	1.6
c. Engaged in work while housekeeping	7,08	80	89.8	12.4	1.5
ii) Not at work	1,52	1,04	59.4	2.7	1.9
B. Unemployed persons	76	1,15	39.8	1.3	2.1
Those seeking job as primary activity	54	93	36.7	0.9	1.7
Not in the labour force (a + b + c)	26,77	15,27	63.7	46.8	28.5
a) Housekeeping	12,40	75	94.3	21.7	1.4
b) Attending school	2,77	3,11	47.1	4.8	5.8
c) Other	11,60	11,41	50.4	20.3	21.3

*Col. = collective, i.e. percentage of total labour force
Source: Ministry of Internal Affairs and Communications (2020a)

Figure 3.1: Ratio of labour force by age group in Japan

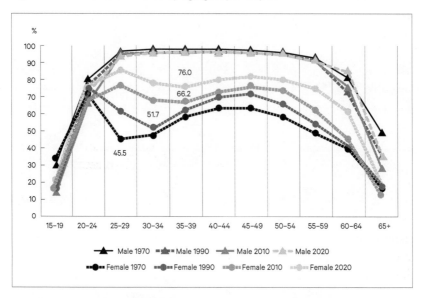

Source: Ministry of Internal Affairs and Communications (2020a)

women, with many filling atypical (part-time and fixed-term) employment, augmenting the long-term trend of an increase of atypical employees as a proportion of all employees. There is concern that many care workers receive insufficient wages due to the financial constraints of the social security budget, although medical care and welfare services are regarded as essential industries in Japan given the ageing population.

Since 2020, the Covid-19 pandemic has heavily impacted on industries in which many women work (Zhou, 2021a, 2021b, 2021c). In this sense, the impact of the virus is gendered. Female workers were more affected than male workers. Some female workers have directly faced the risk of infection at work while others have lost their jobs due to business closures and restructuring. Still others encountered challenges around working from home to avoid infection and balancing this role with that of childcare.

Covid-19 has thus undermined the working life of many women, both revealing and exacerbating gender-gap problems in the Japanese workplace and beyond.

Traditionally, Japanese employment has reflected a male breadwinner system which guarantees male employees sufficient and stable income with long-term employment and seniority-based wages, with women regarded as secondary earners with lower incomes. While the number of double-income couples has been increasing, many wives become part-time workers after childbirth with the expectation that their husband will sustain their household (Ikeda, 2019). Indeed, some mothers fall into poverty following divorce, even if they have a job (Zhou, 2014). Women's dependence on their husband's economic power as the breadwinner has thus placed them in a weak economic position, particularly if they encounter difficulties with their husbands. Arguably, they can choose to engage in work without too much concern for their income when they are in a stable relationship, but poverty affects part-time working single women who can rely on neither husbands nor employers (Kosugi & Miyamoto, 2015; Kosugi et al., 2017).

Thus, while there are increasing numbers of women who participate in Japan's labour market and who stay on in their job after marriage and childbirth, generally speaking, women's income is still lower and their employment is less stable than that of male employees.

EMPLOYMENT REGULATION

The Japanese government has adopted two broad approaches to reducing gender gaps in the workplace. The first emphasises ethical gender equality as justice (Akamatsu, 2003; Gender Equality Bureau Cabinet Office, 2017; Iki, 2011) and draws on a values-based rationale. The second approach is a purpose-based rationale that emphasises economic advantage in the utilisation of female labour for a competitive market and economic growth (Gender Equality Bureau Cabinet Office, 2013; Steinberg & Nakane, 2012; Tsutsui, 2014).

The EEO Act underpins the values-based approach to equity and was established to ratify the United Nations' (UN) Convention on the Elimination of All Forms of Discrimination Against Women. It prohibits a distinction between women and men's retirement age or the dismissal of women due to pregnancy and childbirth (although some employers hire young women on the assumption they will leave their job when they marry or have a child). The statute also prohibits discrimination due to pregnancy or childbirth, such as, for instance, compulsory staying at home, demotion or reduced wages.

Although the government further formulated women's labour policy for the protection and welfare of women in the background of economic recovery and growth after the Second World War, the EEO Act has helped to trigger progress with gender equality in Japan. In Japan's traditional employment system, male workers had experienced a number of advantages over female workers. They were employed as core labour and expected to rise to management or executive positions within a framework of long-term employment that guaranteed their economic stability, while females were peripheral or supplementary paid labour, employed on short-term contracts that supported their family-centred work life (Inagami, 2005). Furthermore, the EEO Act requires that employers review the gendering of their employment practices (Imada, 1996; Takeishi, 2006; Yokoyama, 2002).

Another significant statute, the Child Care Leave Act, was passed in 1991, reflecting the Japanese government's quest since the 1970s to provide support for women's vocational careers. This Act requires that employers provide long-term leave for employees with children under the age of one and entitles both male and female employees to take leave in the interests of promoting gender equality. It thus reinforces the provisions of the EEO Act in encouraging gender equality in both the workplace and the home (Naito, 2008).

However, EEO measures did not expand much in the 1990s due to the long-term recession that followed the bursting of Japan's economic bubble and ensuing political corruption (Takeishi, 2006). Discrimination against female students during recruitment was a notable problem at that time. The 1997 amendment to the EEO Act thus sought to prohibit discrimination between men and women during recruitment or hiring, even though the original Act had required that employers seek to abolish such practices.

Subsequently, in the context of a decreasing birth rate, the Japanese government planned further measures that were designed to support employees' reconciliation of work and childcare roles. The Act on Advancement of Measures to Support Raising Next-Generation Children (Next-Generation Act) was established in 2003 and required that employers make an action plan for supporting employees' childcare needs. All companies that meet government requirements based on the action plan can receive the 'Kurumin Mark' and thus be denoted as an 'excellent' childcare-supporting company. Indeed, companies that achieve the mark use it on their recruitment website and HR employee name cards to appeal to job seekers (Ministry of Health, Labour and Welfare and Immigration Service Agency of Japan, 2021).

By the mid-2000s, with economic recovery, some companies began to stress women's job retention as a key source of labour for company growth (Japan Business Federation, 2014; Ministry of Economic, Trade and Industry, 2003; Sato & Takeishi, 2008). Many companies introduced work–life balance measures, such as childcare leave, to prevent female employees from leaving their jobs due to childbirth and child-rearing and enable them to be promoted to management, executive or highly skilled professional roles.

Against a background of an ageing population, many Japanese employers value women workers and stress their retention, particularly as companies are experiencing labour force shortages due to the decreasing overall population since 2006. To avoid or minimise employee turnover, some employers have tried to improve their working conditions. Employer reforms to address gender discrimination at work via human resource management complement wider regulatory measures. The Japanese government also regards women's labour participation as a source of economic growth. The late prime minister, Shinzo Abe, positioned encouragement of women as one pillar of his economic measures in 2014, and the Act on the Promotion of Female Participation and Career Advancement in the Workplace (Women's Advancement Promotion Law) was established in 2015 to encourage female workers and develop their vocational careers (Cabinet Office, 2014; Eweje & Nagano, 2021).

In this context, the economic approach to encourage women is currently relatively influential. However, these supportive measures in companies do not apply to all working women, many of whom work in marginal or vulnerable positions. Those who are undervalued by employers often face unstable and unfavourable treatment, particularly when compared with that of many male workers. In 2020, the Japanese government established the Act on Improvement of Personnel Management and Conversion of Employment Status for Part-Time Workers and Fixed-Term Workers to prohibit discriminative pay gaps between regular and non-regular employees.

KEY CHALLENGES AND OPPORTUNITIES

Demography

As mentioned, Japan is now the most aged society in the world, with people over 65 years of age forming close to 30 per cent of its total population. The decreasing size of the overall population also contributes to a labour force shortage. The Japanese government has thus stressed labour participation as a key means by which to maintain the economy and productivity levels (e.g. Ministry of Internal Affairs and Communications, 2015).

In this context, women's LFP has become a social issue. In the 1990s, the government began to take measures to counter Japan's falling birth rate. The Child Care Leave Act 1991 and an expansion of nurseries supported mothers' capacity to combine work and childcare. The supply of nurseries for infants under three years of age has been insufficient, particularly in urban areas, though the government has sought to expand their availability to address the increasing number of working mothers since the Second World War (Cabinet Office, 2021; Yokoyama, 2002). Many young couples in Japan live with their parents to receive support with child-rearing and housework, so that young mothers can continue with employment after childbirth. The Japanese government has stressed that such co-residency of adult children and older parents is fundamental to the country's societal welfare (Yokoyama, 2002).

However, changing familial arrangements mean that today's working mothers often face the challenge of insufficient nursery capacity without the option of grandparental care, as an increasing number of young families do not live with their parents nearby. Consequently, taking childcare leave to avoid leaving a job prior to an infant's entry into nursery is key for women who need or wish to continue in paid employment; combining childcare leave and nursery placements is a crucial factor in many Japanese women's endeavours to reconcile work and childcare (Imada & Ikeda, 2007).

Furthermore, it is notable that atypical employees, including part-time or fixed-term contract workers — who are largely women in Japan — find it more difficult to return to the workplace after taking childcare leave compared with employees on open-ended and full-time contracts. Indeed, there is a large gap in the treatment of typical and atypical employees in Japan in terms of their human resource development and wage and employment stability, although the government has sought to tackle inequality between the two. While some women are willing to undertake part-time work or to interrupt their careers for family life, others are reluctant to give up a paid job due to discriminatory treatment (e.g. see Gender Equality Bureau Cabinet Office, 2017). This underscores the unequal employment opportunities among female workers in terms of developing their vocational careers.

To improve many women's work–family life conflict, men's engagement in domestic work has become a social issue since the end of the twentieth century, especially in relation to encouraging Japan's birth rate. However,

Japanese fathers are known for their low commitment to domestic work compared with fathers from other advanced countries (Gender Equality Bureau Cabinet Office, 2020b). Furthermore, the strong cultural norm of the male breadwinner still exists, which requires men to work long hours in paid employment to provide for their wives and children (Hazama, 1996). Thus, Japanese society requires that both husbands and wives assume new work and life roles while they remain tied to deep-rooted, traditional gender roles (Nagai, 2020; Ogasawara, 2009).

On the other hand, unmarried women — who are unable to rely on a husband's income — are growing in number. Some of these women work on fixed-term contracts and/or for wages that are not sufficient for household needs. The Japanese male breadwinner system thus also impacts on single women's working conditions, which are premised on married women as the typical female worker (Ikeda, 2017). Unmarried men also undertake long-term care roles for their elderly parents. While many family caregivers are still wives or daughters, adult sons without wives or sisters, of necessity, increasingly perform these roles (Hirayama, 2014, 2017; Tsudome & Saito, 2007). However, the domestic work associated with eldercare is less time intensive than that required for childcare (Japan Institute for Labour Policy and Training (JILPT), 2015, 2020).

There is also an increasing number of husbands who do not live with dependent children yet provide care to elderly wives. Due to shrinking household arrangements and a decreasing younger population, the number of male workers who provide care to an older family is increasing. About 100,000 employees leave their jobs due to family care each year, and about 10–20 per cent of them are male employees, meaning that, like women, some male workers carry a heavy care burden.

Of middle-aged workers who are likely to need to provide eldercare, many are women in atypical employment, while most of the affected male workers are typical employees who constitute the core labour force of their company. Indeed, the growing number of male family carers is making employers anxious about the departure of their core employees, as single people's combination of paid work and eldercare is increasing as fewer people are getting married (JILPT, 2015, 2020).

Diversification of women's work and wider lives has progressed against a background of social change, including expanding atypical employment, population ageing and increasing numbers of unmarried people. While Japan's government has sought to tackle the protection of married women who try to reconcile full-time work and childcare, its policies have not adequately addressed women's diversification.

Technology

In traditional Japanese work practices, some women have worked from home to undertake manufacturing tasks. More recently, telework, which utilises telecommunication technology, is a growing phenomenon, replacing traditional working from home arrangements (Hashimoto, 2009; Ministry of Internal Affairs and Communications, 2020b). Japanese women have been attracted to work involving computers, with many young female graduates starting their vocational careers as clerical workers in areas such as sales, accounting and judicial affairs (Imada, 1991; Konno, 2000; Ogasawara, 1998). It is thus common for clerical workers to develop skills in using automated office equipment, such as word processors, spreadsheet programs and presentation slides; there is also training for single mothers in Japan who want to learn computer skills to find decent paid work (Zhou, 2014). In these ways, information and telecommunication technology has expanded the suite of occupations available to women in Japan.

Until recently, many young people in Japan's rural areas have had to leave their homes to find jobs in large cities such as Tokyo (Ministry of Internal Affairs and Communications, 2015), with urbanisation a direct result of industrialisation. Population mobility from rural areas to cities has expanded since the 1960s and urbanisation is still occurring during Japan's post-industrialisation phase (Ministry of Land, Infrastructure, Transport and Tourism, 2020). Jobs concerned with information or knowledge are centrally located in large cities. Well-known information technology companies usually set up in Tokyo, and professional and technical services in areas such as law, accounting, consultancy and research and development services are also concentrated in large cities in Japan. However, this urban migration has resulted in social problems in rural areas due to de-population and economic stagnation.

It is anticipated that telework as remote work will encourage women who live in the countryside to pursue job opportunities in any location (Tazawa, 2014). Indeed, jobs that deal in information and knowledge are suited to remote working in rural areas because workers can contact each other through telecommunication technology, overcoming geographical barriers to work that has until recently been largely based in urban areas. Furthermore, some married women who leave employment when their husband transfers jobs can continue in paid work if they can take on remote work for big city organisations while living locally. Telework and remote work can also help to resolve work–life challenges for those women who have to leave their jobs in large cities to provide care to their elderly parents in rural areas (Prime Minister's Office of Japan, 2017).

The Covid-19 pandemic has also stimulated interest in teleworking for those seeking work–life balance and needing to avoid commuting. Just prior to the pandemic, the annual growth rate of telework in Japanese companies was around 20 per cent (in 2019), according to the Communications Usage Trend Survey (Ministry of Internal Affairs and Communications, 2020b). According to a survey by the Cabinet Office on changes in lifestyle and behaviour under pandemic conditions, telework increased after the first declaration of a state of emergency in May 2020 from 10.3 per cent to 27.7 per cent nationwide (Ministry of Internal Affairs and Communications, 2020b). It remained high at 21.5 per cent in December 2020, despite some workers stopping telework after the end of the first emergency declaration. It is notable that the survey results show a higher rate for the metropolitan area around Tokyo than for other localities, implying that the pandemic accelerated the extent of telework in large cities.

Although it was expected that compulsory working from home, driven by state and organisational responses to Covid-19, would accelerate men's engagement in domestic work, it transpired that women spend more hours performing domestic work than men when they are working at home (Gender Equality Bureau Cabinet Office, 2021; Takami, 2020a). Furthermore, full-time male workers with children under 18 years of age (i.e. dependants) have only slightly reduced their working hours, while full-time working women with dependent children have reduced their working hours considerably (Takami, 2020b).

Remote working reinforced gendered roles in relation to paid and unpaid work. However, long-term remote working (i.e. for more than six months) might change this situation in relation to domestic work. Men who continued to work remotely during the pandemic until December 2020 increased their domestic work more than their female partners did (Takami, 2021).

Technology is thus not neutral in its impacts for working women in Japan. It appears to both sustain and change traditional gender roles in the workplace and beyond, and Japan is searching for ways to challenge a gender-biased labour market through telework technologies, among other measures. Information and telecommunication technologies are expected to enable women to mitigate the challenge of conflicts between paid work and domestic work due to the separation of their workplace and residence.

Globalisation

During the 1950s and 1960s, Japan supported emigration, mainly to South America. Emigrants were mostly single men and families. Since the 1990s and the rise of globalisation, the number of long-term overseas residents and overseas permanent residents from Japan has increased (Japanese Association for Migration Studies, 2018). In 2019, the number of long-term overseas residents was about 890,000, 47 per cent of whom were female. The number of permanent residents overseas at that time was about 520,000 (62 per cent female) (Ministry of Foreign Affairs, 2020). A key reason for the high proportion of Japanese women as permanent overseas residents is not thought to be that they work abroad permanently but rather that many have spouses from other countries.

The annual number of Japanese students studying abroad is around 100,000, an increase of 2.5 times since 2010. About 60 per cent of these students are women, their main destinations being Asia, the Pacific region (including Australia), North America and Europe. In Japan, there are few people who can speak a foreign language, including English, so it is advantageous for young men and women workers in the labour market to speak a foreign language. In addition, more women are working in foreign countries where gender equality is more advanced than in Japan.

With regard to inward labour, faced with a declining birth rate and an ageing population, the Japanese government, despite its reluctance to accept immigrants, has considered the need for foreign labour to replenish the domestic labour force. It has promoted the acceptance of highly skilled professional workers to help counter serious labour shortages in certain sectors (Immigration Service Agency of Japan, 2020; Japan Business Federation, 2016; Nagayoshi, 2020; Tomohara, 2020). According to Ministry of Justice statistics for 2020, the employment areas of foreign residents with a particularly high percentage of women include medical care (medical professionals such as doctors, nurses and pharmacists) and long-term care. Of approximately 2500 foreign medical workers, 82 per cent are women, and women form 68.3 per cent of the 1300 long-term care workers in Japan, with both categories of workers being in high demand (see Figure 3.2).

In 2019, the government implemented a new Specified Skilled Workers (SSWs) visa system. It is anticipated that this will bring in a total of 354,000 new migrant workers from 13 Asian countries over a five-year period, helping to fill labour shortages in 14 key industries: nursing care, building cleaning, material processing, industrial machinery manufacturing, electric and electronic information-related industries, construction, shipbuilding and ship-related industries, automobile maintenance, aviation, lodging, agriculture, fisheries, food and beverage manufacturing, and food services

(Immigration Service Agency of Japan, 2021). Among these, nursing care, building cleaning, agriculture, food and beverage manufacturing and food services have a high proportion of female Japanese workers, but due to Japan's ageing population there is an increasing need for foreign workers.

The shortage of nurses and long-term care workers, many of whom are female, is serious given Japan's declining birth rate and ageing population. Japan has signed Economic Partnership Agreements (EPAs) with Indonesia (concluded in 2008), the Philippines (2009) and Vietnam (2014), and has since accepted nurses and Certified Social Worker (CSW) candidates. By 2019, 1421 nurse candidates and 5026 CSW candidates had applied. To work in Japan, they needed to pass the national qualification exam but, due to the Japanese language barrier, their pass rate was only around 11 per cent for nurses and about 45 per cent for CSW in 2019, considerably lower than the pass rate for Japanese candidates. Consequently, there are few nurses and CSWs from the three countries working in Japan (Ministry of Health, Labour and Welfare, 2020b).

At the same time, to transfer skills cultivated in Japan to developing countries and contribute to the economic development of these countries, in 2017 the Japanese government introduced a 'foreign technical intern trainee' system, with the aim of international cooperation (Ministry of Health, Labour and Welfare and Immigration Service Agency of Japan, 2021). However, technical interns are, in practice, utilised as short-term workers, and some companies cannot establish a business without this labour force. Women form 41.6 per cent of these technical trainees. While not officially announced, it is assumed that there are many female trainees in the industries in which many elderly women work, due to a shortage of young domestic workers. The industries facing such problems include textiles (Satoh, 2013) and fish-processing factories (Kong, 2020).

Even prior to the pandemic, some techincal interns were forced to work in poor conditions with low wages. Their efforts to escape, and suicides, became notable social and human rights problems (Nihon Keizai Shimbun, 2018a, 2018b). Due to Covid-19, many are worried that they are

Figure 3.2: Percentage of female resident foreign workers by industry in Japan, 2020

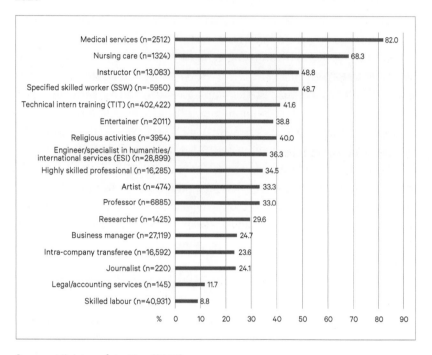

Source: Ministry of Justice (2020)

in workplaces where infection control is inadequate, information on the pandemic is absent, and they cannot return to their home country. It has also been reported that some have lost their jobs due to factory closures, meaning that they live in a vulnerable state (Nagata, 2018; Sunai, 2021). Furthermore, maternity harassment, such as dismissal due to pregnancy, is reported as a problem for female trainees (Sunai, 2020).

In addition, some of these trainees arrived in Japan with a debt of nearly US$10,000 due to the cost of paying intermediaries in their home countries and travel expenses (Sunai, 2019, 2021). The US Department of

State (2021) evaluates that intermediaries exploit foreign workers engaged in the Japanese technical intern training programme, to which the Japanese government's response is inadequate. In other words, this intern training system structurally produces workers who are in debt for the travel costs to come to Japan (Sunai, 2021). While it is difficult to statistically clarify the situation of these female foreign workers, case studies by journalists, sociologists and others (e.g. Iyotani, 2013; Saiki, 2015; Sunai, 2019, 2021; Suzuki, 2021; Tsuzaki, 2018) indicate that they face particular difficulties as both foreign and female workers.

The number of international students coming to Japan exceeded 300,000 in 2019. In 2020, this figure decreased slightly due to the influence of the pandemic on labour mobility. Nonetheless, it has still increased by more than 100,000 in the decade since 2011. The percentage of international students who are female is about 45 per cent (Japan Student Services Organization, 2020). A case study of female employees from Asia who studied at a Japanese university and attained a job at a Japanese company found that, among Japanese companies with large gender role divisions, there are career development difficulties similar to those faced by Japanese female employees and foreign workers (Suzuki, 2017).

International students with weak funding are a source of valuable, unskilled labour for industries dealing with labour shortages. About 1.7 million foreigners worked in Japan in 2020, of whom 17.8 per cent were international students (Ministry of Health, Labour and Welfare, 2020a). In 2019, around 70 per cent of privately funded international students had limited working hours in Japan (a maximum of 28 hours a week legally), engaging predominantly in part-time jobs in restaurants, retail stores and convenience stores (Japan Student Services Organization, 2021). Although the government has not released detailed gender-specific data, a gendered division of roles is likely also affecting the work of international students (e.g. customer service roles are held by females while warehouse operation work is undertaken by males).

Thus, if female workers in Japan are employed as cheap labour due to 'rational' economic arguments and to maintain the male earner model based on gender role divisions, female foreign workers are in a weaker position in the labour market. These contradictory forces converge on these workers, causing them considerable difficulties. In addition, there are challenges for foreign workers that are common to both men and women, such as difficulties caused by differences in language and lifestyle habits, and it can be said that foreign female workers in Japan face double the level of challenges.

Sustainability

Japan has experienced many natural disasters, including frequent earthquakes, tsunamis, volcanic eruptions, heavy rains and floods. These disasters have threatened the sustainability of Japan's economy and society. Indeed, the damage caused by, and ongoing recovery efforts concerning, the earthquake off the Pacific coast of Tohoku and the meltdown of nuclear power plants in March 2011 has been enormous. As of 2021, 19,744 people had been killed, 2556 were missing, and 470,000 were evacuees immediately after the earthquake (Reconstruction Agency, 2021a).

In the wake of major disasters, gender inequities often become apparent. For example, when living in evacuation shelters, women have faced serious human rights challenges including a lack of necessary supplies, shelter management that does not consider women's needs, an increased burden of care roles due to a wider gendered division of labour, and sexual violence (Ikeda, 2012). Even within evacuation shelters, there has been a clear separation of roles based on gender, such as males overseeing decision-making work or physical labour, and females in charge of care work and cooking (Gender Equality Bureau Cabinet Office, 2020a; Hounoki & Okada, 2015; Ikeda, 2012). Even in relief activities at these shelters, women have often taken care of evacuees as medical professionals. As a result, problems have arisen, such as female staff being sexually harassed by male evacuees.

As women often take on family care roles such as housework, child-rearing and long-term care, they tend to give priority to others' needs over their own.

Especially in the event of a disaster — when tragic events occur, women's labour problems are thus often regarded by them and others as 'small things' (Hounoki & Okada, 2015). The labour problems created by disasters for men, as key household earners, are taken more seriously than those for women (Chiba, 2013; Hounoki & Okada, 2015; Okada, 2012; Takenobu, 2012). For example, the unemployment of men is treated more seriously than the unemployment of part-time women workers during disasters.

This approach is premised on women's work not being the main source of livelihood for the family. However, in some cases, such as for single mothers and single women, their livelihoods are sustained by part-time working. Yet, the part-time work of such women is not considered to constitute an earner role but rather is considered a household supplementary role. In other words, the magnitude of the challenge is not assessed from the realities of their lives but from an ideology that emphasises a heterosexual family model where the husband is the main earner and the wife is responsible for family care (Hounoki & Okada, 2015).

Moreover, most leaders of disaster relief, shelter and ordinary disaster-prevention activities in Japan have been men, and women have not participated in important decision-making. As a result, efforts for disaster prevention and disaster/reconstruction support have not reflected the needs and opinions of women, and they have repeatedly faced gender-specific difficulties whenever a disaster occurs (Gender Equality Bureau Cabinet Office, 2020a; Hounoki & Okada, 2015; Ikeda 2012; Takenobu, 2012). However, women are now required to participate in disaster-prevention activities. Some women also participate in reconstruction activities that create new business for supporting people who were affected by the disaster, and make concrete recommendations to incorporate women's viewpoints into local government's disaster-prevention plans (Asano & Tendou, 2021; Gender Equality Bureau Cabinet Office, 2020a; Reconstruction Agency, 2021b).

Assessing volunteer activities, government statistics indicate that men's participation rate is high for security and town planning, and that the number of days in which they engage in volunteer activities is also high. However, there are high levels of participation by women in care areas such as activities for children and senior citizens (Ministry of Internal Affairs and Communications, 2016). Their activities in care areas of work also include security and town planning in relation to children and senior citizens, but they are not recorded as such (Gender Equality Bureau Cabinet Office, 2020a).

As with the gendered division of roles in evacuation shelters, in disaster recovery work in Japan, men dominate in the area of physical labour, such as construction and rubble removal. As a result, paid work in reconstruction projects tends to be allocated to men, sidelining women into part-time, low-paid jobs (Hounoki & Okada, 2015; Ikeda, 2012; Takenobu, 2012). Indeed, the number of female workers engaged in such work is so small that, when female workers are active in reconstruction work, this is reported by the media as a rare event, as in the case of activities involving female radioactive material decontamination workers in Fukushima (Hayasaka, 2015). Of course, many women also perform activities to support the reconstruction work, but this goes unrecorded (Hounoki & Okada, 2015).

Compared with previous catastrophes, the impacts of the Covid-19 pandemic in Japan differ greatly in terms of gender, industry and employment status. Industries that have suffered considerable economic damage include face-to-face service industries that cannot utilise teleworkers (e.g. restaurants and tourism). In these industries, there are many female workers in both regular and non-regular employment.

According to a study of aggregated data on Labor Force Survey Monthly Reports (Zhou, 2021d), the increase in the unemployment rate during the pandemic has been larger for women than for men, and its impact on employment in restaurant and accommodation businesses — and thus on women workers — continues to be severe. Indeed, there is a tendency for women to work in 'recession industries', with this phenomenon being known as a 'she-session'. However, even during the pandemic, the number of women in typical employment has increased. The reason for this is thought to be that medical and welfare recruitment and employment have been strong for women (Zhou, 2021d).

As well as employment trends, it is instructive to examine more qualitative features of the workplace. A recent survey conducted by the Japanese government examined workers' job satisfaction by industry, comparing pre-Covid responses and responses made during the pandemic. According to the report, the satisfaction levels of atypical employees declined more than was the case for typical employees across all industries. By major industry, the decline in employment satisfaction of atypical employees was considerable in fields such as services, medical and nursing care, retail and childcare, where women workers predominate. In care work such as nursery teaching, nursing and caregiving, which also include a high proportion of female workers, significant challenges in terms of work intensification and mental burdens were identified (Gender Equality Bureau Cabinet Office, 2021).

The gendered division of roles is embedded, not only in the labour market but also in society as a whole in Japan. Each time that the sustainability of a society is threatened by disasters, including the Covid-19 pandemic, it brings greater difficulties for female workers than for their male counterparts. However, these challenges have often been regarded as relatively inconsequential.

RECOMMENDATIONS AND CONCLUSIONS

Drawing on the above analysis, we now discuss some recommendations for the Japanese government and other stakeholders, which are aimed at reducing gender gaps and encouraging women in the workplace.

Regarding demographic changes, Japan's government should address labour force shortages that are arising from a decrease in the size of the overall population. It is crucial to encourage women to participate in the labour market and to develop their careers, even during periods when they engage in child- or long-term care. In particular, atypical employees such as part-time or fixed-term workers must be afforded greater support, as they suffer from insecure employment and lower wages which become causal factors of women's poverty. It is, therefore, important that Japanese socio-economic policy emphasises the improvement of women's treatment and workplace opportunities, and supports their economic independence to eliminate gender inequities in Japan's labour market. It is particularly critical that regulation of part-time or fixed-term employment with low wages and job instability is developed.

It is also important for women to learn skills relating to information technology in order to develop their vocational careers and balance their work and family life. It is still common for many women to engage in personal service work without technology, but telework must be designed to assist women's combination of work and caring. Due to Covid-19, some women have been able to work at home while taking care of their children, whose schools are closed, while others have had to work outside their home (e.g. in hospitals, shops and restaurants). Men's way of working and commitment to housework also can be changed through remote working. It is therefore important to develop technology which supports all forms of women's work and family life.

With globalisation, Japan's acceptance of foreign workers will increase to respond to labour shortages due to the ongoing decline in the country's birth rate and its ageing population. Some foreign women who study in Japanese schools are expected to become white-collar workers with higher wages, while others who learn lower skills look to be en route to jobs with lower wages or as trainees. The country must promote a comprehensive and gender-sensitive foreign worker policy (e.g. by including the technical intern training initiative) that supports a competitive economic policy rather than adopt an ad hoc one. As a first step towards achieving this change, there is an urgent need for the government to publish detailed gender statistics on overseas workers and foreigners in Japan.

In relation to sustainability, in Japan, gender roles have been shown to be deepened during a disaster, increasing the burden of women's care work. Central and local governments should ensure equitable access to resources and opportunities for women and men in reconstruction, as this is currently biased against women. While Japan's government often focuses on male-dominanted activities with regard to financial support, it is important that unpaid female volunteer workers who contribute to a sustainable society are adequately supported by the government. In addition, based on experiences in Japan of large-scale natural disasters and the pandemic, which have threatened societal development and sustainability, comprehensive and gender-sensitive policy making in all fields needs to be advanced to help realise gender equality as promoted by the UN's Sustainable Development Goals (SDGs).

Importantly, the state should regulate in a manner that seeks to prohibit gender discrimination in the workplace and beyond. Currently, there is no comprehensive regulation against discrimination. Although the EEO Act seeks to regulate employers' behaviour towards employees, it does not include provisions to prohibit discriminatory behaviour by employees against their colleagues. Rather, its 2016 amendment more specifically requires only that employers seek to prevent colleagues' harassment against pregnant workers. There are also gender-related problems beyond the industrial relations framework (e.g. sexual harassment involving colleagues or customers). It is therefore important to establish a comprehensive framework for eliminating gender discrimination that solves gender-related problems outside the sphere of industrial relations.

In conclusion, the Japanese government should develop policies to empower working women more comprehensively. The deep-rooted nature of gender discrimination in Japan, both in the workplace and beyond, requires that the government and others, such as trade unions, community groups, women's groups and employer bodies, coordinate their activities and focus on both the labour market and other contexts to realise a gender-equal society. Over the years, the government has sought to eliminate discrimination in the workplace and to encourage female workers' empowerment. Overall, however, the scope of regulation has been limited and improvement has been slow.

Moreover, diversification of women's work and lives extends beyond that which has been addressed to date by regulation. The government has sought to support 'typical' women as 'typical' or standard employees. Typical employment in Japan has traditionally concerned full-time and long-term employment wherein workers stay with the same organisation for decades. However, atypical forms of work such as part-time or fixed-term contract roles have grown in significance.

Beyond the workplace, Japanese people have traditionally married, raised children and not sought to divorce. The government has tended to focus its support on married women who wish to continue their paid job at the same organisation. Consequently, some of these women have reduced the employment opportunity gap with their male colleagues, while a growing body of other, less 'typical' working women continue to face gender discrimination beyond the areas addressed by regulation. It is therefore crucial for the Japanese government, employers, unions and others to work together to develop initiatives that will empower all women to eliminate gender discrimination in society and address the increasingly diverse and intertwined nature of women's work and non-work lives.

Japan in focus: Working women and men's changing family responsibilities

Shingou Ikeda and Kazufumi Sakai

This short commentary examines changing gender roles around child- and eldercare and combining work and family life in Japan. It complements Chapter 3 by focusing on male workers' commitment to care.

In relation to women's career development, the Japanese government has supported women's work–life balance since the 1970s, beginning with the Working Women's Welfare Law 1972, which was reformed as the Equal Employment Opportunity Act (EEO Act) 1985. This Act prohibits dismissal and disadvantageous treatment (e.g. compulsory staying at home, demotion, reduced wages) due to pregnancy and childbirth as a counter-measure against gender discrimination. Additionally, the falling birth rate resulted in the establishment of the Child Care Leave Act 1991, which obliges employers to provide long-term leave for employees with children under one year of age. This Act was reformed as the Child Care and Family Care Leave Act in 1995, adding the regulation on family care leave. The government has also expanded the number of nurseries for infants to support working mothers in response to a seriously deficient supply of nurseries in urban areas. It has thus made efforts to expand support by reducing working women's childcare burdens as a response to the falling birth rate, rather than to improve gender equality.

However, as Japan's birth rate did not increase in the 1990s, since the 2000s, the government has promoted further countermeasures, focusing on fathers' commitment to childcare as well as mothers' labour participation. A key issue has been the relatively few male workers who take childcare leave despite the Child Care and Family Leave Act entitling male employees to do so on the basis of gender equality. Furthermore, Japanese fathers' time spent on childcare is shorter than is the case in various other countries, while Japanese mothers spend a longer amount of time on childcare than is the case elsewhere. Some commentators have attributed a work-centred culture to Japanese fathers' avoidance of taking leave for family life, with long work hours preventing them from undertaking childcare, as many fathers go home late at night after their children have gone to sleep (Matsuda, 2002; Saito, 2020). Work–life balance has thus become an issue for fathers as well as for mothers.

In response, the Act on Advancement of Measures to Support Raising Next-Generation Children (the Next-Generation Act), established in 2003, requires that employers make action plans that include both male and female employees taking childcare leave if their company is to receive the 'Kurumin' Mark for excellence in supporting childcare. A well-known governmental campaign, the 'Ikumen' Project, recommends that both employers and male workers take childcare leave, with a commitment to childcare, starting in 2010 in the context of a 2009 amendment to the Child Care and Family Care Leave Act.

Today, an increasing number of fathers are taking childcare leave and the average amount of time they spend on childcare is growing, though husbands' and wives' gender roles have not significantly altered as mothers' time spent child-rearing has also increased (Nagai, 2020). To accelerate the change, therefore, the 2020 amendment of the Child Care Leave and Family Care Leave Act establishes a new kind of paternity leave, entitling fathers to four weeks' leave. This leave can be divided into two time periods so that fathers can take leave more flexibly at the time of childbirth, and couples can take turns with childcare leave.

In 2020, there was some expectation that gender-based family relations would be influenced by the Covid-19 pandemic as it led to an expansion of working from home. However, the pandemic has revealed ongoing, deep-seated gender role divisions in Japan. Some mothers assume a very heavy burden around childcare compared with their husbands, and Japanese fathers often work overtime and late at night, although mandated remote working should increase the time that fathers are able to commit to child-rearing (Takami, 2020).

Despite the increasing number of working women as a result of supportive labour policies in Japan, traditional gender relationships around childcare remain entrenched. Many women still expect their husbands to be the 'breadwinner' rather than adopt a carer role, even if they are working at the time of marriage or childbirth. It still seems to be common for married women to stress their motherhood roles even if they face poverty due to their husband having a low income (Zhou, 2014, 2019). In addition, more attention needs to be paid not only to child-rearing, but also to the care provision of elderly parents if familial gender roles are to change.

While many married couples retain conservative gender roles, there are an increasing number of unmarried men and women in Japan (indeed, the bond between marriage and childbirth is so strong that Japan has few never-married parents who are raising children). Young people may feel that it is disadvantageous to marry if they want to spend their time and money on non-familial matters such as study, work and leisure. While some unmarried workers maintain their household and do their own housework, others live with their parents and receive support with housework (Yamada, 1999), reflecting the strong connections between adult children and their elderly parents in Japanese families, with adult children receiving financial or housework support from their parents, while expected to care for their frail parents in the future.

However, Japan faces long-term care challenges as one of the most aged societies in the world. This is despite the government expanding the country's social care services financed by Long-term Care Insurance since 2000, and statutory long-term leave for caregivers to provide family care being established as part of the Child Care and Family Care Leave Act in 1995. In addition, gendered roles around eldercare are highlighted when there are women in families (Yamato, 2008); long-term care is a key issue for working women in the context of an ageing population (Sodei, 1989; 1995). Those workers who leave their job to provide family care tend to be women, and professional care workers are also mostly women.

Although the government's efforts to expand social support for eldercare could help to alleviate women's heavy family care burdens, this has not been progressed as much as might be expected due to financial constraints on the Long-term Care Insurance system related to an increasing number of service users due to an ageing population. To the contrary, some have observed a 're-familisation' of long-term care in Japan, with restrictions on social care services returning the burden of caregiving to the family (Fujisaki, 2009).

The picture is further complicated by families becoming smaller, decreasing the number of children available to care for elderly parents. Consequently, some families do not have wives or daughters to take on this role that traditionally falls to women, resulting in an increasing number of husbands and single adult sons providing care to their wives or parents (Hirayama, 2014, 2017; Tsudome & Saito, 2007), although married sons often rely on their wives to provide care to their elderly parents.

Thus, while female part-time workers form the mainstay of working carers, male full-time employees are an increasingly important source of such care. This demographic change is encouraging employers to recognise that their support for working carers is a key management issue in the retention of their core labour force. Women's turnover is an equally important issue if women are expected or are to be able to be part of the core labour force, developing their careers as full-time employees and becoming managers. How best to combine work and care roles has become a common concern for both men and women in Japanese companies (Ikeda, 2021).

The expansion of long-term family care roles among male workers encourages new thinking about the assumptions on which policies that support work–family life balance are based. Traditional policies based on a principle of 'no work, no pay' and a childcare policy entitling workers to long-term leave and shorter working hours presuppose that carers have a spouse who is a breadwinner. However, many working men who are carers are also the breadwinners of their households and they cannot sustain long-term leave on a lower or decreased income. As well as undertaking eldercare, single male and female carers must maintain their households, implying that existing long-term leave and shorter working hours with lower incomes are not viable approaches for breadwinner carers.

Amendments in 2016 to the Child Care Leave and Family Care Leave Act reformed the support system for long-term care so that working carers can commit to work as much as possible to keep their income and occupational careers. The long-term care leave of 93 days has become divisible into three timeframes, and the entitled exemption from overtime work supposes that shorter working hours are not necessary as many carers can work their scheduled working hours as usual, even if they cannot work longer hours (Ikeda, 2021).

In summary, couples' gender roles around childcare are deep-rooted and gender equality efforts will not easily change them. However, an increase in the number of unmarried adult sons with care responsibilities for their elderly parents stresses the need to reconsider gender roles concerning family care. Due to Japan's ageing profile, moreover, the need for husbands to care for their sick or frail elderly wives is growing, suggesting that the increase in elderly male carers may help to shift gendered responsibilities more rapidly than will be the case with fathers' increasing commitment to childcare.

4. Working women in China

Huiping Xian

A significant level of progress has been made with gender equality in workplaces in China. Chinese women have one of the highest rates of labour market participation in the world and chairman Mao Zedong proclaimed that they 'uphold half of the sky' (Woodhams et al., 2009; World Economic Forum, 2020). However, their participation rate has fallen since 1990, and gender discrimination at work and in other economic activities has been widely reported (e.g. see Global Entrepreneurship Monitor, 2020; Human Rights Watch, 2018; Kuhn et al., 2020).

This chapter analyses working women (defined as formal and informal workers, the self-employed and those engaged in entrepreneurial activities) with regard to employment regulation and four key themes: globalisation, technology change, demographic change and sustainability. It argues that, given traditional gender norms and weak enforcement of employment regulations, women's employment rights are not well protected.

While the development of internet and mobile internet technologies has provided many women with new entrepreneurial opportunities online, they are also more likely to fall into vulnerable self-employment, especially since the Covid-19 pandemic. Recent demographic trends and new family planning policy, which allows each couple to have up to three children, may further weaken women's labour market position. This chapter calls for government measures and interventions to ensure that the sustainability of Chinese families and society is not achieved at the expense of gender equality.

China is the third largest country in the world in geographic terms, covering approximately 9.6 million square kilometres (World Bank, 2020b). It is the world's most populous country, with more than 1.4 billion people. Females form 48.7 per cent of China's population (World Bank, 2020c), with an imbalance in the country's sex ratio at birth due to China's one-child policy declining to a normal level with the gradually liberalising and multi-stage two-child policy (Fan et al., 2020). Globally, China is the largest economy by GDP, with a forecast indicating that it will become the world's largest economy in nominal GDP by 2028 (Elliot, 2020). China's economy is a developing, market-oriented mixed economy that incorporates economic planning through industrial policies and strategic five-year plans, and is the world's biggest manufacturer and exporter.

The government has conducted a series of economic reforms since 1978 under the leadership of Deng Xiaoping (Galvez, 2012), and entered the World Trade Organization in 2001. It is also a member of the United Nations (UN) Security Council, the BRICS (Brazil, Russia, India, China and South Africa), the G8+5, the G20, the Asia-Pacific Economic Cooperation (APEC) and the East Asia Summit. However, it ranks among the lowest on international measurements of civil liberties, government transparency, freedom of the press, and freedom of religion and ethnic minorities. It is currently governed as a unitary, one-party socialist republic by the Chinese Communist Party (CCP).

EMPLOYMENT REGULATIONS

In many ways, gender equality is at the centre of China's long-term political and ideological project. Since 1954, China has enacted various regulations to protect women's employment rights. Article 48 of the Constitution of the People's Republic of China states:

> Women ... enjoy equal rights with men in all spheres of life, political, economic, cultural and social, and family life. The state protects the rights and interests of women, applies the principle of equal pay for equal work for men and women alike and trains and selects cadres from among women. (UN Women, 2021)

Major pieces of statute relating to women's rights and protection in the workplace include Regulation Governing Labor Protection for Female Staff and Workers (1988), Law on the Protection of Rights and Interests of Women (1992, revised in 2005), Labor Law (1994, revised in 2020), Employment Promotion Law (2008), and Labor Contract Law (2008, revised in 2012). These regulations restate the principle of gender equality at work and aim to guarantee various employment rights for women, including equal pay for equal work, prohibition of recruitment discrimination, an equality principle for promotion, and addressing women's health, wages, benefits and other labour issues.

The Labour Promotion Law (2008) prohibits employers from discriminating against migrant women workers who are moving to urban areas in search of employment. It also provides job-seekers and employees with the right to bring a lawsuit for employment discrimination against a company. Another stream of legislation that is associated with women's protection are Chinese labour regulations which protect the employment status and wages of women during pregnancy, delivery and breastfeeding, and outlaw sexual harassment.

However, some 'protective discrimination' regulations are controversial. For example, current employment regulations include a list of jobs (e.g. mining, scaffolding) that are deemed unsuitable for women. Furthermore, there is a gender-based difference in the state retirement age, where men can remain at work until the age of 60 while women must retire at 55. These practices have been criticised for leading to gender-based occupational segregation and women's under-representation in leadership roles, where promotion to such is based on seniority (Woodhams et al., 2009). Earlier retirement also jeopardises women's income and pension capacity (Yang & Li, 2009).

Moreover, China's anti-discrimination laws and regulations are often criticised for their lack of transparency and enforceability. For example, the term 'gender discrimination' does not have a comprehensive legal definition in China. As a result, it might be difficult to determine what constitutes discrimination and to thus develop a systematic approach to tackling discriminatory workplace practices. Furthermore, most legislation only sets out broad principles for national and local governments rather than outlining specific rules and definitions that inform how those principles are executed in practice (Yang & Li, 2009).

Women who decide to sue their employers also have to go through a tedious process before their cases can be accepted in an employment tribunal. A victim of employment discrimination is often advised to first report to women's organisations (mainly the Women's Federation at local levels), which will communicate and coordinate with the relevant government departments that investigate the case and propose a settlement. Women victims can only seek help in litigation and bring a lawsuit after both sides fail to agree to a settlement. As Yang and Li (2009, p. 304) commented, this process reflects 'the traditional political and administrative means to settle labour disputes', and its effectiveness depends largely on local government officials and judicial staff's gender awareness.

Unlike many Western regulations that prioritise women's empowerment, current Chinese employment regulations have been developed based on paternalistic views and notions. While anti-discrimination laws and regulations protect women's employment rights to some extent, some emphasise biological differences between men and women, reinforcing the presumption that women are 'weaker' and 'intellectually inferior'. These regulations restrict women's choice of work, with a lack of practical guidance providing little remedy to employer violations.

KEY CHALLENGES AND OPPORTUNITIES

In line with the UN Working Group on Discrimination Against Women and Girls' (2020) global thematic report, the following sections consider working women with regard to key globalisation, technological, sustainability and demographic challenges in China.

Globalisation

Globalisation and China's associated market reform have undoubtedly had profound impacts on women's labour market position (Cooke & Xiao, 2014; Woodhams et al., 2015). However, the situation is far from clear cut. On the one hand, a number of positive features for women have been linked to globalisation and the market-led economy. Firstly, large inflows of foreign direct investment (FDI) and foreign ownership are thought to act as a driving force for the dissemination of 'best practice' human resource management (HRM) and the transfer of emancipatory values into contemporary Chinese workplaces (Woodhams et al., 2015).

China has been one of the biggest recipients of FDI among developing economies since the 1990s, with multinational corporations bringing employment opportunities to Chinese women. It has also been suggested that Western HRM policies with an emphasis on formal equality ought to offer some protection from discrimination (Cooke & Xiao, 2014). Globalisation and market reform have also created a competitive and less regulated labour market in China, which may encourage employers to move away from gender-based assumptions and focus more on employees' skills and competencies.

Secondly, globalisation has created opportunities for young Chinese women (especially those from urban, middle-class families) to study abroad, an experience which significantly increases women's human capital. Since 2011, the number of Chinese students studying in the UK has increased by 90 per cent (Bolton, 2021) and, in recent years, more than half of Chinese students studying overseas have been women (Zhang & Xu, 2020). While the Covid-19 pandemic has had a negative impact on international students' visas and mobility, Chinese students' demand for overseas education remains unchanged (Lou, 2021). Many Chinese female students believe that studying in the UK helps them to self-realise and that an overseas qualification will facilitate their early and mid-career development (Matthew, 2014).

On the other hand, there are also less positive developments in China for women workers that link to globalisation trends. Firstly, traditional state supports for women's employment such as free childcare, communal canteens and a gender quota system have been largely removed from the private sector, putting pressure on the dual-earner model and women's participation (Woodhams et al., 2015). Indeed, Chinese women's labour force participation rate dropped from 73.2 per cent in 1990 to 60.5 per cent in 2019 (World Bank, 2019).

Secondly, without job allocation — a national measure to ensure women's full-time employment during the Communist years (1949–79) — women have been segregated into sectors such as food industry, low-skilled manufacturing, domestic service and hospitality where they receive low pay and have limited job security in an increasingly market-orientated economy. Chow and Zuo (2011) observed that globalisation benefits Chinese men more than Chinese women as many (especially migrant) women are employed as cheap labour and are more vulnerable during a global recession due to lower consumer demand from developed economies. As a result, China's gender pay gap (36 per cent in 2019) is one of the largest among industrial countries (World Economic Forum, 2020). Furthermore, although women are now receiving almost the same level of education as men, Chinese women formed only 9.7 per cent of boards of directors in listed companies in 2019 (World Economic Forum, 2020).

Thirdly, globalisation and the liberalisation of the Chinese economy has meant that women have become further distanced from the protection of the state as an employer (Woodhams et al., 2015). Despite legislation against gender discrimination at work, women's employment rights are not guaranteed (Woodhams et al., 2009). For example, 90 per cent of job advertisements for civil service positions in 2018 listed a requirement or preference for male candidates (Human Rights Watch, 2018). Recent evidence suggests that discrimination against women during recruitment has worsened, especially after the one-child policy was replaced by the two-child policy in 2016 because employers expect women to spend more time on childcare and domestic chores (Cooke, 2017). For job advertisements targeting women, many now specify that women should be married with children and/or possess specific physical attributes (e.g. to do with their height, weight, age, voice) that are unrelated to job specifications (Human Rights Watch, 2018; Woodhams et al., 2009). Chow et al. (2011) have been critical of globalisation enabling capitalist expansion driven by neoliberal ideology, policies and practices into China without challenging men's dominance.

Thus, it has been argued that globalisation has not fundamentally challenged traditional gender assumptions in China (Cooke & Xiao, 2014). Rather, it has found a way to accommodate the gendered construction of the 'ideal worker' in the West alongside the Confucian notion of a 'good wife/mother' for the sake of the husband's family. While women are now expected to combine both 'breadwinner' and 'carer' roles, they are also considered to be less productive by most employers and often have to fight against gendered stereotypes, discrimination and exploitation. Related to this, women are more likely to face furloughs, pay cuts, demotion and even sexual harassment (Chow & Zuo, 2011; Woodhams et al., 2015).

Technology

A significant area where technological changes have affected Chinese women's work and economic activities since the turn of the century is in the increasing popularity of digital technologies, including the internet, mobile internet and associated applications. Online retailing in particular has witnessed a rapid increase in women's entrepreneurial activities. A recent study by AliResearch (2019) identifies that at least 49 per cent of Chinese entrepreneurs on the Alibaba platform (China's largest online marketplace) are women. Women's presence in online retailing may be a result of the Chinese government's long-term strategy of moving to e-commerce (Yu & Cui, 2019).

The same study also observes that a large number of young and educated women entrepreneurs have entered the online retailing business. For example, most female shop owners on Taobao (China's equivalent of Amazon) were born in the 1980s and 1990s and around 55 per cent are aged 23–33 years old. In terms of education, 46 per cent of the female store-owners obtained a university degree or higher and many have better skills in foreign languages than their male counterparts (AliResearch, 2019). These enhanced human capital capacities could help young Chinese women entrepreneurs move away from traditional low-skilled household-related services. However, echoing debates elsewhere, there have been mixed views about the extent to which these recent changes reflect actual progress for women's participation in work and entrepreneurial activity. Unlike 'high-tech' entrepreneurial activities, online retailing benefits from such features as low barriers to entry and an abundance of information.

Prior research in other contexts shows that digital technologies offer, to some extent, an opportunity for women to negotiate day-to-day challenges in their offline lives and, in doing so, promote women's empowerment and emancipation (McAdam et al., 2020). In China, digital technologies have been credited with freeing women from the limitations of time, space and pace to engage in entrepreneurial activities and enjoy more flexibility, and may have encouraged Chinese women's willingness and capability in pursuing social mobility through entrepreneurial activities (Zhao & Yang, 2015). Even rural women, who have traditionally received low levels of recognition for their economic contributions, have been incorporated into the digital economy (Yu & Cui, 2019).

On the other hand, it has been recognised that women's entrepreneurial opportunities in the digital economy do not necessarily translate into substantial changes in gender equality, as Chinese women account only for 10.2 per cent of those engaged in entrepreneurial activities (Global

Entrepreneurship Monitor, 2020). Prior research has identified a number of issues affecting women's entrepreneurial activities. Firstly, many Chinese women store-owners have received little training on running businesses online. They also do not anticipate the growth of their businesses which, as a result, have had a much higher rate of failing within the first three years than is the case with men's online businesses (Yu & Cui, 2019). Furthermore, most female store-owners using the Alibaba platform have not seen themselves as entrepreneurs and believe that their digital skills are not transferable to offline environments (Yu & Cui, 2019).

Secondly, while women's involvement in online business helps, to some extent, to redistribute gender-based power and contribute to family income, their contributions tend to 'blend in' with domestic work, childcare and eldercare, resulting in their low recognition and economic status (Yan & Zhou, 2015). Rural women in particular are often confined by traditional patriarchal family norms, with their work in the informal economy also tending to be less visible. Yu and Cui (2019, p. 433) suggest that rural women's involvement in the digital economy is mostly 'in exploitative ways as cheap, underpaid, unpaid and devalued labour' due to traditional patriarchal norms involving self-sacrifice, domesticity and subordination.

Thirdly, the rising number of young and educated women participating in the online retail sector may reflect fierce competition in the labour market and the gender bias that women face in recruitment and selection. Recent evidence suggests that discrimination against women has been exacerbated since the adoption of the two-child policy in China, as will be explored later in this chapter.

Explicit gender-related requests in job advertisements are also commonplace in the Chinese labour market. Kuhn et al. (2020) find that gendered jobs aimed at young and educated women tend to concern low-skilled and low-paid administrative work (e.g. as a receptionist or office clerk), whereas those directed at men include both technical and managerial jobs (e.g. as a technician, production manager or warehouse manager). This gender-stereotypical recruitment, coupled with the uncertainty of employment opportunities in China's transitional economy, can lead young women to engage in self-employed or entrepreneurial activities in sectors of the digital economy that have low barriers to entry but little social protection (Hernandez et al., 2012).

Demography

A key demographic influence on women's work and family in China has been its controversial former one-child policy (OCP) and resultant 4-2-1 family structure (four grandparents, two parents and one child). The impact of the OCP can be examined with regard to three important issues for females who are an only child: education, work and eldercare.

Food shortages and the need for economic reform encouraged China's leaders to develop measures to control population expansion during the 1970s. Against this backdrop, the government introduced the OCP in 1979 as a family planning mechanism designed to limit the number of children born to each family. Nationally, the OCP was promoted as a trade-off between quality and quantity (Falbo & Hooper, 2015), whereby married couples were advised that, instead of having two or more children, they should focus their energies on one child.

The policy applied mainly to the ethnic majority *han* people living in urban cities where social resources were scarce. Some exceptions were allowed, including families in which the first child had a severe disability or both partners were themselves from one-child families. The policy was also sometimes loosely enforced in rural areas, whereby a second child was permitted in the space of five years if the first-born was a girl, a clear indication of the preference for sons.

Compliance with the OCP was underpinned by a series of reward and punishment schemes. 'Only-children' were prioritised for social welfare such as schooling, employment and housing, while violations could result in financial penalties, confiscation of property or dismissal from work (Hesketh et al., 2005). Consequently, by the 1990s, nearly 90 per cent of children from urban areas and almost 60 per cent of children from rural areas had no siblings (Chen, 1994). Four decades after the introduction of this policy, despite only-children employees now being a crucial part of the Chinese labour force, there has been only limited research on related work and gender issues. And although the OCP was repealed late in 2015, only-children will dominate Chinese workplaces for some time to come.

While research is required to develop in-depth understanding of only-child workers in general, extant studies indicate important differences between only-children and those with siblings, and between male and female only-children. Firstly, it has been suggested that the OCP may have enhanced women's access to family resources such as education, thereby helping to level the 'playing field' between men and women in the workplace. In 2019, 52.5 per cent of all undergraduate students and 49.8 per cent of all postgraduate students in Chinese universities were women (National Bureau of Statistics, 2020). This may not be surprising, as in a Confucian tradition that stresses continuous learning and education, most urban parents are willing to invest heavily in the education of their only-children. Furthermore, Falbo and Hooper (2015) reported that only-children achieve higher academic success than those with siblings. However, recent research indicates that many Chinese families continue to prefer male heirs even at the risk of government sanction (Xian et al., 2021).

Secondly, economic and sociological research into the OCP has identified its role in creating an ageing population and in placing an increased burden of eldercare on only-children (especially female only-children). China's total fertility rate dropped from 2.75 in 1979 to 1.66 in 2016, while the proportion of the population aged 65 and above increased dramatically from 4.5 per cent to 9.8 per cent over this period (World Bank, 2016), putting pressure on China's eldercare and pension systems.

In the Confucian tradition of filial piety, children are expected to treat their ageing parents and grandparents with loyalty, respect and physical care (Strom et al., 1996). Thus, one direct effect of the OCP has been that, with an ageing population, an only-child is expected to shoulder the burden of eldercare without sibling support. This increased pressure for eldercare also means that the OCP has changed the gender dynamics within Chinese families, wherein women are expected to go back to their 'feminine roles', for example, as caregivers (Cooke & Xiao, 2014).

Thirdly, and unsurprisingly, limited research suggests that female only-children struggle to meet demands from both work and family domains (Cao et al., 2015; Xian et al., 2022). Many female only-children have high career expectations due to their enhanced education level, yet they are more likely to suffer from work–life conflict compared with their male counterparts. To avoid a backlash, a female only-child will often adopt a 'conformist strategy' and accept traditional gender roles while trying to 'do it all' (Xian et al., 2022). Xian et al. (2022) find a positive relationship between their work–life conflict and career aspirations in that their ability to withstand work–life conflict without dropping out increases their self-belief and career ambition, and their ability to juggle work–life demands works in their favour to advance their career development.

China ended the OCP due to the increasing pressures of an ageing population, low birth rate and rapidly shrinking workforce. It was replaced with a universal two-child policy. In June 2021, China further relaxed control to enable a maximum of three children per couple (see also Fan et al., 2020). While the full effect of this new policy remains to be seen, early evidence suggests that this change has resulted in similar gender discrimination against women in the workplace as encountered under the two-child policy (Cooke, 2017), stressing an apparent tension between gender equality and the sustainability of Chinese families.

Sustainability

Apart from the controversial OCP, China's family policies have not attracted as much attention as its economic and environmental policies. In terms of social sustainability, the OCP and subsequent family policies have impacted on the sustainable development of Chinese families, Chinese women in the workplace, and the incompatibility between gender equality and family policy.

In a Confucian kinship system, a family has always been an important social institution that provides security and support to its members (Sison et al., 2020). Family ties are an important source of *guanxi* (personal trust and reciprocal relationships), which significantly expands an individual's network. The role of the family has become even more crucial since the early 1990s, when the state reduced many welfare supports such as housing, subsidised childcare and pensions — benefits which were popular among women during the Communist years. Pensioners often rely on their children for eldercare and young couples also rely on their ageing parents for childcare provision. However, the OCP and its resultant 4-2-1 family structure have been widely blamed for greatly undermining the sustainability of Chinese families and the traditional function of the family in providing security (Yang & Huang, 2020). Chinese women's relatively high labour market participation rate means that support from family members is on the decline. Thus, in China's 12th Five-Year Plan (2011–2015), policy-makers proposed a commitment to 'increasing family development capacity . . . promoting the construction of population and family planning service systems'.

In response to an ageing population and shrinking labour force, the Chinese government ended the OCP to allow married couples to each have two children from 2016. However, uptake of the two-child policy has been low and China's fertility rate has not significantly increased as expected since the policy's implementation. In 2019, China's fertility rate was 1.7 births per woman, a mere 2.4 per cent increase since 2015 (World Bank, 2020a). Recent research shows that young Chinese women's desires to have a second child have been low due to high living costs, shortages of childcare and healthcare facilities, reduced intergenerational childcare from grandparents and career pressures on women (Zhong & Peng, 2020).

Although many women have opted out of the two-child policy, they inevitably face further gender discrimination in the labour market owing to employers' perception that hiring a woman will incur extra costs. In China, the costs associated with a female employee's child-bearing and child-rearing activity (including time off for pregnancy checks, maternity leave, and for looking after a sick child) are mainly covered by the employer. Unsurprisingly, women, especially those who are an only-child themselves, encounter escalated employment discrimination as employers expect women to accommodate the dual pressures of childcare and eldercare with little support.

More specifically, female university graduates are reported to experience serious discrimination during recruitment and selection stages, with some employers changing recruitment criteria from 'married with a child' to 'married with two children' for female candidates (Cooke, 2017). At the same time, professional women who have a child are frequently denied promotion as employers anticipate that they will soon have a second child (Zhang et al., 2019). Thus, China appears to face a tension between achieving gender equality and sustainable family development.

After reviewing 112 family policies between 1989 and 2019, Yang and Huang (2020) point out that Chinese family policies often involve indirect goal planning at the macro-level but lack direct and effective support for the family responsibilities of both the husband and wife. While the Chinese government has been trying to tackle the ageing population and increase the sustainability of Chinese families, existing family policies have not provided more targeted support for working women in the family, resulting in gender discrimination and a work–family imbalance, with increased risk for families (Yang & Huang, 2020).

IMPACTS OF THE COVID-19 PANDEMIC

Due to the implementation of strict quarantine rules, China has experienced lower social and economic disruption from the Covid-19 pandemic than has been the case in many other countries. While much of the world has been in recession, China has enjoyed economic growth and even surpassed the US to become the largest recipient of FDI by 2020 (Reuters, 2021). Nonetheless, the Covid-19 crisis has further disadvantaged the already vulnerable, including women. While it has affected Chinese women in various ways, the government's response to date has been gender-blind.

The pandemic has led to an increase in women's unpaid household and care work. Before the pandemic, Chinese women spent an average of nearly four hours per day (2.5 times that spent by men) on unpaid care responsibilities, which were considered more tiring than formal office work by two-thirds of women (International Labour Organization [ILO], 2018). It has also been suggested that the closure of schools and childcare facilities during China's lockdown in the first quarter of 2020 significantly increased women's unpaid care work (Trankmann, 2020). Women working from home in particular have frequently had to juggle formal work, home schooling and domestic work (e.g. cooking and cleaning), roles that intensify when a family member becomes ill (Trankmann, 2020). There is a risk that, post-pandemic, women's economic opportunities will be limited as many companies continue to see working mothers as a burden.

Secondly, the pandemic has disproportionately affected low-skilled women workers in both formal and informal sectors. Before the pandemic, many low-skilled Chinese women, especially migrant women from less developed regions, were segregated into working in tourism, hospitality, retail and domestic support — sectors heavily hit by travel restrictions and social distancing during the pandemic.

Reduced consumer demand from developed economies and China's ongoing trade disputes with the US and other countries have also negatively impacted on employment in some manufacturing industries (e.g. fashion, textile, toys) where women are the majority. In February 2020, the urban unemployment rate in China soared to 6.2 per cent, the highest in two decades (Statista, 2021). While the Chinese government provided emergency relief for businesses, except funds paid into medical insurance and pension schemes there has been very little financial support for furloughed workers. Low-skilled and migrant workers typically have no permanent employment contract in China.

The pandemic crisis means that many women have received almost no income during and following the lockdown. Consequently, many have moved from formal sectors to online retailing to quickly generate income but have inevitably fallen into precarious self-employment (Warnecke, 2016). Moreover, women working in informal sectors have faced a greater risk of losing their income, unemployment and exploitation, and many have had to mainly rely on their husband for financial support (Trankmann, 2020). Given that the coronavirus pandemic has significantly impacted travel, production and consumption, its economic impacts on low-skilled Chinese women are likely to last for a long period due to the global slowdown and employers' risk-averse behaviour.

Finally, women's lower economic status, coupled with social issues that emerged during the lockdown, may further deepen inequality in family life. During China's lockdown, domestic violence against women increased by two to three times in some areas (Trankmann, 2020). For example, in Hubei province, where the coronavirus was first identified, reported cases of domestic violence have increased three-fold since the pandemic started (Liu, 2020). In Xi'an, a southwestern city, there has been a spike of divorce requests since March 2020 (Liu, 2020). The disruption of protective networks means victims also had fewer options for escape and weaker social support (Trankmann, 2020). While China legislated against domestic violence in 2016, it has been suggested that the aftermath of physical containment, psychological distress and financial constraints are likely to have a long-term impact on Chinese families (Liu, 2020). Community support and solidarities (e.g. raising awareness, sharing information, maintaining a sense of togetherness) will thus be vital for maintaining a quality family life.

RECOMMENDATIONS AND CONCLUSIONS

Based on the above analysis, a number of policy considerations are recommended. Although some of the initiatives outlined earlier are not directly related to gender equality at work, given the collectivist culture in China, work and family are inseparable for most women. To help them to achieve gender equality in employment, measures need to be taken to ensure the effective implementation of other corresponding policies (e.g. economic development and family-planning policies) so that their impact will not be at the expense of women's work, employment and career development.

The first set of recommendations concerns demographic trends and the sustainability of families in relation to the achievement of gender equality in employment. While the Chinese government now allows each couple to have up to three children, given the ineffectiveness of the two-child policy in raising the national birth rate, parallel measures are needed to support both employers and parents (especially mothers). Some scholars have argued against pushing the bulk of childbirth costs onto employers while blaming them for gender discrimination (Cooke, 2017). Government intervention is thus urged to prevent further deterioration of women's employment and career prospects when they opt to have more children. Moreover, given the pressure of an ageing population, measures need to be taken to ensure the work–life balance of the 'sandwich generation'.

Government interventions suitable for the Chinese context could include tax reductions for families with more than one child to help relieve their financial pressure. Similar to this, maternity leave subsidies (such as in a form of corporate tax reduction) may be provided to law-abiding employers to reduce their financial burden. In addition, the government could regulate to protect employment rights for parents (both men and women). To support family development, paid leave entitlements (e.g. eldercare leave, parental leave, childcare leave) should be available to both men and women to encourage shared care responsibilities within the family and reduce negative impacts on women's careers. Moreover, the government should invest more in providing affordable care facilities (childcare and eldercare) for low-income families, particularly in urban cities where these resources are in high demand.

A second set of recommendations is associated with technological change and the long-term effects of Covid-19 on women's work. As noted, while a large number of Chinese women have entered online retailing businesses, their overall entrepreneurial activities are very low and women-owned businesses are more likely to fail than those owned by men. Thus, government guidance and support for women-led micro businesses are necessary to provide them with a better ecosystem. Similar to measures taken by the Swedish government (Pettersson, 2012), a number of support mechanisms are appropriate in China, including those which support business start-ups by women to promote social inclusion and combat long-term unemployment, especially among low-skilled women. For example, training and business counselling for women who are interested in starting a business would be useful in helping to reduce the business failure rate. Other measures could include mentoring, economic advice for micro-credit financing, and networking activities (Pettersson, 2012).

This chapter examined four interrelated themes regarding working women in China with regard to the employment regulations and Covid-19 pandemic context, and offered recommendations for policy considerations. Research evidence indicates a tension and contradiction between gender equality and economic/family-planning policies in China. While globalisation, market reform and technological changes provide new work and employment opportunities for Chinese women, gender discrimination persists in the workplace and in other economic activities. Paradoxically, the removal of the OCP in an attempt to address the pressure of the ageing population and enhance the sustainability of Chinese families has exacerbated employers' recruitment and promotion discrimination against women of child-rearing age. The failure of the two-child policy since 2016 to increase China's birth rate re-emphasises the production–reproduction dilemma (Moelders, 2019), which has not been properly addressed in Chinese socio-economic debates. The impacts of the recent three-child policy are yet to be fully discerned.

Chinese women have been vulnerable during the Covid-19 pandemic, and many have been pushed into self-employment and contingency work that is characterised by low pay and employment insecurity. The current state of working women in China may not only reflect a waste of human capital but also a setback to reasonable gender equality progress made during the Communist period (Cooke & Xiao, 2014). It is thus argued that a transformation towards a sustainable, equitable and inclusive Chinese society will require a clarification of conflicting goals for economic growth, sustainability and women's empowerment.

5. Working women in Cambodia

Kristy Ward and Michele Ford

Over the past two decades, Cambodian women have made considerable gains in the world of work. No longer willing to toil in the rice fields, they have become the face of the burgeoning garment sector and increased their visibility in the construction and tourism workforces. Women's engagement in paid work in outward-facing industries — and their dominance of the garment sector, in particular — meant that the Covid-19 pandemic had a rapid and profound impact on women workers, even though Cambodia experienced low case numbers in its first year (Ford & Ward, 2021). During this period, many women workers lost their jobs or a substantial proportion of their income. Many of those who remained in work, and those looking for work, had little option but to take up additional care responsibilities due to the closure of public schools.

In this chapter, we argue that the disruption and severity of the pandemic exposed a silent and unfolding crisis of work. This crisis was borne of the Cambodian government's continued reliance on low-skilled, low-value production for economic growth and employment, combined with inadequate regulatory enforcement of labour standards and limited uptake of technology.[1] By comparing the position of women before and during the

---

1   Our analysis draws on author interviews conducted with female workers and

pandemic, we highlight the extent to which globalisation and government inattention to labour, care and social protection policies undermined the economic and social gains made by workers in general, and women workers in particular. It is these same limitations, we conclude, that must urgently be addressed not only to aid recovery from the Covid-19 pandemic, but also to expand and enhance the economic opportunities available to women. Such opportunities must minimise women's role in precarious, low-paid and low-skilled work, and de-link the burden of urban and rural household livelihoods from women's paid and unpaid labour.

In Cambodia, women comprise 51 per cent of the total population. At 77.9 per cent, the country's female labour force participation (LFP) rate is the highest in Southeast Asia (see Table 5.1). In the decade to 2019, the type of work that women performed changed dramatically, with women much more likely to be found in paid employment — up from 14 per cent in 2008 to 29.3 per cent in 2019 (National Institute of Statistics, 2020a).

In addition, there has been a considerable shift of the total workforce from agricultural production to manufacturing, wholesale and retail trade and construction. For almost a decade after the signing of the Paris Peace Agreement in 1991 — which saw the end of more than 19 years of conflict — Cambodia relied on agriculture as its main source of employment. New employment opportunities in the formal sector emerged in the late 1990s, primarily due to rapid industrialisation in the garment sector. By 2019, garment manufacturing accounted for 17 per cent of GDP, 75 per cent of merchandise exports and 45 per cent of waged labour for women (World Bank, 2020). Just prior to the onset of Covid-19 in January 2020, the

---

unionists in the garment, construction and tourism sectors in 2017, 2018 and 2019, as well as follow-up interviews with a small number of garment sector unions in March 2021. Interview data are complemented by secondary data on the economic and social effects of Covid-19 collected and reported on by the Cambodian Government, the ILO, and various labour and non-government organisations, and on analysis of articles in the Cambodian press collected between March 2020 and June 2021. Work on this article was supported by ARC Linkage Project Grant No. LP 200100431, 'Better Responses to Gender-based Violence in Cambodia's Construction Sector'.

Table 5.1: Labour force, unemployment and primary work type by gender in Cambodia, 2019

	Total (%)	Female (%)	Male (%)
Labour force participation rate of population aged 15–59 years	81.7	77.9	85.8
Unemployment rate of population aged 15–59 years	1.2	1.3	1.1
Percentage of population in paid work	31.5	29.3	33.6
Percentage of population performing own account work	42.7	34.7	50.3
Percentage of population performing unpaid family work	25.0	35.4	15.1

Source: National Institute of Statistics (2020a)

garment sector employed almost a million workers and supported many others in associated services for workers, including transport and food vending (World Bank, 2020).

Another important source of employment for women is the tourism industry, which, along with garment manufacturing, is a major contributor to Cambodia's economy. The sector employs over 200,000 workers, 60 per cent of whom are women. In 2019, tourism's contribution to GDP growth outstripped the garment sector at 18.7 per cent (World Bank, 2020).

A third key sector in the Cambodian economy is construction — by far the largest contributor to GDP, accounting for 35 per cent in 2019 alone — in which women comprise almost 40 per cent of the workforce, a rate much higher than that found in most countries (Strickler & Pou, 2016).

Despite these developments, women continue to be found in a narrow range of occupations, and often in low-skilled and low-paid positions (National Institute of Statistics, 2020a). Yet, while the number of women as managers and in professional roles remains low (see Table 5.2), their

Table 5.2: Working population by occupational category and gender in Cambodia, 2019

Occupation	Male (%)	Female (%)
Managers, professionals and technicians	7.3	4.3
Clerical, service and sales workers	13.9	17.8
Agricultural, forestry and fishing	52.0	54.9
Craft and related	15.1	18.1
Plant and machine operators, and assemblers	4.0	0.5
Elementary occupations*	4.4	7.6

*Elementary occupations are mostly routine tasks, often involving the use of simple hand-held tools, and, in some cases, requiring a degree of physical effort (e.g. refuse workers, cleaners, labourers, street and related sales and services workers). Source: National Institute of Statistics (2019, 2020a)

participation has more than doubled in both categories since 2008, reflecting improvements in education and shifts in social values that have positively affected women's role in the workforce (National Institute of Statistics, 2020a).

EMPLOYMENT REGULATION

Cambodia's comprehensive framework of labour regulation was developed in the late 1990s with assistance from the ILO. The 1997 Labour Law covers the core labour standards, including non-discrimination, freedom of association, elimination of all forms of compulsory and forced labour, equal pay for equal work and abolition of child labour. Article 12 of the law contains specific anti-discrimination provisions that address maternity leave, equal pay for equal work and non-discrimination. Article 172 prohibits sexual harassment, including at work.

The Labour Law is implemented through numerous regulations (*prakas*) that specify how the law is to be interpreted and applied. These legal provisions apply to formal sector workplaces but not to workers in the informal sector. Although domestic workers, numbering almost 240,000 in Cambodia, are explicitly excluded by the law (Kunthear, 2019), steps were taken in 2018 by the government, following pressure from labour and non-government organisations, to implement labour regulation covering working conditions (Prakas No. 235). Since 2019, domestic workers have been also covered by the National Social Security Fund.

While relatively comprehensive on paper, this regulatory framework is poorly enforced. Labour standards compliance is rarely monitored by the Ministry of Labour and Vocational Training (MoLVT) and workers have limited options for reporting violations and seeking redress. The Department of Labour Inspection had, in 2019, only 649 inspectors across the country for all sectors (US Department of Labor, 2019). When inspections are conducted, the process is plagued by corrupt behaviour (interviews, 2018; Ward & Mouyly, 2016). Advance warning of inspections, payment of bribes to inspectors and preparation in advance of inspections — including hiding known breaches, such as unacceptable forms of child labour and directing workers to lie to inspectors about labour conditions — are frequently reported by workers (Oka, 2016; interviews, 2018, 2019).

There are also serious problems with the country's mechanisms for dispute resolution. Firm-level processes for resolving disputes between management and workers, such as bipartite grievance committees, exist only in some sectors — and primarily garment manufacturing, as a result of the influence of the ILO's Better Factories Cambodia Programme.

Beyond the firm level, the system is centred on collective disputes brought by unions with Most Representative Status.[2] Cases are first brought to the MoLVT for conciliation. If matters are unresolved, collective disputes can be brought to the Arbitration Council, an independent body funded by external donors, including bilateral aid and multilateral organisations. The

---

2   For a detailed discussion of unions and Most Representative Status, see Ford et al. (2021).

Arbitration Council has a record of neutral and fair adjudication, although its awards are non-binding (unless parties agreed to be bound).[3] However, many matters are not brought to the MoLVT or the Arbitration Council, such as those that pertain to wages and other payments, unfair dismissal or freedom of association (Ford et al., 2021). Matters that disproportionately affect women workers, such as parental leave, gender-based violence and harassment at work, tend not to be investigated and are rarely the subject of dispute resolution claims.

As a consequence of these systemic limitations, women workers experience numerous labour rights violations perpetrated by employers, ranging from non-payment of wages through to union discrimination and violence and harassment at work (interviews, 2017, 2018, 2019). Women have been at the forefront of labour protests to improve working conditions in Cambodia. However, they face considerable marginalisation within formal labour institutions, including unions. While there are no accurate figures on women as a proportion of total union members, union density is estimated to be around 5 per cent of the total workforce and as high as 60 per cent in the garment sector.

In garment manufacturing, most union members are women, reflecting the relative proportion of female employment (around 85 per cent) in the sector (Serrano & Nuon, 2018). In the construction sector, the total number of female union members reflects women's employment in the sector at 40 per cent of the labour force and total union membership. Women's participation in union leadership is low, with most elected and senior positions being held by men in both independent and politically affiliated unions (Ward, 2022; You, 2020).

As such, the employment relations system is highly gendered, sidelining issues that disproportionately affect women in the workplace, such as parental leave, gender-based violence and harassment at work, and

---

3   From 2016, the government moved to weaken the influence of the Arbitration Council (see Ford et al., 2021).

legislative requirements for employer-provided childcare in the garment sector. Moreover, the failure of the employment relations system to address labour rights violations has largely kept women where they are — in precarious and low-paid work, even in the formal sector.

KEY CHALLENGES AND OPPORTUNITIES

Globalisation

Globalisation has provided unprecedented opportunities for Cambodian women to engage in the workforce beyond agriculture, and gain employment in the formal sector, most often producing garments for export. Cambodia's young population is highly engaged in paid work, and a considerable proportion of workers, across all age groups, are women. The shift in women's work from unpaid family labour and agriculture has largely occurred as a result of Cambodia's integration into the global economy following decades of conflict, and the state's imperative to secure international legitimacy (Ford et al., 2021). The impact of Cambodia's demographic challenges and their relationship to the labour market, then, cannot be separated from the impact of globalisation. However, a narrow labour market, slow uptake of technology in manufacturing, a dominant informal sector and persistent gender norms have limited the quality of women's opportunities in the world of work.

The state first turned its attention to market reforms to stimulate the economy and recover from the sudden withdrawal of Soviet aid in the early 1980s (Hughes, 2003). Within two decades, Cambodia became firmly entrenched at the bottom of the world's garment sector supply chains. An increased number of overseas foreign visitors, propelled by political stability and Cambodia's close bilateral relationship with China, stimulated the exponential expansion of Cambodia's tourism sector. Meanwhile, foreign direct investment (FDI) skyrocketed in the construction sector, prompting some women to shift from the garment factories to more flexible, yet more precarious, work arrangements on construction sites (interviews, 2019). By early 2020, these three sectors became Cambodia's economic pillars and primary employers, giving women unprecedented employment opportunities outside of agriculture.

The Cambodian government's over-reliance on the garment sector as an engine of economic growth and jobs has been an issue for some time. Global systems of production are highly organised and spatially divided. Lead firms subcontract different aspects of production to different countries, before goods are assembled and shipped to markets around the world. In a global supply chain, goods may be produced in a sequence, where components from country A are sent to country B, then enhanced before they are sent to country C. Alternatively, parts from multiple sources may be shipped to a central point for assembly (Baldwin & Venables, 2013). The primary objective of this process is to create and capture surplus value.

At the top of the supply chain, lead firms develop strategies aimed at maximising value from design and marketing, while circumventing highly regulated labour markets in their own and similar countries. At the bottom, profits are generated by minimising labour and other costs. This is achieved by contracting suppliers in countries where social and environmental protection is patchy, and wages are low. Vast numbers of waged workers remain in poverty, even as they labour to produce goods and services for consumers in the Global North (Phillips, 2017). It is this unequal distribution of benefits along these supply chains that matters from a global development perspective.

While the long-term effects of the reach of global capital into Cambodia have undoubtedly generated economic and social gains for women, they have also led to an over-reliance on the garment sector for household income across the country. Indeed, such is the importance of female garment workers' economic role in society that it has resulted in a preference for female children, who are seen as better placed than male children to provide for rural families, including well into parents' later years (Norén-Nilsson, 2017).

However, globalisation has also limited women's opportunities in the workplace and, as the Covid-19 pandemic illustrated, entrenched precarity. When the pandemic hit, over 50 per cent of garment factories across the country closed, with many refusing to pay workers compensation and entitlements. Over 40 per cent of workers in the sector were suspended for a period of 11 weeks, on average (Ngo et al., 2021). Furloughed garment and footwear workers received a US$70 per month government subsidy (Ngo et al., 2021), while suspended tourism workers received a US$40 per month payment (Ford & Ward, 2021). By July 2020, half of workers across the tourism, garment and footwear industries had no income other than the government's subsidy payments (Ngo et al., 2021). These payments were insufficient to meet basic living costs, let alone support extended families. Construction workers, of whom there are higher numbers of women employed than in most countries, meanwhile, received nothing.

Women who maintained their jobs in the garment or tourism sectors — in female-headed households or otherwise — faced a range of other pressures. Shifts in the labour market and the fact that women have taken up a primary breadwinner role in many households while continuing to take primary responsibility for care work, means that the squeeze on care dynamics is considerable (Ward, 2017). Most workers in these industries have migrated from rural locations and make a substantial financial contribution to the sustainability of extended families' rural households. Even before the pandemic, they experienced considerable stress as they juggled the high cost of living in the city with demands for remittances on income that was considered below a living wage (interviews, 2018, 2019).[4] The limited availability of market or government preschool and daycare services also meant that they constantly juggled paid labour and unpaid care work. To survive during the pandemic, they reduced household expenditure including food and remittances, took out loans or relied on savings (ActionAid, 2021).

---

4   While this is true for women workers in many sectors, it is particularly salient in the case of garment workers, as factories are located in Phnom Penh or near to a provincial capital.

Demography

Cambodia's demographic profile is the product of two decades of conflict, including four years of totalitarian rule under the Khmer Rouge. The population is young, with almost 50 per cent under 25 years (National Institute of Statistics, 2020a). This means that it was less vulnerable to Covid-19 than many other countries. However, when cases escalated sharply in April 2021 — from almost no cases to over 800 per day — it was mainly young people who contracted the disease. Risks were particularly high for workers in the feminised garment sector, due to the quick spread of the virus through their cramped rental accommodation and overcrowded public transport (*CamboJA*, 2021). Employers' inability, but also unwillingness, to implement the government's hygiene and prevention measures, such as providing handwashing facilities, hand sanitiser and face masks, and distancing within workplaces, has compounded these risks (interviews, 2021).

Another legacy of conflict is the prominence of female-headed households in Cambodia. The number of women heading households has remained steady since 1998 at around 26 per cent of all households (National Institute of Statistics, 2019). Notably, by 2019, a much lower percentage of female-headed households were widowed, divorced or separated (10.2 per cent) and/or never married (4.3 per cent) than the much higher percentage — almost double from 2008, at 85.5 per cent — of female-headed households in which women were married (National Institute of Statistics, 2020a). Women in female-headed households can sometimes be more secure than in other households, as they have greater control over decision-making. For example, outstanding loans of women-headed and indebted households are considerably and consistently lower, year on year, than that of male-headed and indebted households (National Institute of Statistics, 2020b). However, female-headed households tend to have less income-earning capacity. In 2019, approximately 30 per cent of female-headed households had only one member who was economically active. At 7.7 per cent, a much higher proportion of households with women heads have no economically active members when compared with all households, at 3.3 per cent (National Institute of Statistics, 2020a). Those households where the female head had a steady income were also vulnerable in the context of Covid-19 as a consequence of the lack of alternative income sources and inadequate social protection.

Before the pandemic hit, women's role in the labour market was, to a large extent, propelled by the government's inability and unwillingness to implement social protection policy reform. Instead, rural households relied on remittances from family members working away from home. During the pandemic, over 50 per cent of all workers ceased sending remittances to rural households (Ngo et al., 2021). As remittances account for a considerable percentage of household income in rural Cambodia, the abrupt halt of access to remittances had flow-on effects for rural households. There were also gendered effects as most households that receive remittances tend to be headed by older unmarried females and have lower levels of education among all members (Chea, 2021). Impacts for recipient households include decreased agricultural production, inability to repay debts leading to financial stress (interviews, 2019), and increased poverty (Chea, 2021).

Technology

Cambodians have rapidly embraced consumer technology, with 90 per cent of households owning a mobile phone (National Institute of Statistics, 2020b). These consumer technologies have enabled farmers and micro-entrepreneurs to access new markets or exploit their existing customer base.[5] For example, the introduction in 2016 of the ride-hailing mobile

---

5   This access to mobile phone technology has led to the development of apps (usually by overseas companies and academics) that have been instrumental in enhancing the provision of social services, including women's access to sexual and reproductive health advice, tenure registration in informal settlements and agricultural pest identification.

technology, PassApp, transformed traditional *tuk tuk* (motorcycle taxi) transport. PassApp enabled individuals who were not members of worker associations to gain entry to the labour market, aided by the affordability of new Indian-style rickshaws that are cheaper to purchase and run. Overall, however, drivers' fares have decreased as a consequence of market saturation and lower costs per trip (Jack, 2020). Similar mobile technologies have been used to support women entertainment workers — working in sex work, massage parlours, karaoke bars and beer promotion — that face specific occupational health risks, including high rates of HIV and other sexually transmitted infections, as well as gender-based violence at work and psychological distress (Brody et al., 2021).

While the micro-economy has made great strides in relation to technology, uptake among larger-scale businesses has been relatively slow compared with that of a number of other countries in Southeast Asia. Some of this lag relates to Cambodia's reliance on the garment sector, which uses labour-intensive methods to produce low-cost items. Covid-19 further exposed the problem of over-reliance on garment exports propelled by cheap labour. The failure of investors to upgrade production in their supply chains means that there is a risk that Cambodia will get left further behind in manufacturing, given the setbacks posed by the closure of so many factories during the pandemic. And, given the gender imbalance within the garment industry workforce, the impact will fall disproportionately on women.

The rapid increase of Covid-19 cases in April 2021 demonstrated just how problematic Cambodia's reliance on the apparel industry is. The garment sector remains focused on lower-value and lower-priced production, meaning that workers have not benefited from the diversification of skills that accompanies supply chain upgrading (Barrientos, 2019). Most management positions in the sector are held by men, leading to a gender pay gap of around 13 per cent across the sector (Clarke, 2021), while women often remain in the same roles for years on end, with no opportunity for skills development or diversification. The impacts of Covid-19 on the economy and workers have highlighted the need to invest in training and upskilling to expand the available employment options for women, both within and outside of the sector.

Most other formal-sector industries are also relatively low-tech. Most companies use basic technologies such as the internet, email and word-processing packages, but few use more advanced technologies for communication, collaboration and business analytics (Heng, 2019). Companies identify a skills deficit in this area, including managing online information, online collaboration and technology-based analytics. However, very few companies prioritise skills development in this area and employees feel that they are not able to rely on employers for upskilling (Heng, 2019). Even among workers and small businesses in the informal sector, Covid-19 has prompted the need for businesses to adapt and develop new models of working, often requiring skills for digital literacy.

There is also a considerable digital literacy gender divide. Cambodian women are 20 per cent less likely to own a mobile phone than men, and rural women the least likely of all (LIRNEasia, 2018). Expanding opportunities for women in the labour market, particularly post-pandemic, will require considerable investment in digital literacy and in supply chain technology.

Sustainability

The ability of countries to eradicate poverty and achieve sustainable development to a large extent depends on investment in human resources. Investments in primary and secondary education have improved the position of women in society and provided greater opportunities in the labour market. Cambodia has made considerable gains in increasing primary and secondary enrolments for children, particularly girls, with a net enrolment rate of 90.1 per cent for both girls and boys (National Institute of Statistics, 2020b). Primary completion rates for younger Cambodians illustrate that girls are more likely than boys to complete primary school, which is a notable shift from the previous decade (National Institute of Statistics, 2020b).

The pandemic is likely to undermine these gains, with specific gender implications. According to one report, families with an ID 'poor card'[6] had greater difficulty accessing remote learning due to the lack of ICT infrastructure and devices (Ministry of Education, Youth and Sport, 2021). In the short and medium term, there is an increased risk for both girls and boys of child labour in order to provide sufficient household income following job losses or the cessation of remittances.

A further challenge for sustainability is the prevalence of precarious work in Cambodia. The informal sector accounts for around 80 per cent of all employment. Almost 35 per cent of women's labour force participation is own-account work such as street and market vending. Informal waged workers include those who work for and are paid by companies but who do not have secure contracts and are not protected by existing regulatory systems, such as those in the construction industry and entertainment workers (e.g. massage, karaoke, beer promotion), along with domestic workers. Before the pandemic, these women had access to regular income despite the precarity of their work situation. However, they also faced numerous challenges, including wage theft, job and income insecurity, lack of social protection, and exclusion from industrial relations institutions and protections (ILO, 2006).

When Covid-19 hit, women in entertainment, transportation and street vending lost over half of their monthly income, with 20 per cent earning less than US$1.90 a day (ActionAid, 2021). While over half of workers in the sector reported high levels of depression owing to the impacts of the pandemic, rates were considerably higher among women workers (ActionAid, 2021). This situation escalated in April 2021, when case numbers rose from zero to over 800 per day, prompting the government to lock down the country and declare neighbourhoods with higher risk of infection 'red zones'. Over 300,000 residents in these red zones were given stay-at-home orders, which permitted to leave only for specific medical reasons, thus rendering them unable to work (Human Rights Watch, 2021).

---

6   IDPoor is a poverty identification programme designed to support cross-sectoral collaboration on maternal and child health.

The constrained and narrow labour market within the country also pushes women and men across the border into neighbouring Thailand, or further afield to Malaysia, South Korea and the Middle East in search of work. In March 2020, when the pandemic first began, there were a reported 1.2 million Cambodian workers in Thailand, representing around 93 per cent of all Cambodians working abroad (CARE, 2020). These migrant workers tend to be young and low-skilled, and just under half are women. They often experience physical and sexual assault, forced labour, wage theft and unpaid overtime due to an ineffective or non-existent legal and regulatory framework (OECD and Cambodia Development Resource Institute, 2017). They are also particularly vulnerable to exogenous shocks.

With the onset of the pandemic, migrant workers either returned home by choice or were prevented from travelling due to heightened border controls. For example, Thai authorities permitted migrant workers to legally remain in the country on the condition that they had provided biometric data to officials and had applied for health insurance and work permits. However, not all migrant workers were willing or able to comply (*Khmer Times*, 2021). Consequently, remittances from migrant workers dropped by 17 per cent in 2021 to US$1.2 billion (Kunmakara, 2021), placing even further pressure on rural Cambodian households, as those who returned found themselves without work. As Covid-19 has undermined the availability of work in Cambodia's formal and informal sector, there is a very real risk that gender gains in the world of work will be eroded in the short and medium term.

RECOMMENDATIONS AND CONCLUSIONS

Cambodia has become trapped in producing high-volume, low-cost garments for export. The effect on the mostly female workforce has included a gender pay gap, limited opportunities to develop skills and for career advancement, and a high rate of gender-based violence and harassment (Clarke, 2021). The country's reliance on foreign direct investment in the garment and construction sectors has resulted in a reluctance on the part of the government to mandate better wages and conditions in these sectors, despite increasing political pressure from garment workers (Ward & Ford, 2021). Covid-19 has exacerbated women's position in the sector, increasing unpaid care work and stress, and limiting women's work options.

The legacies of the pandemic will likely continue to have a major impact on economic progress and poverty reduction, rolling back gains made in the past two decades, during which time women increasingly became the primary, if not sole, income earner for their family. Equally, the pandemic has revealed deep structural problems with women's employment. Not only have employers failed to provide opportunities for career advancement and skills development, including in the area of digital literacy, but women also have limited time due to care pressures and no social-protection safety net to take risks. The impacts of Covid-19 have demonstrated that better practices are needed in the industries that employ women to build human resources, thereby enabling skills development and transfer across industries. A reconfiguration of the formal-sector economy is also required at the macro level to diversify and expand labour market opportunities for women, and also within workplaces to provide upskilling and career progression.

The reality remains that 80 per cent of Cambodia's workforce is employed in the informal sector. Until this changes, policy reform is urgently needed so that women engaged in precarious work have some access to social protection. In order to relieve the burden of remittances on women workers, better social protection is also required to provide a social safety net for rural and extended households. Finally, the Covid-19 pandemic has shown, yet again, that for women to be engaged in decent work, a radical transformation of care responsibilities is required. This means shifting some responsibility to men so that there is a more equitable division of labour in the household, and also providing low-cost, high-quality state or market care. Given the analysis in preceding sections, potential multiparty responses involving workplace parties such as employers, employees, unions, the state and community groups are required to ensure that strategies implemented are responsive and sustainable.

6. Working women in India

Vibhuti Patel

In twenty-first-century India, the greatest policy concern has been the declining percentage of women in the workforce and their invisibility in the care economy (Mehrotra & Parida, 2017). Between 2005 and 2019, the proportion of Indian women in paid employment reduced from 32 per cent to 21 per cent (International Labour Organization (ILO), 2021). According to a 'time use' survey conducted during 2019–2020, only 20.6 per cent of women and 70 per cent of men in the age group 15–59 years were engaged in paid work (Kasliwal, 2021). When it comes to unpaid work for the same age bracket, 94 per cent of women and 49 per cent of men participated in unpaid work (Ministry of Statistics and Programme Implementation [MoSPI], 2020).

In 1991, India adopted a new economic policy, defined by a structural adjustment programme for economic stabilisation and economic policies of liberalisation, privatisation and globalisation (Patel, 1994). As a result, major changes occurred in the Indian economy, including the introduction of information technology at micro-, meso- and macro-economic levels; the growth of gig work[1] and a platform-based service sector; growth in

---

1   Gig work or temping signifies a temporary assignment. Gig workers include freelancers, casual labour, temporary employees, part-time workers, independent contractors and project-based workers.

e-commerce; technological advancements in the manufacturing sector; and agricultural mechanisation. In addition, corporatisation of the education and health sectors, as well as the introduction of artificial intelligence, robotics and machine learning in the corporate sector, have had major implications for working women's employment prospects, work conditions and remuneration, as 94 per cent of India's working women are in the informal sector of the economy, where they are not protected by labour laws (Patel, 2021).

Alongside India's economic reforms, a number of demographic changes have taken place, most importantly the decline in total fertility rate. The average number of children born to a woman in her lifetime has fallen from 3.2 in 2000 to 2.1 in 2020 (PRS Legislative Research, 2020). Since 2018, there has also been an increase in the working-age population (those between 15 and 64 years of age) of India, as compared with its dependent population (children aged 14 or below and those above 65 years of age) (Thakur, 2019). Demographers have estimated that this bulge in the working-age population is going to last until 2055, or 37 years from its beginning (PRS Legislative Research, 2020).

In this context, the chapter encompasses a wide range of issues touching on the livelihoods and survival struggles of Indian women in the post-colonial period. For the past two years (to the beginning of 2022), the Covid-19 pandemic and lockdowns have drastically impacted the paid and unpaid work of women in India, with the closure of schools, 'work from home' conditions and recurrent illnesses in families. New employment regulations, defined by labour intensity and informalisation of the economy, technological challenges and erosion of women's entitlements in the farm sector, demand concerted efforts by the state and non-state actors to ensure a bottom-up approach to policy formulation and programme implementation.

India, officially the Republic of India, is the most populous democracy and the second-most populated country in the world. British Crown rule began in 1858 and rights promised to Indians were granted slowly

(Taylor, 2016). Technological changes were introduced, along with ideas of education, modernity and public life (Embree et al., 1988). India has been a federal republic since 1950, governed by a democratic parliamentary system. It is a country of socio-cultural, ethno-religious diversity where the caste system plays a dominant role in all spheres of society. Post-colonial India is committed to secular and democratic principles and its constitution guarantees fundamental rights of equality, freedom, non-discrimination and affirmative action for gender equity (Government of India, 2020).

Over the period from 1951 to 2021, its nominal per capita annual income grew from US$64 to US$1498 and it has become a fast-growing major economy and hub for information technology (services). Over the same period, India's literacy rate rose substantially from 16.6 per cent to 74 per cent. It has also substantially reduced its poverty rate, though economic inequality has increased (Dyson, 2018). However, gender inequality is one of India's key socio-economic challenges, along with child malnutrition and air pollution.

EMPLOYMENT REGULATION

An overarching framework of protective labour legislation informed by the Constitution of India was adopted by the Indian Parliament in 1950 after much public debate. In accordance with the Indian Constitution's Fundamental Rights Article 14 Equality before law, men and women have equal rights and opportunities in political, economic and social spheres. Article 15(1) prohibits discrimination against any citizen on such grounds as religion, race, caste, sex or date of birth. Article 15(3) has special provisions that enable the State to make affirmative discrimination in favour of women, while Article 16 provides for equality of opportunities in the matter of public employment for all citizens.

Furthermore, directive principles of the Constitution, as per Article 39(a), recommend that the State should direct its policy towards securing for all citizens the right to a means of livelihood/the right to work and, under Article 39(d), equal pay for equal work for men and women. Provisions under Article 39(d) were fulfilled when the Ministry of Labour enacted the Equal Remuneration Act 1976, that promised equal opportunity, equal treatment in the workplace, and equal remuneration to men and women for work of similar nature. Article 41 of the Constitution provides that

> the State shall within the limits of its economic capacity and development, make effective provision for securing the right to work to education and to public assistance in cases of unemployment, old age, sickness and disablement, and in other cases of undeserved want.

This pledge has resulted in the passing of the National Rural Employment Guarantee Act 2005. Article 42 also directs the State to make provision for ensuring just and humane conditions of work and maternity relief, resulting in the enactment of the Maternity Benefit Act 1961, which stipulated that a woman must be paid a maternity benefit at the rate of her average daily wage for the three months preceding her maternity leave. However, under the Act, a woman needs to have worked for her employer for at least 80 days in the 12 months preceding the date of her expected delivery. As per the ILO's Maternity Protection Convention 2000 (No. 183), in 2017, the Parliament of India amended the Act to extend the period to 26 weeks, wherein up to eight weeks can be claimed before delivery. Only women in the statutory sector (who happen to be 6 per cent of the total female workforce), are entitled to maternity leave benefits that grant paid leave for 26 weeks.

Under the Constitution of India 1950, Article 51(A)(e) renounced practices that are derogatory to the dignity of women; indeed, it took the Indian women's rights movement four decades to secure legislation aimed at securing workplace safety for women workers (Government of India [GoI], 1950). After several efforts to introduce legislation addressing workplace sexual harassment, in 2013 the Indian Parliament unanimously passed the Prevention of Sexual Harassment at Workplace Act 2013.

The Indian Government has passed various Acts to ensure equal pay and equal treatment in the workplace. The Workmen's Compensation Act 1923 aimed to provide financial protection to all men and women workers and their dependants in case of accidental injury by means of payment of compensation by a certain class of employers. For its part, the Minimum Wages Act 1948 provides for statutory minimum wages to all men and women workers since many workers are poorly organised and have little bargaining power in India (Ministry of Labour and Employment, 1948). The Factories Act 1948 is important for regulating the condition of labourers employed in factories while the Contract Labour (Regulation and Abolition) Act 1970 makes separate provision for utilities and fixed working hours for women. Due to the efforts of the LGBTQIA+ movement, the Indian Parliament passed the Transgender Persons (Protection of Rights) Act 2019, which prohibits discrimination against transgender people in employment, education, housing, healthcare and other services.

However, a major challenge faced by working women in India is the limited application of protective legislation that applies to only 6 per cent of the workforce. The unorganised sector of the workforce, hired as casual, temporary, contract, daily wage and piece-rate workers, is not covered by these legislative employment protections.

Furthermore, India was a signatory to the Convention on the Elimination of All Forms of Discrimination Against Women (CEDAW) in 1980 and ratified it in 1993. The Women Empowerment Policy, passed by the Parliament of India in 2001, ensured a reduction in gender gaps in education, employment, health and the political decision-making processes. Both the CEDAW and the Women Empowerment Policy have exhaustive recommendations on social security and social protection, labour standards and safety of working women.

In recent times, there has been a significant reversal of all collective bargaining gains for the working class that were gained over the previous 150 years. The State recently introduced three statutes for farm sectors concerning agricultural product pricing, contract farming and agricultural subsidies, and four new labour codes regarding wages, industrial relations, social security occupational safety, health and working conditions, and the freezing of 48 central and 200 State-specific labour laws. These hastily passed, crudely drafted and gender-blind farm laws and labour codes violate the ILO Covenant, C190 — Violence and Harassment Convention 2019, to which India is a signatory (Patel, 2021). Trade unions, farmers' associations, human rights groups, social movements of Dalits (Encyclopaedia Britannica, 2021), tribes, minorities, the feminist movement and transnational solidarity movements have vigorously opposed them.

KEY CHALLENGES AND OPPORTUNITIES

Demography

India's population stands at 1399 million, of which 722 million are men and 677 million (or 48.4 per cent) are women (Census of India, 2021). There is, thus, a deficit of 45 million women and the sex ratio is skewed in favour of men. The sex ratio of the total population is 937 women for every 1000 men and sex ratio at birth in India is 910 girls for every 1000 boys, which is alarmingly low for girls (United Nations Population Fund [UNFPA], 2020). There have also been major reductions in the birth rate, the price of which is paid by Indian girls in terms of sex-selective abortions of female foetuses (PRS Legislative Research, 2020).

The extremely low labour force participation (LFP) rate for women in paid employment from 1955 to 2017, as revealed in Figure 6.1, is a major challenge for the Indian economy (Desai & Joshi, 2019). In 1955, the LFP rate showed that less than one-quarter of Indian women aged between 15 and 59 years were employed; by 1972, the LFP rate for women had peaked at one-third, mainly due to the feminisation of the agricultural labour force in India. The female LFP rate has remained below 30 per cent and, in 2017, it dropped to an abysmally low level of 18 per cent (World Factbook, 2020).

Despite anticipated growth of the working-age population — expected to climb to over 800 million people by 2050 (Kamdar, 2020) — less than one-quarter (20.3 per cent) of women aged 15 and older participate in the labour force as of 2020 (World Bank, 2020b), compared with 76 per cent of men (World Bank, 2020c). Women account for only 19.9 per cent of the total labour force in India (World Bank, 2020b), due in part to restrictive cultural norms regarding women's work, a gender wage gap, an increase in time spent by women continuing their education, and a lack of safety policies and flexible work offerings (Ratho, 2020). The LFP rate for women fell to 16.1 per cent during the July–September 2020 quarter, the lowest among major economies, according to a recent government report, reflecting the impact of the pandemic and a widening job crisis (Kumar, 2021). The unemployment rate among women reached 15.8 per cent, compared with 12.6 per cent among male workers during the three months to September 2020 (Vyas, 2022).

Recent job stagnation and high unemployment rates for women, worsened by the Covid-19 pandemic, have also kept women out of the labour force, with rural women leaving the workforce at a faster rate than urban women (Kamdar, 2020). Table 6.1 shows the unemployment rates for females and males in urban and rural work from 1972 to 2018 in India.

As Table 6.1 reveals, in urban areas, female unemployment rates have been higher than those of their male counterparts for both current weekly status (CWS) and usual status.[2] In rural India, for both categories, unemployment among women is less than that of their male counterparts due to a gender-based division of labour that assigns collection of fuel, fodder, water, forest produce and innumerable agrarian pre-cultivation and post-harvest chores to women, while men only operate ploughs, tractors and sprayers for pesticides, tube wells and so forth (Bhattacharya, 2002). In the landmark report *Towards Equality Report,* commissioned by the UN in 1972, it was found that with artisanal work and the cottage industry where men use tools and technologies, labour-intensive chores

---

2   If a person has engaged in any economic activity for a period of 30 days or more during the preceding 365 days, that person is considered employed, according to the Periodic Labour Force Survey.

Figure 6.1: Labour force participation rate (%) by gender and all age groups in India, 1955–2017

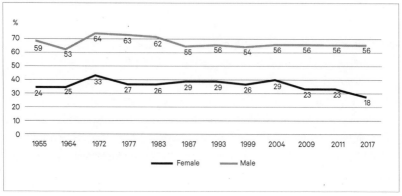

Source: MoSPI (2017)

are assigned to women of the households and categorised as 'unpaid family work' (Government of India, 1974).

Furthermore, a recent time-use survey by MoSPI (2020) revealed that Indian men spend 97 minutes on unpaid domestic work every day, while Indian women spend 299 minutes. During 2019, India's overall participation rate in unpaid activities was 63.6 per cent, with an average time of 289 minutes spent on unpaid activities. The participation rate in unpaid activities for rural women was 85 per cent while, for urban women, it was 81.7 per cent. However, the participation rates for rural and urban men were just 47.8 per cent and 35.1 per cent, respectively. Furthermore, an average Indian woman spends around one-fifth of her time every day in unpaid work, including in housework and caregiving, compared with just 2.5 per cent of time spent by men. Figure 6.2 shows the time spent by women and men on different activities in a given day.

The disproportionately high burden of unpaid care work as well as unpaid family labour in household-based enterprises, due to rigid gender segregation and cultural mores, greatly impacts women's educational and

Table 6.1: Unemployment rates (%) according to usual status and current weekly status (CWS) from 1972–73 to 2017–18

Round (year)	Rural				Urban			
	Male		Female		Male		Female	
	Usual status	CWS	Usual status	CWS	Usual status	CWS	Usual status	CWS
2017–18	5.8	8.8	3.8	7.7	7.1	8.8	10.8	12.8
2011–12	1.7	3.3	1.7	3.5	3.0	3.8	5.2	6.7
2009–10	1.6	3.2	1.6	3.7	2.8	3.6	5.7	7.2
2004–05	1.6	3.8	1.8	4.3	3.8	5.2	6.9	9.0
1999–00	1.7	3.9	1.0	3.7	4.5	5.6	5.7	7.3
1993–94	1.4	3.1	0.9	2.9	4.1	5.2	6.1	7.9
1987–88	1.8	4.2	2.4	4.4	5.2	6.6	6.2	9.2
1983	1.4	3.7	0.7	4.3	5.1	6.7	4.9	7.5
1977–78	1.3	3.6	2.0	4.1	5.4	7.1	12.4	10.9
1972–73	1.2	3.0	0.5	5.5	4.8	6.0	6.0	9.2

Source: MoSPI (2017)

career opportunities in India. Gender norms in India force women to be responsible for childcare, eldercare and household chores, while at the same time women are not allowed to move out of their house unescorted by male family members (Dey et al., 2022). There is also limited occupational diversification among women workers, who are often ghettoised in monotonous, semi-skilled, unskilled or dead-end jobs at the bottom of the pyramid of the burgeoning informal sector (Harriss-White & Prakash, 2019).

In India's manufacturing sector, women workers can be found in textile, garment, leather and shoe factories, and in electrical and food-processing facilities. In household industries, women are weavers, knitters, spinners, tailors, embroiderers, cloth cutters, finishers and leather-product artisans. In these activities, the gender-based division of labour is extremely

Figure 6.2: Percentage share of total time spent on different activities in a day by gender in India, 2019

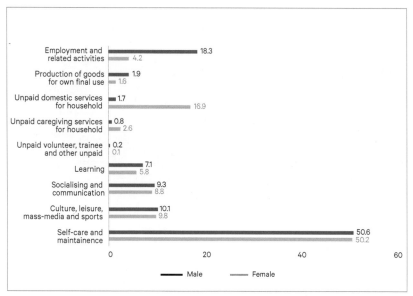

Source: MoSPI (2020)

pronounced within semi-skilled manufacturing employment, where women are deprived of up-skilling opportunities by their employers and government-controlled Industrial Training Institutes (ITIs) (Ratho, 2020).

Gender stereotypes held by parents that girls have to be homemakers and boys will be income earners result in boys joining ITIs and a general aversion to sending girls to these institutes. Such stereotyping is strengthened by schools making gender-based divisions right from the 5th Standard (the first year of middle school, when children are around 11 years old), when girls have to learn needlework and flower arrangements while boys are trained in carpentry and in the operation of lathe machines and electrical equipment. In a study by Ernst Young (EY) India (2020), 77 per cent of students mentioned that they learnt about the ITIs through the internet and schools. Hence, employment opportunities for women in chemical, electrical, power, rubber and plastic products production remains low. A similar scenario exists in sales, services, manufacturing, mining, brick kiln and construction sectors where women are employed as the cheapest labour for temporary work of a casual nature.

Poor self-employed women usually assume work roles as cooked-meal suppliers, vendors and waste picker-cum-recycling workers. In addition, the significant increase in the purchasing power of the upwardly mobile and digitally connected Indian middle class (Metcalf & Metcalf, 2012) has resulted in the hiring of poor women domestic workers who are forced to migrate to urban areas due to agrarian distress, resulting in the de-feminisation of agricultural labour (Pachauri, 2018).

Furthermore, India's gig economy is thriving from its use of the cheap labour of women. In the personal services sector, women are employed as hairdressers, beauticians, masseuses, housekeepers, cooks and back-end restaurant service workers; in the travel industry, they are engaged in tourism-related work as babysitters; in tutoring services and other educational services, they work as restaurant and cafeteria workers in catering services and in hostels, boarding houses and correctional homes. Platform-based service providers use age-old gender stereotypes associated with women's work to extend care work in a commercialised manner (Ghosh et al., 2021).

It is also notable that more than 2 million women workers on government schemes are forced to work for honoraria rather than market-rate wages. For example, public programmes such as the Integrated Child Development Scheme employs more than 1 million women, and the National Rural Health Mission around 1 million women, in roles that include motivating women to give birth in hospitals, bringing children to immunisation clinics, encouraging family planning (e.g. surgical sterilisation), treating basic illness and injury with first aid, keeping demographic records and improving village sanitation (Ministry of Women and Child Development, 2019). Although the government is the employer, women receive abysmally low remuneration, termed 'honoraria', wherein they are classified as 'volunteers' and not as workers (Mondal et al., 2018). Yet, in the context of the Covid-19 pandemic, these overworked and underpaid 'volunteers' have formed the backbone of the overstretched public health delivery system (Kidangoor, 2020).

The share of women in high-skilled roles (e.g. as doctors, lawyers, architects, engineers, managers and teachers) is increasing but not in proportion to their increasing percentage as university degree holders across all disciplines. For instance, women entrepreneurs constitute only 9 per cent of India's entrepreneurs, and mostly work for tiny, micro and small-scale producers. According to the World Bank (2020d), which uses indicators such as mobility, workplace, pay parity, marriage, parenthood, entrepreneurship, assets and pension to rank 190 countries, India was positioned 117th in this index.

Women's low representation in decision-making roles in corporate jobs in India has been a key concern in the past few years, though the Company's Act 2013 made it mandatory for listed companies to have one woman director. By 2020, Indian women held just 17 per cent of board positions in corporate India, and only 11 per cent were in leadership roles, according to the *Egon Zehnder Global Diversity Report 2020* (Shekhar, 2020). Although the number of women degree holders in all disciplines has increased drastically since 2000 (MHRD, 2020), the number of highly qualified, educated women has not translated into an increase in their presence in professional careers (McKinsey Global Institute, 2018).

Increasing incidences of sexual harassment, misogynistic workplace ecosystems, and male-chauvinist and victim-blaming biases in grievance systems within workplaces have driven Indian working women to use social media's #MeToo movement to air their grievances against sexual harassment in workplaces and to draw attention to their suffering (Jain, 2020).

Globalisation

Neoliberal economic globalisation is characterised by the removal of all trade barriers to international and domestic trade and commerce; privatisation of all available services, resources and sectors of micro, meso and macro economy; and the unleashing of market forces for profit maximisation and capitalist expansion, and super-exploitation of foreign workers and marginalised people (Patel, 1994). Globalisation has increased human, financial, economic and technological transactions and communications across countries and regions (Patel & Karne, 2006). Since the 1990s, studies have revealed that globalisation accompanied by liberalisation and privatisation have accentuated inequality and poverty. In India, this has dramatically influenced the urban–rural divide, where Dalit/ tribal poor women, as paid, underpaid and unpaid workers, experience deplorable conditions as migrant workers (Bakker & Silvey, 2008).

As homemakers, poor women have also shouldered a disproportionate burden due to commercialisation and marketisation of day-to-day needs, such as drinking water and sanitation, alongside the degradation of the environment and erosion of public health services and cash-controlled privatised education by corporate-driven economic policies (Acharya, 2008). Furthermore, galloping inflation on essential items for daily consumption, expensive transport, the dismantling of the public distribution system that provides items such as grains, cooking fuel, cloth material and soap, have exacerbated the hardships and labour intensity of millions of poor women (Floro & Hoppe, 2008).

The liberalisation of Indian agriculture to service the global market has increased the volatility of agrarian prices. The price makers are global agro-businesses who have contributed to impoverished farmers' suicides (Reddy, 2018). According to the National Crimes Record Bureau (NCRB) (2018), an average of 28 Indian farmers commit suicide every day due to agrarian distress. Women farmers, who are mostly small and marginal farmers, suffer as prices crash at the time of harvesting. Poor women peasants end up with few sales of their crops, resulting in a persistent vicious cycle of indebtedness

(Sengupta, 2020). Furthermore, predatory private microfinance institutions backed by global financial powers mercilessly exploit women farmers for land-grab (Reserve Bank of India, 2019), and disposed-of, landless women farmers are inducted as daily wage workers by agro-businesses, supported by global players (Tongia, 2019).

The ILO (2017) report on work participation of women in India showed a massive fall in their work participation rate from 34 per cent in 1999 to 27 per cent in 2017. New robotic and automation technologies are further transforming global supply chains and production processes, putting many jobs that are typically held by women at risk (Bakker & Gill, 2019). Rather than increasing access to decent work in the Global South, the reality is that these jobs are disaggregated into micro-tasks performed by contractors and their sub-contractors in low-income countries where the workers have no labour contracts or workplace protections and are often underpaid (Dasgupta & Singh, 2016).

Digitalisation amd automation thus risk perpetuating old forms of discrimination, exploitation and informal work for women in the Global South (Raman & Rizvi, 2021). Restrictive social norms result in physical and economic isolation of women; even when women discover new jobs, they face continued pressure from their families to give up their jobs, get married if single, and stay at home (Uniyal, 2019).

Technology
Globalisation has brought rapid changes to technologies and the environment (Wheebox, 2021). Since 2010, technological developments in and the modernisation of India have resulted in the retrenchment of women workers who have not received the skills training to cope with new technologies (Chandrasekhar & Ghosh, 2015). It is only in the information technology sector that women are accessing employment as computer operators, call-centre employees and tele-workers (Gothoskar, 2000).

The role played by women in electronics, information technology, food processing, agro-industry and textile industries has been crucial to the development of these sectors. Their employers, who dominated sunrise sectors (i.e. rising sectors in the Indian economy such as pharmaceuticals, green energy and digital economies (which have the advantage of both scale and reach, creating job opportunities, and poised to move up the value chain), have been granted comprehensive support: state subsidies; the relaxation of labour legislation provisions regarding social security that covers medical care, sickness benefits, unemployment benefit, old-age pension, employment injury compensation, family leave, maternity benefit, invalid compensation and survivors' benefit; and other support services such as subsidised transport, canteen and rental housing (Mehta & Awasthi, 2019).

Indeed, the opening of the Indian economy due to globalisation has facilitated major technology transfer. Women of the third world are seen as the most flexible of those in the world's labour force (Patel, 2020). There are large numbers of poor and desperately needy women in many countries looking for work within the narrow confines of a socially imposed, inequitable demand for labour and strict taboos on mobility. These women have become ideal workers for this kind of international division of labour (Patel, 2004). In India's newly expanding export-oriented industries of leather goods, toys, food products, garments, diamonds and jewellery, piece-rate female labour is utilised, and women work in either sweatshops or from home. This process has also intensified the immiserisation and hunger due to food shortages for the women workers in rural areas who are left to do agrarian chores, animal care and eldercare (Kamdar, 2020).

Women have also been displaced from India's traditional manufacturing sector, which constitutes textile, jute and small-scale industries, due to the introduction of semi-automated and automated machinery (Abraham, 2017). The government's ITIs only provide women with training in tailoring and screen printing. India's southern states have started to recruit women to handle new industrial technologies because of male labour shortages due to men's migration to Gulf countries. However, all industrial technologies have been designed with the average height and body of men in mind. As a consequence, the recommendations of the Shramshakti Report (1988) and National Commission of Enterprises in the Unorganised Sector (NCEUS) (2015) was that women workers be given technical training to handle new machinery so that they could enter gainful employment in all industrial categories.

Furthermore, due to the introduction of agricultural technologies and mechanisation, and high yielding varieties (the Green Revolution),[3] women have been eased out of agricultural tasks in the Punjab and Haryana (Bhalla, 1989). The employment elasticity of output (i.e. the ability to absorb more workforce) in India's agricultural industry has reduced to 0.64 per cent as a result of agricultural mechanisation (Misra & Suresh, 2014). This has resulted in women's employment declining in both urban and rural areas, a phenomenon referred to as 'de-feminisation' (Dewan et al., 2019). Unemployment and under-employment in rural areas have increased because, in the New Economic Policy of 1991, schemes for rural development and rural industrialisation were not considered (Dasgupta & Singh, 2016).

Introducing computers and office automation has reduced manual administrative chores, while the internet has eased communication. Many internet-savvy women get piece-rate paid work, either in office or in a work-from-home arrangement. The mobile revolution has made women more secure as they can coordinate their work and home lives more efficiently and with a sense of security. A new range of easily manageable automobiles have encouraged women with purchasing power to own vehicles so that they can remain mobile at all times. Women entrepreneurs are reaping the benefits of new technologies of video-conferencing, tele-conferencing, e-commerce, ATMs and credit cards. Self-help groups for women and Rural Women Banks in India are using

---

3   The Green Revolution in India was initiated in the 1960s by introducing high-yielding varieties of rice and wheat to increase food production in order to alleviate hunger and poverty.

smart cards, which facilitate financial transactions for women.

However, much of the discourse on the 'future of work' that envisions economic growth fuelled by the mainstreaming of artificial intelligence and robotics in the manufacturing sector and agriculture is gender blind. Precarity of working women in the gig economy and cyber coolies[4] in the IT-enabled services makes it imperative to deconstruct the concept of 'flexibility' (Babu, 2004).

Gig work is touted as suitable for Indian women, as gender norms demand women's labour for unpaid childcare, eldercare and care of sick family members, along with daily household chores of cooking, cleaning and the provision of fuel, water, vegetables and other groceries for daily consumption. However, with gig work, women continue to be deprived of any social or legal protection in new work arrangements, and the gender pay gap and occupational segregation have followed Indian women into gig employment as was the case in their earlier work in the unorganised sector (Ghosh et al., 2021). Moreover, in gig work, women's employment, incentives and disincentives are governed by algorithms and IT, hence the moment they are unlogged by the owner from their computer network, they are out.

Atomisation of gig workers, where each worker is working in isolation, makes it extremely difficult for them to organise. There is not a single union of women workers in the gig economy, they have only WhatsApp groups in which to discuss sexual harassment at work and safety concerns (Chakraborty, 2020). They have to put up with pay gaps, career stagnation and micro-aggression in their day-to-day life, and within five years many quit their jobs (Gupta, 2020). With able-bodied men searching for livelihood opportunities in the cities, more women than ever are left to do low-paying agricultural jobs, including activities that were earlier prohibited to them, such as ploughing (Shiva, 2005).

---

4   'Cyber coolie' is increasingly being used to describe a typical Indian data-entry operator and IT worker doing what might be considered a dead-end job.

Sustainability

The poorest of the poor, mostly Dalit, Muslim and tribal women, are the main force in the collection and processing of waste material (both solid and organic) disposed of by individual consumers, communities and industries. In India, campaigns against single-use plastic have remained on paper (Mhapsekar, 2006). Civil society organisations have taken the initiative to clean public places and collective plastic waste from the seashores and riversides by involving student volunteers and through mandatory programmes, such as the National Service Scheme, which demands 100 hours of social work from undergraduate students (Chikarmane & Narayan, 2006).

Micro, small and medium industries employ waste management contractors who are not concerned with the occupational health and safety of the workers, as shown by studies of the Indo Global Social Service Organisation (IGSSS, 2019). The Covid-19 pandemic has had a major toll on women waste pickers and sanitation workers due to the careless disposal of items such as medical waste, personal protection kits and used masks.

In most Indian states, 50 per cent of seats are reserved for women in the urban local self-government bodies (ULBs), such as municipal corporations in mega-cities, municipal councils of tier-two cities, and rural local self-government bodies (RLBs), such as village, block and district councils. The ULBs and RLBs have initiated training programmes for the women elected as representatives on recycling solid waste management, energy generation from organic waste, and the safe disposal of contaminated material and medical waste. Women's organisations and elected women representatives are at the forefront of local initiatives (Kidangoor, 2020), and a gendered discourse on the green economy in India has begun among Fortune 500 companies due to increased global awareness (Bhamra, 2018).

The devastating impacts of climate change have placed greater pressure on women to shoulder the adverse consequences on their households. Women, thus, face a double challenge when confronted with climate change as they are on the receiving end of these consequences, and also responsible for the survival needs and care of family members, community, plants and domestic animals. Women also often have unequal access to information and resources, and are under-represented in decision-making, making them even more vulnerable to natural disasters and extreme weather events.

THE COVID-19 PANDEMIC

The current health emergency created by the Covid-19 pandemic has triggered a slowing down of the Indian economy, negatively affecting Indian working women three times more than men (Dixit & Chavan, 2020). Poorer women lost the highest percentage of jobs and suffered malnutrition due to eating last, least and leftovers (Bloomberg, 2021). Sex workers and transgender persons face increased stigma and social exclusion. In the rebuilding efforts of the post-Covid economy, they are not even considered as citizens in the economic planning.

As a result of the pandemic more generally, many working women have been pushed out of the labour market and are taking longer to re-enter the workforce, due to the closure of schools and the wider responsibilities of home schooling, eldercare, care of sick family members and increased housework (Mamgain, 2021).

Job losses among low-income households have also been greater for women than for men (Makol, 2021). Total employment in India for November 2020 was 2.4 per cent lower than in November 2019, but among urban women it was down by 22.8 per cent. Of the 6.7 million women displaced from the labour force during this period, 2.3 million were rural women while 4.4 million were urban women. Urban women faced the deepest losses with a labour force contraction of 27.2 per cent. For urban men, the contraction was 2.8 per cent (Vyas, 2022). Furthermore, a rapid masculinisation of the Indian workforce under pandemic conditions, at all levels and in all sectors of the economy, is pushing women out of such careers as managers, entrepreneurs, beauticians, fitness trainers, tourist guides and restaurant owners (Rukmini, 2019).

Another recent study found that, after the announcement of lockdown in India, when much work shifted from workplaces to domestic locations, many women reported an inability to differentiate between paid work and unpaid and household work (Jasrotia & Meena, 2021). During 2020, when work was conducted from home, the number of complaints of crime against women and domestic violence cases rose substantially (Joy, 2020).

According to the 2011 census, more than 41 million daily wage earners had migrated from rural to urban areas for work. The Covid-19 crisis and lockdown compounded their difficulties and blurred their motives to stay (Nair & Verma, 2020). Most of the workforce in India is located in the unorganised sector. In the Indian economy, only 8 per cent of women workers/employees have permanent jobs and therefore receive the protection of labour legislation. Within the category of informal workers, the largest group is self-employed workers (32 per cent), followed by informal employees in the informal sector (30 per cent) and contributing family workers (18 per cent) (ILO, 2017). This informalisation is highly pronounced for women. In India, 94 per cent of women are employed in the unorganised sector and involved in work which lacks dignity of labour, social security, decent and timely wages, and, in some cases, even the right to be called a 'worker' (Banerjee, 2019).

Migrant women workers who are at the bottom of the informal employment pyramid work as part-time, contract, unregistered, home-based workers — most of whom do not have official status. While those who are unemployed vary significantly by gender and socio-economic status, there has been a flight of migrant industrial workers from larger cities and urban agglomerations to states dominating the agriculture-based subsistence economy. Adding to the precarity of the migrants losing their jobs in towns, villages do not have the employment capacity to absorb so many returning migrants.

RECOMMENDATIONS AND CONCLUSIONS

The current economic downturn due to complete lockdown for a year and partial lockdown of the economy intermittently in different parts of the country during three waves of the pandemic, has caused tremendous human misery among working women in India, who are often positioned at the bottom of the employment pyramid (Deshpande, 2022). The biggest impact has been on the lives of the bottom 80 per cent of the population, mainly agricultural labourers and the urban informal sector workers, of which 60 per cent are women. The collective efforts of employers, employees, unions, the state, community groups and feminist economists, among others, can help to ensure gender-sensitive workplace initiatives and enhance the work participation of women in all sectors of the Indian economy.

In response to the Covid-triggered crisis, income support must be provided to women-headed households, where women shoulder the main economic responsibilities, including those who are widowed, single, deserted and divorced. More specifically, the socially excluded and stigmatised communities of 3 million women sex workers (Mahapatra et al., 2018) and over 500,000 transgender persons (Census of India, 2021) must be assisted through the provision of free ration kits, food from state-supported community kitchens, and medical facilities for vaccination and Covid-19 related care.

In India's agrarian sector, asset ownership by women farmers of land and irrigated areas is crucial for them to undertake sustainable economic activities. The participation of women from Dalit, tribal and religious-minority communities self-employed in agriculture must be promoted through the distribution of surplus government land to these women for cultivation.

Top priority must be given to enhancing the skills and education of women workers living in rural areas through existing industrial training institutions across India by ensuring a 30 per cent quota in admission for women. In addition, public education to counter gender stereotypes is required so that women can take advantage of growing employment opportunities in the non-farm sectors, and in mechanised harvesting, weeding and food-processing activities, to improve women's productivity rather than encourage further de-feminisation of the agricultural sector.

In the National Rural Livelihood Mission (NRLM), a poverty-alleviation project implemented by the Ministry of Rural Development for promoting self-employment and organisation of the rural poor, skills are imparted for entrepreneurship development with a focus on middle-educated rural youth, both women and men (NRLM, 2017).

Furthermore, legislative protection for gig-platform women workers in this fast-developing, under-regulated economy in India is a must. Hence the demands of the gig workers for a new legislation for operationalising universal and portable social security schemes as per ILO's Employment Relationship Recommendation, 2006 (No. 198) on Platform work and the employment relationship (De Stefano et al., 2021). There is also a need to start information kiosks for women in rural and urban centres promoting various schemes and programmes in different sectors of the economy by both private and public sector enterprises.

Industrial training centres must provide opportunities for women to deal with all traditional and modern technologies in the cottage industries, dairy development, organic farming, the poultry business, orchid cultivation, floriculture, horticulture, block printing, pottery and so forth. India's Department of Science and Technology needs to target school and college girls for advanced scientific training in core subjects that impart foundational knowledge and skills and application of STEMM subjects — science, technology, engineering, mathsematics and medicine — as well as computer science in the enterprise development.

Women entrepreneurs must be given orientation in new technologies by the government as well as entrepreneurship development opportunities. Information, education and communication (IEC) policy in modern technologies and scientific development must have a strong gender component in its design and implementation. Global, national, regional- and local-level information about job opportunities, career advancement and training opportunities should also be announced in both print and electronic media in order to encourage women to seek such opportunities. Training women in modern technology should be viewed as an investment rather than simply as expenditure (India Skills Report, 2021).

Despite women's vulnerabilities, women's knowledge and social practices could be used to build community resilience if women were included in the efforts at adaptation and mitigation. For this to happen, we need to train our decision-makers to identify strategic gender needs and practical gender needs in matters concerning climate change and sustainable development (Moser, 1993).

The government needs to place a moratorium on rent and utilities payments and at the same time, given top priority for state-owned, low-cost rented homes for the workers, enhance social protection systems, including child- and eldercare programmes and provide credit to women's cooperatives and self-employed women to rebuild their businesses wiped out due to the pandemic.

As per the commitment of the UN and other multilateral organisations at the Generation Equality Forum held in Paris in 2021 to commemorate the 25th anniversary of the Beijing Declaration and Platform for Action (UN Women, 1995), the Indian economy needs to focus on: gender-responsive budgeting to reduce women's burden of poverty; inequalities and inadequacies in access to education, skill training, food security, healthcare, employment, and political decision-making; gender-based violence; and the promotion and protection of the human rights of girls, women and gender minorities. All gender commitments need to be translated into financial commitments and allocation of specific function and functionaries to address gender gaps in education, health, employ-ment and skills, security and political participation that results in not only getting back the historic gains lost due to the pandemic but also to ensure the advancement of women.

The expansion of internal and external markets for horticultural and floricultural products have encouraged many farmers to use their land for fruit and flower cultivation. The introduction of biotechnology, food, fruit and flower preservation and processing technologies has given a boost to rural and tribal women entrepreneurs getting into this field. But they face difficulties in accessing markets. Hence, the state should establish women's markets with infrastructural facilities such as credit, low interest rate loans, transport, storage space and publicity. Enhancing women's capabilities and participation in national policy and economic governance as well as in social practices of equality and non-discrimination, accompanied by concerted gender sensitisation, are key to women's empowerment in the globalised world of work (World Bank, 2020d).

India's future trajectory for working women in a pandemic/post-pandemic context demands state policies to combat structural and systemic discrimination. Judicious implementation of progressive legislations, mass-scale gender-sensitisation programmes to promote gender equity and equality in the family, community, economy and political decision-making are required to challenge existing inequalities for women. The approach to date of adding women into the masculinist structure of work and the economy has failed to realise women's human rights and will continue to do so in a changing world of work that is guided by massive automation, artificial intelligence and robotics.

Equal value for paid employment and unpaid care work, changes in gender norms to promote sharing of care work by women and men, universalisation of healthcare with special emphasis on comprehensive sexual and reproductive healthcare, regularisation of the gig economy, universal social security, social protections for childcare, paid parental, sick and family-care leave, a pension for the elderly, and the universal applicability of labour legislation by the integration of informal workers into the formal sector have been demanded by women's movements in India (Velayudhan, 2020). Furthermore, the need for a bottom-up approach to policy formulation and programme implementation with all 'stack' groups — namely, women's rights organisations, trade unions, women's cooperatives, self-help groups, employers' associations and the concerned ministries and departments of the state governments and central government — has been continuously stressed by community-based organisations.

India in focus: Women, technology and the future of work

Binitha V. Thampi

As the preceding chapter highlights, with rapid population growth and economic development, over the past four decades India has experienced key demographic changes, often linked to urbanisation. Its fertility rate has declined considerably and the share of women enrolled in educational institutions has increased, although subject segregation on the basis of gender continues. Such structural changes have not resulted in improvements to women's participation in India's labour force, which fell to a record low of 15.5 per cent in April–June 2020, reflecting the impact of the pandemic and a widening job crisis (Kumar, 2021). Furthermore, recent technological developments will have a gendered effect on the future of work and workers in India, and it is pertinent to reflect on some of their likely impacts on women in this country.

This account focuses on the influence of new technologies on Indian working women's experiences during the Covid-19 pandemic, and discusses the likely trajectories for women workers in India and policy suggestions aimed at gender equality in the workplace.

TECHNOLOGICAL CHANGE AND COVID-19

India has experienced considerable technological advancements in recent decades. During the 1960s, the country faced a major food deficit due to a combination of relative neglect of agriculture (inadequacy of long-term planning for agriculture development and an erroneous pricing policy that adversely affected terms of trade), and two successive droughts in the mid-1960s. The Green Revolution, a period that began in the 1960s, during which agriculture in India was converted into a modern industrial system by the adoption of technology, aimed to increase the country's rice and wheat yields, and technical inputs have increasingly replaced human inputs.

However, women have been marginalised in and by these changes in terms of their participation and knowledge input in the workplace, often reduced to becoming secondary producers. Despite working longer hours and exerting more physical effort, they are often not recognised for their work. Cultural norms and stigma also play a large role in the non-recognition of women's work (Bardhan, 1985; Jayachandran, 2021), with Nirmala and Parthasarathy's (1999) study suggesting that cultural factors play a greater part than technology in women's marginalisation in the Indian labour market (Esteve-Volart, 2004).

Similarly, the introduction of information technology has had a major impact on women's employment due to differential access to it for women and men, and a resultant gendered digital divide. Indeed, within the Asia Pacific region, India has the widest gender gap in terms of internet usage. Women's mobile internet use rose from 21 per cent in 2020 to 30 per cent in 2021 (compared to an increase from 42 per cent to 45 per cent for Indian men), pushed by greater internet affordability, and Covid-19 restrictions and lockdowns resulting in more women going online. However, in 2022, women's mobile internet use stalled at 30 per cent while men's continued to rise to 50 per cent. The plateauing of women's mobile internet use in India as the pandemic has progressed has meant that livelihoods have suffered, particularly for women, and the country's internet gender gap has 'also widened the overall gender gap in South Asia and across LMICs [low and middle income countries]' (GSM Association, 2022).

The pandemic has also exacerbated other existing gender-based inequalities in India's labour market. The *State of Working India Report 2021* tracks India's workforce from December 2019 to December 2020 (Basole et al., 2021), straddling pre-Covid and lockdown contexts. It found that, as in many countries, the contrast in employment experiences between men and women was stark, with job losses higher and the recovery slower for women. While 61 per cent of men's employment was unaffected by the pandemic and subsequent lockdown, the corresponding figure for women was just 19 per cent. Similarly, while only 7 per cent of men were unable to recover from job loss, the figure for women was much higher at 47 per cent. Having lost employment during the lockdown, men were eight times more likely to return to work compared to women.

Chauhan's (2021) survey showed that, among women, marital and employment status are key determinants of their unpaid work burden, with time spent on unpaid work having increased most for married women and unemployed women, both of whom were already spending the highest amount of time on such work prior to the lockdown. These results are also reflected in the India National Sample Survey Office's (NSSO) Time Use Survey (2019). The proportion of females engaged in unpaid domestic services was 81.2 per cent compared to only 26.1 per cent for males, hinting at the invisibility of female labour. Furthermore, the proportion of females engaged in such work in rural areas was higher (82.1 per cent) than those in cities (79.2 per cent).

However, a brief report in 2021 by the Observer Research Foundation notes that, while Covid-19 propelled a 500 per cent increase in tele-health consultations and a structural shift towards online shopping — with e-retail reaching 95 per cent of Indian districts and digital payments nearing 100 million transactions per day — it also amplified the impacts of a gendered digital divide (Nikore and Ishita, 2021). In order for women to gain their rightful share of these opportunities, they thus need to acquire skills in newly opening fields (see also Chapter 6).

WOMEN AND THE FUTURE OF WORK IN INDIA

New digital technologies such as artificial intelligence, cloud computing, machine learning, the Internet of Things, 3D technologies and advanced robotics play a key role in determining labour market outcomes in the future. Literature on the future of work explores various mega-trends, including the impact of technological change on work, the potential for job loss, and changes in industry and organisational structures (e.g. Hill et al., 2019). Digital technologies can result in the destruction of jobs or the expansion of jobs, depending on how fast new jobs are matched with corresponding skills. There may be a lag in generating the skills needed to match newer forms of technology, resulting in unemployment.

Two conflicting narratives characterise debates around the effect of technology on the world of work in the Global South. The first sees technology as an enabler that allows developing countries to fast-track their development. Increased productivity and efficiency can contribute to economic growth. At a time when many countries in the Global South struggle to create more jobs for a large and growing youth population, technological advancements provide new employment opportunities (Madgavkar et al., 2019).

The second, however, has a more sombre tone. It has been argued that technology has induced capital intensification that has fuelled economic growth but has not been able to absorb the surplus labour that is characteristic of many developing countries. At the risk of being left behind are those without access to technology or skills and those unable to participate in a digitally driven economy. This narrative posits that disruptive technologies will fuel inequalities in income, productivity and wellbeing between and within countries (Dewan & Ernst, 2020).

Given that women in the Global South tend to have lower educational levels than their male counterparts, computerisation and automation will probably result in them losing their jobs due to not being able to gain access to jobs that are require higher qualifications. In the absence of conscious measures, this eventually leads to new patterns of gender inequality in the labour market. It is important to note, however, that the impact of new technologies on the future of work will be mediated by political, legal and social frameworks at the local level, and the actual adoption of technologies will be driven by these local conditions (ILO, 2018).

In India, studies argue that much of the workforce is still involved in the low-skilled and low-paid informal sector while relatively few work in the country's formal or organised sectors (Mehta & Awasthi, 2019; ILO, 2018). Nathan and Ahmed (2018) have thus contended that new technologies will impact less on India's larger informal sector, while the formal/organised sector will face greater change, similar to that experienced by industrialised countries, particularly in terms of the loss of routine task jobs in the manufacturing and services sectors.

Furthermore, women's work participation rates and the proportion of women in regular salaried, self-employed and casual wage categories differ substantially across Indian states. Across 28 states and nine union territories, the female labour force participation rate varies markedly, with the highest at 47 per cent in Himachal Pradesh and the lowest at just 3 per cent in Bihar, while the all-India average is 19.5 per cent (MoSPI, 2021). In addition, the proportion of women in regular salaried, self-employed and casual labour categories varies widely between states, with the effects of new technologies more apparent in states such as Delhi, Goa, Punjab, Kerala, Haryana, Maharashtra and Gujarat, which have a relatively high proportion of women in skilled or semi-skilled occupations (Mehta et al., 2021).

However, while the future impacts of technological change on job loss have been studied extensively, comparatively little analysis exists on the gendered implications of the work and labour market change that it brings about, and how this will impact on the reproduction of social structures and systems — despite women's increased participation in the labour market and gender equality at work becoming key government objectives around the world. McKinsey's 2019 Global Institute report on the future of women at work argues that, world-wide, to achieve gender equality 40–160 million women may need to transition between occupations by 2030, often into higher-skilled roles, as 20 per cent of working women risk having their jobs displaced by automation (Madgavkar et al., 2019).

In 2018, an ILO report on digital labour platforms and the future of work found gender differences in the propensity to do crowd work, where outsourcing of tasks is organised using online platforms; women represent only one out of every three workers (ILO, 2018). In developing countries, including India, the gender balance is particularly skewed, with only one in five workers being a woman. Strong gender differences for those who could 'only work from home' were attributed to gendered care responsibilities (13 per cent of women workers gave this reason compared to just 5 per cent of men). Indeed, many women combined crowd work with care responsibilities, and one in five female workers had small children (0–5 years). These women nonetheless spent 20 hours per week on the platform, just five hours fewer than the sample as a whole. Many worked during the evenings and at night, reflecting a long-term practice by women of accommodating greater domestic responsibilities than those held by many men so as to engage like men in the world of paid work (Berg et al., 2018).

It is also pertinent to investigate how the Covid-19 pandemic will influence the future of women's working lives. A recent study that examined the impact of lockdowns on the gender division of labour in India found that it has resulted in a shift in the gender composition of domestic work, with more male participation (Deshpande, 2020). Despite this, at least in the short term, it remains to be seen whether it will have a major impact on longer-term social norms.

Due to the nature of the occupations that they perform, a large proportion of people who work from home are women, and India has a greater proportion of work-from-home workers in urban areas than in rural areas. The share of women employed in work-from-home occupations (23 per cent) is higher than the share of men (18 per cent) (Bhatt, Grover & Sharma, 2020). Such a pattern may reflect gender roles assigned to occupations and female preferences for flexible occupations (also Berg et al., 2018). Using American Time Use Survey data, Mongey et al.'s (2021) study shows that workers in work-from-home jobs (i.e. predominantly women) are more economically vulnerable.

There are also specific pandemic-induced changes in the school system that impact on working mothers. In many schools, additional shifts were introduced after reopening to ensure physical separation, and the workload of the staff has increased significantly. Therefore, much of the teaching and supervision responsibilities have been transferred to parents. These additional responsibilities affect women working from home with children. According to anecdotal evidence, many women with childcare responsibilities had to leave their jobs during lockdown and the subsequent adjustment period after schools opened.

In India, it is also useful to identify occupations that need to be modernised and mechanised due to their low dignity status and associated social stigma. Women face double discrimination as gender inequalities and caste converge. The vast majority of those who engage in manual scavenging in India are women (more than 95 per cent), and deploying technology to relieve them from such inhumane work is key (Kumar & Preet, 2020). In spite of the Prohibition of Employment as Manual Scavengers and Their Rehabilitation Act 2013 (PEMSR) and subsequent orders of the Supreme Court of India, manual scavengers continue to work in certain pockets in India. To ensure decent work for women engaged in such occupations, concerted collective action is required (also Chapter 6).

In addition, there is limited understanding of the consequences of digitalisation and new technologies on labour mobility and migration. The ways in which online platforms are altering the organisation of work for migrants in sectors heavily dependent on their labour, and the type of work that cannot be automated, such as nursing and delivery services, are under-studied. This will have an impact on female labour migration from India to North America, Europe and Middle East countries.

ADDITIONAL POLICY SUGGESTIONS

In Chapter 6, recommendations are made to help improve the situation of working women in India, the overwhelming majority of whom are employed in its large informal and unorganised sector. The first step towards better understanding the constraints that women face in the labour market is to use more comprehensive measures of female labour force participation. While India is making progress in terms of systematically collecting better labour force statistics via the Periodic Labour Force Survey and the Time Use Survey (e.g. India Ministry of Statistics and Program Implementation, 2021; India National Statistical Office and Ministry of Statistics and Program Implementation, 2019), extant labour force surveys often underestimate the work performed by women as labour force measurements comply with accepted international definitions, which do not consistently apply a distinction between unpaid family workers and those exclusively engaged in domestic duties (Deshpande & Kabeer, 2019). Much of the work undertaken by women is rendered invisible, as they often engage in overlapping activities such as formal/informal employment, cooking, taking care of children and elderly dependents, and other domestic tasks. More refined indices of women's engagement in work are still needed.

Despite many attempts by India's government to mainstream skill formation in the formal education system and to develop innovative approaches to skill creation outside the formal education system (Nayana & Kumar, 2019), there remains a dearth in skills programmes, and this functions to gendered effect. As Patel has noted in Chapter 6, legislative protection for gig-platform women workers in this fast-developing, under-regulated economy, and a targeted range of skill measures to assist women and girls in India. In addition, Fletcher, Pande and Moore (2017) have argued that, since women's engagement in manufacturing employment has grown over the last decade (as opposed to their employment levels in agriculture), government-funded expansion of the sector would benefit women.

Beyond skill development, it is also argued by Patel and emphasised here that formalising India's informal and unorganised sector by implementing social security systems would help to ensure that women are better protected at work (Nair et al., 2020). The Centre for Sustainable Employment's (2019) report proposed the creation of a National Urban Employment Guarantee Scheme to address underemployment and low wages in the informal sector, unemployment, and the lack of skills held by the educated labour force, among other issues (Basole et al., 2019). While the rights-based framework of India's major employment guarantee programme MGNREGA is retained, they argue for varied forms of employment. One policy challenge is thus to encourage the upskilling of women and the creation of opportunities in regular wage work, and to address other constraints that women face in the labour market, including those concerning their workplace safety, a need for greater support to conduct their burden of domestic chores and care work, and the inadequate availability of flexible working arrangements.

7. Working women in Sri Lanka

Kasuni Weerasinghe and Thilini Meegaswatta

Sri Lanka, formerly known as Ceylon, and officially the Democratic Socialist Republic of Sri Lanka, is a developing island country in South Asia. On the surface, Sri Lanka's track record in gender equality and women's empowerment seems rather impressive: this tiny island nation produced the world's first female prime minister — Sirimavo Bandaranaike (1960–65, 1970–77, 1994–2000) — and one of the longest-serving female executive presidents — Chandrika Bandaranaike Kumaratunga (1994–2005). It also has the third-highest gender equality ranking in South Asia (World Economic Forum, 2021). However, women still face considerable challenges compared with those of their male counterparts, especially in terms of economic activity.

Sri Lanka has been named among the top 10 countries in the world in its handling of Covid-19 (Economynext, 2021), but the socio-economic impact of the pandemic has exacerbated existing hurdles to gender equity. While the country effectively managed the first outbreak of the virus in early 2020, since then its citizenry has suffered the brunt of the second and third waves,[1] with the pandemic particularly affecting women.

---

1   As this book was in production, Sri Lanka was facing its biggest post-independence economic and political crisis. The country defaulted on its debts in May 2022 and the

In this chapter, we explore the issues and challenges faced by the working women of Sri Lanka with regard to demographic, technological, globalisation and sustainability trends and issues in the context of the Covid-19 pandemic. Drawing on key findings, we then advance a range of policy recommendations with an eye to improving Sri Lankan working women's situation in the workplace and beyond.

Sri Lanka's documented history extends back three millennia. Its location as a long-standing trading hub has helped to create the country's diverse cultures, languages and ethnicities. Sri Lanka has a population of 21.8 million, of whom 51.8 per cent are women (Department of Census and Statistics [DCS], 2019a). The Sinhalese form the majority of the nation's population, with the Tamils, a large minority group, having played a key role in the island's history.

Sri Lanka's free market economy experienced annual growth of 6.4 per cent from 2003 to 2012, above its regional peers, driven by the growth of non-tradeable sectors. Growth has subsequently slowed and, in July 2020, the country was downgraded to a lower middle-income classification by the World Bank exactly a year after it was upgraded to a upper middle-income country (*Daily Financial Times*, 2020, July).

Following the Sri Lankan civil war (1983–2009), the country had striven to transition back to this higher status, but has faced various challenges in social inclusion, governance and sustainability (World Bank, 2016). Services made up more than half (58.2 per cent) of the Sri Lankan economy in 2019 while industry formed 27.4 per cent and agriculture 7.4 per cent (DCS, 2021), though rising trade protection in recent years has encouraged

---

economy has almost ground to a halt, with depleted foreign reserves. The government has been unable to pay for essential imports of fuel, medicine and food. Inflation is at a record high, with the National Consumer Price Index rising from 5.7 per cent in September 2021 to 54.6 per cent in June 2022 (Central Bank of Sri Lanka, 2022). The UN has called for international assistance in Sri Lanka, citing urgent humanitarian needs (UN, 2022). A deep frustration at the mismanagement at the highest level of government led to months-long protests in Colombo that ousted both the prime minister and the president.

Figure 7.1: Labour force participation (%) by gender in Sri Lanka, 2012–19

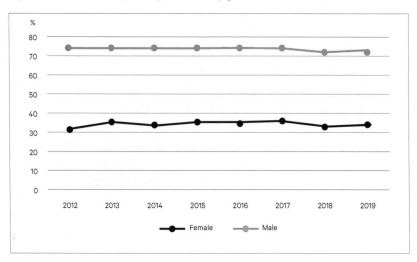

Source: DCS Annual Labour Force Survey reports (various years)

a resurgence of inward-looking policies (Athukorala, 2012).

As Figure 7.1 indicates, the female labour force participation (LFP) in Sri Lanka seldom exceeds 35 per cent (DCS, 2019b). Moreover, a gender parity score of 0.48 in work, which takes into consideration five indicators (LFP rate, professional and technical jobs, perceived wage gap for similar work, leadership positions and unpaid care work) puts Sri Lanka into the 'extremely high inequality' category in Asia Pacific, despite being ahead of most South Asian countries (McKinsey Global Institute, 2018).

Sector-wise, women comprise the majority (over 60 per cent) of Sri Lanka's health workforce and face increased health risks in fighting the battle against Covid-19. Working women also carry a heavier burden on the home front, including increased care responsibility for homebound family members during lockdowns (Meegaswatta, 2021). In addition, Covid-19 has shown the precarity of many women's employment and the exploitative conditions in which they work. Indeed, women in informal work (e.g. housemaids) and low-skilled jobs (e.g. the apparel sector where 70–80 per cent of employees are women) are among the vulnerable majority who have lost or are at risk of losing their jobs, thus facing increased financial difficulties.

EMPLOYMENT REGULATION

From a legislative perspective, employed women in Sri Lanka enjoy the same, if not greater, rights as men. In addition to blanket laws and regulations, there are targeted statutes, ordinances and provisions which seek to encourage better working conditions or more security and access, particularly for women. Legislation that specifically relates to women includes the Employment of Women, Young Persons, and Children Act of 1956; the Maternity Benefits Ordinance of 1941; and additional protections afforded through special provisions in the Factories Ordinance of 1942 and the Shop and Office Employees Act of 1954 (Department of Labour, n.d.).

Sri Lanka is a signatory to various international labour conventions that aim for equality of opportunity and treatment of women, occupational safety and health, and maternity protection. Examples include the Equal Remuneration Convention of 1951 (signatory since 1993), Discrimination (Employment and Occupation) Convention of 1958 (1998); Underground Work (Women) Convention of 1935 (1950); and Maternity Protection Convention (Revised) of 1952 (1993) (ILO, n.d.).

Women's welfare and work constantly feature in mainstream political agendas and, as such, are sometimes part of public discourse. The policy documents of presidential candidates have routinely focused — either comprehensively or more tokenistically — on equality, empowerment and decent work for women. For example, two-term former President Mahinda Rajapaksa's policy document promised 'pride of place to the mother', and 'higher priority' rather than 'equal status' for women, expressing plans to establish financial support to enhance self-employment, equal wages for equal work, and measures to increase women's participation in politics and decision-making (Rajapaksa, 2010). Some of these plans, especially those relating to financial support, have been repeated in President Gotabaya Rajapaksa's manifesto, which promised to 'assign high priority to increasing the labour force participation of women and to promoting women entrepreneurs' (Rajapaksa, 2019, p. 27).[2]

Hence, superficially, employed women in Sri Lanka appear to be well-supported and -protected by a comprehensive legal and policy framework. However, it has been suggested that 'the gap between the de jure equality in law and de facto practice persists [and that] equality in employment remains to be an elusive goal' (Otobe, 2013, p. 25). For instance, while Sri Lankan law stipulates that women should not lose their job due to pregnancy or childbirth, it is likely that the unavailability of quality care options for young children, coupled with social pressures, force mothers to give up their paid role. While appearing voluntary, their decisions are, in reality, constrained by circumstances grounded in gendered structural inequalities.

At the same time, Sri Lanka's legal and regulatory frameworks are far from faultless. For example, there are no laws on sexual harassment in the workplace; labour law does not extend to the informal sector where the majority of workers are women; and almost all labour laws and regulations exclude (often explicitly) domestic workers, who are mostly women (ILO, 2020a). Furthermore, Sri Lanka has not ratified a number of ILO conventions that relate to women, including C156 — Workers with Family Responsibilities Convention (1981), C177 — Home Work Convention (1996), C189 — Domestic Workers Convention (2011), and C190 — Violence and Harassment Convention (2019).

Conditions of employment and benefits are also variously applied to women working in certain sectors. For instance, according to the Shop and Office Employees Act of 1954, women are granted 84 days of maternity

---

2   Whether these election promises have resulted in tangible outcomes and concrete policy commitments is open to debate. For instance, Gotabaya Rajapaksa's pledge to provide rural women with relief from predatory micro-financial schemes has resulted in a series of hunger protests in different parts of the country by groups of women who have demanded the cancellation of their debts.

leave excluding holidays whereas, according to the Factories Ordinance of 1942, the 84 days are inclusive of holidays. In addition, the Sri Lankan legal regime does not afford protection to overseas workers, a significant proportion of whom are women employed as domestic workers in Middle Eastern countries and who are often vulnerable to exploitation and grave harm (Amnesty International, 2021; Human Rights Watch, 2007; Tidball, 2011). Loopholes in the law have also been exploited by some industries, especially in Free Trade Zones (FTZ), to deny basic rights and benefits to workers, most of whom are women.

The unjust practices of the FTZ came under scrutiny when the sector was hit hard by the second wave of Covid-19 in Sri Lanka. This wave was reported to have originated in the country's apparel sector, where the vast majority of workers are young women with no formal employment contracts on account of being recruited through employment agencies, and who were thus susceptible to being dismissed without warning or compensation when disaster struck (Dabindu Collective, 2021; *Daily Financial Times*, 2020, October; Forum-Asia, 2021).

KEY CHALLENGES AND OPPORTUNITIES

Demography

Sri Lanka's population is largely defined by the steady rise in life expectancy and the slow but sure decrease in fertility rate over the years, which, conjointly, translate into the overall ageing of a society. While having a larger working-age population has been identified as a 'demographic bonus' that lasted until around 2017, population forecasts suggest that Sri Lanka is set to have the oldest population in South Asia by 2041 (World Bank, 2012). This increase in the population share of the over 60s, which would outpace the decline in youth dependency, is expected to significantly increase the overall dependent ratio, putting pressure on the working-age population, particularly women.

Indeed, a key demographic, educational and socio-cultural reason for the comparatively low female LFP rate in Sri Lanka is the burden of care work that disproportionately falls to women. Sri Lankan society is traditional in that working women often engage in a 'double shift' as the primary or sole caretakers of domestic responsibilities while engaging in waged labour outside the home.

The first Sri Lankan national survey on the use of time in 2017 showed that the proportion of time spent in a day on unpaid domestic and care work by women was significantly higher than that for men (5.6 hours a day for women compared with 30 minutes for men) (DCS, 2017). Hence, women who enter the workforce, especially in the private sector, often tend to leave the workforce after marriage and particularly after motherhood, reflecting a lack of policy, infrastructure and services support for working mothers in terms of anti-discrimination policies, state-funded childcare, extended periods of maternity leave for private sector workers and paternity leave, which is not granted in the private sector and is limited to three days for state sector employees. On the other hand, women's extensive care roles form part of the 'invisible' work that is not formally quantified; the female LFP rate has stagnated around 30–36 per cent for decades, partly due to the invisibility of different forms of women's work in formal records, especially in the agrarian sector (Kumara & Weerakkody, 2011; Sirisena, 1986).

In this scenario, Sri Lanka's decreasing fertility rate might be expected to increase the chances for women to enter the workforce. A two-way relationship exists between women's employment and fertility: with fewer children, female participation in paid work could rise but, as women increasingly participate in the labour market, they would seek to have fewer children due to a rising opportunity cost (Roser, 2014).

Even if low fertility positively relates to female employment, the rising proportion of the population aged over 60 seems to exert growing pressure on women's care responsibilities. In Sri Lanka, families are close-knit, and elderly parents are the responsibility of the children; admitting parents to an old-age home is largely taboo. Although sons are seen as primarily responsible for the care of elderly parents, in practice this duty is largely performed by women: daughters and daughters-in-law. At the same time, parental presence and support have been found to be a significant contributor to Sri Lankan-employed women's successful navigation of work–life balance during Covid-19 lockdowns:

> straddling of both worlds seems to be possible in most cases — especially for married women with children — given the support structures available to women in the traditional South Asian home in the form of retired parents or parents-in-law. (Meegaswatta, 2021, p. 168)

Nevertheless, the burden of care work means that women often tend to work part-time or in the country's sizeable informal sector where flexible working hours are likely. However, much of women's employment in this sector can be characterised as precarious, as emphasised by the unprecedented impact of Covid-19 in terms of loss of employment. Drawing on DCS data for the first quarter of 2019 and 2020, Meegaswatta (2021) notes how the decrease in employment levels in 2020 mostly affected women (a fall of 229,029 compared with a slight rise in the number of employed men). Further, women made up 67 per cent of those who lost their job in all segments of the informal and formal tourism sectors in Sri Lanka (United Nations Development Program (UNDP), cited in Meegaswatta, 2021).

However, a steady increase in women's achievement in higher education may see an increase in their LFP rate. Over the last few years, women have comprised over 60 per cent of the total university admissions and have outnumbered their male counterparts in most faculties by a significant margin, with the gender gap in science, technology, engineering, mathematics and medicine (STEMM) — traditionally male-dominated areas of study — steadily closing or fully closing (University Grants Commission, 2019). When women have higher levels of education, participation in the labour force increases significantly: according to data segregated by gender and education level, the gap between men and women sits at just 1.2 per cent at graduate level and above (DCS, 2019b).

Figure 7.2: Unemployment rate (%) by level of education in Sri Lanka, 2020 first quarter

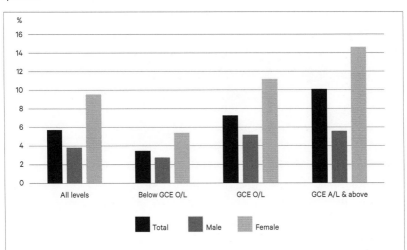

GCE = General Certificate of Education. O/L = Ordinary Level. A/L = Advanced Level. Source: DCS (2020)

This could be because women with more qualifications earn more, in turn enabling them to afford childcare, eldercare and domestic help, which are instrumental in creating the space and time for them to enter the workforce (Arunatillake, 2017).

However, the extent to which this is reflected in the overall female LFP rate is unknown given that women's pursuit of higher education (which is at a higher level than men's), and their high expectations for starting salaries due to high levels of education attainment has also been identified as reasons for their low labour force participation (Gunatilaka, cited in Asian Development Bank (ADB) and ILO, 2017; Semasinghe, 2017). For instance, while female unemployment rates exceed those for males at all levels of education, the problem of unemployment is more acute in the case of educated females than of educated males (see Figure 7.2).

Further, due to extended periods of full-time study, over the years women have consistently entered the workforce later than their male counterparts have (DCS, 2020). However, a definitive statement on the overall effect of higher education on LFP is difficult to make as quantitative research has not been able to establish a statistically significant relationship between LFP and education (Semasinghe, 2017).

Technology

Globally, the proliferation of digital platforms and technology over the past decade, specifically information and communication technologies (ICT) that facilitate effective collaborations and communication, has affected women's employment. The use of ICT can leverage more women's participation in paid work because it enables flexible work arrangements whereby women can continue to work, and to balance paid work with care work for their family (ILO, 2016). However, some evidence suggests that teleworking arrangements in Sri Lanka have not seen an increase in the number of women in the workforce, and that employers are not in favour of remote working as they claim that workers are not committed, responsible or disciplined enough to work from home, leading to cost and productivity issues for companies (ILO, 2016). Also, Sri Lankan labour legislation does not recognise or provide for special conditions of flexible work such as remote working (ILO, 2016), further discouraging employers from offering it. Nonetheless, due to the effects of the Covid-19 pandemic, many Sri Lankan organisations have been more open to offering their employees the option to work from home (Liyanage & Ekanayake, 2021).

Over the past decade, the Sri Lankan government has taken a number of steps to facilitate the use of IT, primarily through the Information and Communication Technology Association (ICTA) (Dissanayake, 2017). Higher education institutes, too, are increasingly promoting IT education in the country. In turn, IT-related work opportunities have been very popular among the labour force in Sri Lanka. This could result in increased female LFP, especially in a context where rigid work arrangements and difficulty in balancing personal and professional commitments in the past have led women to leave the workforce or experience counter-productive physical and mental wellbeing issues (Dissanayake, 2017).

In addition to remote working, other key types of flexible work include online freelancing, micro-work and gig work. Online freelancing refers to production and delivery of services through online means, utilising digital platforms. Micro-work is work that requires low skill levels (e.g. ad-clicking),[3] while gig work involves services provided by individual contractors, such as food delivery (Bandaranayake et al., 2020). A national survey by Galpaya et al. (2018) identified that, compared with men, women are significantly less aware of the opportunities around online freelancing, micro-work and gig work in Sri Lanka. If these types of opportunities are well promoted, they can become good avenues of income for Sri Lankan women who are looking to work flexibly.

In developing countries like Sri Lanka, access to ICT infrastructure, such as an effective telecommunication service, uninterrupted internet connectivity and access to required peripheral devices and associated costs are challenges in both rural and urban areas (Dissanayake, 2017). Telecentres, first introduced in 2002 (called NenaSala), were intended in rural Sri Lanka to provide computer and internet facilities that enable villages to take advantage of information sharing, government information and healthcare, to access education, and other services (Hansson et al., 2010). While NenaSala has laid groundwork to empower rural women to use ICTs and has opened up new work opportunities for women, the gender considerations for rural workers using these telecentres has not been explicitly explored (Kottegoda et al., 2012). As a result, it has been challenging for women to effectively participate in such spaces given difficulties for them, for instance, around negotiating their social roles in this context (Kottegoda et al., 2012).

The global pandemic has accelerated the technology-based transfor-

---

3 This involves paid work for clicking on advertisements on websites.

mation of many workplaces. In Sri Lanka, travel restrictions and social-distancing measures designed to curb the spread of Covid-19 have forced both employers and employees, even in the most traditional settings, to adopt and adapt new technologies and remote working practices. Challenges with this are far from absent. For instance, limited IT facilities and literacy, and the nature of the business (e.g. in the apparel industry and hospitality sector) have made remote work difficult or impossible (Robinson & Kengatharan, 2020). Furthermore, during extended lockdowns, there has been greater pressure on limited IT resources in households (especially for families with working adults and school-age children), with women more likely to miss out or have less access to or time on such devices (Meegaswatta, 2021).

Covid-related changes in workplace practices, especially flexible working from home, are likely, in the long run, to have an overall positive impact on women's workforce engagement as they help employers and employees to better capitalise on saved time and energy, and better manage multiple responsibilities. The pandemic has thus forced employers to rethink workplace practices and to develop new skill sets, encouraging positive policy developments in the future with respect to IT-enabled flexible work.

Globalisation

Globalisation has brought opportunities for Sri Lankan working women, particularly those in the country's apparel industry which produces international clothing brands. While workplaces in FTZ and Export Processing Zones (EPZ) face unique problems and often harbour exploitative conditions, they also provide a way out for thousands of women who are looking to earn a living (Madurawala, 2017). However, the second Covid-19 wave in Sri Lanka escalated within the FTZ, much of which comprises a feminised workforce in garment factories. Since the advent of the pandemic, the fragile nature of work for women in this sector, among others, has been more clearly revealed with the termination of job contracts, non-payment of wages and bonuses, and employer negligence with regard to worker health and wellbeing.

A key benefit of globalisation for women is the opportunity to find employment outside of the country. Sri Lanka, as a low-income country, is known for its high migration rates, with approximately 250,000 migrant workers leaving Sri Lanka each year, 34 per cent of whom are women (Sri Lanka Bureau of Foreign Employment, 2016). As a South Asian country, Sri Lanka has had one of the highest migration outflows and foreign remittance inflows in the 10 years since 2012, and it has long depended upon international remittances from migrants (Karunaratne, 2012). In 2019, incoming international remittances equalled 8 per cent of the country's GDP (World Bank, 2021b). Skilled and low-skilled types of migrant work present different sets of challenges to women who are looking to improve their economic opportunities and living standards by opting to work overseas.

The migration of skilled workers with higher qualifications typically involves middle- to high-income families who move to developed countries for higher incomes and better lifestyles. While official data are unavailable, a recent online survey provides a glimpse into the scale of the phenomenon. Women form significant proportions — 53 per cent and 20 per cent — of the high- and medium-skilled migrants to Western countries and the Middle East respectively (Weeraratne, 2019, 2020). A lack of facilities and infrastructure, poor salary rates, and corruption in politics and the public sector are key drivers for more highly qualified people to move to developed or fast-developing countries.

People who obtain higher education through the free system in Sri Lanka are among the majority of those who migrate as skilled workers. Perceived prospects of better opportunities and a better quality of life were cited as key reasons for mobility by skilled migrants, resulting in 'brain drain'. However, this form of migration also has advantages, such as international remittances. But skilled migrant women, particularly mothers, face greater difficulties in maintaining work–life balance due to a lack of available support. The Covid-19 pandemic, lockdowns, border closures and new national migration policies have exacerbated challenges for female migrants who face issues such as the need to hold on to jobs amidst challenges, their inability to find flexible work and their inability to access support from extended families at home.

Due to income inequality between different strata of the society, a significant number of women from low-income families in Sri Lanka also go overseas as low-skilled workers, hoping to supplement family income and access decent living conditions for themselves and their impoverished families. While the number of overall female migrants declined from 48.8 per cent in 2008 to 38.6 per cent in 2018 (Sri Lanka Bureau of Foreign Employment, 2018), the vast majority of these migrants (78.8 per cent in 2016) belong to the low-skilled category and were employed as domestic workers in the Middle East (Sri Lanka Bureau of Foreign Employment, 2016).

Women who migrate as low-skilled labourers and domestic workers often have to endure inhumane working conditions and treatment, without any possibility of demanding better conditions due to a lack of legal protection and bargaining power. Furthermore, they are easily replaced in a competitive and abundant labour market (Aoun, 2020). And as Covid-19 has spread, the workplace and wider conditions for female migrant workers have further deteriorated. Female migrant domestic workers in the Middle East are facing increased risks as a combined result of the kafala (sponsorship) system[4] and the pandemic. Hundreds of female domestic workers reportedly lost their jobs and accommodation due to the Covid-19 pandemic while waiting (some as long as 18 months) for the Sri Lankan

---

4   According to Amnesty International (2021), the Saudi Arabian kafala system, which ties migrant workers to their employer, is 'an abusive sponsorship system that facilitates exploitation and abuse'. Under this system, domestic workers are expected to obtain permission from their employer to change jobs or leave the country, 'which makes the workers extremely dependent on them and increases their vulnerability to abuses of rights, including forced labour and physical and sexual assault'. Failure to secure this permission can be grounds for indefinite detention. Although limited reforms were introduced in March 2021, Amnesty International argues that 'these will do little to eliminate the risk of labour abuses and exploitation faced by migrant workers who continue to be tied to employers who retain tremendous control over them'.

government to bring them home, and have been subjected to ill treatment including abuse and deprived of medical attention (Amnesty International, 2021). With Covid-19 also disrupting the flow of international remittances, this is likely to threaten the welfare of low-income families who are highly dependent on them (Withers et al., 2021).

Sustainability

A primary concern for Sri Lanka is its pursuit of sustainable economic growth. After explosive development in the immediate aftermath of the global financial crisis and the Eelam war in 2009, the country's economy showed an overall downward trend, hitting an all-time low during the pandemic when it contracted by 3.6 per cent in 2020 (World Bank, 2021a). While the pandemic has wreaked economic havoc globally, Sri Lanka's downward trend in a context of what had been regional growth is particularly worrying. A key contributory factor has been the country's supply of untapped female labour, despite the benefits that women have reaped from positive human development trends in Sri Lanka. A success story in the region, the country has exceeded a number of other South Asian countries, notably, in terms of mortality, life expectancy, literacy and fertility rate (UNDP, 2020). UNDP statistics for 2019 indicate that women's life expectancy was 80.3 years while, for men, it was 73.6 years. In addition, expected years of schooling are slightly higher for girls at 14.5 years, compared with 13.8 years for boys. However, as reiterated in the section above, women's participation in the labour force remains low.

Reports emphasise the huge economic costs of gender inequalities that keep women out of the labour force and exacerbate challenges for countries seeking to reduce poverty and achieve sustainable development (International Finance Corporation [IFC], 2019). A recent ILO report on Sri Lanka's potential for green growth highlighted five sectors. In three of these sectors — tourism, agriculture and the apparel industry — women form a significant proportion of employees. If sectors like the apparel industry were to seriously commit to a 'green' transformation to stay abreast of the demand for 'clean' or 'guilt-free' clothing, this would not only involve environmentally friendly practices but also 'reforms aimed at improving workers' wages, non-exploitative working conditions, women's safety and mechanisms for organising and collective bargaining' (ILO, 2020b, p. 18). Currently, however, the situation is far from ideal; in particular, the conditions surrounding the pandemic have brought to light the precarity of employment in the sector, exploitative working conditions and safety concerns.

Another pressing sustainability concern is the destructive use of natural resources in Sri Lanka, particularly forest land, in the name of development and economic growth. The arbitrary and intensified use of land for agriculture, settlements and other development activities, and the resultant loss of forest cover, especially in post-war Sri Lanka, has been dubbed an 'ecocide' by an increasingly concerned public.

More recent environmental controversies have included housing developments in Wilpattu National Wildlife Park; and road constructions and plans to construct two irrigation tanks, each spanning an area of five acres, inside the Sinharaja rainforest, a biodiversity hotspot and a UNESCO World Heritage site. Sri Lanka has lost 188,000 hectares, or a 4.8 per cent decrease, of tree cover since 2000. More alarmingly, the loss of humid primary forest constitutes 5.5 per cent of the total tree cover loss, with commodity-driven deforestation the most significant reason for permanent deforestation (Global Forest Watch, n.d.). This, together with poor seasonal farming practices, leads to land degradation and is likely to have an adverse, long-term impact on local weather patterns, water and food security, and biodiversity.

The spillover of such unsustainable use of natural resources differentially impacts on women and men. Global data suggest that women are more vulnerable when disaster strikes and, as primary caregivers and providers of food and fuel, they are more likely than men to be affected by climate change and related natural adversities such as floods and droughts (Halton, 2018). In the context of land degradation, for example, women contribute an increasing number of hours in cultivation that, eventually, will not yield the expected harvest or income. This, in turn, will make them more vulnerable to exploitation and debt traps.

In addition, populist and short-sighted policy measures to address harmful farming and cultivation practices can have a devastating impact on agricultural workers. For instance, research and news reports have revealed that the Sri Lankan government's 2015 ban on glyphosate, a weedicide regularly used on tea plantations, led to a drop in tea production and loss in income in the plantation sector (Abeywickrama et al., 2017; Marambe & Herath, 2020). This affected women workers acutely as the estate sector is where women's LFP is consistently the highest, particularly in the tea sector where 75–85 per cent of the workforce are women, with only 7 per cent engaged as regular employees (Central Bank of Sri Lanka, cited in Otobe, 2013; Kotikula & Solotaroff, 2006; Ranraja, cited in Otobe, 2013). A ban imposed on the importation of chemical fertilisers, pesticides and herbicides in April 2021 in a bid to promote 100 per cent organic production without a transition plan has had detrimental impacts on agriculture,[5] a sector that has become more feminised over the years (Otobe, 2013), with women playing an increasingly key role as either waged labourers or unpaid family workers.

However, anticipated bans of agro-chemicals and fertilisers could also bring to light the sustainable and environmentally friendly nature of small-scale farming practices (e.g. home gardens) adopted by women with the primary aim of providing their families with toxin-free produce (Padmasiri, 2020). It has been observed that women's farming practices and activism show a more ecological approach in their promotion of organic

---

5 As of July 2022, this short-sighted and sudden decision to convert to 100 per cent organic farming has been dubbed as one of the key reasons for the economic crisis in Sri Lanka. It has been reported that within months of this decision, the volume of tea exports had halved and rice yields had plummeted, leading to an unprecedented requirement to import rice for local consumption, which together made grounds for the collapse of the currency (Ridley, 2022).

and traditional farming methods against the neoliberal, profit-oriented agriculture industry that is monopolised by a handful of multinational companies in Sri Lanka. It is thus 'a pragmatic use of resources leading to sustainability and protection of the environment' (Padmasiri, 2020) that is promoted by women activists working with women in agrarian communities. Equipped with the relevant knowledge and skills, women may indeed have increased local as well as global opportunities in the agricultural sector, particularly given rising consumer awareness and global demand for organic and sustainable produce, and consumers' desire for a personal connection with small-scale farmers (ILO, 2019, 2020b).

Heightened environmental consciousness among urban populations; sustainability practices enforced through state policy initiatives such as reduced usage of single-use plastics, polythene and other such non-biodegradable material usage; and a growing preference for biodegradable local products could create small-scale employment and entrepreneurial opportunities for women in Sri Lanka.

RECOMMENDATIONS AND CONCLUSIONS

Our analysis of key challenges for working women in Sri Lanka reveals a need for a psycho-social shift in attitudes to help address problems such as gender role traditions that relegate women to the domestic sphere, and discrimination in hiring and promotion that restricts women's entry into the paid workforce, as well as to opportunities and paths to advance in their chosen career.

Given the challenges that women face, more pragmatic and concrete suggestions might include the provision of greater structural support of women's engagement with paid work through laws, policies and infrastructure. Indeed, it has been identified that by addressing issues around safety, equity and work–life balance the private sector can better support working women (Solotaroff et al., 2017). Steps in this direction could include improving maternity leave and introducing paternity leave to help acknowledge the child-rearing responsibilities of both parents and lessen the gendered pressures on working mothers and the discrimination they face during workplace recruitment following their take-up of special leave to which they are entitled. In addition, the introduction of state-subsidised childcare services and the implementation of crèches in workplaces could prevent well-qualified women from leaving work due to family commitments, thereby improving the retention rate of female workers and reducing the under-utilisation levels of female labour. Policy support for flexible work arrangements, too, especially in the pandemic context, might play a significant role in enabling women to remain and thrive in the workforce in Sri Lanka.

These measures could be flanked by encouragement for and the facilitation of women's acquisition of relevant and sought-after skills and qualifications to reduce human capital mismatches that have been identified as a key hindrance to women's entry to and progress in Sri Lanka's labour force (Solotaroff et al., 2017). State-led action to ensure that women acquire skills and qualifications that are in demand in the labour market could be instrumental in this regard. Skill upgrading is also necessary if women are to reap the full benefits of a shift towards a green economy. Similarly, more support is required to bolster female entrepreneurship; existing programmes could be further strengthened so that they provide relevant and timely information, knowledge, technology, equipment and financial assistance to women who aspire to set up small-scale industries and businesses.

Such encouragement of a higher female LFP rate is expected to have a significant positive impact on economic growth. The World Bank has identified increasing the number of working women as the most equitable and sustainable way to grow Sri Lanka's overall workforce (Solotaroff et al., 2017) and it is predicted that equal participation by men and women in the economy could add up to US$20 billion to Sri Lanka's GDP (McKinsey, cited in IFC, 2019). Hence, policy and strategy recommendations to pursue growth need to constructively address gender parity in the workplace.

Against this background, the UN-backed green economy agenda, which combines economic development, environmental sustainability, decent work and social inclusion (ILO, 2020b), could spell positive changes for women and work in Sri Lanka and beyond.

More specifically, in the Covid-19 context, employers must acknowledge the dual, and sometimes multiple, burdens that many women carry. The pandemic has presented extreme and unprecedented conditions. Sri Lankan women have been under high levels of pressure during lockdowns, with often overwhelming levels of housework, spousal, elder- and childcare alongside their paid work. The working culture in Sri Lanka has been performance- and commitment-oriented, showing little interest in employees' work–life balance (Dissanayaka & Hussain, 2013). It is, thus, high time that Sri Lankan organisations and managers acknowledge and appreciate that the pandemic has created an era in which women are 'at home trying to work' rather than 'working from home'.

As a developing South Asian country, Sri Lanka has a rather positive record for working women, with laws, policies and ratified conventions in place to encourage and facilitate their participation in the labour force. In reality, however, the country's female LFP rate has stubbornly remained at around 35 per cent, largely due to deep-seated conventions pertaining to the nature of 'women's work' that subtly underpin the type of education that women receive, the skills that they develop, the kinds of work in which they engage, the hurdles that they encounter in the workplace and beyond and the overall ways in which women negotiate the world of work. It is these gendered roles and traditions that have made a burgeoning dependent population a key challenge for working women, given the disproportionately high burden of care and domestic responsibilities that they shoulder.

Often, internalised traditional notions about what a wife and a mother should be prevent women from obtaining the long-term benefits of increased educational and economic opportunities. This eventually translates into an issue of economic sustainability, with a large precariously employed — as well as unemployed — segment of women constituting an untapped labour resource in Sri Lanka. The Covid-19 pandemic has further exposed the inherent vulnerability of the country's economy and exacerbated the challenges that are faced by employed and unemployed women. Nevertheless, the unprecedented circumstances of the pandemic have also created opportunities in the world of work, some particularly so for women, as indicated by increasingly flexible working arrangements. Multilateral efforts and steps in the right direction at this point of transition will help to ensure that Sri Lanka emerges from this disastrous pandemic with wins for women and work.

8. Working women in Fiji

Natalia D'Souza

Fiji is an island nation in the southwest Pacific comprising more than 330 islands (110 of which are inhabited) and has a population of 902,906 (Macrotrends, 2021), with indigenous Fijians (iTaukei) (57 per cent) and Indo-Fijians (38 per cent) forming the two largest ethnic groups (Farran, 2020). Despite being one of the more economically developed nations in the Pacific region — ranking 93rd out of 189 countries on the Human Development Index (UNDP, 2020) — Fiji fares relatively poorly on gender equality measures such as the Global Gender Gap Index, with a rank of 113th out of 156 countries (World Economic Forum, 2021).

As with many other countries, cultural norms and values in Fiji have historically reflected patriarchal ideals that govern women's roles within the household and society, and influence their occupational segregation, mobility and access to decent work (Fiji Women's Rights Movement [FWRM], 2018). In the context of political coups in recent decades, economic development and living standards have been in decline, particularly for women (Chand et al., 2020), further weakening their labour market positions and outcomes. Moreover, research increasingly demonstrates the economic, social and environmental costs associated with gender inequalities (Kaur & Prasad, 2020). Given Fiji's commitment to the UN's sustainable development goals, it remains imperative that gender inequality is addressed, especially as the ongoing Covid-19 pandemic presents additional health, economic and socio-political challenges for this Pacific state (UN, 2020).

From the outset, it is important to note that Fiji has a sizeable informal economy (Dahal & Wagle, 2020) comprising more than two-thirds of all workers (International Labour Organization (ILO), 2021a), most of whom are women. Indeed, there is considerable evidence that women are disproportionately employed in 'vulnerable' and subsistence forms of work, often for income-supplementation, provision of household food or bartering (Loumoli & Bhati, 2015; Vunisea, 2016; World Bank, 2020). Broader national-level factors, such as increasing political instability (N. Gounder, 2020), reduced collective organisation, labour market deregulation, and limited representation, voice and participation of women in the civic and political spheres (Asian Development Bank [ADB], 2018; Bennett et al., 2020; Parker & Arrowsmith, 2014; Parliament of the Republic of Fiji, 2019) have further contributed to a 'feminisation' of the workforce in recent decades. In this context, women's increased engagement in paid work has coincided with reduced earnings and greater employment insecurity (Chand, 2000; Chattier, 2013; Leckie, 2000).

In Fiji, as in many nations, unpaid care and domestic work continue to remain largely the remit of women. Data from 2016 indicate that females in this country spent approximately three times as much of their day on unpaid care and domestic work (15.2 per cent of their day) than did males (5.2 per cent) (World Bank, 2020). This unpaid work simultaneously subsidises men's economic activity (Leckie, 2000), while constraining women from entering and advancing within the workforce (Boccuzzi, 2021). Cultural and religious values and the role and 'place' of women in Fiji reinforce this gendered division of labour, further exacerbating disparities at work. Together, this paints a compelling picture of women's reduced participation and access to the formal labour market, and consequently the protections that this can offer.

As with most small island developing states in the Pacific, data are missing for key population and labour market statistics in Fiji. Where recent information is available, it is not always disaggregated by gender, age, ethnicity or other relevant dimensions (Fiji Bureau of Statistics, 2018; Parker & Arrowsmith, 2014), making it difficult to track, let alone compare, progress. Furthermore, the absence of unpaid labour in workforce statistics and gross domestic product calculations has implications for the distribution of resources and benefits, which can further reinforce gender inequities (Narsey, 2007; Waring, 2020).

Equally, scholars have questioned the relevance of traditional gender equity metrics in countries like Fiji where a largely informal economy and socio-cultural structures reinforce the gendered division of labour (Carnegie, Gibson & Rowland, 2016; McKinnon et al., 2016; Novaczek & Stuart, 2006). Indeed, women in Fiji may differentially possess power — through access to finances, resources, land and decision-making abilities — by virtue of their ethnicity, age, religion, geography and family dynamics (Parker et al., 2011). Empirical evidence permitting, this chapter thus adopts an intersectional approach in the analysis of current and future predictions for women and work in Fiji, outlining various implications for different groups of women where relevant.

EMPLOYMENT REGULATION

Compared with many Pacific states, Fiji has historically had a relatively well-developed and progressive employment framework (Parker & Arrowsmith, 2014), ratifying several international labour standards and all eight fundamental conventions, including the UN Convention on the Elimination of All Forms of Discrimination Against Women (CEDAW) (ILO & ADB, 2015; Malo, 2017). The Employment Relations Promulgation of 2007 covers the conditions of employment across both the public and private sector and forms the backbone of Fiji's employment regulatory context.

However, the steady deregulation of the labour market since 1991 (Chand, 2000), in combination with ongoing political coups in recent years, has increasingly destabilised the regulatory context, particularly in relation to trade unionism (Fiji Trades Union Congress [FTUC], 2020). For instance, the introduction of the Employment Relations (Amendment) Act No. 4 in 2015 imposed further barriers to collective bargaining and industrial action for those employed in 'essential industries', including the public services, and has led to recent arrests of Fijian trade unionists (International Trade Union Confederation, 2019). Unionisation has also tended to be higher among those in formal employment, particularly urban, white-collar workers; predominantly men (Malo, 2017), although overall union membership has seen a steady decline in recent decades (Parker & Arrowsmith, 2014).

Despite these challenges, there have been efforts to organise at a broader societal level, and groups such as the Fiji Women's Rights Movement (FWRM) continue to remain a leading voice in advocating for gender equality and the promotion of women's rights (FWRM, n.d.).

As a result of the economic hardships faced by businesses due to Covid-19, in May 2020 Fiji's Parliament introduced the Employment Relations (Amendment) Act 2020 in response to increased job and income loss and reductions (FTUC, 2020), with a view to facilitating continuity of work despite ongoing economic instability. These amendments have enabled employers to adjust wages, increase contributions to employees' medical insurance, and reduce the number of paternity and family care days from five to two working days. Thus, there has been a worsening of labour market conditions (FTUC, 2020) and certain social protections in the interests of promoting employment continuity, potentially resulting in mixed outcomes for women, although their immediate effectiveness and long-term impacts are yet to be fully determined. Additionally, workers in the informal economy — predominantly women — have traditionally remained beyond the remit of the trade union movement (ILO, 2006) and have experienced further challenges to their job and income security, as well as with organisation during the pandemic (ILO, 2021b).

The combined effects of these labour market conditions in the current regulatory context means that many working women in Fiji continue to remain at a considerable disadvantage. Despite being guided by eight key international agreements on gender equality, and the introduction of the Fiji National Gender Policy in 2014 to help enhance women's economic empowerment (Ministry for Social Welfare, Women and Poverty Alleviation, 2014), progress with gender equity has not only stalled, but has taken a back seat due to ongoing issues with freedom of association as well as the current Covid-19 crisis. In response, the government has recently announced it will undertake a Country Gender Assessment with a goal of providing an overview of various gender-related issues (Fijian Government, 2020).

KEY CHALLENGES AND OPPORTUNITIES

Globalisation

Many countries in the Pacific were at the height of integration into global markets just prior to the pandemic (Kabutaulaka, 2020) so its impact on these economies has been dramatic. In Fiji, many industries have been affected, with the economy declining by approximately 20 per cent (Connell, 2021). Importantly, the closure of international borders has substantially affected tourism, a key contributor (40 per cent) to Fiji's gross domestic product (Dahal & Wagle, 2020), creating wider ripple effects for accommodation providers as well as the farmers and fishers who supply them (Connell, 2021). As a result, workers in the predominantly female informal economy, as well as in micro- and small businesses, have been most affected economically.

For those in formal paid employment, the Fijian government announced a series of relief packages in March 2020, estimated at approximately FJ$1 billion, to help with employment and income continuity through business assistance schemes, and other social protections such as early withdrawals from retirement schemes via the Fiji National Provident Fund (Gerasimova, 2020). However, aside from a one-off payment of FJ$1000 for workers who contract Covid-19, once again the significant number of informal workers engaged within the tourism industry have been left to fend for themselves. Traditional reliance on international aid and remittances is also unlikely to eventuate due to the global economic downturn (Farrell et al., 2020; Herr, 2020), indicative of a slow and prolonged recovery for Fiji. However, at the time of writing (2022), quarantine-free 'travel bubbles' have been established — for example, between New Zealand and Rarotonga, and the New Zealand borders have since re-opened for travel with many Pacific Island countries, including Fiji (New Zealand Government, 2022).

Border closures have also prevented Fijians from emigrating, presenting both benefits and challenges. On the positive side, the halting of emigration has combatted the 'brain drain' experienced by the country in recent years, wherein approximately one-third of tertiary-educated workers were exiting the country (ILO, 2017). However, it has also curtailed opportunities to engage in seasonal work in nearby Australia and Aotearoa New Zealand or to seek employment elsewhere. In late 2020, the New Zealand government announced a limited opening of the borders to the Pacific (restricted to 2000 seasonal workers), with living wage provisions, to fill labour shortages in the horticulture industry.

Within seasonal horticulture work, the low quality of jobs and wages continues to remain an issue, with risks to worker health and safety increasing in recent years (*One News*, 2021). Thus, seasonal employment opportunities do not necessarily equate to opportunities for decent work or adequate pay, despite the remittances sent home by these workers forming a substantial portion of many families' incomes (Fagaiava-Muller, 2021). Since opportunities for seasonal work are predominantly taken up by men, the migration of male family members places additional domestic demands on the women and children who stay behind (Carswell, 2003), and reflects a trend whereby men's employment is frequently prioritised over women's during periods of employment shortages (FTUC, 2020).

Encouragingly, there is emerging evidence that many Pacific people — including Fijians — are embracing new opportunities afforded by the pandemic as a means of reinvigorating traditional cultural values and relationships with the land. Emerging anecdotal case studies indicate that the setbacks experienced by the tourism industry in Fiji offer an opportunity to rethink what progress and development looks like within the industry when sustainable, indigenous philosophies of collective community needs and long-term wellbeing are prioritised over individualistic profit seeking and growth (Kabutaulaka, 2020; Movono & Hughes, 2020).

Other research has found that those engaged in tourism in the Pacific region have also noted improvements in their financial management, and physical and social wellbeing (Scheyvens et al., 2020). Many respondents in this same study (predominantly from Fiji) also demonstrated incredible resilience to current circumstances and were optimistic about wages and conditions of work improving within the tourism sector in the future (Scheyvens et al., 2020).

Demography

As of 2020, Fiji's labour force participation rate was 56.1 per cent, with unemployment at 4.8 per cent (World Bank, 2020). However, data from 2019 indicate that women had considerably lower labour force participation (38.2 per cent) than men (76.5 per cent), as well as higher levels of unemployment (5.3 per cent versus 3.5 per cent, respectively) (World Bank, 2020).

Another striking feature of Fiji's labour market is its relatively high and persistent youth unemployment rate (20 per cent), even prior to the Covid-19 pandemic (Dahal & Wagle, 2020), mirroring gendered patterns once again with nearly twice as many females (22.2 per cent) compared with males (11.5 per cent) being unemployed in 2019 (World Bank, 2020).

The pandemic itself has disproportionately impacted on sectors where young workers, especially women, are over-represented (ILO, 2020) — most notably tourism (FTUC, 2020), — with youth unemployment rates predicted to double (ADB, 2020). The FTUC (2020) summarises challenges for this group as tri-fold: disruptions to education and training, barriers to employment continuity or movements across jobs, and impediments to accessing the labour market in the first instance.

Women also comprise a greater proportion of the ageing population and are thus more likely to experience economic insecurity, poverty and vulnerability to illness, especially if based in rural regions (Dodd et al., 2021). These outcomes represent the cumulative lifespan effects of gender inequities in education, paid work, income, assets and access to healthcare in Fijian society (Dodd et al., 2021), further illustrating the disadvantages experienced by women.

Interestingly, from 2017, there is not a huge gender discrepancy between the educational rates at the upper secondary (46.8 per cent female, 42.3 per cent male) or bachelor's (5 per cent female, 5.4 per cent male) levels, and the gap increases only slightly at master's (0.8 per cent female, 1.3 per cent male), and doctoral (0.05 per cent female, 0.1 per cent male) levels (World Bank, 2020). This suggests that post-education, women may encounter challenges in joining the paid workforce due to structural biases (Bennett et al., 2020; Leckie, 2000), and these may be compounded by ethnic, geographic, economic or family influences. For instance, a significant portion of indigenous Fijians live in rural areas, compared with Indo-Fijians who live near or in urban areas. The former may therefore experience additional barriers in accessing education, formal employment and other key resources (Singh, 2020).

Indeed, studies have highlighted differences in employment patterns based on geography, with women based in rural or coastal villages found to form a significant portion of the fisheries (Loumoli & Bhati, 2015; Vunisea, 2016) and agriculture (Chand et al., 2020) sectors, and to predominantly engage in multiple forms of subsistence work such as seaweed harvesting, handicrafts and farming (Chand et al., 2020; Loumoli & Bhati, 2015). Due to patrilineal land ownership customs, these women may also have differential access to rights in accessing marine resources and participating in selling or bartering, based on birth versus marriage (Vunisea, 2016).

Finally, rural women may be more likely to experience economic abuse from their partner which can further impede their economic empowerment (Fleming et al., 2019).

For women engaged in formal employment, gendered trends in horizontal and vertical occupational segregation persist (R. Gounder, 2020), with women concentrated in entry or low-skilled positions (Chand et al., 2020; Market Development Facility, 2020) in sectors such as fisheries (Michalena et al., 2020; Vunisea, 2016). The significant proportion of these women simultaneously engaged in subsistence and care work also means that career advancement is not always prioritised or possible (Vunisea, 2016). Indeed, data from 2016 indicates that only 38.6 per cent of middle and senior management roles were occupied by females (World Bank, 2020). Thus, although women's labour force participation had been incrementally increasing in the years prior to Covid-19 (Naidu, 2016), for many, engagement with paid work does not alleviate their level of other allocated duties (Vunisea, 2016), indicating that as long as gendered division of labour remains the norm, there is little hope for gender equity progress.

Structural barriers also perpetuate these inequities. For instance, the persistent gender pay gap in Fiji produces a differential earning potential. Therefore, for many families, it becomes more practically and economically viable for women to undertake domestic and other unpaid work (Bennett et al., 2020). This 'triple burden of work' (in productive, reproductive and community roles) for women is further amplified by the increasing urbanisation and emergence of nuclear families in recent decades (Boege & Shibata, 2020; Leckie, 2000), inhibiting the sharing of domestic work and child-rearing.

Further, Fiji continues to be plagued by above-average rates of physical and/or sexual abuse (Kline, 2021), and the country saw increased reports of domestic and gender-based violence over the Covid-19 period (Cliffe, 2020; McMichael & Powell, 2021) due to the direct and indirect stressors associated with the pandemic: job and income losses, food insecurity, and restrictions associated with lockdowns and curfews (Cliffe, 2020).

Yet, due to the tenuous economic and social protections afforded to women, in addition to cultural stigmas, many may be reluctant to leave violent domestic situations (Kline, 2021). The UN Population Fund (2020) also predicts an increase in unplanned pregnancies resulting from the lockdown due to increased barriers to accessing reproductive health services and supply chain issues with contraceptives, which could further affect women's health and wellbeing outcomes. Combined, these findings point to the cumulative lifespan challenges experienced by women of all demographic groups, amplifying their precarity both within and beyond the context of paid work.

Technology

Information and communication technologies (ICT) serve as both a challenge to, and as a potential lever for, Fiji's post-pandemic economic and social recovery. In 2017, approximately 50 per cent of the population were internet users (Dahal & Wagle, 2020) with internet penetration increasing to 70.5 per cent in 2021 (DataReportal, 2021). However, a digital divide prevails, particularly in rural regions (Khosla & Pillay, 2020). Beyond access to the internet alone, there are second- and third-level digital divides representing gaps in online skills and outcomes, respectively (Van Deursen et al., 2017). These digital divides remain a key challenge for Fiji, with a clear gender gap also evident (Boccuzzi, 2021).

While improved access to knowledge and information in community decision-making has been identified as essential for alleviating poverty in rural communities and for women, these same groups have historically been excluded from access to ICT infrastructure and involvement in decision-making by the State (Rahman & Naz, 2006), with ramifications for training, education, workforce development and political voice.

Digital divides also have implications for data gathering, particularly from remote or hard-to-access regions. As evidenced throughout this chapter, the absence of such data creates challenges in identifying and supporting vulnerable groups, assessing the full extent of the Covid-19 pandemic impacts, as well as in the development of a broader recovery strategy that prioritises working women (ILO, 2020).

The onset of the Covid-19 pandemic has also highlighted the centrality of ICT for communication, social connection, education, remote work and e-commerce purposes. For instance, the 'Barter for Better Fiji' was a female-led grassroots movement established via social media to facilitate the exchange of goods and services during the pandemic without relying on monetary transactions (Kabutaulaka, 2020), enabling self-determination through indigenous values of reciprocity and accountability (Finau & Scobie, 2021). However, while the use of social media platforms such as Facebook have been critical in exchanging information during particularly significant events such as in prior elections and disaster contexts, as with the rest of the world, it has also had a role to play in the spread of misinformation during the pandemic (Khosla & Pillay, 2020).

A recent report outlines five potential scenarios through which technology is likely to impact on Fiji's future economy, with most offering opportunities for job creation and filling a niche in global value chains (Dahal & Wagle, 2020). Outsourcing services to Fiji, for example, may be particularly attractive given the nation's proximity to other industrialised economies in the Asia Pacific region, and may be effective in targeting Fiji's youth unemployment problem (Boccuzzi, 2021). However, the eventuation of these opportunities requires significant investment in technological infrastructure and upskilling of ICT literacy to 'future-proof' workers' skills (Boccuzzi, 2021; Dahal & Wagle, 2020).

Education alone does not translate into improved labour market opportunities and outcomes for women in Fiji — as matters stand, men are better positioned to reap the advantages of any technological developments and investments. Indeed, in a 2020 report by the UN on women's rights in the changing world of work, the trend of 'defeminisation' is outlined wherein an overall decline in women's employment is inverse to technological advancements (UN, 2020). This defeminisation is likely to occur due to occupational segregation, women being employed in jobs that are at greater risk of automation, and in sectors that have already been impacted due to disruptions to global supply chains since the pandemic began (Boccuzzi, 2021). Further, whereas remote working was established as a new way of working during the lockdown, in Fiji, women in particular are likely to be negatively impacted by potential digital skills gaps (Boccuzzi, 2021) as well as being employed in forms of work less amenable to telework (Dahal & Wagle, 2020).

Sustainability

Sustainability-related issues continue to remain a priority for Fiji's future (World Health Organization, 2021), with environmental rights embedded in Fiji's Bill of Rights (Farran, 2020). This suggests State-level commitment to addressing the 'wicked' problem of climate change. Unfortunately, the greatest impacts of global climate change are borne by the very nations — Fiji and other Pacific Island countries — that contribute the least to climate emissions (Leal Filho et al., 2020). In Fiji, climate change brings with it increasing risks of natural disasters and disease outbreaks (McMichael & Powell, 2021), as well as the erosion of land and marine resources (Farran, 2020), which directly impact on significant sectors such as fisheries and indirectly affect related sectors such as tourism (Leal Filho et al., 2020).

There are parallels between the impacts of the Covid-19 pandemic and climate change in Fiji. At greatest risk are those sectors relying on land and coastal resources — fisheries, agriculture, mining and tourism — with the impacts of climate change on workers playing out in a similar vein of those from the pandemic. Several coastal villages have already been affected by rising sea levels and coastal erosion (Boege & Shibata, 2020), and recent natural disasters such as Tropical Cyclone Winston in 2016 have left devastating trails, including the loss of lives and the destruction of property and crops (Bennett et al., 2020).

Given Fiji's reliance on cultivation and extraction-based industries, climate change threatens the future of the economy. Left unchecked, it poses challenges for food, livelihood and employment security. Beyond being a source of food and livelihood, these natural resources are also integral to iTaukei culture and ways of life (McMichael & Powell, 2021; Singh, 2020).

Women are more susceptible to the impacts of climate change for several reasons. First, the gendered division of labour means that they are more likely to engage in 'climate-sensitive activities' such as collecting water or working on farms and at fisheries, while also experiencing reduced ownership and access to these resources (Aipira et al., 2017). The impacts of climate change and natural disasters, therefore, disrupt opportunities for work as well as access to resources (Michalena et al., 2020), an effect referred to as the 'feminisation of vulnerability and disaster' (Bennett et al., 2020). Crucially, women themselves remain 'the cornerstone of climate change adaptation' (Bennett et al., 2020, p. 89), contributing to social, economic and ecological resilience to climate change at a community level (Singh, 2020). Rural and indigenous women, in particular, possess knowledge that is vital to survival and recovery during natural disasters, such as knowing how and where to access clean water and the suitability of growing certain crops, and they frequently prepare in advance for seasonal weather events, thereby ensuring their family and community's survival (Aipira et al., 2017).

Through their engagement in informal or subsistence work in fishing and agriculture, women are also able to establish community social networks where goods and services can be exchanged and assistance provided to the community, in the absence or shortfall of aid or relief during disasters (Bennett et al., 2020). Yet, women experience an expansion of their roles during disasters without necessarily being afforded increases in their power or voice. In the civic and political realms in Fiji, they continue to remain excluded from having input into key decision-making that could impact on entire communities' survival (Bennett et al., 2020; Kopf et al., 2020), making rural women in particular most vulnerable to the impacts of climate change.

In recent years, the Fijian government has proactively engaged in the relocation of communities in response to rising sea levels, with many more planned in the future (Boege & Shibata, 2020). These relocations are inherently complex and challenging, disrupting psychological and spiritual connections to the land for indigenous groups (Boege & Shibata, 2020; McMichael & Powell, 2021). While rural and indigenous communities in Fiji have historically demonstrated significant resilience in the face of natural disasters, shifts away from traditional ways of living and the unravelling of cultural knowledge around marine resource management threaten this resilience in future post-disaster recovery scenarios (Bennett et al., 2020), particularly with a predicted increase in relocation and urbanisation (Boege & Shibata, 2020). Relocations may further amplify issues for working women due to the increased care burden, gendered division of labour in the harvesting of food and collection of water, women's greater role in preserving food security, and their consistent exclusion from decision-making (Kline, 2021; Kopf et al., 2020; Singh, 2020).

There are also concerns around the threat of increased gender-based violence, with the shift away from the protections of communal living to nuclear families (McMichael & Powell, 2021), although women are at greater risk of experiencing violence within disaster contexts more generally (Kopf et al., 2020). Initial investigations of relocations have indicated mixed findings on health outcomes, with some opportunities to move away from environmental health risks and access better resources and health services, while also presenting other risks to wellbeing such as violence and diet-related issues due to a greater reliance on processed foods (McMichael & Powell, 2021). Urbanisation will also likely create additional challenges including crowding and pressures on the labour market; as discussed earlier, women are among those most likely to be locked out of jobs.

RECOMMENDATIONS AND CONCLUSIONS

Despite several State-level initiatives and policies, the ongoing political instability, reduced representation of women in Parliament, declining social dialogue and protections, and cultural barriers continue to hinder gender-equity progress in Fiji (FWRM, 2018; Parker & Arrowsmith, 2014). The Covid-19 pandemic has also differentially impacted women and created further setbacks for women and work, likely leading to a greater gender divide than ever before (Boccuzzi, 2021; Cliffe, 2020; Farrell et al., 2020). Indeed, the FTUC (2020, p. 9) notes that 'the bigger [women's] losses in employment . . . and the greater the scarcity of jobs in the aftermath of the Covid-19 crisis, the harder it will be for women's employment to recover'. It is more crucial than ever that Fiji's recovery strategy places women at the forefront, in line with recommendations from key international bodies (e.g. OECD, 2020; UN Women, 2021; World Economic Forum, 2020).

First, while job creation will no doubt be prioritised, efforts should focus not just on increasing women's labour market participation but equally on ensuring that work roles provide opportunities for decent work (FWRM, 2018). This may necessitate changes to employment law frameworks, including better facilitation of worker representation and social dialogue mechanisms (Parker et al., 2011), and monitoring and enforcement of legislation (ILO & ADB, 2015).

Alongside formal institutional mechanisms, there is scope to expand the skill base and opportunities for those in informal work to engage in other forms of income generation (ILO & ADB, 2015). Extending the coverage and effectiveness of social protections such as access to healthcare services and basic income security will also protect these workers in the event of a disruption to employment (ILO & ADB, 2015).

Women engaged in the informal economy can be supported through initiatives that promote their engagement in entrepreneurial micro and small enterprises, including in financial institutions, with regard to financial literacy and management, as well as access to loans and grants at a state level (ADB, 2018). Such initiatives will need to be supported by improved metrics to capture women's participation over time in the labour market — both formal and informal — as well as their contributions at a household level (ADB, 2018).

Second, democratic processes that prioritise women's knowledge, roles and needs (Michalena et al., 2020) will be essential for improving women's working and living situations in Fiji (Parker & Arrowsmith, 2014). Thus, there is a need to increase opportunities for women to be included in civic decision-making at a state level in Parliament (Kline, 2021; Pacific Women, 2020) and at local and community levels; for example, in climate change consultations (Bennett et al., 2020; Kopf et al., 2020). Facilitating women's ownership of and control over resources such as land or fishing areas (UN, 2020; Vunisea, 2016) will empower them to engage in entrepreneurial activity, not only in establishing microbusinesses (Market Development Facility, 2020; Novaczek & Stuart, 2006) but also in affording women opportunities to grow their business operations (UN Women, 2021).

Third, significant investments in technology and infrastructure, as well as in skill development, will be required to ensure a capable and future-proofed workforce in a post-Covid economy (Dahal & Wagle, 2020; R. Gounder, 2020). Part of this investment will also require that digital literacy and outcome gaps are closed in rural regions and for women, ensuring these groups are trained in other income-generating skills (ILO & ADB, 2015). This could thereby provide a wider and more sustainable range of employment opportunities, particularly for women workers in regions that are overshadowed by the ever-growing threat of unemployment or disruptions to work due to climate change (Boccuzzi, 2021).

Finally, it is important that recovery is framed within iTaukei worldviews and values, working towards the three pillars of sustainable development: economic, cultural and environmental. Indigenous knowledge around marine resource management remains the bedrock in achieving sustainable development in a region threatened by climate change (Farran, 2020). Community social networks and values around reciprocity have also proved instrumental in insulating against vulnerability (of food and other resources) during natural disasters and in post-pandemic recovery, providing an essential safety net for many communities (Bennett et al., 2020; Leweniqila & Vunibola, 2020).

Equally, it is important to address broader socio-cultural and religious attitudes that constrain gender roles and behaviour for women in Fiji, particularly when examining the dynamic ways in which religion, ethnicity, age and geography intersect with gender (Chand et al., 2020). A societal-wide change is required, one that is enacted by and empowers all actors in society to move towards a more gender-equal Fiji. The Pacific Women (2020) strategy highlights some ways forward in this regard, including the elimination of discrimination and violence experienced by women and enhancing their agency more broadly.

Recent years have seen growing inequities for women and work within Fiji in terms of accessing opportunities for decent work, progressing within the labour market and being excluded from the social protections traditionally restricted to those in formal employment; all of which are likely to be further exacerbated by the four global megatrends shaping the future of work.

First, women in Fiji have been over-represented in those industries which have been most directly impacted by Covid-19 (Cliffe, 2020); indicating that women continue to disproportionately experience the negative impacts of globalisation while simultaneously being excluded from the potential opportunities that it offers.

Second, demographic factors such as ethnicity, geography and cultural values interact in dynamic ways, resulting in differential access to formal paid employment and its related social protections for different groups of Fijian women.

Third, the rapid rate of technological change itself creates both challenges — in further excluding certain groups of women from its use, involvement in decision-making and allocation of resources — as well as opportunities for economic advancement, contingent on how this is managed and resourced by the State. Finally, sustainability challenges created by climate change are disproportionately experienced by women in terms of threats to their livelihood, wellbeing and work.

The ongoing pandemic presents further challenges to the nation's focus on addressing gender equality and other sustainable development goals. Yet it has also been argued, somewhat optimistically, that the pandemic presents an opportunity to redesign policies and practices within and beyond the workplace, including a re-envisioning of women's roles within different spheres (UN Women, 2021).

A sustainable recovery strategy will involve the creation of decent-quality jobs; enhanced opportunities for collective organisation and social dialogue, especially for those in the informal economy; increased investments in technological infrastructure and upskilling; and support for women's roles beyond just the workplace. Part of this may also involve a re-envisioning of what 'gender equity' looks like within the Fijian context and with consideration of iTaukei worldviews — whether this reflects a desire for equality versus a desire to have women's unique roles, knowledge and contributions valued on a par with those of their male counterparts.

9. Working women in Pakistan

Fatima Junaid and Afia Saleem

Statistically, Pakistan provides a comparatively bleak picture of human existence, particularly for working women. However, beyond the figures, there are many encouraging initiatives and inspirational achievements for and by women in Pakistan, including the election of Prime Minister Benazir Bhutto (1988–90 and 1993–96), the first woman elected to head a democratic government in a Muslim-majority country; Pakistani activist Malala Yousafzai, who was the 2014 Nobel Peace Prize laureate, the youngest ever to achieve this; Oscar wins by movie director Sharmeen Obaid-Chinoy; and others who have made the BBC's list of the world's 100 most influential women (BBC, 2014, 2021). This chapter evidences the resilience and hope in the lives of Pakistani women.

Pakistan is the world's fifth most populous country and South Asia's second largest. After being a British colony for 150 years, Pakistan became an independent Islamic State in 1947, differing from Hindu India on the basis of Islamic ideology. Pakistan's first constitution, approved in 1956, evolved between 1971 and 1973, and Sharia (Islamic) Law was incorporated in 1988 (Government of Pakistan, 2012). The existing constitution upholds Islamic principles of social justice and provides the legislative framework for the country. Pakistan has experienced political turbulence in its short life, including military coups and dictatorships involving martial law enforcement in 1958, 1969, 1977 and 1999, each lasting at least a decade (BBC, 2019). In 2007, democracy was restored due to local and global pressure.

Pakistan inherited its labour laws from its colonial rulers. With legislative amendments made over time, statutes are centrally regulated and provincial governments can amend and make rules pertinent to their context (International Labour Organization [ILO], 2020b). The current constitution provides protection for women and children; fairness in access to public places, and equal employment opportunities to enable women's participation in all spheres of life and social activities (Women Development Department, 2020). However, despite efforts since the turn of the century, Pakistan is struggling to achieve ILO standards and the United Nations' (UN) Sustainable Development Goals (SDGs) (UN Women Asia Pacific, 2021). Furthermore, Pakistan is currently the seventh most unsafe place in the world (Institute for Economics and Peace, 2020), with this taking a huge toll on the society's wellbeing (Junaid et al., 2018).

Pakistan falls short on various ILO standards, including Conventions 87 (Freedom of Association) and 98 (the Right to Organise and Bargain Collectively) (Ijaz, 2019). Pakistani trade unions have faced several significant challenges since 1947, when independence was achieved (Malik et al., 2011). In 1951, there were 209 registered unions with 393,137 members (Khalil, 2018), yet they were not formally recognised by many organisations and institutions. While the Industrial Relations Ordinance enforced the recognition of unions in 1969, union membership has remained relatively muted. By 2000, although there were 7204 unions in Pakistan, just 3 per cent of the workforce were members (Khalil, 2018). Military coups and dictatorships negatively affected unions' membership and influence, with unions under the control of armed forces. In 2016, the unionised workforce of 2 million represented only 2.3 per cent of the national workforce (Khalil, 2018). The majority of unionised labour is located in the Sindh and Punjab provinces, while the less developed provinces of Khyber Pakhtunkhwa (KPK) and Balochistan make up the remainder.

Significantly, the majority (72.4 per cent) of Pakistan's 68.8 million-strong workforce is found in its informal sector (Pakistan Bureau of Statistics [PBS], 2019), to whom labour laws have little application. The 77 per cent of women who are employed in the informal sector or as home workers often do not have contracts, cannot join unions and/or have no other means of protection (Naz, 2020). In the smaller formal sector of 9 million workers, 15.5 per cent of the workforce is unionised (statistics for women's union membership are not available) (Khalil, 2018).

Sector-wise, 39.2 per cent of workers are employed in agriculture, 37.8 per cent in services and 23 per cent in other industries (Khalil, 2018). The current minimum wage is between US$175 and $200 per month, with some provinces having a minimum of US$130 per month for minors aged 13–17 (Malik et al., 2021).

Pakistan is a gendered society (Sadaquat & Sheikh, 2011) that scores highly on collectivism, power distance, patriarchy and religiosity indices (Bhattacharya, 2014). It is the world's sixth most unsafe place for women (Thomson Reuters Foundation, 2018). Patriarchal approaches are deeply embedded and widely upheld by its culture, religious norms and social biases, and women are appreciated for their subservience to men and society. They often face discrimination, structural exclusion and social acceptance of violations of human rights, all of which restrict their freedoms (Asian Development Bank [ADB], 2016).

Most women in Pakistan are expected to live in their homes in a state of subordination, behind their *purdah* (veil), assigned to the role of reproduction, and they do not inherit property. By contrast, men are the formally productive earners of society. Thus, women are severely dependent on men and require the permission of male members of the household to make nearly every decision in their lives, including visits to family or relatives (Jatoi, 2020).

Furthermore, women's independence and sexuality are often associated with male/family honour, and any act against the accepted norms can taint this honour. This can lead to severe consequences, including so-called 'honour' killings (FitzGerald, 2021), with an estimated toll of 1000 women per year (Human Rights Watch, 2021). Concerningly, a recent UN report shows that 44 per cent of young (15–24-year-old) married men and women in Pakistan see no harm in wife beating (Asghar, 2020). The introduction of Pakistan's Domestic Violence Bill in 2021 is yet to be implemented due to the Pakistan Council of Islamic Ideology's critical stance of it (*Business Insider*, 2021).

Both at macro and meso levels, women are, thus, not expected to be on a par with men. With respect to SDG 5 (Gender Equity and Women's Empowerment), Pakistan ranks poorly. For example, it:

- ranks 164th out of 167 countries on the 'Women Peace and Security Index' 2019/20, although Pakistan is not classified as fragile and conflict inflicted (i.e. it has an elected government and is not considered to be a war zone);
- has the lowest ranking in South Asia in terms of women's financial inclusion (Klugman et al., 2019); and
- ranks 151st out of 153 countries on the Gender Inequality Index (UN, 2020).

Social narratives devalue women's labour in Pakistan (Amir, 2020), affecting women's work, career choices and progress (Mustafa et al., 2019). Although Pakistani women continue to fight for basic human legislative rights, and the Protection Against Harassment of Women at the Workplace Act has been in place since 2010, many do not report sexual harassment because it is culturally inappropriate and goes against female modesty (Amir & Pande, 2018).

Favouritism or nepotism, the 'maternal wall', a 'glass ceiling' (Tanwir & Khemka, 2018) and social mores also prevent women from pursuing careers. For example, family pressures often cause female doctors to discontinue their profession when they start a family (Zafar, 2017).

In addition, women's interaction with men becomes potentially problematic for their safety and reputation. Women are often blamed when strangers (men) stare, pass rude remarks, touch, harass and, in some cases, rape, burn or kill them (Amir, 2020). Many influential women have also been publicly ridiculed for how they conduct their personal lives. Unmarried women face particular hardships, including character assassination, as marriage is a universal norm (Zakariya, 2019). The Covid-19 pandemic is exacerbating these dire circumstances, with a 'shadow pandemic' of gender-based violence. In one province, a 25 per cent increase in reported domestic violence was recorded, and there is a likelihood that such figures might be much higher as such violence often goes unreported (Safdar & Yasmin, 2020).

Against the odds, however, some women have made tremendous contributions in various sectors of Pakistan's economy, including in education, academia, government, the armed forces, medicine and the corporate sector, with some even reaching senior positions (Jamal, 2021). These women are able to achieve these positions due to grassroots activity in Pakistan by international and local bodies, the growth of technology (discussed later), some progressive families enabling their women to progress in the workplace, and some women seeking to break barriers for their own and their children's survival. These developments support the notion of 'womenomics' — the idea that advancing women's equality will improve the wider economy in developing countries like Pakistan (United Nations Development Programme [UNDP], 2021).

KEY CHALLENGES AND OPPORTUNITIES

Demography

Pakistan's population increased by 57 per cent from 132.3 million in 1998 to 207.7 million in 2017, of whom men form 51 per cent and women 49 per cent (PBS, 2018). Women's labour force participation rate nearly doubled from 13.4 per cent in 1990 to 24.5 per cent in 2016, although this is still well below those in similar economies (Redaelli & Rahman, 2021). Of those aged 15–24, 48 per cent of women are not in education, employment or training compared with just 7 per cent of men (Asghar, 2020). Pakistan also ranks as the world's worst country in terms of its gender pay gap (ILO, 2018), and third lowest on the 'Global Gender Gap' index (World Economic Forum, 2020) against which 90 per cent of organisations measure the gender pay gap (Sarfaraz, 2020).

Most Pakistani women work in the informal sector in agriculture in low or unpaid jobs (see Table 9.1), with the proportion holding these precarious roles in significantly higher numbers than for men. In this sector, women are likely to experience the worst working conditions and encounter high levels of exploitation, mistreatment or abuse, particularly during the pandemic lockdown periods (Naz, 2020), while also having no access to union membership.

Table 9.1: Proportion of women and men working in agriculture in four of Pakistan's provinces, 2017

	Sindh (%)	Punjab (%)	Balochistan (%)	KPK (%)
Men	34.1	32.4	27.3	48.8
Women	77.0	74.6	75.9	65.2

Source: PBS (2018)

In the country's large agricultural sector, the social status of women's work is undervalued (Mohiuddin et al., 2020). Pakistani society generally abhors working women, and it is generally those with no or low education engaged in paid work due to poverty and inflation. Only a handful of women from higher social, educational and economic strata work in the public and private sectors; 71 per cent of the female population with degree qualifications are not part of Pakistan's formal labour force (Sadaquat & Sheikh, 2011). Just 25 per cent of educated women engage in paid work, underutilising many women's skills and thereby negatively impacting on productivity and economic growth (Tanaka & Muzones, 2016).

Sadly, less than 5 per cent of women in Pakistan are included in its formal financial sector, compared with South Asia's average of 37 per cent (Mustafa et al., 2019), and more than 70 per cent of corporates do not have any women on their boards. Overall, in Pakistani-listed companies, a mere 1.3 per cent of CEOs and 1.8 percent of CFOs are women, compared with the global average of 4.4 and 12.7 per cent respectively (Sarfaraz, 2020). Furthermore, most senior female managers work in human resources (Pakistan Business Council [PBC], 2017), a heavily feminised management function in many countries. Table 9.2 shows women's representation in Pakistan's business sector.

Table 9.2: Women's representation in Pakistan's business sector, 2017[1]

Companies (%)	Women employees (%)
40	Less than 10
50	10–20
10	More than 20

Source: PBC (2017)

Technology

Globally, Pakistan is ranked fourth as a freelance gig market (Pofeldt, 2019). Its digital gig economy growth is the fastest in Asia and fourth fastest in the world, contributing 8 per cent to the worldwide digital gig economy, and trailing only India, Bangladesh and the United States (Toppa, 2018). It has surged 69 per cent during the pandemic, placing Pakistan among the world's top four online freelancer markets (Payoneer, 2020). As Haq (2020) notes, the rapid expansion of Pakistan's gig economy has been driven by several factors, including the country's very young population (70 per cent is under 30 years of age), improvements in science and technical education,

---

1 Defined as local, international, multinational private sector organisations or institutions.

and the expansion of high-speed broadband access. Indeed, Pakistani freelancers under the age of 35 generated 77 per cent of the revenue in the second quarter of 2019 (Haq, 2020).

Despite their comparatively weak standing in workplaces generally, within the gig economy, some Pakistani women earn twice as much as men. Some, thus, argue that this economy is a means for Pakistani women to gain a foothold in the digital economy and seek empowerment (Malik, 2019). Yet, it is a small proportion of the total employed workforce of women who are doing very well in the gig economy. For example, just 39 per cent of Pakistani women own a mobile phone, compared with 93 per cent of men (Jatoi, 2020), and only 13 per cent have internet access, compared with 29 per cent of women in India (Viqar, 2019). Those women who have internet access also face challenges of discrimination and cyber bullying; many never voice their experiences of inequity, fearing blame for family dishonour (FitzGerald, 2021).

More widely, South Asia has not done well in terms of the level of gender imbalance in the tech or digital arena, and Pakistan does not score well on innovation or technology indices, such as education, infrastructure, environmental performance, entertainment and media (Dutta & Lanvin, 2020; Shabbar, 2022). The bulk of Pakistani women are employed in informal jobs, and formal low-skill jobs involving repetitive or administrative tasks (Viqar, 2019). Many are at high risk of losing their jobs due to either automation or a lack of skills.

Pakistan has long lagged behind countries such as the Philippines and Malaysia in terms of women working in information, communication and technology (ICT) (Tanwir & Khemka, 2018). Slow ICT adoption in Pakistan (Hafeez et al., 2018) can be attributed to a lack of capital investment and expertise, limited availability of the latest technology, and poor governance, which has led to a lack of the skills required to use ICTs optimally (Khan et al., 2020). Furthermore, the public education sector is weak on ICT adoption due to poor funding, dated content and the non-English medium of instruction in overcrowded classrooms (Salam et al., 2018).

Many initiatives in Pakistan's public–private and humanitarian sectors have sought to alleviate women's situations, including 'Girls Learn Women Earn' (World Bank Blog, 2020). In 2020, the government, along with the World Bank, developed a project to revive micro-enterprises by providing smartphones, especially to women, to access online training and launch their own businesses (Quresh, 2020). Furthermore, the state's legal protection of women and girls encourages online participation and promotes their use of ICT, enhancing their economic empowerment and bridging the digital divide (Naz, 2020).

Among the 13 per cent of women with internet access, many have started initiatives. One of which, Circle, is a nationwide non-profit organisation which helps women to learn JavaScript, web design and web page development, and provides life skills such as CV building, writing and communication, increasing their chances of employment and financial independence (Empower Foundation, 2018). Another initiative is Pakistani Women in Computing (PWiC), a global community of Pakistani women who aim to collaborate, research, grow, inspire, mentor and celebrate each other. Others, including TechKaro, CodeGirls and WomenInTeckPK, reflect how women have helped and enabled themselves and others to use technology to their advantage (Ebrahim, 2020).

While such initiatives may be commonplace in the developed world, they are major achievements in Pakistan. During the tumult of the pandemic, internet usage and technology have enabled Pakistani women (with access) to work from home and on projects connecting them with a large community inside and outside the country.

Globalisation

Pakistan's migration and remittance figures have been growing since the 1990s, helping to build the country's economic resilience (ILO, 2020a). From 1971 to 2019, more than 10.5 million Pakistanis undertook overseas employment. In 2019 alone, their remittances amounted to US$21.8 billion, and grew 26 per cent in 2021. The Gulf oil boom has further enabled the migration of Pakistanis, with Gulf Cooperation Council (GCC) countries hosting about half of Pakistan's migrant workforce (Seigmann, 2010). However, the vast majority of these workers are men: between 1971 and 2019, just 0.4 per cent of migrant workers from Pakistan were women (ILO, 2020a).

Pakistani migrant women face many challenges. Some struggle with their identity as immigrants, finding themselves culturally distant and in conflict with a host country's values (Sarwar & Jadoon, 2020). For instance, some Pakistani migrant women stay anchored to their own culture and find divorce difficult as it is culturally stigmatised (Accordini et al., 2018). Those who have lived in a foreign, especially Western, country for a decade, adapt somewhat but still struggle with differing religious values and practices. Challenges are compounded by language barriers, especially if host country natives do not speak English (Arora et al., 2019). Migrant adolescents living with parents also feel pressure from their parents, who encourage their daughters to abide strictly by cultural norms of modesty and stay at home, while sons are pushed to attain higher education and earnings (Giuliani et al., 2017).

Two provincial studies reveal very contrasting perspectives, partly reflective of their differing cultures. In the Punjab, a study posited that globalisation has had an overall positive impact on women's social, health, educational and economic empowerment as it leads to more information, ease of business, and support through ICT, which empowers women in the long term (Sarwar & Jadoon, 2020).

Moreover, globalisation reportedly eases communication and migration, making parents more open to sending female family members abroad for work and education (Mohyuddin & Begum, 2013). In contrast, a large study of the KPK province shows that most migrant workers in the GCC are men who hail from the rural part of the province and leave their wives to care for the household (Seigmann, 2010). They also assign money management to a patriarch, leaving women with even less agency and greater subordination. This leads to negative outcomes, such as decisions about and access to education and the healthcare of women being further compromised.

Thus far, globalisation has not brought about changes for the betterment of most Pakistani women. Trade liberalisation, globalisation, international buyers and exports have not been able to alleviate the conditions that they face as workers at the lower end of the labour market and/or the informal sector, and many remain largely invisible and vulnerable (Tanwir & Sidebottom, 2019).

Sustainability

Since 2013, Pakistan has made some progress on various SDGs as a part of its political Agenda 2030 (Kiani, 2017), with special taskforce teams focusing on SDGs 3, 5, 8 and 13 (Bakhtyar, 2019), seeking to promote inclusive economic growth, social development, gender equality and empowerment. Recent progressive legislation and workplace policies encourage more women to enter the labour market (Bakhtyar, 2019). Consequently, the gross number of female enrolments in schools has increased, although the female literacy rate remains low due to a high number of dropouts.

Focusing on SDG 5, women's vulnerability and sustainability in Pakistan is a complex issue. Of the country's estimated 20 million home workers, 12 million (60 per cent) are women and they account for 65 per cent of home workers' US$2.8 billion contribution to Pakistan's economy (UN Climate Change, 2021). Yet, most receive low wages and are denied legal protection and social security (Bari, 2020).

With mostly unpaid, informal or lower levels of work, entrepreneurship could be an area that can assist women's sustainability. Pakistan scores low on the Global Entrepreneurship Index with a rank of 120th out of 137 (Ács et al., 2018), yet some female entrepreneurs have used technology to set up businesses, and have successfully overcome social barriers (Mustafa et al., 2019). Success stories are found in industries such as fashion, IT, non-profit/human rights, media and engineering (Ghani, 2020).

Aligning with SDG 16 (peace, justice and strong institutions), many

Pakistani women are seeking to reduce extremism through grassroot programmes. For example, Paiman and the Institute of Inclusive Society have worked on building coalitions with groups of women from different provinces, educating them against extremism and terrorism (Peters & Saeed, 2017).

With climate change, Pakistan is the world's fifth most vulnerable country (Eckstein et al., 2020). Between 1999 and 2018, climate change cost Pakistan almost 10,000 lives and US$3.8 billion in economic losses (Eckstein et al., 2020). The government is currently focusing on climate change and has undertaken several initiatives with goals out to 2030. To this end, the UN Climate Change (a sustainability initiative) created a 'Ladiesfund' in 2007 to support women's financial sustainability by developing environmentally sustainable small businesses (UN Climate Change, 2021). The initiative is run by women using innovative strategies to empower women. For instance, local start-up consulting group 'Stimulus' collaborated with the government and Climate Launchpad to work on building clean-tech initiatives (ClimateLaunchPad, 2020). The fund now has 1000 direct and 100,000 indirect beneficiaries.

Many tech-oriented initiatives also enable sustainability for women in Pakistan, providing ecosystems for networking, mentoring and wellbeing, such as the Women in Power Sector Professional Network in South Asia and Women Engineers Pakistan (Qureshi & Hameed, 2019). They provide visibility and support platforms for other aspiring women to work in globally under-represented sectors. Sehat Kahani is an all-female online healthcare provider that collaborated with global funders (Palmer & Ajadi, 2020) and now assists under-served communities (Sehat Kahani, 2021). These initiatives are valuable for employing and serving women, as Pakistan scores very low on 'access and quality of healthcare' indices (Baker, 2019).

Social media support groups for women such as 'Soul Sisters Pakistan', 'She Power She Works', 'Readers Lounge', and 'Pakistani Women in Academia' aim to improve women's wellbeing and position by providing a safe space for communication, women's employability, literature and reading, and mentoring in higher education and academia respectively.

Considering sustainability in relation to Covid-19, the pandemic has resulted in a larger proportion of women than men being pushed into extreme poverty (Tariq & Bibler, 2020). Amid the pandemic, many female workers within small and medium-sized organisations have encountered major pay cuts and layoffs where employers have been unable to compensate their workers. In addition, lockdowns have hindered mobility. This has created a major crisis for women workers who lack independent means of transportation, with many consequently losing their jobs (Shaikh, 2021).

Additionally, thousands of self-employed Pakistani businesswomen have suffered drastic revenue losses, reduced household income and worsening mental health during lockdowns under Covid-19, wiping out the demand for the products of many women-owned micro-enterprises (Mustafa et al., 2021; Quresh, 2020). However, some women have taken their business online, upskilling to do online/mobile banking and having supplies delivered to their home by males, thereby breaking the tradition of communicating with strangers (men), as well (Afshan et al., 2021). During the pandemic, education has gone online, meaning that female teachers have been challenged to upskill themselves at the same time as their domestic caretaking responsibilities and duties have amplified, and they have had limited access to the internet (Kalsoom, 2021). Notwithstanding this, women have reportedly coped better than males in response to Covid-19 (Rana et al., 2021).

RECOMMENDATIONS AND CONCLUSIONS

Based on our analysis, for women to attain decent work and gender equality, Pakistan will need to take an array of macro-, meso- and micro-steps. Human Rights Watch (2021) suggests that there should be a focus on nurturing, protecting, preserving and empowering women in Pakistan. Effective implementation of anti-rape and anti-honour killing bills in the country are important (e.g. see Zahra-Malik, 2016). Knowing that only

1 per cent of young females (aged 15–24) can make decisions regarding their own marriage, 16 per cent are consulted by their family, and the remainder are married without any say in the decision (Asghar, 2020), it is crucial to have mass education about the right to choose a partner. Contextually, Asghar (2020) recommends that there should be an integration of sectoral policies and programmes, and a clear focus on the elimination of barriers in implementation of laws and policies related to:

- women's rights; recognition and registration of agricultural workers, daily wagers, domestic workers, home-based workers and self-employed females;
- inclusion of women's productive and reproductive work in labour force statistics, and to ensure higher completion rates for secondary and tertiary education;
- support for girls and women to acquire non-conventional skills, with a focus on STEMM fields; and
- recognition of women aged 18 years and above as adults with full citizenship rights.

Demographically, many countries' institutions and governments emphasise equal opportunity goals based on a 50:50 gender balance. In Pakistan, recommendations have focused on starting with 33 per cent female representation, with local government, public and private sector boards promoting young women's leadership. This is realistic given that, initially at least, there may not be enough female candidates to fill more than one-third of organisations' boards. Furthermore, women may be qualified but not want to work in those positions (e.g. they may not seek high positions if their husbands do not allow them to as it goes against social mores concerning their modesty) (Hasan, 2015).

Technologically, women in Pakistan need greater digital literacy to capitalise on existing and future opportunities while feeling confident rather than vulnerable about their capabilities and job security. The government's commitment to digital literacy, and to the protection and empowerment of women, aims to reduce the existing digital gender divide and related gender pay gaps (FitzGerald, 2021). Globally, with Covid-19, some gender-based inequities have been worsening for women, but in the digital world unprecedented opportunities for all, including women, have been created. Pakistan's public and private sectors need to develop initiatives to upskill and connect women with these opportunities. The Pak-China Economic Corridor presents a huge opportunity for women in terms of job opportunities at different levels and in different sectors, including online work opportunities (Ali, 2018).

In relation to sustainability, women might be assisted in the workplace through various measures. For instance, positive discrimination could help to bolster entrepreneurship initiatives and quotas for women, networking opportunities, positive role models and mentoring (Tanwir & Khemka, 2018). Micro-financing (particularly Islamic micro-financing)[2] could further benefit women to operate small sustainable businesses (e.g. running a home-cooked food service, or a beauty parlour from home). These initiatives might afford opportunities to those who are less educated and cannot manage or access online business initiatives. Many women in Pakistan need home-based work opportunities, with minimal disruption to their daily lives, and least possible contact with men outside their homes, so that they can become economically independent.

Aggregately, women in Pakistan work 10 times more hours than men (Shaikh, 2021). Thus, their mental and physical wellbeing needs urgent

---

2   The core belief in Islamic finance is that money is not an earning asset in and of itself. Importantly, risk must be present in the commercial or productive venture, and transactions should be directly or indirectly linked to tangible economic activity and not financial speculation and excessive uncertainty. The profit or loss is shared by both the lender and borrower. Furthermore, the product bought or sold must be clear to both parties and only socially productive activities that are not exploitative and socially or morally harmful should be funded. Selling what one does not own is impermissible, and financial risk must lie solely with the lenders of capital and not with the manager or agents who work with the capital (Kustin, 2015).

attention and support, especially in the context of the Covid-19 pandemic. Shaikh recommends that gender disaggregated data should be publicly available to help organisations come up with relevant solutions. As part of the Covid-19 response, Government could also support the return of women to work and girls to their education. A timely response from the public and private sectors would also help to reduce the devastating impact of the pandemic on woman's wellbeing and growth.

Unless the main societal narratives in Pakistan are addressed, the status of women will not change. There are opportunities for women in Pakistan, particularly in a context of policy and systemic reform. Through upskilling and training, women can avail the economic, entrepreneurial and social networking opportunities that they need for their self-development and empowerment (Farooq et al., 2018).

10. Working women in the Philippines

Daisy Arago, Jane Brock and Peter Brock

Philippine society is strongly defined by the co-existence of a semi-feudal system of rural land ownership amid rural poverty; urbanisation accompanied by poverty and under-employment; and a shift to a low value-added export economy premised on raw materials and labour services. Working women experience an array of social inequalities and economic disadvantages, with less access than men to education and employment opportunities. Concomitantly, there has been growing efforts to achieve progress towards equity for women in the Philippines.

The Philippines' population is 111,368,677, 49.9 per cent of which are women (World Bank, 2019). The workforce comprises those living in the Philippines and those working overseas. Within the Philippines, 59.8 per cent of the population aged 15 and over participated in the labour force in 2021 (Philippine Statistics Authority [PSA], 2021b). By major industry group and class of worker, the decline in the agricultural workforce and increase in the service sector, and wage and salary earners, reflect a long-term trend (PSA, 2021b) (see Table 10.1).

In 2017, a year after Duterte's Partido Demokratiko Pilipino–Lakas ng Bayan (PDP–Laban) political party assumed office, the country's unemployment rate stood at 5.3 per cent (3.78 million) (PSA, 2018a). It remained around this level until the onset of the Covid-19 pandemic in

Table 10.1: Persons employed by major industry groups in the Philippines

Employed persons by sector	July 2020 (%)	April 2021 (%)	July 2021 (%)
Agriculture	26.3	24.4	22.1
Industry	18.8	18.2	20.0
Services	54.8	57.4	57.9
Employed persons by class of worker			
Wage and salary workers	60.4	61.0	67.1
Self-employed without any paid employee	29.3	28.4	26.0
Employer in family-operated farm or business	2.6	2.6	3.0
Unpaid family workers	7.7	7.9	3.9

Source: PSA (2021b)

early 2020. The unemployment rate in July 2021 was 6.9 per cent (3.1 million) and the underemployment rate 20.9 per cent (8.7 million) (PSA 2021a). Amid the pandemic, women's unemployment rate rose to 10 per cent in July 2020, while their under-employment rate reached 14.5 per cent during that time (PSA, 2020b).

From 2013–17, the male workforce grew steadily from 25 to 26.7 million, while the female labour force stagnated at just over 16 million (PSA, 2018b).[1] In 2017, women's labour force participation (LFP) rate was 46.2 per cent, compared with 76.2 percent for men. The October 2020 *Labor Force Survey* (PSA, 2020a) reported those aged 25–34 years as the largest single age group of employed persons (27.6 per cent) at 39.8 million workers.

---

1   This report has not been updated since 2018, reportedly due to budget constraint reasons, though this may also reflect a lack of commitment to addressing women's lower level of labour force participation.

According to the PSA (2018b), women aged 45 years and over had LFP rates of at least 40 per cent. However, those under 45 years had a lower LFP rate, these being women's primary years of child-bearing and-rearing, and the years of peak deployment of women overseas to work. The PSA's (2022) January quarterly *Labor Force Survey* indicates that men's LFP rate was 72.9 per cent compared with 48.1 per cent for women. The under-employment rate among men was higher at 16.4 per cent than for women (12.5 per cent).

A study commissioned by the National Economic Development Agency (NEDA) attributed the low LFP rate of women to 'stereotyped gender roles of ascribing to women the primary responsibility of taking care of homes and to men, as the provider of the family'. These stereotyped roles undermine the LFP rate of women (World Economic Forum, 2019). Indeed, the Philippine Commission on Women (PCW) states that gender-based discrimination at work, particularly discrimination in the hiring, retention and advancement of women workers, sexual harassment, wage gap and limited flexible work arrangements, contribute to the low level of women in employment (Arago, 2021). Furthermore, traditional gendered roles are often performed by poor women who leave the labour force to undertake domestic and care roles, prompted by traditions that enable male family members, as the 'breadwinners', to engage in paid productive labour.

Among those women who have a job, most are concentrated in low-waged, low-productivity and insecure work in service, manufacturing and agro-corporations. 'Contractualisation' — where workers are directly employed on five-month contracts, or are hired indirectly by the company to evade legislation that mandates that workers be made permanent after working for six months and one day — and other precarious working conditions also prevail in these sectors.[2]

---

2   Women WISE3 is a network of factory women workers. They have chapters in Camarin, Caloocan city — a relocation site, Novaliches, Quezon city and Valenzuela — an industrial area in the National Capital Region. They organise women workers in manufacturing sectors and communities, as well as women's families and victims of human rights violations.

In the service sector, women mostly engage in the business process outsourcing (BPO) industry. BPO includes contact centre work, back-office services, data transcription, animation, software development, engineering and game development (Ortiguero, 2018). Women in this industry mostly dominate its largest sub-segment sector: contact centre or customer relations management. Government data also show that, in other sub-segments, women are concentrated in medical transcription (74.5 per cent of these workers are women) and data processing (65.2 per cent) (PSA, 2009). The BPO industry mainly exports to the US (86 per cent) (Ecumenical Institute for Labor Education and Research, 2012).

In manufacturing, women are concentrated in industrial areas or special economic zones (SEZs), engaging in packaging, garment production and electronics (75–85 per cent of all people directly employed in the electronics sector are women, a figure that has stayed the same since the sector's rise in the 1970s). Many employers and researchers attribute this 'preference' to 'characteristics' of female labour such as dexterity and patience to undertake repetitive work required in chip making — with women traditionally perceived by employers to be cheap, docile, non-complaining and less interested in workers' organising (e.g. Center for Trade Union and Human Rights [CTUHR], 2020). In large agricultural corporations, women work on agri-business plantations for bananas and pineapples in harvesting and pesticide application roles. Similarly, in palm oil plantations, women perform fertiliser and pesticide applications or work in the nursery without protective clothing or equipment.

Another key characteristic for Filipinos is their engagement in migrant labour. Of the estimated 10.2 million Filipinos living outside the country in 2017, 4.9 million were permanent migrants, 4.2 million were temporary migrants, and 1.2 million were irregular migrants (Department of Foreign Affair, 2015; OECD/Scalabrini Migration Center, 2017). The PSA's annual survey conservatively estimated that there were 2.2 million overseas Filipino workers (OFW) between April and September 2019 (PSA, 2022), the vast majority of whom (93.2 per cent) were working without an employment contract. OFWs remitted a record US$31.4 billion back to the Philippines in 2021, up 5.1 per cent from 2020, with remittances accounting for nearly 9 per cent of the Philippines' GDP (Venzon, 2021). Furthermore, women comprised the majority of OFWs (56 per cent). They were more strongly represented in younger age groups (15–34 years), the largest OFW age cohort, while men formed the majority of the over-40 age group (PSA, 2020a).

While various factors may encourage people to migrate for employment, the United Nation's (UN) Women's *Policy Brief* (2017), providing an overview of women's migration from Mexico, Moldova and the Philippines, observed that a lack of adequate employment opportunities in the Philippines is driving people to migrate. Only 40 per cent of women were in paid employment in the preceding decade, making migration necessary for many. Furthermore, the Philippines has a 'legacy of State-sponsored women's mobility with migration into "feminised" labour sectors being promoted as an opportunity for women' (UN Women, 2017, p. 3). However, de-skilling of migrant women was reported to remain 'a significant issue with many Filipino women who have trained as nurses or teachers migrating to work in low-skilled sectors' (UN Women, 2017, p. 3). The impacts are a loss of more highly trained and skilled workers; a skewing of education and vocational training towards the needs of overseas countries rather than local needs; and women tending to find employment abroad only in occupations for which they are overqualified (OECD/Scalabrini Migration Centre, 2017).

Since the 1970s and the Marcos dictatorship's promotion of female labour emigration, gendered ideas of women in the Philippines have impacted on its labour export policy. Mohyuddin (2017, p. 93) claimed, for instance, that when advertising to Filipina women, government agencies use existing Filipino and global ideas of femininity, such as women's role as caretakers and taking responsibility for household work, and 'strive to fulfill the wishes of employers abroad by following reductive, stereotypical ideas of Filipina women being dutiful and a desirable labor population for the service sector'.

Women in the Philippines form the majority of those who are not in the labour force (i.e. not available and not looking for paid work, such as housewives, students, people with a disability and retirees). Over two-fifths (43.2 per cent) of this group are aged 15–24 years old, and many are women who have dropped out of the labour force, not because they were disinterested in paid work but because they, rather than their male counterparts, were expected by their family to perform unpaid domestic care work. An absence of childcare and breastfeeding facilities in workplaces, particularly in SEZs, has also pushed women into unpaid work (Arago, 2021). These women, their children and elderly depend on the meagre income of household members that is insufficient for their needs. Their limited and unequal participation in economic opportunity thus perpetuates a cycle of poverty and directly impacts on the country's growth and development (e.g. Arago, 2021; ADB and ILO, 2011).

Many Filipinos work in the informal economy, defined by the ILO (2013, p. 34) as 'all economic activities by workers and economic units that are — in law or practice — not covered or insufficiently covered by formal arrangements'. The informal economy accounts for as much as 61 per cent of the Philippine gross domestic product (Porras & Maningat, 2015). Women form a large proportion of the Philippines' informal sector, and are mostly found in small home businesses, contractual jobs in the manufacturing and service sectors, and in other under-developed sectors of the economy. A total of 70.2 per cent of women workers engage in informal employment in the non-agricultural employment sector (ILO and Women in Informal Employment: Globalizing and Organizing [WIEGO], 2013).

In 2012, women formed 37 per cent (8 million) of the Philippines' total wage and salary workers, with 4.8 million working in private establishments and 1.7 million as helpers in private households with compensation below a minimum wage (PCW, 2019a). About 4 million self-employed Filipino women workers are engaged in home businesses or 'sari-sari stores', home-based work for garments and shoemakers, direct selling and personal services. Furthermore, home-based subcontracting was reported to be on the rise, with women undertaking 'low-paying, back-breaking production work in garments, handicraft, shoes, and toy manufacturing; food processing; metal craft, leathercraft, and furniture making' (Frianeza, 2003, p. 180). In the informal service economy, retail stores, food and beverages, accommodation and their supply chains feature prominently, and women play a vital role in food distribution. They work on the streets selling items such as *kakanin* (rice cake sweets), vegetables and fruit to supplement household income. Many are considered to work illegally, being unregistered and not covered by the labour laws. As such, they are vulnerable to police harassment and confiscation of their goods.

EMPLOYMENT REGULATION

The women's movement in the Philippines is making inroads towards equity for working women. This is shown in the passage of the Anti-Sexual Harassment Act of 1995, the Safe Spaces Act of 2019, local government ordinances that illegalise cat-calling in Quezon city, and the comprehensive Magna Carta of Women (Republic Act (RA) 9710). The latter was issued in 2009 by the Philippine government through the PCW and includes women workers in marginalised sectors of the informal economy who should be given particular attention to guarantee that their human rights are respected, protected, fulfilled and promoted. The law provides for the realisation of decent work standards for women that involve the creation of jobs of acceptable quality in conditions of freedom, equity, security and human dignity (PCW, 2019b).

Furthermore, the Philippines has been a signatory to the UN Convention on the Elimination of All Forms of Discrimination Against Women (CEDAW) since 1981; the Beijing Declaration and Platform for Action; the UN Security Council Resolutions (UNSCR) on Women, Peace, and Security; and the 2030 Global Agenda for Sustainable Development (see UN Office of the High Commissioner for Human Rights [UNOHCHR], 2022). The Duterte administration has also claimed that a gender equality plan is integral to the Philippine Development Plan (PDP) 2017–2022. The

Gender Equality and Women's Empowerment (GEWE) Plan 2019–2025 covers four years of this plan and the remaining years of the Philippine Plan for Gender-Responsive Development 1995–2025 (UNOHCHR, 2022). Every March, banners hang from fences and on walls of government offices paying tribute to women. However, the president himself, in spite of these commitments, is notorious for his much-publicised misogynistic remarks (ABC, 2019). In 2018, he ordered soldiers to shoot female rebels in their vaginas (Regencia, 2018). This was followed by remarks about the presidency not being a job for women (Ranada, 2021).

Despite regulatory developments, progress towards equity for working women in the Philippines has been slow and patchy. For example, both women and men workers covered by the Magna Carta of Workers in the Informal Economy encounter challenges that are often multiple and overlapping. The vulnerabilities faced by informal workers, particularly women, stem from the lack of formal work arrangements. Women informal workers have intersecting roles 'as informal workers [who are either] wage, self-employed or sub-contracted workers, and as members of poor households and disadvantaged communities'. Housing is 'doubly important' for home-based workers 'both as a place of residence and place of work', and, thus, there is need 'to secure tenure, basic infrastructure services in the home and capital to improve the home-as-workplace' (PCW, 2019b). Poor women in the informal economy face particular challenges of violence in the workplace, low wages often below minimum legal standards, greater exposure to health and safety risks, and abuses when seeking loans in times of economic crisis (Lazo, 2015).

The Philippines' ranking in the *Global Gender Gap (GGG) Report 2021* reflects a concomitant decline to 17th place on the GGG index (World Economic Forum, 2021), due to lower political participation by women. The country's political empowerment of women fell from 41.6 per cent in 2019 to 35.3 per cent in 2020 and a similar percentage in 2021 (PCW, 2019c). In terms of economic participation, women in the workplace continue to experience a gendered division of labour in various sectors, with women often found in the packaging section or on assembly lines in manufacturing, sales or services and receiving unequal pay. For instance, in the industrial area, women workers receive only P500 (US$10) against P630 (US$10.74) for male workers, for 12 hours' work simply because they are women.

KEY CHALLENGES AND OPPORTUNITIES

In the following sections, we examine working women's situation in the Philippines with regard to challenges presented by globalisation, demographic changes, sustainability and technological development changes in the context of the Covid-19 pandemic.

Globalisation

Globalisation in the Philippines can be traced back to the 1970s policies of the Marcos dictatorship. It has precipitated privatisation of hospitals, utilities and other public institutions and seen a reduction in government subsidies. With the rise of neoliberalism, regulations and restrictions in the economy and labour market have been removed and prices have been subject to market dictate rather than government rules. The country has experienced considerable liberalisation (of trade, investment and finance) and the creation of SEZs in the mid-1990s.

For many workers and poor Filipinos, globalisation has presented some opportunities but also many challenges, which are often synonymous with joblessness and/or under-employment. In 2017, one year after Duterte assumed office, unemployment stood at 5.3% or 3.8 million (PSA, 2018a). Except for relatively easier access to cellphones (84 million in towns and urban centres — Statista, 2022a), working people have witnessed an increase in precarious jobs, non-standard employment, declining union density and an increase of corporate power in all spheres of life. In Mindanao, the onset of globalisation has resulted in an increase in agri-business plantations (Ocampo, 2015) and mining (Dela Cruz, 2021). Indigenous people, farmers and fisherfolk have been displaced and women in plantations relegated to roles such as fertiliser and pesticide application (on oil palm plantations) and packing (on banana plantations) where they have no protection from harmful chemicals.

Crop and land conversion policies worsened the displacement of Filipino peasant women. In 1998, plans for 3 million hectares of rice and corn-producing lands to be converted threatened the livelihood of two-thirds of the total population of peasant women (GABRIELA, 1998).

In the Philippines' expanding global fashion and footwear industry, and its service industry (accommodation, health and retail), ongoing unequal relations between workers and social norms and practices intersect to impact negatively on women, including in terms of gender-based violence.

There is little centralised provision for childcare and no budget for paid parental leave, which would assist women's equity progress in the workplace and beyond. Thus, 'government policies continually taper the already narrow opportunities for Filipino women' (GABRIELA, 1998). Privatisation of hospitals and health institutions has diminished health services for women, particularly those in the poorer sections of society. And poor women and children who migrate from rural to urban areas have also become targets of sex trade syndicates.

The remittances of Filipino women who are OFWs generate a significant proportion of the country's currency deposits. However, due to their weak protection in labour law, a number of these women, particularly domestic helpers and entertainers, are vulnerable to sexual exploitation and physical abuse. Trafficking of Filipino women in other countries for labour bondage, prostitution and sex slavery has also become widespread, and many enter other countries as mail-order brides. 'From the rural areas to urban centers, in and outside the country, Filipino women are being displaced and commodified' (Parreñas, 2000; GABRIELA, 1998).

Demography

Among Southeast Asian nations, the Philippines was the most affected in terms of Covid-19 cases, and economic and labour market impacts

(ADB, 2021). As in many countries, women workers (and the young) in the Philippines have been disproportionately impacted by the pandemic in terms of their employment, health, family, education and other spheres of life (Ibañez, 2021). Already dire conditions for working women have worsened, and the gender and social inequalities that they experience, including multiple burdens at home, were exacerbated while they also faced dismissal from jobs.

Women in both the formal and informal sectors are seeking to balance work, increased unpaid care and domestic workloads (UN Women Asia Pacific, 2020a, 2020b). The burden of unpaid care work (housework, childcare and eldercare) on women has increased during the pandemic. They increasingly provide even greater support to family members, including maintaining sanitary conditions in the home and caring for family members who are ill, putting themselves at increased risk of becoming infected with the virus (UN Women Asia Pacific, 2020b). Besides performing domestic work at home, they are burdened with the multiple tasks of managing a shrinking budget (with women often acting as the economic manager of their home), rising household expenses, and teaching, as children stay home for their online classes (see below), underscoring how lockdowns have exacerbated women's multiple burdens at home and disproportionately high level of dismissal from jobs (UN Women Asia Pacific, 2020b).

The Center for Women's Resources (CWR) reported that, before the pandemic, 16 million Filipino women were already economically insecure, contending with 'multiple burdens of ensuring health and education of the family while seeking means to augment meagre income amid loss of jobs and livelihood' (CWR, 2021a). The Center estimates that the number of economically insecure women increased to 19.5 million during Covid-19 (Ellao, 2021).

LIFE IN THE TIME OF THE PANDEMIC:
THE STORY OF PRECY LAGING

Precy Laging, her husband, Lando, and their 13-year-old son rent a single room in Valenzuela, north of Manila for 2700 pesos (or about US$48) a month. Both lost their jobs in March 2020. At the start of the pandemic, Lando was a delivery driver with a government department, and Precy worked in an administrative role for a signage company, collecting payments from clients. Lando was required to stay at his workplace in Manila during the week, so Precy took care of their son while also working. Precy says:

'The wage that [my employer] paid me and my husband's wage were not sufficient for our daily needs, with skyrocketing prices of commodities like rice, vegetables, fish or pork, so our food is a mixture of eggs, cans of sardines and instant noodles. Electricity and water rates were going up — we were spending P1500 (US$27) for electricity and around P500 (US$9) for water. Days before pay day my salary is already gone as my list of debts to pay is long. My wage is almost gone without it even touching my hands.

'With Covid, my son's schooling went online with added expenses, such as a tablet for school, (and) data load for internet. Then I watch and assist or help my son in his homework and see to it that his modules are completed. Without a wage, we depend on relief goods that seldom come, like rain during the summer. For Government relief we have to undergo a long process before affected families can benefit and, like many affected families, we cannot get the assistance we need.

'We don't see any hope of returning to our previous jobs — not enough vaccines and we still don't see any clear plan from the government for mass testing and vaccination for workers and the poor like us. The people endure long queues often to find there are no more vaccines at the vaccination centre. Even if there are vaccines available, a list of who should be vaccinated excludes many vulnerable workers and their families. There is always chaos. When does the government plan to have us, the poor, vaccinated?

'Inspired by community pantries in different parts of the country and despite our fear of being 'red tagged' as rebels or terrorists, Women WISE3 Valenzuela set up a small pantry to receive donated foodstuffs to help the hungry. Goods ran out so quickly and we had difficulty sustaining it. But we do the best we can. But it is terrible that our government claims our actions to help our community is like terrorism, because it shows how they are failing workers and the poor.

'But I never stop thinking how my family can survive and how to maintain at least three meals a day.'

Precy Laging is a member of Women Workers in Struggle for Employment, Empowerment and Emancipation (Women WISE3), Valenzuela. As an active member and community leader, she initiated the community pantry in her neighbourhood.

Women's larger share of job losses was due in part to their predominance in jobs requiring greater human interaction, or in work that cannot be performed remotely (ADB, 2021). Women's re-entry to the labour force is more likely to be in the informal sector and in employment of lower 'quality' than they held before the pandemic (ADB, 2021; UN Women, 2020a, 2020b).

In terms of formal work, the ILO (2020, p. xiv) recently noted that in the Philippines '4.1 million [employed women] are likely to face job disruption [due to Covid-19], particularly in industries such as wholesale and retail, accommodation and food service activities'. Health workers, seven out of 10 of whom are women, are particularly vulnerable. The health workers who are on the frontlines of the battle against Covid-19 lack support, benefits and facilities. In the words of a nurse from a public hospital that is the main referral centre for Covid-19 infected persons, it feels like they are 'being tossed to the sharks', due to insufficient support by government (Tomacruz, 2020). Indeed, more than 15,000 healthcare workers have been infected with Covid-19 at the time of writing (Gonzales, 2021). One nurse, a 47-year-old mother of three who had health conditions died before she received the hazard pay that was being demanded from the government. She had worked 10–12 hours per day and sought only P500/day (NZ$15/day) hazard pay (Ranada, 2020).

Women WISE3 (n.d.) reported that women in the BPO and export industries, who are required to report to work despite quarantine measures, experienced reduced working hours or rotational shifts and prolonged 'floating' status for six months to a year. Those who were not technically dismissed but found themselves without work or income due to a temporary closure or other adjustments made by their employers suffered an income loss due to policies of 'no work, no pay' and no paid leave — despite some even needing to quarantine due to contracting Covid-19. Others faced a lack of social protection and additional costs associated with needing extra electricity, equipment (e.g. laptops, headsets), health-related items such as face masks and shields, sanitiser, personal protective equipment (PPE), and internet expenses for those working from home, while receiving no hazard pay during the pandemic.

The electronics industry in the Philippines is a sizeable economic contributor and considered a feminised industry. However, it pays low wages and has serious health and safety challenges for women (e.g. in terms of the impacts of chemical use and hazards for women's reproductive health). It is also one of the most unorganised sectors in the country, mostly located in anti-union SEZs[3] (e.g. International Trade Union Confederation [ITUC], 2012), impeding collective action for change around gender inequities, which have been exacerbated during the pandemic. Indeed, the government has used the country's Anti-Terrorism Law (ATL) to repress workers and to union bust. Unionists have been visited and harassed by the National Task Force to End Local Communist Armed Conflict (NTF-ELCAC), with illegal arrests and filing of trumped-up charges against unionists and labour organisers, and the killing of more, a significant number of whom were women (ITUC, 2019).

By April 2020, 1,089,649 workers in the formal sector were displaced by closures or flexible work arrangements (Department of Labour and Employment [DOLE], 2020). In the same period, 250,000 informal sector workers sought assistance from the DOLE's programme for displaced workers (DOLE, 2020) as the Covid-19 impacts on the informal sector were more pronounced (ILO, 2020). While men dominate much of this sector, women are often found in its lower-paying and more vulnerable categories of work and have been affected more by the lockdowns due to their work and wider, gendered roles. Lockdowns have, for example, prohibited many informal workers from going out and curtailed their opportunity to make a living. The same situation also forced women to initiate community kitchens or community pantries to address the needs of their local areas (e.g. Leyesa & Obanil, 2021).

While the ILO (2020) report noted that men's employment was negatively affected during the pandemic, it pointed out that 'a broader gender view indicates that the socio-economic ramifications of Covid-19 for women goes beyond the story gleaned from the data. The pandemic has exacerbated gender-based violence' (p. 58). This is due to centuries of domination by patriarchal society fuelled by fundamentalism, militarism and latterly a neoliberal system of so-called 'development'. The economic strains of

---

3   SEZs in the 1980s and 1990s in the Philippines were notorious for 'lay off or lay down' policies as conditions of continuous employment or hiring.

the pandemic have led to greater levels of domestic conflict, which may result in more abuse of women and children, and act as a further cause of child poverty, forced labour and a cycle of violence among children. As deepening poverty, hunger and male joblessness during the country's Enhanced Community Quarantine (ECQ) or strict lockdown have increased the risk of domestic violence, the Philippines' Commission on Human Rights (CHR) released the following statement of concern in April 2020:

> Women and children who experience abuse are trapped inside their homes with their abusers, and have nowhere to go. Most of these women are not able to seek help because they fear being overheard by their abusive partners or are stopped from leaving home. An exact figure of cases of domestic violence involving their partners is hard to obtain as they go unreported due to the sensitivity of the issue and the stigma that it entails. (CHR, 2020)

Quezon City Mayor Joy Belmonte confirmed that reports of around 602 women, an average of eight per day, were maltreated or raped across the city between 17 March and 23 May 2020. The women and children's desk receives at least 12 complaints of domestic abuse per week, escalating from around five per week before the pandemic (Calleja, 2020).

Sustainability

The latest Philippine Workers' and Trade Union Report in 2019 on the UN Sustainable Development Goals (SDGs) identifies a number of stumbling blocks (ITUC, 2019). Philippine workers face neglect of their fundamental freedoms and gross human rights violations that are perpetrated by the government (SDG 16). At the time of the report, there had been 200 victims of extrajudicial killings since Duterte's election, half of whom were peasants. Forty-two labour rights defenders were killed and 'no one was served justice' (ITUC, 2019, pp. 14–15).

Women are included among the victims. They include Cora Molave Lina and Arlyn Almonicar (with her husband, Arman), members of the peasant organisation in Mabini, Compostela Valley (Mindanao), who were tagged by the military as 'subversive' and gunned down in March 2017 (Karapatan, 2017). Also among rights defenders who were killed were Mariam Uy Acob from the Moro Kawagib's Human Rights organisation. Acob was killed in Mamasapano, Maguindanao (Mindanao) on 23 September 2018 (Unson, 2018). After the report's release, Zara Alvarez was shot dead in Bacolod City, Negros Island, on 17 August 2020 (CNN Philippines, 2020).

As the government has pursued a war against its perceived enemies, with numerous human rights violations, democratic space in the Philippines has shrunk, putting the lives and safety of human rights defenders at risk. In January 2020, the Philippine National Police (PNP) and the Philippine Economic Zone Authority (PEZA) launched the Joint Industrial Peace and Concern Office (JIPCO) in the Clark Freeport Zone in Pampanga, north of Manila. PNP Brigadier General Rhodel Sermonia described the JIPCO as 'the first line of defense from radical labor infiltration of the labor force and the industrial zones' (Malig, 2020). Unions and human rights organisations condemned the JIPCO as an instrument to inhibit union organising against unfair labour practices in the economic zones (Karapatan, 2020). The JIPCO was noted by the ITUC when it cited the Philippines as one of the 10 worst countries for working people in its 2020 global rights index (Buan, 2020).

In the Covid-19 pandemic context, according to CTUHR (2020), the government's militaristic lockdown focused more on ordering people to follow protocols and punishing violations than on providing social protection and financial aid to the people. As early as July 2020, 233,172 people were arrested due to quarantine orders violations, with 31 per cent officially charged and at least 3000 yet to be released from prison (CTUHR, 2020). According to the CWR (2021b), during the pandemic, 54 women human rights defenders were arrested and eight were killed between January 2020 and February 2021.

In the Philippines, against stagnant real wages and attacks on the rights of vulnerable workers, there is no clear mechanism for monitoring labour and human rights compliance at any level. An expensive and circuitous legal system does not offer workers justice. The government's 'wars' on drugs, terrorism and insurgency include as 'targets' trade unionists, labour leaders and organisers, resulting in not only discrimination against unions, but also endangering the safety, liberty and lives of those accused, sometimes mistakenly, of being targets (ITUC, 2019).

In terms of socio-economic sustainability, women in this country, as in many others, suffer from the gender wage gap and are more affected by poverty than men are. They are also more likely than men to be in low-paid work and are paid less than men in occupations where women predominate. Socio-economic issues for women are exacerbated by a difference in the retirement ages for women and men. Furthermore, it can be noted that many of the indicators of SDG 10 targets are not disaggregated by sex in data and reports from the Philippine Government (ITUC, 2019). And in relation to SDG 8, significant use of non-regular forms of employment tends to undermine the rights of workers to regular employment and security of tenure, with government data lacking and only available up to 2015 (ITUC, 2019).

A general observation throughout the report is the Philippine government's failure to collect and report basic data that allow monitoring and measurement of performance against the majority of the SDGs. This, and the government's practice of condoning attacks on union and workers' rights, is consistent with a low level of engagement by public institutions with trade unions (ITUC, 2019).

In addition, union membership and the number of unionised workplaces in the Philippines have declined during and prior to the report period. Consequently, economic growth and growth in productivity have not translated into real wage growth. A dramatic decline in union membership from 2003 has also seen the erosion of workers' bargaining power, collective bargaining, impact and access to policy making, and defence against workplace abuses (ITUC, 2019). Rampant contractualisation and informal employment stem from employers' deliberate disregard of workers' rights to freedom of association and collective bargaining (ITUC, 2019).

With respect to SDG 4, quality education, this has not been attainable in the Philippines due to the country's education expenditure lagging far behind the international standard of 6 per cent of GDP. Only 2.6 per cent of the 2018 national government budget was set aside for education, health and social development combined. Again, data disaggregated by sex, disability or indigenous background are not available, inhibiting the mapping of progress on this goal. Similarly, measures of the supply of qualified teachers and support for quality teaching, including by women, who form the majority of school teachers in the Philippines, cannot be provided due to the absence of general and disaggregated data from the government (ITUC, 2019).

While the Philippine Government may undertake a Voluntary National Review of its implementation of the UN's 2030 Agenda for SDGs, its practices reflect hostility to rights-based goals and targets, and an institutional failure to implement policies and practices that enable measurement and analysis of progress across multiple goals and targets, including those that are specific to women workers.

Technology

Technological change has played its part in limiting the independence and social power that women enjoyed in pre-colonial society in the Philippines. As well as providing some opportunities, long term it has served to enmesh women in the patriarchal structures of Spanish colonial rule and the twentieth century's colonial and neo-colonial structures.

Women weavers dominated industry in the Philippines at the turn of the twentieth century. In 1903, 1 million women (or 70 per cent of female productive workers) had independent incomes. Technological change had already seen cheaper imported fabrics from Chinese traders and England impacting the Philippines (Eviota, 1992). Landed oligarchy and US capital expanded imports and production in local mechanised factories by using male workers, and by 1939 women represented just 24 per cent of the country's manufacturing workforce (Eviota, 1992).

Women workers dominated the country's micro-electronics and chip industry, which emerged with technological advancements from the 1970s, forming 90 per cent of the 35,000 people employed in this field in 1981. Factories were located in SEZs, where foreign firms sought cheap labour for intensive aspects of production (Eviota, 1992). Indeed, most of the 25,000 workers at the Bataan Export Processing Zone were women. The national minimum wage did not apply, authorities repressed unions, and worker's rights enjoyed outside the zones were flouted. Women paid for accommodation in crowded dormitories. Many suffered from blurred vision, and the 'skills' that they acquired in the factories were not transferable to other employment. In effect, the zones cut women workers off from the support system that existed in their home communities (Eviota, 1992).

With automation de-skilling women's work in micro-electronics, and as multinational corporations have seen little advantage to moving or keeping operations in the Third World, employment in the field has declined in the Philippines (Eviota, 1992).

Technological development has also informed land use in the Philippines, with implications for working women and others in particular industries. The oppressive land tenure system at the end of Spanish colonial rule was reinforced by the Philippine landed oligarchy's integration into the colonial system imposed by the US (Putzel, 1992). Unlike in Japan, Taiwan and South Korea in the 1940s, in the Philippines, attempts at redistributive land reform were successfully repelled by the landed oligarchy such that, by the start of World War II, tenancy had risen to 35 per cent of the farming population compared with 16 per cent in 1903 (Putzel, 1992). Tenant farmers had little incentive to employ new technology as half of any productive gains went to landlords, and high lending rates meant fertilisers and insecticides were out of reach. Landed rentiers acquired more land rather than providing capital for industrialisation (Putzel, 1992), which remained export-oriented and subject to international dynamics.

Technological change ushered in by the 'Green Revolution' high-yielding varieties (HYVs) of rice offered only short-term production increases that were later dwarfed by environmental damage and a fall in the real income of farmers in the 1970s due to the high cost of fertilisers and other inputs. The HYVs and associated changes in loan and work arrangements meant that women lost income and economic power. HYVs required more intensive farm labour; tenants and sharecroppers could not afford to pay for more hired labour so families turned to women as unpaid labourers, and landless women farm labourers were less likely to be hired. The tasks performed by women were thus affected. For example, weeding shifted from waged work to arrangements where a portion of the harvest was allocated — if the crop failed, weeding work of landless workers went unpaid. Women undertook more transplanting of rice seedlings than men did. Thus, direct dry-seeding of HYVs cut women out of this form of gainful employment, increasing the loss of income and economic power landless women workers experienced due to the Green Revolution (Eviota, 1992).

In another key sector, telecommunications, it is noteworthy that the Philippines has one of the lowest rates of fibre-to-home connection while fixed-line penetration stagnates growth (Statista, 2022b). In 2022, Duterte removed the Constitutional cap on foreign ownership, particularly in relation to utilities, with amendments to the Public Service Act allowing 100 per cent ownership of telecommunications (Venzon, 2022). The pandemic has deepened the divide between rich and poor and urban and rural women in terms of access to internet-based/network-dependent technology.

Call centres in the Philippines constitute a feminised workforce that serves 16–18 per cent of the global market (Concepcion, 2021). Presently, these centres offer women workers an income that is considerably higher than the average Philippine wage, thereby attracting women with tertiary qualifications (e.g. in education and nursing). Unionisation has been low, although some organising has begun (Concepcion, 2021). With Covid, workers more acutely sense that their health and safety are neglected, and that job insecurity has increased, as the pandemic has impacted on business and clients have been lost, with 'no work, no pay' provisions enforced in these scenarios (Concepcion, 2021). In addition, technology that allows performance monitoring engenders stress and anxiety around employment tenure and 'steadily increased' quotas are used to get workers to take on additional tasks or be terminated, allowing 'trainees' to be hired on lower pay (Concepcion, 2021; Sainato, 2018). For instance, Telstra, which has call centres throughout India and the Philippines, has committed to 'answering all voice calls in Australia by the end of June 2022' (Cotter, 2021).

RECOMMENDATIONS AND CONCLUSIONS

Based on the preceding analysis, we advocate for the broad approaches adopted by the UN CEDAW and Committee on Economic, Social and Cultural Rights (CESCR), urging the government to develop and strengthen a clear legal framework with which to eliminate discrimination against women in relation to their right to work. The Covid-19 pandemic context has highlighted and exacerbated the challenges of neoliberalism to worker protection, with this particularly evident for women in the Philippines. Measures are also needed to ensure equality between men and women at work, noting in particular the persistent gender wage gap and the difference in retirement ages for men and women workers. Employers should be subject to unannounced labour rights spot inspections to uncover any unequal pay rates between women and men. As women predominate in flexible work, flexible workers should be accorded the same protections as formal and permanent workers.

Reflecting demographic and cultural contextual sensitivities, our findings also highlight the need for women's under-employment in the labour force and their under-representation in specific professions to be addressed. Alongside this, the negative impacts of entrenched gender stereotypes and resulting lack of equal employment opportunities for women warrants urgent multilateral attention involving government and other agencies.

As emphasised by the impacts of the Covid-19 pandemic, working parents, particularly women, need to be enabled to reconcile their professional and family responsibilities through measures that protect them against discrimination based on their marital status or pregnancy, address the current lack of sufficient childcare facilities and ensure increased educational opportunities for women.

Relating to sustainability, measures are needed within and beyond the workplace. Women in the Philippines need to continue to resist oppressive measures against women's and workers' organising, and to raise the level of consciousness to organise in order to bring social change towards an equitable distribution of wealth, resourcing and social support. Within the workplace, initiatives might include those which seek to eliminate sexual harassment, exploitative employment practices, and inadequate or unsafe working conditions, to each of which women workers are particularly vulnerable. Concomitantly, among women, there needs to be a focus on the issues faced by the most vulnerable groups of women, including women migrant workers, women living with disabilities, rural women, elderly women, unpaid domestic child labourers, and others in vulnerable work in the informal economy. Indeed, with the latter, multilevel measures must address the impacts for working women caused by a lack of regulation.

Coupled with sustainability concerns, the government must examine the gendered development and impacts of technological advancements for workers. Coordinated workplace, social and other protections are needed to ensure a level playing field at work and beyond. Related to this, the Philippines' international commitments, particularly in recognising the right of workers to join and participate in trade unions, and to take collective action, must be consistently upheld; a call from workers, including women, to abolish the ATL and disband the NTF-ELCAC is noted.

Finally, underpinning each of these recommendations is an urgent need to collect a greater body of disaggregated data about working women's situation in the Philippines to enable empirically grounded and meaningful policy development, the impacts of which can peg working women's equity progress — or otherwise — over time. The history of this vast and diverse country emphasises that such progress is not always linear, and equity gains need to be made secure, particularly amid the excoriating and gendered impacts of Covid-19.

The Philippines in focus: Breaking-in — union women and young leaders

Cedric Bagtas

Leaders come and go — in governments, the corporate world, organisations and unions. In the Philippines, there are leaders who have chosen to remain, to continue contributing and helping. And even as those union leaders age, they are not retiring, despite many reaching their pensionable ages. Union members regard their leaders as important, and are perhaps fearful as to what could happen to their union should they leave. Or perhaps union leaders feel they have not yet completed their job, with their subordinates, except for a few, often feeling the same. And while the latter often express privately their desire to strike out on their own, they rarely do so, not wanting to upset the existing order.

These phenomena, among others outlined here and elsewhere (e.g. International Trade Union Confederation — Asia Pacific [ITUC-AP]/ Deutscher Gewerkschaftsbund Bildungswerk [DBG BW][4]/ASEAN[5] Trade Union Council [ATUC], 2020a),[6] feed into the low numbers of women and youth in unions and union leadership.

In 2019, a baseline survey of ASEAN national centres and confederations, was conducted by the ITUC-AP/DGB BW/ATUC. The total membership of the 15 responding centres at that time stood at 19,770,654 (ITUC-AP/DGB BW/ATUC, 2020b). Despite a large membership, the study found that

---

4   DGB BW is the nationwide training organisation of the German Trade Union Confederation (DGB) for general, political and trade union knowledge transfer. Founded in 1972 as a non-profit association, it has demonstrated expertise in many different professional, labour law, business, social and political fields. It offers various target groups a comprehensive range of educational opportunities that is open to anyone interested.

5   ASEAN is the Association of Southeast Asian Nations.

6   ATUC is the sub-regional organisation of 18 national confederations in ASEAN countries and Timor Leste, with a combined membership of 13 million.

average women and youth memberships (54 per cent and 37 per cent respectively) were not reflected in governing bodies.[7] Furthermore, the numbers (and proportions) are lower for federations, and even lower again for local unions (Bagtas, 2019). In fact, there remain unions in women-dominated enterprises in which presidents are men.

The ITUC-AP sees the problem of women's and youth's low representation in union leadership as linked to a lack of policies (union statutes and frameworks); structures (women and youth committees); and resources/capacities in Asian unions. This situation prevents the development of women and youth leaders to their full potential, and contributes to difficulties in promoting decent work, social and core labour rights, further placing women and youth at a disadvantage (ITUC-AP/DGB BW/ATUC, 2020b).

The ITUC-AP frameworks for women (see 'Platform of Action for Gender Equality') and youth (see 'Youth Charter'), as well as the ITUC-AP women and youth agendas, thus outline the terms for building women and youth leadership (ITUC-AP, 2019, pp. 63–65, 65–69). Furthermore, the ATUC has a youth and women committee whose four-point work plan for 2018–22 includes 'organizing and strengthening youth and women representation in trade unions' (ATUC, 2018).

CHANGING STRUCTURES, CHANGING LEADERS

Changing structures and changing leaders are easier said than done, although most agree with a periodic recast in governance. Unions talk of succession, but many have not given way to women or younger leaders. There are cases where younger leaders nudge older leaders from their position, but many have too much respect for their leaders. Directed research or external influences provide a range of recommendations and much advice but, like many projects, technical support for leadership

---

7   Female membership ranges from 90 per cent down to 36 per cent, while youth membership ranges from 80 per cent down to 20 per cent (ITUC-AP/DGB DW/ATUC, 2020b).

building could be better. Indeed, leadership development and transition cannot be left to the natural course of events. Building leaders requires a proactive project that is well intentioned, and has direct action, an explicit action plan and faithful implementation.

In certain environments, including the Philippines, it is agreed that 'Matagal ang building nang leaders' or 'It takes a long time to build leaders'. Time, patience and perseverance are needed to develop and nurture leaders; leaders do not emerge overnight. Those who would be leaders need study, mentoring, experience in and exposure to different aspects of union principles and operations. There are various issues for consideration regarding leadership and development, particularly for women and youth.

Moreover, women and youth in unions come and go. Many do not stay long enough to rise to positions of responsibility. They may leave a company for various reasons — other opportunities beckon or they go their own ways, leaving their union. At times, they simply get tired of their static status as 'plain women and youth' in unions. Anecdotal reports suggest turnover is high. Exacerbating this, women and youth have multiple responsibilities — at home, work and in communities. The Covid-19 pandemic has further complicated their fulfilment of these multiple responsibilities, involving working from home, managing online schooling for children, and increased risk of domestic and gender-based violence.

Unions are resigned to people having competing priorities and being unable to cope with union realities and environments. Indeed, for the realities of women and youth participation in unions, the president of the National Trade Union Centre of the Philippines (NTUC Phl) said: 'Pabilisan 'lang pag-replace' or 'We just replace them [those we lose] as fast as we can'. How to maintain participation is as challenging as attracting women and youth to unions in the first place, underscoring that their needs, wants and interests have yet to be addressed.

Members need to see unions as nurturing, mentoring and caring organisations. Women and youth need guidance from their organisation and leaders, and to see that they have a future in that organisation. As noted, however, there are barriers to union participation for women and youth. There are seemingly unending demands on their time — a continuing tug-of-war in their many engagements. Furthermore, in the hierarchy of personal priorities, unions are not clear winners and, often, women and youth are not seen or appreciated enough, with leaders seemingly oblivious to their difficulties. The following sections relate an example of intentioned direct action to develop women and youth leaders in a union setting.

THE NATIONAL TRADE UNION CENTER OF THE PHILIPPINES' PROJECT

The National Trade Union Center of the Philippines (NTUC Phl), in striving to break inertia, demonstrates a less painful way of making changes to structures and operations (NTUC Phl, 2019b). The initiative is supported by the ITUC-AP/DGB BW project on women and youth participation in unions and elsewhere (see an outline of the project brief below).

The project is supported by the DGB BW and implemented in cooperation with the ATUC. The NTUC Phl subscribed to the project in the opening assembly along with other ATUC affiliates. It nominated three women and youth representatives (WYRs)[8] for training and expected to help lead and coordinate project implementation.

From day one, the union's leaders have been involved in this project. NTUC Phl's governing body, the general council, confirmed participation terms and proposed actions in three meetings, including its very first online meeting, six days after the country declared a Covid-triggered lockdown on 12 March 2020. At the meetings, the women and youth committees proposed a draft action plan from weeks of intense discussions and preparation. The general council was favourably disposed to the draft

---

8   WYRs are initially trained by the project to coordinate unions' activities under the participation project.

plan. As a measure of its enthusiasm, perhaps to keep people excited and on their toes, it added to the proposed programme and asked for progress reports at every general council meeting.

BRIEF OF THE ITUC-AP/DGB BW'S PROJECT ON WOMEN AND YOUTH PARTICIPATION IN UNIONS AND ELSEWHERE

The women and youth participation project (2019–21) supports the initiatives of ITUC-AP and its affiliates to strengthen women and youth leadership within the union movement in Southeast Asia. The project trains and guides potential women and youth leaders to effect changes in union policies and structures towards equitable representation of women and youth. Trained participants are helping, through social dialogue, to address women and youth concerns about more appropriate organising approaches, responsive collective bargaining agreements, and better national regulation. They are strengthening their representation within their unions and national confederations and improving the conditions of work and life for women and young workers.

Source: ITUC-AP/DGB BW/ATUC (2020b)

Indeed, the NTUC Phl is very ambitious, angling to address many issues. The plan's indicators may seem formidable (see NTUC Phl project indicators below) but outlining indicator components (sub-indicators) has helped to clarify the direction of the plan. From this, those involved gained traction. Preliminary activities were conducted to provide a baseline to measure progress, and to assess where quick victories could be won, to help prime interest and enthusiasm.

NTUC PHL PROJECT INDICATORS

- Additional women and youth in new or higher positions or responsibilities in their organisations (end 2020).
- Additional women and youth in decision- and policy-making bodies of their unions or in collective bargaining and other negotiations and activities (end 2020).
- Additional women and youth participating in social dialogues with government agencies on selected women and youth and other social and labour standards (end 2020) — initially for ratification of ILO C190 (Violence and Harassment Convention).
- Additional women and youth committees in federations and local unions (end 2021).
- Additional women and youth participating in advocacy for improvements in gender- and youth-related national or local regulations (end 2021).
- Increased women and youth representation to 35 per cent of their chosen governing bodies or operating bodies (end 2021).
- Federations and local unions have made use of project's best practices in pushing for women and youth and other concerns (June 2021).

Source: NTUC Phl (2019a)

The union implemented a series of activities, followed up action, and monitored results. They tracked indicators, building a database to show progress.

Table 10.2: The NTUC Phl's activities, 2019–21

Activities	Dates
National project committee set-up	February 2019
National project committee meetings	January–December 2019–20
Preliminary activities Phl baseline survey Analysis of constitutions and bylaws (CBLs) and governing bodies Analysis of collective bargaining March–May 2020 agreements (CBAs)	February–April 2020 March–May 2020 March–May 2020
National workshop on women and youth concerns, project assembly and planning workshop	August 2020
Writeshops (workshops) for women and youth leadership modules	October 2020, November 2020, December 2020, February 2021
Tripartite discussions on ILO Convention 190 on violence and harassment at work	December 2020
National training workshop of women and youth representatives	October 2020, Part 1; December 2020, Part 2
National project committee meetings	January, February, March, June, August 2021
National workshop on good women and youth in CBAs in the Philippines	April 2021
Joint (all affiliates) representation and advocacy workshop on women and youth participation in the Philippines	May 2021
Federation-level representation and advocacy workshops on women and youth participation	April–September 2021

Local union-level representation and advocacy workshops on women and youth participation	April–September 2021
National workshop on enterprise-based mechanisms and violence/harassment risk assessment	July 2021
Online advocacy and campaigns concerning Covid-19 labour issues in sector/industries, and ratification of ILO Convention 190	April–September 2021
National small events representation and Advocacy for the ratification of ILO Convention 190 — Review conference on	August 2021
Second monitoring workshop	September 2021
Small other stakeholders' representation and advocacy	April–September 2021
National advocacy sustainability workshop	October 2021
Validation workshop for two- to three-day leadership modules	November 2021

The union's WYRs comprise two teachers and an NGO representative. The national project committee (NPC),[9] comprising 15 women of whom five are youths; and three men (of whom two are youths) is multidimensional, coming from the NTUC Phl, federations and local unions, and includes the WYRs. Members appreciate the direction (from the committees), and appear to engage heartily, building on each other's strengths.

The NTUC Phl included all affiliates in preliminary activities, and in the national workshop, which validated the union's action plan. Requirements for formal participation of organisations in the project were stringent,

---

9   The NPC steers the implementation of national and sub-national activities and tracks progress with the assistance of focal points.

and only eight federations qualified, remarkably higher than the target. However, those affiliates not formally engaged continue to participate in project activities that they find useful. The project is not another of the usual seminars-and-social activities followed by another series of seminars leading to more recommendations, and then inactivity; the NPC and the focal points were determined to improve on practices. Indeed, they have been relentless in following up actions on recommendations, and monitoring activities, results and accomplishments.

There were weekly meetings in the initial months to discuss where those involved were going, how best to get there, what had been happening, and what had been achieved. There were meetings to prepare for activities, go through checklists, and for dry runs of seminars, all of which went online from March 2020. Initially, the implementers had little experience with Zoom meetings. The leadership stressed that the situation would probably not revert to how it was pre-pandemic and that there was no choice but to adapt to the then current environment. The NPC developed competence and confidence as they implemented online activities and are developing a Zoom manual to ensure that the union's affiliates do not encounter similar learning difficulties. Although the pandemic limited what could be achieved, and while implementation could have been better with in-person activities, the NTUC Phl have persisted.

The NPC developed training modules (through online 'writeshops' or workshops), adapting those in the region-wide project manual. The training modules were purposely tailored to the lower level of preparation of intended users in enterprise-based unions. As perpetual works-in-progress, these modules were used at the national workshop, where trainees appeared to gladly receive them.

The union's training modules
- Our world of work (decent work)
- International labour standards and the future of work
- Climate justice and just transition

- Economics and statistics for unionists
- Gender mainstreaming/sensitivity (women and youth are in this together)
- Why am I here? (Trade unionism and me)
- Leadership in trade unions
- Education for trade unions and stakeholders
- Leadership is communication
- Communication is participation
- Advocacy and campaigns
- ILO Convention No. 190 on violence and harassment in the world of work
- Negotiation is fun
- SMART action planning, including monitoring, evaluation and reporting

The national workshop trained 35 women and youth trainees (WYTs), of whom 70 per cent were women and nearly 60 per cent were youth. They were nominated by their organisations, presumably as second- or third-level leaders (of the 25 women, 13 were youths, while of the 10 men, seven were youths). They underwent training online for four hours across four afternoons in December 2020 to prepare them for implementing their action plans and activities, and the long grind to leadership. There will also be online monthly refreshers on many issues.

A MEASURE OF INITIAL SUCCESS AND MUCH PRIDE

After five months, of the 35 WYTs, 10 have new responsibilities or assignments in their unions, and 16 are serving or will serve in panels negotiating their union's collective bargaining agreements (CBAs). Federations and local bodies are modifying union structures as embodied in the union statutes (constitution and by-laws [CBLs] in the Philippines), putting more women and youth in their governing bodies. Federations and locals have created new women and youth committees or are rebuilding them. Committees are crafting action plans and implementing them. Some good practices have been identified, disseminated and are being applied. There is a clear demonstration effect, with federations learning from each other, replicating good practices and 'socialising' issues and actions.

The union is engaged in advocacy and campaigns for the ratification of International Labour Organization (ILO) Convention 190 on violence and harassment at work. While pushing for ratification, its local affiliates are working for enterprise-based mechanisms against violence and harassment through negotiations and collective bargaining. Four unions have already reached agreement with their employers for formal seating[10] within 90 days of signing of the agreement to craft measures against violence and harassment.

The NPC gathered 'good' CBA provisions (particularly for women and youth) from its analysis of CBAs in 2020 and presented them at a workshop in April 2021. Seven unions have reached agreement with their employers on 'good' women and youth (WaY) provisions; and at least five others have WaY provisions under negotiation. These are good alternatives to improvements in wages and benefits, which have been largely precluded because of the pandemic.

WHY HAS THIS SEEMING INTEREST, EXCITEMENT, ENGAGEMENT NOT BEEN SEEN BEFORE?

Part of the reason is to do with saving face, which is important in Filipino culture. Union leaders agreed, therefore, that they need to act and deliver. Furthermore, they were motivated in part by seeing others doing and demonstrating good things. They were also likely enthused by the union of leaders who are determined to lead by example.

In addition, the organisation, roused by its past successes, showed renewed vigour and was driven and pushed to show results. There were

---

10 'Seating' is the term used in CBAs to refer to formal discussions, almost equivalent to formal CBA negotiations.

also interactions between the leaders and trainees that indicated acceptance and recognition. Trainees are accepted for who they are, what they do, and what they might achieve. Indeed, it was gratifying to see established leaders yielding to trainees, urging them to take over certain roles and assignments. It also helps that trainees were already embedded in their organisation(s), and were known to be involved in the NTUC Phl and federation actions rather than new recruits from the outside world.

Other factors concern the trainees themselves, all young or young-ish, with many wanting to try new union activities. Exuding enthusiasm behind their masks, their depersonalised images on Zoom suggested, related and catalysed actions starting at the 'grassroots' within their local unions. It is a pleasant surprise to see existing leaders listen, engage, encourage and start to bond with their trainees.

Finally, the NTUC Phl's WaY agenda (2019–23), consolidated in 2019, outlines the union's terms for action, with all 13 points (many with sub-points) contributing to building people, leaders, participation and direct action. The project is helping to fulfil some aims while facilitating others in its agenda. Furthermore, the agenda is subject to full reviews in conjunction with assemblies for the Centre's milestones and celebrations. As the woman chair noted, 'There are those who guide', nudging people to do what they have planned and pledged. Enablers help to ensure that the right things are done better, with those in a strategic position in the organisation reminding and cajoling leaders about their commitments.

WHAT'S NEXT?

There is a long way to go. Much more needs to be done. The next challenge will concern how to deepen the existing actions of and commitment in more federations and local unions.

Timely implementation of actions is planned. For example, on 30 May 2021 seven unions recorded what they will do for the rest of the year. Replication of good practices is emerging. Already a non-affiliate federation and two of its local unions have learned and are using modules and participation practices. The application of modules in the training and mentoring actions of the WYRs and the WYTs for their union members will hold and retain them in union activities. And there will be sustained efforts beyond the project's life. Changes in structures, governance, processes and practices will continue.

However, challenges persist. The union has lost NPC members and one of the three WYRs. The NPC lost one of its leading lights, with all her accumulated wisdom on women and unions, to a non-pandemic illness. It lost one of its target federations and local unions as the pandemic led to the closure of three of its companies and their unions, and must focus efforts on rebuilding. It also lost two young NPC members: one young man who lost in his union elections, and a young woman who went freelance. And the short-handed NGO represented in the NPC could not spare the time to continuing engagement as the pandemic hit harder.

Online activities in the Philippines have limited participation, being accessed largely by those with devices and internet access. Members also have to cope with poor internet connections and costly internet access. Indeed, it is not uncommon to see trainees, some using only mobiles, from signal-challenged locations far from the capitals, being disconnected. One observer said it was amazing to see them scramble to get back online — several times.

There is also the challenge of union leave to attend the many leadership activities, reaching the maximum under agreements. Federations and unions, with reduced union dues under the pandemic, have the additional burden of reimbursing their participants for lost pay. As leaders continue with their tutelage, it is a delight to be reminded that 'it is the responsibility of leaders to enable their followers to rise above them'. The union's women and youth trainees are well on their way to making their leaders proud.

References

FOREWORD

UN Office of the High Commissioner for Human Rights. (2022). *Working Group on Discrimination Against Women and Girls.* www.ohchr.org/en/special-procedures/wg-women-and-girls

UN Working Group on Discrimination Against Women and Girls. (2020, April 16). *Report on women's human rights in the changing world of work.* Presented at the UN General Assembly Human Rights Council 44th session, 15 June–3 July 2020. www.ohchr.org/en/calls-for-input/reports/2020/report-womens-human-rights-changing-world-work

INTRODUCTION: WORKING WOMEN IN ASIA PACIFIC

de Stefano, V., Durri, I., Stylogiannis, C., & Wouters, M. (2021). Platform work and the employment relationship. ILO. www.ilo.org/wcmsp5/groups/public/---ed_protect/---protrav/---travail/documents/publication/wcms_777866.pdf

Duerto Valero, S. (2019, September 12). Why are gender statistics important? UN Women Presentation, Nadi, Fiji. www.unescap.org/sites/default/files/Why%20are%20gender%20statistics%20important.pdf

Elson, D. (2017). Recognize, reduce, and redistribute unpaid care work: How to close the gender gap. *New Labor Forum, 26*(2): 52–61.

Foley, M., & Cooper, R. (2021). Workplace gender equality in the post pandemic era: Where to next? *Journal of Industrial Relations, 63*(4): 463–476.

Gray, M., Kittilson, M., & Sandholtz, W. (2006). Women and globalization: A study of 180 countries, 1975–2000, *International Organization, 60*(2): 293–333.

Halton, M. (2018, March 8). Climate change 'impacts women more than men'. *BBC News.* www.bbc.com/news/science-environment-43294221

Hansen, A. (2021, August 12). Spotlight on Asia: What does gender diversity in Asia look like in 2021? GlassHammer. https://theglasshammer.com/2021/08/spotlight-on-asia-what-does-gender-diversity-in-asia-look-like-in-2021

Institute for Economics and Peace (IEP). (2022). *Global Terrorism Index 2022: Measuring the impact of terrorism.* https://reliefweb.int/report/world/global-terrorism-index-2022

International Labour Organization (ILO). (2018). *Women and men in the informal economy: A statistical picture.* Third edition. ILO.

International Labour Organization (ILO). (2012). *Gender equality and decent work: Selected ILO conventions and recommendations that promote gender equality as of 2012.* International Labour Office, Bureau for Gender Equality, International Labour Standards Department, ILO.

International Labour Organization (ILO). (not dated). Decent work and the 2030 Agenda for Sustainable Development. Department of Communication and Public Information. www.ilo.org/wcmsp5/groups/public/---europe/---ro-geneva/---ilo-lisbon/documents/event/wcms_667247.pdf

International Labour Organization (ILO) and Asian Development Bank (ADB). (2015). *Fiji: Creating quality jobs — Employment diagnostic study.* www.adb.org/publications/fiji-creating-quality-jobs-employment-diagnostic-study

Legge, S., & Lukaszuk, P. (2021). Regionalization versus globalization: What is the future direction of trade? World Economic Forum. www.weforum.org/agenda/2021/07/regionalization-globalization-future-direction-trade

McKinsey Global Institute. (2019). *Globalization in transition: The future of trade and global value chains.* www.mckinsey.com/featured-insights/innovation-and-growth/globalization-in-transition-the-future-of-trade-and-value-chains

Ortiz-Ospina, E., Tzvetkova, S., & Roser, M. (2018). Women's employment. Our World In Data. https://ourworldindata.org/female-labor-supply

Parker, J., Nemani, M., Arrowsmith, J., Douglas, J., with Cooper, R., & McDonnell., N. (2011). Comparative study on social dialogue and gender equality in New Zealand, Australia and Fiji. ILO Working Papers 994634123402676, International Labour Organization.

Parker, J., Sayers, J., Loga, P., Paea, S., Donnelly, N. (forthcoming). The potential of gender (and intersectional) equity indexes: The case of Aotearoa New Zealand's public service. Manuscript under review.

Parker, J., Sayers, J., Young-Hauser, A., Barnett, S., Loga, P., & Paea, S. (2022). Gender and ethnic equity in Aotearoa New Zealand's public service before and since Covid-19: Towards intersectional inclusion? *Gender, Work and Organization, 29*(1): 110–30.

Sachs, D., Lafortune, G., Kroll, C., Fuller, G., & Woelm, F. (2021). *Sustainable development report 2021: The decade of action for the Sustainable Development Goals.* Cambridge University Press.

Statista. (2022, February 8). *The countries with the largest percentage of total population over 65 years in 2021.* https://www.statista.com/statistics/264729/countries-with-the-largest-percentage-of-total-population-over-65-years/#:~:text=Japan%20has%20the%20oldest%20population,of%20Japanese%20being%20over%2065

UN Working Group on Discrimination Against Women and Girls. (2020, April 16). Women's human rights in the changing world of work: Report of the Working Group on discrimination against women and girls. Presented at the UN General Assembly Human Rights Council 44th session, 15 June–3 July 2020, A/HRC/44/51. https://documents-dds-ny.un.org/doc/UNDOC/GEN/G20/094/80/PDF/G2009480.pdf?OpenElement

UN Women. (not dated). *The shadow pandemic: Violence against women during COVID-19.* https://www.unwomen.org/en/news/in-focus/in-focus-gender-equality-in-covid-19-response/violence-against-women-during-covid-19

UN Women. (2021). *Why women should be at the forefront of world's sustainable Covid-19 recovery.* https://asiapacific.unwomen.org/en/news-and-events/stories/2021/06/why-women-should-be-at-the-forefront-of-worlds-sustainable-covid-19-recovery

UN Economic and Social Commission for Asia and the Pacific. (2021, March 31). *ESCAP's input to the thematic review of the High-Level Political Forum 2021.* https://sustainabledevelopment.un.org/content/documents/27482ESCAP_inputs_HLPF.pdf

UN Global Compact. (2022). *Women's employment and business 2022 — trends and opportunities: Progress amid pandemic challenges across regions.* UN Global Compact.

Walby, S. (2020). Varieties of gender regimes. *Social Politics: International Studies in Gender, State & Society, 27*(3): 414–31.

World Bank. (2020). *Women, business and the law.* https://openknowledge.worldbank.org/bitstream/handle/10986/32639/9781464815324.pdf?sequence=10

World Bank. (2011, September). *Globalization's impact on gender equality:*

What's happened and what's needed. https://elibrary.worldbank.org/
doi/10.1596/9780821388105_ch6

Zanko, M. (2003). Change and diversity: HRM issues and trends in the Asia-Pacific region.
Asia Pacific Journal of Human Resources, 41(1): 75–87.

1. WORKING WOMEN IN AOTEAROA NEW ZEALAND

AI Forum of New Zealand. (2018). *Artificial Intelligence: Shaping a future New Zealand.*
www.mbie.govt.nz/dmsdocument/5754-artificial-intelligence-shaping-a-future-new-
zealand-pdf

Anderson, D., & Naidu, K. (2010). The land of milk and honey? The contemporary working
lives of contingent youth labour. *New Zealand Journal of Employment Relations, 35*(3),
61–79.

Badkar, J., Callister, P., & Didham, R. (2008). *Ageing New Zealand: The growing reliance on
migrant caregivers.* IPS Working Paper 09/08. Institute of Policy Studies.

Belong Aotearoa. (2020). *Migrant experiences in the time of Covid.* https://static1.
squarespace.com/static/5cca54599e483d0001fff53b/t/6036e88e787d3713
6315aa1e/1614211227802/Migrant+Experiences+in+the+time+of+COVID_
Belong+Aotearoa+Survey+Report+2020.pdf

BMW Group. (2021). *Next generation leadership report April 2021.* www.press.bmwgroup.
com/new-zealand/article/detail/T0330470EN/new-zealand-business-leaders-say-
sustainability-trumps-profit-in-ground-breaking-leadership-report?language=en

Bollard, A. (2020). Globalisation in the time of Coronavirus or one hundred years of
solitude for New Zealand? *Policy Quarterly, 16*(3), 15–19.

Carey, D. (2019, September 6). *Improving well-being in New Zealand through
migration.* Economics Department Working Papers No. 1566. OECD. www.
oecd.org/officialdocuments/publicdisplaydocumentpdf/?cote=ECO/
WKP(2019)35&docLanguage=En

Caritas Aotearoa New Zealand. (2003). *Protecting children at work: Children's work survey.*
Caritas.

Caritas Aotearoa New Zealand. (2020, February 27). *Risk that child poverty is becoming ingrained.* https://caritas.org.nz/newsroom/media-releases/risk-child-poverty-becoming-ingrained

Carroll, M. (2020a, October 12). Covid-19 boosts NZ union membership, but aviation job losses hit E tū numbers. *Stuff.* www.stuff.co.nz/business/industries/123048137/covid19-boosts-nz-union-membership-but-aviation-job-losses-hit-e-t-numbers

Carroll, M. (2020b, August 9). Women bearing brunt of Covid-19 job losses. *Stuff.* www.stuff.co.nz/business/women-of-influence/122366842/women-bearing-brunt-of-covid19-job-losses

Central Intelligence Agency. (2021). *The World Factbook: New Zealand.* www.cia.gov/the-world-factbook/countries/new-zealand/#economy

Chartered Accountants of Australia and New Zealand and New Zealand Institute of Economic Research (NZIER). (2015). *Disruptive technologies: Risks, opportunities — Can New Zealand make the most of them?* www.charteredaccountantsanz.com/-/media/ba904c297f9842b0acadd82d18b864a5.ashx

Climate Change Response (Zero Carbon) Amendment Act, No. 61. (2019). www.legislation.govt.nz/act/public/2019/0061/latest/LMS183736.html

Colmar Brunton. (2019). *Better futures.* https://static.colmarbrunton.co.nz/wp-content/uploads/2019/05/Colmar-Brunton-Better-Futures-2019-MASTER-FINAL-REPORT.pdf

Council of Trade Unions (CTU). (2013, October). *Under pressure: A detailed report into insecure work in New Zealand.* www.union.org.nz/wp-content/uploads/2016/12/CTU-Under-Pressure-Detailed-Report-2.pdf

Council of Trade Unions (CTU). (2019). *Next steps on just transition to good, green jobs: CTU agenda for 2020 and into the new parliamentary term — People power for our planet.* www.ituc-csi.org/IMG/pdf/191014_-_ppl_power_for_our_planet_-_next-steps-on-just-transition-oct-2019.pdf

Council of Trade Unions (CTU). (2021, May 21). *Budget report 2021: A working people's analysis of the 2021 Budget.* www.union.org.nz/wp-content/uploads/2021/05/CTU-Budget-Report-2021.pdf

Dale, M., & St John, S. (2020). *Women and retirement in a post Covid-19 world.* University of Auckland Business School Research Paper No. 2020–1.

Deeks, J., Parker, J., & Ryan, R. (1994). *Labour and employment relations in New Zealand.* Longman Paul.

Deloitte. (2021). *Women in the boardroom: A global perspective.* www2.deloitte.com/nz/
en/pages/risk/articles/women-in-the-boardroom5th-edition.html

Domestic Violence — Victims' Protection Act, No. 21. (2018). www.legislation.govt.nz/act/
public/2018/0021/latest/DLM7054315.html

Elson, D. (2017). Recognize, reduce, and redistribute unpaid care work: How to close the
gender gap. *New Labor Forum, 26*(2), 52–61.

Employment New Zealand. (2020, July 28). *Tackling temporary migrant worker
exploitation.* www.employment.govt.nz/about/news-and-updates/tackling-
temporary-migrant-worker-exploitation

Employment Contracts Act, No. 22. (1991). www.nzlii.org/nz/legis/hist_act/
eca19911991n22280

Employment Relations Act, No. 24 (2000). www.legislation.govt.nz/act/
public/2000/0024/latest/DLM58317.html

Equal Pay Amendment Act, No. 45. (2020). www.legislation.govt.nz/act/
public/2020/0045/latest/LMS86440.html

Fair Pay Agreements (FPA) Working Group. (2018). *Fair pay agreements: Supporting
workers and firms to drive productivity growth and share the benefits.* www.mbie.
govt.nz/dmsdocument/4393-working-group-report-pdf

Family Violence Act, No. 46. (2018). www.legislation.govt.nz/act/public/2018/0046/latest/
whole.html

Fanslow, J., & Robinson, E. (2011). Sticks, stones, or words? Counting the prevalence of
different types of Intimate Partner Violence reported by New Zealand women. *Journal
of Aggression, Maltreatment & Trauma, 20*(7), 741–59.

Financial Services Council of New Zealand. (2018). *Women and finance in New Zealand.*
www.fsc.org.nz/Consumer+Information/blog/women-finance-new-zealand.html

Grant Thornton. (2018). *Women in business: Beyond policy to progress.* https://
grantthornton.co.nz/insights/women-in-business-2018

Halteh, J., Arrowsmith, J., Parker, J., Zorn, T., & Bentley, T. (2018). The impact of
technology on employment: A research agenda for New Zealand and beyond. *Labour
and Industry, 28*(3), 203–16.

Harawira, M. (1999, May). *Economic globalisation, indigenous peoples, and the role of
indigenous women.* Paper presented at the Hague Appeal for Peace Conference (panel:

'Women and Globalisation'), Women's International League for Peace and Freedom. www.apc.org.nz/pma/Mak.htm

Harbridge, R., May, R., & Thickett, A. (2003). The current state of play: Collective bargaining and union membership under the Employment Relations Act 2000. *New Zealand Journal of Industrial Relations, 28*(2), 140–49.

Healy, J., Nicholson, N., & Parker, J. (2017). Technological disruption and the future of employment relations. *Labour and Industry, 27*(3), 1–8.

Hyslop, D., Rice, A., & Skilling, H. (2019). *Understanding labour market developments in New Zealand, 1986–2017.* Reserve Bank of New Zealand Discussion Paper. www.rbnz.govt.nz/-/media/ReserveBank/Files/Publications/Discussion%20 papers/2019/DP2019-02.pdf?revision=7ffc50ab-2fd0-40e7-a706-a3acd17f0e09

Iles, J. (2019, February 28). Government commissions new study on the future of work. *Dominion Post.* www.stuff.co.nz/dominion-post/news/110919733/government-commissions-new-study-on-the-future-of-work

International Labour Organization (ILO). (2020). *ILOSTAT data.* https://ilostat.ilo.org/data

Kanengoni, B., Andajani-Sutjahjo, S., & Holroyd, E. (2018, August 23). Setting the stage: Reviewing current knowledge on health of New Zealand immigrants — an integrative review. *PeerJ.* https://doi.org/10.7717/peerj.5184

La Croce, C. (2020, 4 November). Women in tech: Supporting women during COVID-19. IDC. https://blog-idcuk.com/women-in-tech-supporting-women-during-covid-19

Madgavkar, A., Manyika, J., Krishnan, M., Ellingrud, K., Yee, L., Woetzel, J., Chui, M., Hunt, V., & Balakrishnan, S. (2019, June). *The future of women at work: Transitions in the age of automation.* McKinsey & Company. www.mckinsey.com/featured-insights/gender-equality/the-future-of-women-at-work-transitions-in-the-age-of-automation

Manch, T. (2019, September 23). Census 2018: New Zealand population is larger and more diverse. *Stuff.* www.stuff.co.nz/national/politics/116005822/census-2018-new-zealand-population-is-larger-and-more-diverse

McGregor, J., Bell, S., & Wilson, M. (2015). Fault lines: Human rights in New Zealand. *New Zealand Law Foundation Research Reports.* www.nzlii.org/nz/journals/NZLFRRp/2015/2.html

Ministry for Business, Innovation & Employment (MBIE). (2021, March 16). Plan of action against forced labour, people trafficking and slavery. Cabinet paper. www.mbie.govt.

nz/dmsdocument/13607-plan-of-action-against-forced-labour-people-trafficking-and-slavery-proactiverelease-pdf

Ministry for Women (MfW). (2016). *Effect of motherhood on pay — methodology and full results: June 2016 quarter.* www.stats.govt.nz/assets/Reports/Effect-of-motherhood-on-pay-methodology-and-full-results/effect-of-motherhood-on-pay-methodology-full-results.pdf

Ministry for Women (MfW). (2019, August 19). *Gender inequality and unpaid work.* https://women.govt.nz/sites/public_files/Gender%20inequality%20and%20unpaid%20work%20.pdf

Ministry for Women (MfW). (2020, May 31). *COVID-19 and women.* https://women.govt.nz/news/covid-19-and-women

Ministry for Women (MfW). (2021, May 17). *Women's Employment Action Plan.* https://women.govt.nz/news/womens-employment-action-plan

National Advisory Council on the Employment of Women (NACEW). (2010). *Flexible work arrangements literature review.*

New Zealand Companies Office. (2022). *Union membership return report 2020.* www.companiesoffice.govt.nz/all-registers/registered-unions/annual-return-membership-reports/

New Zealand Government. (2019). *He Waka Eke Noa: Towards a better future, together: New Zealand's progress towards the SDGs — 2019.* https://sustainabledevelopment.un.org/content/documents/23333New_Zealand_Voluntary_National_Review_2019_Final.pdf

New Zealand Institute of Economic Research (NZIER). (2017, July). *Is peak globalisation upon us? Globalisation is much more than trade in goods.* NZIER Public Discussion Paper 2017/1. www.nzier.org.nz/news/is-peak-globalisation-upon-us-nzier-public-discussion-paper-20171

New Zealand Parliament. (1996, November 1). *The Employment Contracts Act and its economic impact.* www.parliament.nz/en/pb/research-papers/document/00PLSocRP96021/the-employment-contracts-act-and-its-economic-impact

New Zealand Productivity Commission. (2020). *Technological change and the future of work: Final report.* www.productivity.govt.nz/assets/Documents/0634858491/Final-report_Technological-change-and-the-future-of-work.pdf

Notz, G. (1999). *Women's work under the conditions of globalisation.* Workshop on Women and globalisation: A Brazilian-German-South African trade union dialogue. Hattingen, Germany, 20–24 September. https://library.fes.de/pdf-files/netzquelle/01779.pdf

OECD. (2019, February). *Measuring women's economic empowerment: Time use data and gender inequality.* OECD Development Policy Papers No. 16. www.oecd.org/dev/development-gender/MEASURING-WOMENS-ECONOMIC-EMPOWERMENT-Gender-Policy-Paper-No-16.pdf

O'Kane, P., Walton, S., & Ruwhiu, D. (2020). *Remote working during COVID-19: New Zealand National Survey: Initial report July 2020.* A Work Futures Otago report. www.otago.ac.nz/management/research/covid-survey/otago741202.pdf

Ongley, P., Lum, R., Lynch, C., & Lu, E. (2013). *A snapshot of New Zealand's temporary workers: Results from the 2012 Survey of Working Life.* StatsNZ.

Palmer, G. (1980). *Unbridled power?* Oxford University Press.

Parker, J., & Arrowsmith, J. (2012). Are we being served? Women in New Zealand's service sector. *Equality, Diversity and Inclusion: An International Journal, 31*(7), 663–680.

Parker, J., Arrowsmith, J., Young-Hauser, A., Hodgetts, D., Haar, J., Carr, S., & Alefaio-Tugia, S. (2022). Perceptions of living wage impacts in Aotearoa New Zealand: Towards a multi-level, contextualised conceptualisation. *Personnel Review* (ahead-of-print). https://doi.org/10.1108/PR-01-2021-0037.

Parker, J., & Donnelly, N. (2020). The revival and refashioning of gender pay equity in New Zealand. *Journal of Industrial Relations, 62*(4), 560–81.

Parker, J., Donnelly, N., Young-Hauser, A., Barnett, S., Sayers, J., Loga, P., & Paea, S. (in press). Women's progress in Aotearoa New Zealand's public service. In H. Conley & P. Koskinen (Eds.), *International handbook on gender and public sector employment.* Routledge.

Parker, J., Young-Hauser, A., Loga, P., & Paea, S. (2022). Gender and ethnic equity in Aotearoa New Zealand's public service: Where is the progress amid the pandemic? *Labour and Industry, 32*(2), 156–77. https://doi.org/10.1080/10301763.2022.2091198

Phillips, J. (2015, August 1). History of immigration — Many leave, fewer arrive: 1975 to 1991. *Te Ara — the Encyclopaedia of NZ.* https://teara.govt.nz/en/history-of-immigration/page-16

Proctor-Thomson, S., Donnelly, N., & Parker, J. (2021). Bargaining for gender equality in Aotearoa New Zealand: Flexible work arrangements in collective agreements, 2007–2019. *Journal of Industrial Relations, 63*(4), 614–40.

Public Service Act, No. 40 (2020). www.legislation.govt.nz/act/public/2020/0040/latest/LMS106159.html

Public Service Commission (PSC). (2020, December 9). *Gender pay gap comparison.* www.publicservice.govt.nz/our-work/workforce-data/gender-pay-gap-comparison

Public Service Commission (PSC). (2021). *Pay gaps and pay equity.* www.publicservice.govt.nz/our-work/pay-gaps-and-pay-equity

Robson, S. (2021, May 25). Unemployment insurance scheme could cost up to $5 billion a year. *Radio New Zealand.* www.rnz.co.nz/news/political/443283/unemployment-insurance-scheme-could-cost-up-to-5-billion-a-year

Ryall, S., & Blumenfeld, S. (2016). *Unions and union membership in New Zealand — report on 2015 Survey.* Centre for Labour, Employment and Work, Victoria University of Wellington. www.wgtn.ac.nz/__data/assets/pdf_file/0009/1816308/new-zealand-union-membership-survey-report.pdf

Scott, A. (2020). Surviving post-separation financial violence despite the Family Court: Complex money matters as entrapment. *New Zealand Family Law Journal, 10,* 27–35.

Spoonley, P. (2021, June). *A changing New Zealand has major impacts for our infrastructure.* Speech to the New Zealand Infrastructure Commission, Te Waihanga's Looking Ahead Symposium. www.tewaihanga.govt.nz/news/commission-news/a-changing-new-zealand-has-major-impacts-for-our-infrastructure

StatsNZ. (2011). *Time use survey 2009/10.* www.stats.govt.nz/reports/caring-for-children-findings-from-the-200910-time-use-survey

StatsNZ. (2019a, September 10). Kiwis work hard at multiple jobs. Press Release. *Scoop Business.* www.scoop.co.nz/stories/BU1909/S00226/kiwis-work-hard-at-multiple-jobs.htm

StatsNZ. (2019b, July 3). *Over half of employees in New Zealand have flexible work hours.* www.stats.govt.nz/news/over-half-of-employees-in-new-zealand-have-flexible-work-hours

StatsNZ. (2019c). *Parenting and fertility trends in New Zealand: 2018.* www.stats.govt.nz/reports/parenting-and-fertility-trends-in-new-zealand-2018

StatsNZ. (2020a, November 4). *Covid-19's impact on women and work.* www.stats.govt.nz/news/covid-19s-impact-on-women-and-work

StatsNZ. (2020b, September 3). *Ethnic group summaries reveal New Zealand's multicultural make-up.* www.stats.govt.nz/news/ethnic-group-summaries-reveal-new-zealands-multicultural-make-up

StatsNZ. (2020c, August 21). *Fewer women working in key tourism industries.* www.stats.govt.nz/news/fewer-women-working-in-tourism-industries

StatsNZ. (2020d, November 9). *Māori women look after whānau and whenua.* www.stats.govt.nz/news/maori-women-look-after-whanau-and-whenua

StatsNZ. (2020e, September 14). *Migration flows down to a trickle.* www.stats.govt.nz/news/migration-flows-down-to-a-trickle

StatsNZ. (2020f, March 6). *Women in Aotearoa.* www.stats.govt.nz/infographics/women-in-aotearoa

StatsNZ. (2021a, August 18). *Gender pay gap unchanged.* www.stats.govt.nz/news/gender-pay-gap-unchanged

StatsNZ. (2021b, August 4). *Labour market statistics: June 2021 quarter.* www.stats.govt.nz/information-releases/labour-market-statistics-june-2021-quarter

StatsNZ. (2021c, July 15). *More women taking up self-employment.* www.stats.govt.nz/news/more-women-taking-up-self-employment

StatsNZ. (2021d, November 3). *Unemployment and underutilisation continue to fall.* www.stats.govt.nz/news/unemployment-and-underutilisation-continue-to-fall

Stillman, S. (2011). *Labour market outcomes for immigrants and the New Zealand-born 1997–2009.* Department of Labour.

Stillman, S., & Maré, D. (2009). *The labour market adjustment of immigrants in New Zealand.* Motu Economic and Public Policy Research. www.motu.nz/our-research/population-and-labour/migration/the-labour-market-adjustment-of-immigrants-in-new-zealand/

Sustainable Business Council. (2019, February). *Future of work: Are you equipped to lead your organisation to thrive in the new realities of work?* www.sbc.org.nz/__data/assets/pdf_file/0009/162495/14022019-FoW-Boardroom-think-piece.pdf

Treasury. (2017, August 17). *Chances, choices and challenges: New Zealand's response to globalisation.* Address by Gabriel Makhlouf, Secretary to the Treasury. www.treasury.

govt.nz/sites/default/files/2018-03/sp-response-globalisation-17aug17.pdf

Thomson, A. (2021, November 15). New Zealand's public sector Gender Pay Gap narrows to record low. *Bloomberg* (Asia edition). www.bloomberg.com/news/articles/2021-11-15/new-zealand-s-public-sector-gender-pay-gap-narrows-to-record-low

Thornton, G. (2021, May 21). *Summary: Budget 2021, fast facts.* www.grantthornton.co.nz/insights/budget-2021-summary

UN Committee on the Elimination of All Forms of Discrimination Against Women (CEDAW). (2020). *Follow-up information on New Zealand's progress in addressing four recommendations from the Committee on the Elimination of All Forms of Discrimination Against Women.* https://women.govt.nz/sites/public_files/SIGNED%20Interim%20CEDAW%20report%2022%20July%202020.PDF

UN Conference on Trade and Development (UNCTAD). (2012). *Trade and development report, 2012.* https://unctad.org/system/files/official-document/tdr2012_en.pdf

UN Working Group on Discrimination Against Women and Girls. (2020, April 16). *Report on women's human rights in the changing world of work.* Presented at the UN General Assembly Human Rights Council 44th session, 15 June–3 July 2020. www.ohchr.org/en/calls-for-input/reports/2020/report-womens-human-rights-changing-world-work

UN Women Aotearoa New Zealand. (2021). *The sustainable development goals.* https://unwomen.org.nz/the-sustainable-development-goals

Vergara, M. (2020, August 5). 11,000 New Zealanders have lost their jobs — and 10,000 of them were women. *The Spinoff.* https://thespinoff.co.nz/business/05-08-2020/11000-new-zealanders-have-lost-their-jobs-and-10000-of-them-were-women

Weatherall, R., Jury, A., & Thorburn, N. (2017). 'What's his is his and what's mine is his': Financial power and economic abuse of women in Aotearoa. *Aotearoa New Zealand Social Work Review, 29*(2), 69–82.

Yadav, U. (2021). *A sharp reversal in migration trends.* BERL. https://berl.co.nz/economic-insights/government-and-fiscal-policy-migration-and-population/sharp-reversal-migration

2. WORKING WOMEN IN AUSTRALIA

Anxo, D., Baird, M., & Erhel, C. (2017). Work and care regimes and women's employment outcomes: Australia, France and Sweden compared. In D. Grimshaw, C. Fagan, G. Hebson, & I. Tavora (Eds.), *Making work more equal: A new labour market segmentation approach* (pp. 309–29). Manchester University Press.

Australian Bureau of Statistics (ABS). (2016). *2016 Census all persons QuickStats*. https://quickstats.censusdata.abs.gov.au/census_services/getproduct/census/2016/quickstat/036

Australian Bureau of Statistics (ABS). (2017). *One in 20 dads take primary parental leave*. www.abs.gov.au/ausstats/abs@.nsf/Lookup/by%20Subject/4125.0~Sep%202017~Media%20Release~One%20in%2020%20dads%20take%20primary%20parental%20leave%20(Media%20Release)~11

Australian Bureau of Statistics (ABS). (2019a). *Australian demographic statistics, June 2018*. Cat. No. 3101.0.

Australian Bureau of Statistics (ABS). (2019b). *Australian historical population statistics*. Cat. No. 3105.0.65.001.

Australian Bureau of Statistics (ABS). (2019c). *Births, Australia, reference period 2018*. Cat. No. 3301.0.

Australian Bureau of Statistics (ABS). (2019d). *6401.0 — Consumer Price Index, Australia, Jun 2019*. Cat. no.

Australian Bureau of Statistics (ABS). (2020a, December). *Gender indicators, Australia*. www.abs.gov.au/statistics/people/people-and-communities/gender-indicators-australia/latest-release

Australian Bureau of Statistics (ABS). (2020b). *Twenty years of population change*. www.abs.gov.au/articles/twenty-years-population-change

Australian Bureau of Statistics (ABS). (2021a). *Births, Australia, reference period 2020*. Cat. no. 3301.0.

Australian Bureau of Statistics (ABS). (2021b). *Household impacts of COVID-19 survey*. Cat. no. 4940.0.

Australian Bureau of Statistics (ABS). (2021c). *Labour force survey 2021, industry data — employment by industry by gender*. https://lmip.gov.au/default.aspx?LMIP/EmploymentRegion/EmploymentbyIndustrybyGender

Australian Bureau of Statistics (ABS). (2021d). *Regional internal and overseas migration estimates, provisional March 2021*.

Australian Bureau of Statistics (ABS). (2022). *Labour force, Australia*, November 2021, Cat. no. 6202.0.

Australian Department of Home Affairs. (2021). *Temporary relaxation of working hours for student visa holders*. https://immi.homeaffairs.gov.au/visas/getting-a-visa/visa-listing/student-500/temporary-relaxation-of-working-hours-for-student-visa-holders

Australian Government. (2020). *Women's economic security statement, Budget 2021 Statement*. Australian Government.

Australian Institute of Family Studies. (2021, July). *Families in Australia survey: Towards COVID normal*. Report No. 4. https://aifs.gov.au/sites/default/files/publication-documents/2106_4_fias_pregnancy_and_fertility_intentions.pdf

Australian Productivity Commission. (2021). *Working from home*. Research paper. www.pc.gov.au/research/completed/working-from-home

Australian Women's Health Network. (2014). *The impact on women's health of climatic and economic disaster*. www.genderanddisaster.com.au/wp-content/uploads/2015/06/Doc-043-Impact-on-Women-Position-Paper.pdf

Baird, M., & Heron, A. (2020). The life cycle of women's employment in Australia and inequality markers. In R. D. Lansbury, A. Johnson, & D. van den Broek (Eds.), *Contemporary issues in work and organisations: Actors and institutions* (pp. 42–56). Routledge.

Baird, M., & Hill, E. (2020, May). *Covid-19 and women's economic participation: A rapid analysis on Covid-19 and implications for women's economic participation*. University of Sydney Business School.

Baird, M., Hamilton, M., & Constantin, A. (2021). Gender equality and paid parental leave in Australia: A decade of giant leaps or baby steps? *Journal of Industrial Relations, 63*(4), 546–67.

Bastion. (2021). *Adapting to the new normal: Hybrid working 2021*. Special Report. Bastion Insights/Pitcher Partners.

Bureau of Meteorology (2019). *State of the climate 2018*. Australian Government. www.bom.gov.au/state-of-the-climate/2018

Bureau of Meteorology. (2021). *Special climate statement 74 — extreme rainfall and flooding in eastern and central Australia in March 2021.* Australian Government.

Charlesworth, S., & Heron, A. (2012). New Australian working time minimum standards: Reproducing the same old gendered architecture? *Journal of Industrial Relations, 54*(2), 164–81.

Chester, L., & Morris, A. (2011). A new form of energy poverty is the hallmark of liberalised electricity sectors. *Australian Journal of Social Issues, 46*(4), 435–59.

Chief Executive Women. (2021). *Equitable flexibility: Reshaping our workforce.* https://cew.org.au/wp-content/uploads/2021/06/CEW-Report-2021_all.pdf

Chomik, R. (2021). *Tapping into Australia's ageing workforce: Insights from recent research.* ARC Centre of Excellence in Population Ageing Research. https://cepar.edu.au/sites/default/files/cepar-research-brief-ageing-workforce-australia.pdf

Clibborn, S. (2021). Multiple frames of reference: Why international student workers in Australia tolerate underpayment. *Economic and Industrial Democracy, 42*(2), 336–54.

Clibborn, S., & Wright, C. (2020). Covid-19 and the policy-induced vulnerabilities of temporary migrant workers in Australia. *Journal of Australian Political Economy, 85,* 62–70.

Commonwealth Scientific and Industrial Research Organisation (CSIRO). (2020). *The 2019–20 bushfires: A CSIRO explainer.* www.csiro.au/en/research/natural-disasters/bushfires/2019-20-bushfires-explainer

Cooper, R., & Baird, M. (2015). Bringing the 'right to request' flexible working arrangements to life: From policies to practices. *Employee Relations, 37*(5), 568–81.

Cooper, R., Baird, M., Foley, M., & Oxenbridge, S. (2021). Normative collusion in the industry ecosystem: Explaining women's career pathways and outcomes in investment management. *Human Relations, 74*(11), 1916–41.

Craig, L., & Churchill, B. (2021). Dual earner parent couples' work and care during Covid-19. *Gender, Work, and Organization, 28*(S1), 66–79.

Dantas, G., Siciliano, B., França, B. B., da Silva, C. M., & Arbilla, G. (2020). The impact of COVID-19 partial lockdown on the air quality of the city of Rio de Janeiro, Brazil. *The Science of the Total Environment, 729,* 139,085. https://doi.org/10.1016/j.scitotenv.2020.139085

Department of Social Services (DSS). (2020). *Multicultural Australia: United, strong, successful — Australia's multicultural statement.* www.homeaffairs.gov.au/mca/

Statements/english-multicultural-statement.pdf

Diversity Council of Australia (DCA). (2012). *Get flexible.* www.dca.org.au/research/project/get-flexible

Economic Security4Women. (2020). *The impact on women in disaster affected areas in Australia: Summary of the 2014 Canberra Roundtable discussion.* www.security4women.org.au/wp-content/uploads/2020/07/eS4WNRWC_4PageSummaryImpactWomenDisasterAffectedAreas-AustraliaFinal20140907.pdf

Eisenstein, H. (2010). Feminism seduced: Globalisation and the uses of gender. *Australian Feminist Studies, 25*(66), 413–31.

Fair Work Act, No. 33. (2009). www.legislation.gov.au/Details/C2017C00323

Foley, M., & Cooper, R. (2021). Workplace gender equality in the post-pandemic era: Where to next? *Journal of Industrial Relations, 63*(4), 463–76.

Foley, M., Oxenbridge, S., Cooper, R., & Baird, M. (2020). 'I'll never be one of the boys': Gender harassment of women working as pilots and automotive tradespeople. *Gender, Work and Organization, 4*(1), 1–16. https://doi.org/10.1111/gwao.12443

Food and Agriculture Organization of the United Nations. (2011). *The state of food insecurity in the world: How does international price volatility affect domestic economies and food security?* https://reliefweb.int/sites/reliefweb.int/files/resources/Full%20Report_266.pdf

Gillett, J. E., & Crisp, D. A. (2017). Examining coping style and the relationship between stress and subjective well-being in Australia's 'sandwich generation'. *Australasian Journal on Ageing, 36*(3), 222–27.

Heard, G., & Arunachalam, D. (Eds.). (2015). *Family formation in 21st century Australia.* Springer.

Infrastructure Australia. (2019). *An assessment of Australia's future infrastructure needs: The Australian Infrastructure Audit 2019.* www.infrastructureaustralia.gov.au/sites/default/files/2019-08/Australian%20Infrastructure%20Audit%202019.pdf

Internal Displacement Monitoring Centre. (2020). *The 2019–20 Australian bushfires: From temporary evacuation to longer-term displacement.* www.internal-displacement.org/sites/default/files/publications/documents/Australian%20bushfires_Final.pdf

International Labour Organization (ILO). (2020). SDG indicator 5.5.2 — Proportion of women in managerial positions (%) — Annual, SDG – SDG labour market indicators (ILOSDG), ID: SDG_T552_NOC_RT_A.

Jewkes, R. (2002). Intimate partner violence: Causes and prevention. *The Lancet*, *359*(9315), 1423–29.

Kaspura, A. (2019). *The engineering profession: A statistical overview* (14th ed.). Institution of Engineers Australia.

Macdonald, F. (2021). *Individualising risk: Paid care work in the new gig economy*. Palgrave Macmillan.

Macdonald, F., & Charlesworth, S. (2021). Regulating for gender-equitable decent work in social and community services: Bringing the state back. *Journal of Industrial Relations, 63*(4), 1–24.

Male Champions of Change. (2017). *Male Champions of Change STEM: Progress report, 2016/2017*. Australian Government.

Male Champions of Change. (2019). *Harnessing our innovation potential: Gender equality in STEM*. https://championsofchangecoalition.org/wp-content/uploads/2019/08/Harnessing-Our-Innovation-Potential_Stem-Survey-Report-2019.pdf

McDonald, P. (2000a). Gender equity in theories of fertility transition. *Population and Development Review, 26*(3), 427–39.

McDonald, P. (2000b). Gender equity, social institutions and the future of fertility. *Journal of Population Research, 17*(1), 1–16.

McDonald, P. (2013). Societal foundations for explaining low fertility: Gender equity. *Demographic Research, 28*(34), 981–94.

McDonald, P. (2020). *A projection of Australia's future fertility rates*. Centre for Population Research Paper, The Australian Government, Canberra.

McDonald, P., & Moyle, H. (2020). The cessation of rising employment rates at older ages in Australia, 2000–2019. *Australian Population Studies, 4*(1), 20–36.

McKinnon, M. (2020). The absence of evidence of the effectiveness of Australian gender equity in STEM initiatives. *Australian Journal of Social Issues, 57*(1), 1–14.

Norton, A., Cherastidtham, I., & Mackey, W. (2018). *Mapping Australian higher education 2018*. Grattan Institute.

Office of the Chief Scientist. (2020). *Australia's STEM workforce: Science, technology, engineering and mathematics*. Australian Government.

O'Loughlin, K., Loh, V., & Kendig, H. (2017). Carer characteristics and health, wellbeing and employment outcomes of older Australian Baby Boomers. *Journal of Cross-Cultural Gerontology, 32*(3), 339–56.

Paid Parental Leave Act, No. 32. (2010). www.legislation.gov.au/Details/C2019C00071

Parker, J., Sayers, J., Young-Hauser, A., Barnett, S., Loga, P., & Paea, S. (2022). Gender and ethnic equity in Aotearoa New Zealand's public service before and since Covid-19: Toward intersectional inclusion? *Gender, Work and Organization, 29*(1), 110–30.

Parkinson, D., Duncan, A., Davie, S., Archer, F., Sutherland, A., O'Malley, S., Jeffrey, J., Pease, B., Wilson, A., & Gough, M. (2018). Victoria's gender and disaster taskforce: A retrospective analysis. *Australian Journal of Emergency Management, 33*(3), 50–57.

Pocock, B., & Charlesworth, S. (2017). Multilevel work–family interventions: Creating good-quality employment over the life course. *Work and Occupations, 44*(1), 23–46.

Priestly, A. (2021). *Will men dominate the office? We can't risk a hybrid work gender gap.* https://womensagenda.com.au/business/will-men-dominate-the-office-we-cant-risk-a-hybrid-work-gender-gap

Rindfuss, R., & Choe, M. (2015). *Low and lower fertility: Variations across developed countries.* Springer.

Risse, L., & Jackson, A. (2021). A gender lens on the workforce impacts of the Covid-19 pandemic in Australia. *Australian Journal of Labour Economics, 24*(2), 111–43.

Ruppaner, L., Collins, C., & Scarborough, W. (2020, July 21). COVID-19 is a disaster for mothers' employment. And no, working from home is not the solution. *The Conversation.* https://theconversation.com/covid-19-is-a-disaster-for-mothers-employment-and-no-working-from-home-is-not-the-solution-142650

Smith, M., & Whitehouse, G. (2020). Wage-setting and gender pay equality in Australia: Advances, retreats and future prospects. *Journal of Industrial Relations, 62*(4), 533–59.

Thevenon, O. (2011). Family policies in OECD countries: A comparative analysis. *Population and Development Review, 37*(1), 57–87.

Ticona, J., & Mateescu, A. (2018). Trusted strangers: Carework platforms' cultural entrepreneurship in the on-demand economy. *New Media and Society, 20*(11), 4384–04.

Treasury. (2021). *Budget strategy and outlook: Budget paper no. 1 2021–22. Budget 2021–22.* https://archive.budget.gov.au/2021-22/bp1/download/bp1_2021-22.pdf

UN Development Program (UNDP). (2020). *Gender climate change and food security,* Policy brief. UNDP.

UN Working Group on Discrimination Against Women and Girls. (2020, April 16). *Report on women's human rights in the changing world of work.* Presented at the UN General Assembly Human Rights Council 44th session, 15 June–3 July 2020. www.ohchr.org/en/calls-for-input/reports/2020/report-womens-human-rights-changing-world-work

van den Broek, D., & Groutsis, D. (2020). *Women, work and migration: Nursing in Australia.* Routledge.

VicHealth. (2009). *National survey on community attitudes to violence against women 2009: Changing cultures, changing attitudes — preventing violence against women: A summary of findings.* Victorian Health Promotion Foundation. www.vichealth.vic.gov.au/~/media/ResourceCentre/PublicationsandResources/PVAW/NCAS_CommunityAttitudes_report_2010.ashx

Workplace Gender Equality Act, No. 20. (2012). www.legislation.gov.au/Details/C2016C00895

Workplace Gender Equality Agency. (2020). *Governing bodies.* https://data.wgea.gov.au/industries/1#governing_bodies_content

World Bank. (2021). *Employment (as a % of total employment) (modelled ILO estimate).* https://data.worldbank.org/indicator/SL.SRV.EMPL.ZS

Wright, C., Wailes, N., Bamber, G., & Lansbury, R. (2017). Beyond national systems, towards a 'gig economy'? A research agenda for international and comparative employment relations. *Employee Responsibilities and Rights Journal, 29*(4), 247–57.

3. WORKING WOMEN IN JAPAN

Act on Advancement of Measures to Support Raising Next-Generation Children (Next-Generation Act). (2003). Revised 2015. www.mhlw.go.jp/english/policy/children/children-childrearing/dl/150407-01.pdf

Akamatsu, R. (2003). *Making the Equal Employment Opportunity Act.* Keiso-Shobo.

Asano, F., & Tendou, M. (2021). *Making disaster women's studies.* Seikatsushisosya. [Published in Japanese].

Bishop, B. (2000). The diversification of employment and women's work in contemporary Japan. In J. S. Eads, T. Gill, & H. Befu (Eds.), *Globalization and social change in contemporary Japan* (pp. 93–109). Trans Pacific Press.

Cabinet Office. (2014). *Basic policy of economic and financial management and reform 2014.* [Published in Japanese].

Cabinet Office. (2021). *Reiwa 3 Annual report on the declining birthrate 2021.*

Chiba, E. (2013). Employment and gender in rural mountain village families: From the disaster-stricken areas of Fukushima Prefecture. *The Bulletin of the Society for the Study of Working Women, 57*, 122–33. [Published in Japanese].

Child Care and Family Leave Act. (1995). *Outline.* www.mhlw.go.jp/english/policy/children/work-family/dl/190410-01e.pdf

Dalton, E. (2017). Womenomics, 'equality' and Abe's neo-liberal strategy to make Japanese women shine. *Social Science Japan Journal, 20*(1), 95–105.

Equal Employment Opportunity Act (EEO Act). (1972). www.mhlw.go.jp/file/06-Seisakujouhou-11900000-Koyoukintoujidoukateikyoku/0000133458.pdf

Eweje, G., & Nagano, S. (Eds.). (2021). *Corporate social responsibility and gender equality in Japan: Historical and current perspectives.* Springer.

Fujimoto, M. (2017). What is the Japanese long-term employment system? Has it vanished? *Japan Labor Press, 1*(1), 22–25.

Gender Equality Bureau Cabinet Office. (2013). *White paper on gender equality 2013.*

Gender Equality Bureau Cabinet Office. (2017). Utilizing the Act to promote women's participation to accelerate and expand the advancement of women. In *White paper on gender equality 2017.* www.gender.go.jp/english_contents/about_danjo/whitepaper/pdf/ewp2017.pdf

Gender Equality Bureau Cabinet Office. (2020a). *White paper on gender equality 2020.* [Published in Japanese]. www.gender.go.jp/about_danjo/whitepaper/r02/zentai/index.html#pdf

Gender Equality Bureau Cabinet Office. (2020b). *Women's perspectives to strengthen disaster response capabilities: Guidelines for disaster prevention and reconstruction from the viewpoint of gender equality.* [Published in Japanese].

Gender Equality Bureau Cabinet Office. (2021). *Research report on the effects of the spread of Covid-19 from the viewpoint of gender equality in 2020.* [Published in Japanese].

www.gender.go.jp/research/kenkyu/pdf/covid19_r02/03.pdf

Gordon, A. (2017). New and enduring dual structures of employment in Japan: The rise of non-regular labor, 1980s–2010s. *Social Science Japan Journal, 20*(1), 9–36.

Hashimoto, Y. (2009). The history behind: Why is there a family labour law only for internal employment? *The Japanese Journal of Labour Studies, 585*, 34–37. [Published in Japanese].

Hayasaka, Y. (2015, August 11). Decontamination NADESHIKO, midsummer struggle 70 women beyond the boundaries of the company. *Sankei Shinbun*. [Published in Japanese]. www.sankei.com/photo/photojournal/news/150811/jnl1508110001-n1.html

Hazama, H. (1996). *The thought which made a Japanese economic miracle: Labor ethos in high economic growth*. Bunshin-do.

Hirayama, R. (2014). *The coming of age of 'son's elderly care': 28 carers site*. Kobunsha-Shinsho. [Published in Japanese].

Hirayama, R. (2017). *Caring sons: Blindside of masculism and gender analysis of care*. Keisho-shobo. [Published in Japanese].

Hounoki, K., & Okada, J. (2015). What the earthquake has done to women's labour. *The Bulletin of the Society for the Study of Working Women, 59*, 66–81. [Published in Japanese].

Ikeda, K. (2012). Understanding needs and concerns of affected women: Experiences of humanitarian and reconstruction workers in the great East Japan earthquake and tsunami. *Japanese Journal of International Society for Gender studies, 10*, 9–23. [Published in Japanese].

Ikeda, S. (2017). The problems on relaxing non-regular single women's insufficiency on life: They need over 3 million yen a year. In R. Kosugi, A. Suzuki, & T. Noyori (Eds.), *Poverty of single women: Work, life and social support of women in non-regular work*. Akashi Shoten.

Ikeda, S. (2019). Women's employment status and family responsibility in Japan: Focusing on the breadwinner role. *Japan Labor Issues, 3*(17), 47–55.

Iki, N. (2011). *The development of women's labour policy in Japan, No. 9*. [Published in Japanese].

Imada, S. (1991). Careers for women and the future way of working life. *The Japanese Journal of Labour Studies, 381*, 12–24. [Published in Japanese].

Imada, S. (1996). Women's employment and job continuity. *The Japanese Journal of Labour Studies, 433*, 37–48. [Published in Japanese].

Imada, S., & Ikeda, S. (2007). The problem of women's job continuity and the childcare leave system. *Japan Labor Review, 4*(2), 139–60.

Immigration Service Agency of Japan. (2020). *2020 immigration control and residency management.*

Immigration Service Agency of Japan. (2021). *Efforts for acceptance of foreign nationals and harmonious coexistence.* [Published in Japanese].

Improvement of Personnel Management and Conversion of Employment Status for Part-Time Workers and Fixed-Term Workers Act. (2020).

Inagami, T. (2005). *Post-industrial society and Japanese corporate society.* MINERVA Shobo. [Published in Japanese].

Iwata, M., & Osawa, M. (Eds.). (2015). *Why do women quit their jobs? From the trajectories of 5155 women.* Sei-Kyu-Sha.

Iyotani, T. (Ed.). (2013). *The experience of mobility: The challenges of 'immigration' research in Japan.* Yushindo. [Published in Japanese].

Japan Business Federation. (2014). *Action plan for women's participation: Improving corporate competitiveness and sustainable economic growth.* www.keidanren.or.jp/policy/2014/029.html

Japan Business Federation. (2016). *Basic concept for promoting the acceptance of foreign human resources.* [Published in Japanese]. www.keidanren.or.jp/policy/2016/110.html

Japan Institute for Labour Policy and Training (JILPT). (2015). *Combining work and care.* Research Reports No. 170. [Published in Japanese].

Japan Institute for Labour Policy and Training (JILPT). (2020). *Combining work and care under the re-familization of elderly care in Japan.* Research Reports No. 204. [Published in Japanese].

Japan Student Services Organization. (2019). *Survey on study abroad of Japanese students.* [Published in Japanese]. www.studyinjapan.go.jp/ja/statistics/nippon/index.html

Japan Student Services Organization. (2020). *Annual survey of international students in Japan.* [Published in Japanese]. www.studyinjapan.go.jp/ja/statistics/nenkan/index.html

Japan Student Services Organization. (2021). *Outline of survey on living conditions of privately-funded international students.* [Published in Japanese].

Japanese Association for Migration Studies. (2018). *Emigration and the Japanese: Migrants' history, present, and future.* Akashi-shoten.

Kawaguchi, A. (2008). *Gender inequality in economic status.* Keisoshobo.

Kong L. (2020). Current status of acceptance of technical intern trainees in the fishery processing industry in Southern Hokkaido and the possibility of shifting to specified skilled workers. *Kaihatsu Kouhou, 688*, 14–17. [Published in Japanese].

Konno, M. (2000). *The creation of office lady: Gender as meaning world.* Keiso-shobo. [Published in Japanese].

Kosugi, R., & Miyamoto, M. (Eds.). (2015). *Women in poverty: Exclusion from work and home.* Keiso Shobo.

Kosugi, R., Suzuki, A., & Noyori, T. (Eds.). (2017). *Poverty of single women: Work, life and social support of women in non-regular work.* Akashi Shoten.

Levonian, M. (2013). Contemporary women's employment in Japan: The effects of state-mandated gender roles, wars, and Japan. *CMC Senior Theses.* Paper 618.

Ministry of Economic, Trade and Industry. (2003). *Women's participation and performance of companies: Report of the gender equality study group.* [Published in Japanese]. warp.da.ndl.go.jp/info:ndljp/pid/1052065/www.meti.go.jp/kohosys/press/0004204/1/030627danjo-honbun.pdf

Ministry of Foreign Affairs. (2020). *Annual report of statistics on Japanese nationals overseas.*

Ministry of Health, Labour and Welfare. (2020a). *Employment status of foreigners.*

Ministry of Health, Labour and Welfare. (2020b). *Overview of the accepting of candidates for foreign nurses and care workers based on EPA.* [Published in Japanese].

Ministry of Health, Labour and Welfare and Immigration Service Agency of Japan. (2021). *Technical intern training system operation procedure.* [Published in Japanese].

Ministry of Internal Affairs and Communications. (2015). *White paper on information and communications in Japan.* [Published in Japanese]. www.soumu.go.jp/johotsusintokei/whitepaper/ja/h27/html/nc231120.html

Ministry of Internal Affairs and Communications. (2016). *Survey on time use and leisure activities 2016.* [Published in Japanese].

Ministry of Internal Affairs and Communications. (2020a). *Annual report on the labour force survey.* [Published in Japanese].

Ministry of Internal Affairs and Communications. (2020b). *Reiwa 2nd year information and communication white paper.* [Published in Japanese].

Ministry of Justice. (2020). *Statistics of foreign residents.* [Published in Japanese].

Ministry of Land, Infrastructure, Transport and Tourism. (2020). *White paper on land, infrastructure, transport and tourism in Japan, 2020.* [Published in Japanese]. www.mlit.go.jp/statistics/hakusyo.mlit.r2.html

Nagai, A. (2020). Marital relationship on paid work and domestic work. *Journal of Japanese Labor Studies, 719,* 38–45.

Nagata, H. (2018). People supporting Japanese-made clothes-making. In K. Tsuzaki (Ed.). *Changes in industrial structure and foreign workers: The actual conditions and historical perspectives of the labor site.* Akashi Syoten. [Published in Japanese].

Nagayoshi, K. (2020). *Immigration and Japanese society: Facts and future.* Chuo Koron Shin-Sha. [Published in Japanese].

Naito, S. (2008). *Regulation on supporting work–family balance, supporting work and child care: Supporting child rearing in Japan,* Vol. 2. Gyosei. [Published in Japanese].

Nihon Keizai Shimbun. (2018a, December 13). *174 People died in 8 years of trainees, Ministry of Justice tabulation, many unknown background.* [Published in Japanese]. www.nikkei.com/article/DGXMZO38898420T11C18A2CC1000

Nihon Keizai Shimbun. (2018b, November 18). *Motivation for disappearance of technical intern trainees 'low wage' 67% survey by Ministry of Justice.* [Published in Japanese]. www.nikkei.com/article/DGXMZO37904810X11C18A1EA3000

Ogasawara, Y. (1998). *Office ladies and salaried men: Power, gender, and work in Japanese companies.* University of California Press.

Ogasawara, Y. (2009). Seibetsu-yakuwari ishiki no tagensei to chichi-oyano shigoto to ikuji no chousei (Consciousness on gender role and father's reconciliation between work and childcare). *Journal of Household Studies, 81,* 34–42.

Okada, H. (2012). Facing opportunistic large-scale dismissal and anxious living: Working women assailed by personnel retrenchment in the afflicted Miyagi Prefecture. *The Bulletin of the Society for the Study of Working Women, 56,* 84–89. [Published in Japanese].

Part-time Workers Act. (1993). https://www.mhlw.go.jp/english/policy/employ-labour/fixed-term-workers/dl/210401-01.pdf

Prime Ministers' Office of Japan. (2017). *The action plan for the realization of work style reform.* [Published in Japanese]. www.kantei.go.jp/jp/headline/pdf/20170328/01.pdf

Promotion of Female Participation and Career Advancement in the Workplace Act. (2015).

Overview. www.mhlw.go.jp/english/wp/wp-hw13/dl/07e.pdf

Reconstruction Agency. (2021a). *Current status of reconstruction and future efforts.* [Published in Japanese]. www.reconstruction.go.jp/topics/main-cat1/sub-cat1-1/20211201_02_genjoutorikumi.pdf

Reconstruction Agency. (2021b). *Reconstruction from the perspective of gender equality: Reference casebook.* [Published in Japanese]. www.reconstruction.go.jp/topics/main-cat1/sub-cat1-16/20130626164021.html

Saiki, Y. (2015). *Migrant women and human rights: From a sociological perspective.* Syougakusya. [Published in Japanese].

Sato, H., & Takeishi, E. (Eds.). (2008). *Work–life balance as managemental strategy: Forward companies growth.* Keiso-shobo.

Satoh, S. (2013). Foreign workers in the apparel industry in Japan. *Journal of Ohara Institute for Social Research, 652,* 46–62. [Published in Japanese].

Sunai, N. (2019). *Dorei roudou: Betonamu-jin ginoujissyuusei no zittai [Slave labor: The actual condition of Vietnamese technical intern trainees].* Kadensya.

Sunai, N. (2020). Vietnamese female technical intern trainees and pregnancy challenges: Corona, continued sexual management, right to be deprived. *F visions, 2,* 70–73. Asia-Japan Women's Resource Center. [Published in Japanese].

Sunai, N. (2021). Possibility of multi-layered difficulties and solidarity before and after Corona: From a survey of Vietnamese technical intern trainees. In E. Suzuki (Ed.), *Andaa korona no imin-tachi: Nihonsyakai no zeijyakusei ga arawareta basyo [Immigrants under COVID-19 pandemic: Where the vulnerability of Japanese society has appeared]* (pp. 52–73). Akashi Syoten.

Suzuki, E. (Ed.). (2021). *Andaa korona no imin-tachi: Nihonsyakai no zeijyakusei ga arawareta basyo [Immigrants under COVID-19 pandemic: Where the vulnerability of Japanese society has appeared].* Akashi Syoten.

Suzuki, N. (2017). Career development processes and the gender role of foreign female employees: Working for Japanese companies: Interviews with those who have graduated from university in Japan. *Journal of Gender Studies, 20.* Ochanomizu University. [Published in Japanese].

Steinberg, C., & Nakane, M. (2012). *Can women save Japan?* IMF, Working Paper WP/12/248.

Takahashi, K. (2018). The future of the Japanese-style employment system: Continued long-term employment and the challenges it faces. *Japan Labor Issues, 2*(6), 6–15.

Takami, T. (2020a). Corona shock that hit full-time work. *JILPT Research Eye, 39.* English translation: Impact of the COVID-19 recession on full-time workers: Shortened work hours, working from home, and possible widening of income disparities. *Japan Labor Issues, 5*(28), January 2021.

Takami, T. (2020b). Who is working from home? Reading changes after 'emergency'. *JILPT Research Eye, 46.* [Published in Japanese].

Takami, T. (2021). A new form of work–life balance by working from home. *JILPT Research Eye, 57.* [Published in Japanese].

Takeishi, E. (2006). *Employment system and women's career.* Keiso Shobo. [Published in Japanese].

Takenobu, M. (2012). The barrier of 'women's care work' revealed through the disaster: Voices of working women in the afflicted area. *The Bulletin of the Society for the Study of Working Women, 56,* 64–74. [Published in Japanese].

Tazawa, Y. (2014). *Homeworking relieves your company: New strategy for encouraging employees.* Toyo Keizai Shinpo-sha Press. [Published in Japanese].

Tomohara, A. (2020). *The economics of immigration: From employment and economic growth to public safety, will Japan change?* Chuo Koron Shin-sha.

Trading Economics. (2021). *Japan labor force participation rate.* https://tradingeconomics.com/japan/labor-force-participation-rate#:~:text=Labor%20Force%20Participation%20Rate%20in%20Japan%20averaged%2063.73%20percent%20from,percent%20in%20December%20of%202012

Tsudome, M., & Saito, M. (2007). *White paper on male carers.* Kamogawa-Press. [Published in Japanese].

Tsutsui, J. (2014). Female labor participation and sexual division of labor: A consideration on the persistent male-breadwinner model. *The Monthly Journal of the Japan Institute of Labour, 56*(7), 70–83.

Tsuzaki, K. (Ed.). (2018). *Changes in industrial structure and foreign workers: The actual conditions and historical perspectives of the labor site.* Akashi Syoten. [Published in Japanese].

US Department of State. (2021). *Country reports on human rights 2020: Japan.* https://jp.usembassy.gov/ja/human-rights-report-2020-japan-ja

World Bank. (2020). *Japan — population, female (% of total)*. Retrieved from Trading Economics: https://tradingeconomics.com/japan/population-female-percent-of-total-wb-data.html

Yokoyama, F. (2002). *Postwar Japan's women's policy*. Keiso Shobo. [Published in Japanese].

Zhou, Y. (2014). *Single mother's working life and economical self-standing*. JILPT Research Publish Series, Japan Institute for Labor Policy and Training. [Published in Japanese].

Zhou, Y. (2021a). How women bear the brunt of COVID-19's damages on work. *Japan Labor Issues, 5*(28), 2–8.

Zhou, Y. (2021b). How women bear the brunt of COVID-19's damages on work (continued): The gender gap in employment recovery. *Japan Labor Issues, 5*(29), 2–10.

Zhou, Y. (2021c). How women bear the brunt of COVID-19's damages on work (continued): Part II: Catch up with men on the employment recovery. *Japan Labor Issues, 5*(31), 11–19.

Zhou, Y. (2021d). Women under COVID-19 pandemic: From both macro and micro statistics. Labor policy forum 2021: Impact of the new Corona on women's employment and life and how to support it. *JILPT*. [Published in Japanese]. www.jil.go.jp/event/ro_forum/20210629/resume/01-kenkyu-shu.pdf

Japan in focus: Working women and men's changing family responsibilities

Act on Advancement of Measures to Support Raising Next-Generation Children (Next-Generation Act). (2003). Revised 2015. www.mhlw.go.jp/english/policy/children/children-childrearing/dl/150407-01.pdf

Child Care and Family Care Leave Act. (1995). *Outline*. www.mhlw.go.jp/english/policy/children/work-family/dl/190410-01e.pdf

Equal Employment Opportunity Between Men and Women Act (EEO Act). (1995). www.mhlw.go.jp/bunya/koyoukintou/pamphlet/dl/01_en.pdf

Fujisaki, H. (2009). The long-term care insurance and defamilization and refamilization of elderly care. *Japanese Journal of Welfare Studies, 6*, 41–57.

Hirayama, R. (2014). *The coming of age of 'son's elderly care': 28 carers site*. Kobunsha-Shinsho.

Hirayama, R. (2017). *Caring son's: Blindside of masculism and gender analysis of care.* Keisho-shobo.

Ikeda, S. (2021). *Combining work and family care.* Diversity Management Series. Chuo-Keizai-Sha.

Matsuda, S. (2002). The directions of promoting fathers' commitment to childcare. In National Institute for Social Security and Demography (Ed.), *Child care support in a childless society* (pp. 313–30). University of Tokyo Press. [Published in Japanese].

Nagai, A. (2020). Relationship between husbands and wives around work and housework. *Japanese Journal of Labor Studies, 719,* 38–45. [Published in Japanese].

Saito, S. (2020). *The problem with men's child care leave: The atmospheres in the workplace which prevent male workers from taking the leave.* Seikyu-Sha. [Published in Japanese].

Sodei, T. (1989). Women and elderly care. In M. Ozawa, N. Kumura, & H. Ibu (Eds.), *Women's lifecycle: Comparing income security between Japan and US* (pp. 127–149). University of Tokyo Press. [Published in Japanese].

Sodei, T. (1995). The issues and meanings of the family care leave system. *Japanese Journal of Labor Studies, 427,* 12–20.

Takami, T. (2020). Who is working from home? Reading changes after 'emergency'. *Japanese Institute for Labor Policy and Training (JILPT) Research Eye, 46.* [Published in Japanese].

Tsudome, M., & Saito, M. (2007). *White paper on male carers.* Kamogawa-Press. [Published in Japanese].

Yamada, M. (1999). *The age of the parasite single.* Chikuma-Shinsho.

Yamato, R. (2008). *The making of life-long carers in Japan: Reconstructed generational relationship and strong rooted gender relationships.* Gakubun-Sha. [Published in Japanese].

Zhou, Y. (2014). *Single mothers' working life and economic independence.* Japan Institute for Labor Policy and Training (JILPT). [Published in Japanese].

Zhou, Y. (2019). *Full-time housewives in poverty.* Shincho-sha. [Published in Japanese].

4. WORKING WOMEN IN CHINA

AliResearch. (2019). *How digital platform enterprises contribute to sustainable development in digital economy — the case of Alibaba Group.* www.aliresearch.com/en/Reports/Reportsdetails?articleCode=21878

Bolton, P. (2021). *Higher education student numbers.* House of Commons Library.

Cao, J., Cumming, D., & Wang, X. (2015). One-child policy and family firms in China. *Journal of Corporate Finance, 33,* 317–29.

Chen, X. F. (1994). The social impact of China's one-child policy. *Harvard Asia Pacific Review, 23*(2), 74–76.

Chow, E. N., & Zuo, Y. (2011). Globalization and locality: The gendered impact on the economic crisis on intersectionality, migration and work in China. In E. Ngan-ling Chow, M. Texler Segal & L. Tan (Eds.), *Analyzing gender, intersectionality and multiple inequalities: Global, transnational and local contexts* (pp. 95–120). Emerald.

Chow, E. N., Segal, M. T., & Tan, L. (2011). *Analyzing gender, intersectionality, and multiple inequalities: Global, transnational and local contexts.* Emerald.

Constitution of the People's Republic of China (PRC). (1982). Adopted at the Fifth Session of the Fifth National People's Congress on 4 December 1982. Instrument A1. www.elegislation.gov.hk/hk/A1!en.assist.pdf

Cooke, F. L. (2017). The two-child policy in China: A blessing or a curse for the employment of female university graduates. In D. Grimshaw, C. Fagan, G. Hebson & I. Tavora (Eds.), *Making work more equal: A new market segmentation approach* (pp. 227–245). Manchester University Press.

Cooke, F. L., & Xiao, Y. (2014). Gender roles and organizational HR practices: The case of women's careers in accountancy and consultancy firms in China. *Human Resource Management, 53*(1), 23–44.

Elliot, L. (2020, December 26). China to overtake US as world's biggest economy by 2028, report predicts. *The Guardian.* www.theguardian.com/world/2020/dec/26/china-to-overtake-us-as-worlds-biggest-economy-by-2028-report-predicts

Employment Promotion Law. (2008). www.lawinfochina.com/display.aspx?lib=law&id=6382&CGid=

Falbo, T., & Hooper, S. Y. (2015). China's only children and psychopathology:

A quantitative synthesis. *American Journal of Orthopsychiatry, 85*(3), 259–74.

Fan, S., Xiao, C., Zhang, Y., Li, Y., Wang, X., & Wang, L. (2020). How does the two-child policy affect the sex ratio at birth in China? A cross-sectional study. *BMC Public Health, 20*(789), 1–11.

Galvez, D. (2012, December 6). The changing of the guard: China's new leadership. *Knowledge.* https://knowledge.insead.edu/economics-politics/the-changing-of-the-guard-chinas-new-leadership-2359

Global Entrepreneurship Monitor. (2020). *Global entrepreneurship monitor 2019/2020 global report.* Global Entrepreneurship Research Association. www.gemconsortium.org/report/gem-2019-2020-global-report

Hernandez, L., Nunn, N., & Warnecke, T. (2012). Female entrepreneurship in China: Opportunity-or necessity-based? *International Journal of Entrepreneurship and Small Business, 15*(4), 411–34.

Hesketh, T., Lu, L., & Xing, Z. W. (2005). The effect of China's one-child family policy after 25 years. *The New England Journal of Medicine, 353*(11), 1171–76.

Human Rights Watch. (2018). *'Only men need apply': Gender discrimination in job advertisements in China.* www.hrw.org/report/2018/04/23/only-men-need-apply/gender-discrimination-job-advertisements-china

International Labour Organization (ILO). (2018). *Care work and care jobs: For the future of decent work.*

Kuhn, P., Shen, K., & Zhang, S. (2020). Gender-targeted job ads in the recruitment process: Facts from a Chinese job board. *Journal of Development Economics, 147*, 102531.

Labor Law. (1994, revised in 2020). www.lawinfochina.com/Display.aspx?LookType=3&Lib=law&Cgid=9587&Id=705&SearchKeyword=&SearchCKey-word=&paycode=

Law on the Protection of Rights and Interests of Women. (1992, revised in 2005). www.china.org.cn/english/government/207405.htm

Liu, Y. L. (2020). Is Covid-19 changing our relationships? *BBC.* www.bbc.com/future/article/20200601-how-is-covid-19-is-affecting-relationships

Lou, K. (2021, May 20). 216,000 Chinese students study in UK as a result of US visa restrictions. *Global Times.* www.globaltimes.cn/page/202105/1224057.shtml

Matthew, B. (2014). What motivates Chinese women to study in the UK and how do they perceive their experience? *Higher Education, 68*(1), 47–68.

McAdam, M., Crowley, C., & Harrison, R. T. (2020). Digital girl: Cyberfeminism and the emancipatory potential of digital entrepreneurship in emerging economies. *Small Business Economics, 55*(2), 349–62.

Moelders, T. (2019). Rethinking gender: Feminist perspectives on Sustainable Development Goals in the light of (re)productivity. *Gaia, 28*(2), 95–99.

National Bureau of Statistics. (2020). *Women and men in China: Facts and figures 2019.* National Bureau of Statistics, Department of Social, Science, Technology and Cultural Statistics.

Pettersson, K. (2012). Support for women's entrepreneurship: A Nordic spectrum. *International Journal of Gender and Entrepreneurship, 4*(1), 4–19.

Regulation Governing Labour Protection for Female Staff and Workers, Order of the State Council (No. 619). (1988). http://english.mofcom.gov.cn/aarticle/lawsdata/chineselaw/200211/20021100050536.html

Reuters. (2021). *China was largest recipient of FDI in 2020: Report.* www.reuters.com/article/us-china-economy-fdi-idUSKBN29T0TC

Sison, A. J. G., Ferrero, I., & Redín, D. M. (2020). Some virtue ethics implications from aristotelian and confucian perspectives on family and business. *Journal of Business Ethics, 165*(2), 241–54.

Statista. (2021). *Monthly surveyed urban unemployment rate in China from March 2019 to March 2021.* www.statista.com/statistics/1109881/surveyed-monthly-unemployment-rate-in-china

Strom, R. D., Strom, S. K., & Xie, Q. (1996). Parent expectations In China. *International Journal of Sociology of the Family, 26*(1), 37–49.

Trankmann, B. (2020). *How gender inequality harms Our COVID-19 recovery: Views from China.* www.cn.undp.org/content/china/en/home/ourperspective/ourperspectivearticles/2020/how-gender-inequality-harms-our-covid-19-recovery--views-from-ch.html

UN Women. (2021). *Constitution of the People's Republic of China 1982, as amended to 2018.* https://constitutions.unwomen.org/en/countries/asia/china?provisioncategory=67a14b9bc7ae451b9ff2bdd8050c3561

UN Working Group on Discrimination Against Women and Girls. (2020, April 16). *Report on women's human rights in the changing world of work.* Presented at the UN General Assembly Human Rights Council 44th session, 15 June–3 July 2020. www.ohchr.org/

en/calls-for-input/reports/2020/report-womens-human-rights-changing-world-work

Warnecke, T. (2016). Informal sector entrepreneurship for women in China and India: Building networks, gaining recognition, and obtaining support. *Journal of Small Business and Entrepreneurship, 28*(6), 479–91.

Woodhams, C., Lupton, B., & Xian, H. (2009). The persistence of gender discrimination in China — evidence from recruitment advertisements. *International Journal of Human Resource Management, 20*(10), 2084–109.

Woodhams, C., Xian, H., & Lupton, B. (2015). Women managers' careers in China: Theorizing the influence of gender and collectivism. *Human Resource Management, 54*(6), 913–31.

World Bank. (2016). *Population ages 65 and above (% of total population), China.* https://data.worldbank.org/indicator/SP.POP.65UP.TO.ZS?locations=CN

World Bank. (2019). *Labor force, female (% of total labor force), China, 2019.* https://data.worldbank.org/indicator/SL.TLF.CACT.FE.ZS?locations=CN

World Bank. (2020a). *Fertility rate, total (births per woman) China.* https://data.worldbank.org/indicator/SP.DYN.TFRT.IN?locations=CN

World Bank. (2020b). *Land area — sq. km (China).* https://data.worldbank.org/indicator/AG.LND.TOTL.K2?locations=CN

World Bank. (2020c). *Population, female (% of total population) — China.* https://data.worldbank.org/indicator/SP.POP.TOTL.FE.ZS?locations=CN

World Economic Forum. (2020). *The global gender gap report 2020.*

Xian, H., Atkinson, C., & Meng-Lewis, Y. (2022). How work–life conflict affects employee outcomes of Chinese only-children academics: The moderating roles of gender and family structure. *Personnel Review, 51*(2), 731–49. https://doi.org/10.1108/PR-05-2020-0330

Xian, H., Jiang, N., & McAdam, M. (2021). Negotiating the female successor-leader role within family business succession in China. *International Small Business Journal, 39*(2), 157–83.

Yan, A., & Zhou, L. (2015, May 22). The rise of she-commerce: Chinese women rock the trend as online entrepreneurs. *South China Morning Post.*

Yang, Q., & Huang, J. (2020). Content analysis of family policy instruments to promote the sustainable development of families in China from 1989–2019. *Sustainability, 12*(2), 693–713.

Yang, S., & Li, A. (2009). Legal protection against gender discrimination in the workplace in China. *Gender and Development, 17*(2), 295–308.

Yu, H., & Cui, L. (2019). China's e-commerce: Empowering rural women? *The China Quarterly, 238*, 418–37.

Zhang, S., & Xu, C. L. (2020). The making of transnational distinction: An embodied cultural capital perspective on Chinese women students' mobility. *British Journal of Sociology of Education, 41*(8), 1251–67.

Zhang, X., Guo, F., & Zhai, Z. (2019). China's demographic future under the new two-child policy. *Population Research and Policy Review, 38*(4), 537–63.

Zhong, X., & Peng, M. (2020). The grandmothers' farewell to childcare provision under china's two-child policy: Evidence from Guangzhou middle-class families. *Social Inclusion, 8*(2), 36–46.

Zhao, Y., & Yang, Y. (2015). Entrepreneurship and new venture creation in China: Focusing on ICT sectors. In R. Lèbre La Rovere, L. de Magalhães Ozório & L. de Jesus Melo (Eds.), *Entrepreneurship in BRICS* (pp. 91–103). Springer.

5. WORKING WOMEN IN CAMBODIA

ActionAid. (2021). *Socio-economic impacts of Covid-19 on workers in informal sector of Cambodia.* ActionAid.

Baldwin, R., & Venables, A. (2013). Spiders and snakes: Offshoring and agglomeration in the global economy. *Journal of International Economics, 90*(2), 245–54.

Barrientos, S. (2019). *Gender and work in global value chains: Capturing the gains?* Cambridge University Press.

Brody, C., Chhoun, P., Sovannary, T., Fehrenbacher, A., Moran, A., Swendeman, D., & Yi, S. (2021). Improving access to health services for female entertainment workers in Cambodia: Findings from the mobile link randomised controlled trial. *The Lancet Global Health, 9*, S15.

CamboJA. (2021, June 3). Most new COVID-19 infections found among factory workers. https://cambojanews.com/most-new-covid-19-infections-found-among-factory-workers

CARE. (2020). *Rapid gender analysis during Covid-19 pandemic, Mekong sub-regional report: Cambodia, Lao People's Democratic Republic, Myanmar, Thailand and Viet Nam.*

Chea, V. (2021, May 10). Effects of remittances on household poverty and inequality in Cambodia. *Journal of the Asia Pacific Economy*, 1–25. https://doi.org/10.1080/1354786 0.2021.1905200

Clarke, D. (2021). *Moving the needle: Gender equality and decent work in Asia's garment sector.* ILO.

Ford, M., Gillan, M., & Ward, K. (2021). Authoritarian innovations in labor governance: The case of Cambodia. *Governance, 34*(4), 1255–71.

Ford, M., & Ward, K. (2021). Covid-19 in Southeast Asia: Implications for workers and unions. *Journal of Industrial Relations, 63*(3), 432–50.

Heng, P. (2019). *Preparing Cambodia's workforce for a digital economy.* Konrad-Adenauer-Stiftung.

Hughes, C. (2003). *The political economy of Cambodia's transition: 1991–2001.* Routledge.

Human Rights Watch. (2021, June 8). *Cambodia: Lockdowns hit low-income families hard.* www.hrw.org/news/2021/06/08/cambodia-lockdowns-hit-low-income-families-hard

International Labour Organization (ILO). (2006). *Decent work for women and men in the informal economy: Profile and good practices in Cambodia.* www.ilo.org/wcmsp5/ groups/public/---asia/---ro-bangkok/documents/publication/wcms_bk_pb_134_ en.pdf

Jack, M. (2020). The socio-spatial installed base: Ride-hailing applications, parking associations, and precarity in tuk tuk driving in Phnom Penh, Cambodia. *The Information Society, 36*(5), 252–65.

Khmer Times. (2021, June 9). Thailand extends Cambodian migrant workers' deadline. www.khmertimeskh.com/50870636/thailand-extends-cambodian-migrant-workers-deadline

Kunmakara, M. (2021, June 3). Remittances fall 17% to $1.2B in 2020: NBC Data. *Phnom Penh Post.* www.phnompenhpost.com/business/remittances-fall-17-12b-2020-nbc-data

Kunthear, M. (2019, June 17). Ministry supports domestic workers. *Khmer Times.* https:// www.khmertimeskh.com/50614792/ministry-supports-domestic-workers

Labour law. (1997). www.ilo.org/dyn/travail/docs/701/labour

LIRNEasia. (2018). *After access: ICT access and use in Cambodia and the Global South.* Presentation.

Ministry of Education, Youth and Sport. (2021). *Cambodia Covid-19 joint education needs assessment.* Ministry of Education, Youth and Sport and the Education Sector Working Group.

National Institute of Statistics. (2019). *General population census of the Kingdom of Cambodia 2008: National report on final census results.* Ministry of Planning.

National Institute of Statistics. (2020a). *General population census of the Kingdom of Cambodia 2019: National report on final census results.* Ministry of Planning.

National Institute of Statistics. (2020b). *Report of Cambodia socio-economic survey 2019/20.* National Institute of Statistics.

Ngo, S., Khon, L., Sour, M., Nuth, S., & Khun, S. (2021). *The Covid-19 pandemic and workers in Cambodia: Magnitude of impact on suspended workers and implication for policy and programme intervention.* Centre for Policy Studies.

Norén-Nilsson, A. (2017). Elections and emerging citizenship in Cambodia. In W. Berenschot, H. S. Nordholt, & L. Bakker (Eds.), *Citizenship and democratization in Southeast Asia* (pp. 68–95). Brill.

OECD, and Cambodia Development Resource Institute. (2017). *Interrelations between public policies, migration and development in Cambodia.* OECD Publishing.

Oka, C. (2016). Improving working conditions in garment supply chains: The role of unions in Cambodia. *British Journal of Industrial Relations, 54*(3), 647–72.

Phillips, N. (2017). Power and inequality in the global political economy. *International Affairs, 93*(2), 429–44.

Serrano, M., & Nuon, V. (2018). *Unions and development in Cambodia.* Friedrich Ebert Stiftung.

Strickler, C., & Pou, S. (2016). *Labour rights for female construction workers: Baseline assessment report.* CARE Cambodia.

US Department of Labor. (2019). *2019 Findings on the worst forms of child labor: Cambodia.* Bureau of International Labor Affairs.

Ward, K. (2017). Cambodia: Managing work and care in a post-conflict context. In M. Baird, M. Ford, & E. Hill (Eds.), *Women, work and care in the Asia-Pacific* (pp. 102–17). Routledge.

Ward, K. (2022). Gender regimes and Cambodian labour unions. *Gender and Society, 36*(4), 578–601. https://doi.org/10.1177/08912432221102155

Ward, K., & Ford, M. (2021). Labour and electoral politics in Cambodia. *Journal of Contemporary Asia.* https://doi.org/10.1080/00472336.2021.1963810

Ward, K., & Mouyly, V. (2016). Employment relations and political transition in Cambodia. *Journal of Industrial Relations, 58*(2), 258–72.

World Bank. (2020). *Cambodia economic update May 2020: Cambodia in the time of Covid-19.*

You, S. (2020). *A Khmer mother, wife, unionist, and woman: Gender analysis of leadership in Cambodia's union.* Solidarity Center.

6. WORKING WOMEN IN INDIA

Abraham, V. (2017). Stagnant employment growth — last three years may have been the worst. *Economic and Political Weekly, 52*(38), 13–17.

Acharya, M. (2008). Global integration of subsistence economies and women's empowerment. In I. Bakker & R. Silvey (Eds.), *Beyond states and markets: The challenges of social reproduction.* Routledge.

Azim Premaji University. (2021). *State of Working in India.* https://cse. azimpremjiuniversity.edu.in/state-of-working-india/swi-2021

Babu, R. P. (2004). 'Cyber coolies' in BPO: Insecurities and vulnerabilities of non-standard work. *Economic and Political Weekly, 39*(5), 492–97.

Bakker, I. & Gill, S. (2019). Rethinking power, production, and social reproduction: Toward variegated social reproduction. *Capital & Class, 43*(4), 503–23. https://doi. org/10.1177%2F0309816819880783

Bakker, I., & Silvey, R. (2008). Social reproduction and global transformations — from the everyday to the global. In I. Bakker & R. Silvey (Eds.), *Beyond states and markets: The challenges of social reproduction.* Routledge.

Banerjee, M. (2019, June 7). What work choices are Indian women making and why? *Wire.* https://thewire.in/women/indian-women-work-care-informal-sector

Bhalla, S. (1989, October 28). Technological change and women workers: Evidence from the expansionary phase in Haryana agriculture. *Economic and Political Weekly, 24*(43), WS67-WS73+WS75-WS78.

Bhamra, A. (2018). *India's Green Economy barometer, Delhi: Development alternatives.* www.greeneconomycoalition.org.

Bhattacharya, D. (2002). The material impact of economic globalisation on women: Exploding few myths. In V. Patel (Ed.), *Discourse on women and empowerment* (pp. 75–107). The Women Press.

Bloomberg. (2021). Covid-19: Poorer Indian women lost more jobs, ate less amid the pandemic. www.bloomberg.com/news/articles/2021-07-05/poorer-indian-women-lost-more-jobs-ate-less-amid-the-pandemic

Census of India. (2021). *India population clock (current population).* https://countrymeters.info/en/India

Chakraborty, S. (2020). *Working paper on Digital India.* ISST Working Paper series. www.isstindia.org/publications/1595487058_pub_Digital_India_Working_Paper_Shiney_Chakraborty__-_Final_1.pdf

Chandrasekhar, C. P., & Ghosh, J. (2015) *Growth, employment patterns and inequality in Asia* (ebook). International Labour Organization. http://ilo.org/wcmsp5/groups/public/---asia/---ro-bangkok/documents/publication/wcms_334063.pdf

Chikarmane, P., & Narayan, L. (2006). *Top of Form.*

Chikarmane, P., & Narayan, L. (2005). *Organising the unorganised: A case study of the Kagad Kach Patra Kashtakari Panchayat-trade union of waste-pickers.* Women in Informal Employment: Globalizing and Organizing (WIEGO). www.wiego.org/sites/default/files/migrated/resources/files/Chikarmane_Narayan_case-kkpkp.pdf

Committee on Status of Women in India. (1974). *Towards Equality Report, New Delhi: Government of India.* https://indianculture.gov.in/towards-equality-report-committee-status-women-india

Constitution of India. (2020). *List of All Articles (1–395) and Parts (1–22).* Government of India, Ministry of Law and Justice, Legislative Department. https://legislative.gov.in/sites/default/files/COI.pdf

Contract Labour (Regulation and Abolition) Act. (1970). www.indiacode.nic.in/handle/123456789/1467?sam_handle=123456789/1362

Dasgupta, S., & Singh, S. (2016). Introduction. In S. Dasgupta, & S. Singh (Eds.),

Transformation of women at work in Asia: An unfinished development agenda. Sage Publications India.

De Stefano, V., Ilda, D., Charalampos, S., & Mathias, W. (2021, March). *Platform work and the employment relationship.* International Labour Organization. www.ilo.org/wcmsp5/groups/public/---ed_protect/---protrav/---travail/documents/publication/wcms_777866.pdf

Desai, S., & Joshi, O. (2019). The paradox of declining female work participation in an era of economic growth. *The Indian Journal of Labour Economics, 62*(1), 55–71.

Deshpande, A. (2022). The Covid-19 pandemic and gendered division of paid work, domestic chores and leisure: Evidence from India's first wave. https://pubmed.ncbi.nlm.nih.gov/35422589

Dewan, R., Sehgal, R., Kanchi, A., & Swati, R. (2019). *Invisible work, invisible workers: The sub-economies of unpaid work and paid work — action research on women's unpaid labour.* UN Women and ActionAid. www.actionaidindia.org/wp-content/uploads/2018/07/Invisible-Work-Invisible-Workers-correction_e-book.pdf

Dey, I., Singh, S., & Panda, S. S. (2022). *Social norms, gender and collective behaviour: Development paradigms in India.* Palgrave Macmillan.

Dixit, M., & Chavan, D. (2020). Gendering the COVID-19 pandemic: Women locked and down. *Economic and Political Weekly, 55*(17), 13–16.

Dyson, T. (2018). *A population history of India: From the first modern people to the present day.* Oxford University Press.

Embree, A. T., Hay, S. N. & De Bary, W. T. (1988). *Sources of Indian tradition.* Columbia University Press.

Encyclopaedia Britannica. (2021). *Untouchable social class, India: Alternate titles: Dalit, Harijan, Panchama, Scheduled Caste, exterior caste.* www.britannica.com/topic/untouchable

Equal Remuneration Act. (1976). Ministry of Labour and Employment. https://labour.gov.in

Ernst and Young (EY) India. (2020). *Gender study to identify constraints on female participation in skills training and labour market in India.*

Factories Act. (1948). Labour Commissioner. https://labour.delhi.gov.in

Floro, M. S., & Hoppe, H. (2008). Towards globalization with a human face engendering policy coherence for development. In I. Bakker & R. Silvey (Eds.), *Beyond states and markets: The challenges of social reproduction* (pp. 34–52). Routledge.

Ghosh, A., Ramchandran, R., & Zaidi, M. (2021). *Women workers in the gig economy in India: An exploratory study.* Indian Social Studies Trust.

Gothoskar, S. (2000). Teleworking and gender. *Economic and Political Weekly, 35*(28), 2293–98.

Government of India (GoI). (1950). *Constitution of India, Article 51 (A)(e).* www.legalserviceindia.com/legal/article-5780-fundamental-duties-in-india-article-51-a-.html

Government of India (GoI). (1974). *Towards equality report (1974) report of the committee on status of women in India.*

Government of India (GoI). (2020). *The Constitution of India.* Ministry of Law and Justice, Legislative Department. https://legislative.gov.in/sites/default/files/COI.pdf

Gupta, N. (2020, February 20). *Indian IT industry attracts more women, but many exit within first 5 years in the job.* https://theprint.in/pageturner/excerpt/indian-it-industry-attracts-more-women-but-many-exit-within-first-5-years-in-the-job/368504/

Harriss-White, B., & Prakash, A. (2019). Social discrimination and economic citizenship. In S. Janakarajan, L. Venkatachalam, & R. Maria Saleth (Eds.), *The Indian economy in transition: Essays in honour of CT Kurien* (pp. 294–26). Sage Publications.

India Skills Report. (2021). *Key insights into the post-Covid landscape of talent demand and supply in India.* All India Council for Technology Education (AICTE), Association of Indian Universities (AIU) and United Nations Development Programme. https://indiaeducationforum.org/pdf/ISR-2021.pdf

Indo Global Social Service Organisation (IGSSS). (2019). *A mirage: Assessment of Swachh Bharat Abhiyan and SWM Rules 2016: Waste pickers perspective across India.* The Alliance of Indian Waste-pickers and IGSSS. https://igsss.org/wp-content/uploads/2020/01/A-Mirage_22Nov1.pdf

International Labour Organization (ILO). (2017). *Indian labour market update.* www.ilo.org/newdelhi/whatwedo/publications/WCMS_568701/lang--en/index.htm

International Labour Organization (ILO). (2021). *Labour force participation rate, female (% of female population ages 15+).* ILOSTAT Database. https://data.worldbank.org/indicator/SL.TLF.CACT.FE.ZS?locations=IN

International Trade Union Confederation (ITUC). (2016, January 18). *Frontlines report*

2016 — scandal. www.ituc-csi.org/frontlines-report-2016-scandal

Jain, J. (2020, February 3). *India and its #MeToo movement in 2020: Where are we now?* https://feminisminindia.com/2020/02/03/india-metoo-movement-2020

Jasrotia, A., & Meena, J. (2021). Women, work and pandemic: An impact study of COVID-19 lockdown on working women in India. *Social Work and Policy, 15*(3), 282–91. https://doi.org/10.1111/aswp.12240

Joy, S. (2020, September 27). 4,300 cases of domestic violence reported with NCW since March. *Deccan Herald.* www.deccanherald.com/national/4300-cases-of-domestic-violence-reported-with-ncw-since-march-893807.html

Kamdar, B. (2020, July 31). Women left behind: India's falling female labor participation. *The Diplomat.* https://thediplomat.com/2020/07/women-left-behind-indias-falling-female-labor-participation

Kasliwal, R. (2021, May 28). *The case of missing women in India's formal economy.* ORF. www.orfonline.org/expert-speak/the-case-of-missing-women-in-indias-formal-economy

Kidangoor, A. (2020, November 1). 1 million women healthcare workers have been drafted to fight COVID-19 in India — for as little as $40 a month. *TIME.* https://time.com/5904706/india-female-healthcare-workers-covid19

Kumar, M. (2021, August 3). India's female labour participation rate falls to 16.1% as pandemic hits jobs. *Reuters.* www.reuters.com/world/india/indias-female-labour-participation-rate-falls-161-pandemic-hits-jobs-2021-08-03

Mahapatra, B., Bhattacharya, R., Atmavilas, Y., & Saggurti, N. (2018). Measuring vulnerability among female sex workers in India using a multidimensional framework. *PLoS One, 13*(9), e0204055. https://doi.org/10.1371/journal.pone.0204055

Makol, M. K. (2021, July 5). Poorer Indian women lost more jobs, ate less amid the pandemic. *Bloomberg.* https://economictimes.indiatimes.com/news/india/poorer-indian-women-lost-more-jobs-ate-less-amid-the-pandemic/articleshow/84137515.cms?from=mdr

Mamgain, R. P. (2021). Understanding labour market disruptions and job losses amidst COVID-19. *Journal of Social and Economic Development 23,* 301–19.

Maternity Benefit Act. (1961). Ministry of Labour & Employment. https://labour.gov.in

McKinsey Global Institute. (2018, May 1). *The power of parity: Advancing women's equality in India.* www.mckinsey.com/featured-insights/gender-equality/the-power-of-parity-advancing-womens-equality-in-india-2018

Mehrotra, S., & Parida. J. K. (2017). Why is the labour force participation of women declining in India? *World Development, 98*(C), 360–80.

Mehta, B. S., & Awasthi, I. C. (2019). *Women and labour market dynamics: New insights and evidences.* Springer.

Metcalf, B. D., & Metcalf, T. R. (2012). *A concise history of modern India.* Cambridge University Press.

Mhapsekar, J. (2006). Environment entrepreneurship programme for urban poor. In V. Patel & M. Karne (Eds.), *The macro economic policies and the Millennium Development Goals.* Gyan Publications.

Minimum Wages Act 1948. Ministry of Labour and Employment. https://labour.gov.in

Ministry of Human Resource Development (MHRD). (2020). *National education policy 2020.* Government of India. www.education.gov.in

Ministry of Labour and Employment. (1948). Minimum Wages Act, 1948. https://labour.gov.in

Ministry of Statistics and Programme Implementation (MoSPI). (2014). *Men and women in India. Chapter 4: Participation in economy, Delhi.* Government of India. http://mospi.nic.in/sites/default/files/reports_and_publication/cso_social_statices_division/Chapter_4_2014.pdf

Ministry of Statistics and Programme Implementation (MoSPI). (2017). *Periodic Labour Force Participation Survey, National Sample Survey Organisation Annual Report.* Government of India. https://mospi.gov.in

Ministry of Statistics and Programme Implementation (MoSPI). (2020). *The Time-Use Survey, Delhi.* Government of India. https://mospi.gov.in/web/mospi/time-use-survey

Ministry of Women and Child Development. (2019). *Integrated Child Development Scheme.* Government of India. http://icds-wcd.nic.in/icds.aspx

Misra, S., & Suresh, A. K. (2014, June 24). *Estimating employment elasticity of growth for the Indian economy.* Reserve Bank of India, RBI Working Paper Series No. 06. https://www.rbi.org.in/SCRIPTS/PublicationsView.aspx?id=15763

Mondal, B., Ghosh, J., Chakraborty, S., & Mitra, S. (2018). *Women workers in India: Labour force trends, occupational diversification and wage gaps.* Centre for Sustainable Employment, Azim Premji University.

Moser, C. (1993). *Gender planning and development-theory, practice and training.* Routledge.

Nair, S., & Verma, D. (2020, May 19). *A policy framework for India's Covid-19 migration.* International Labour Organization. www.ilo.org/newdelhi/info/public/fs/WCMS_746654/lang--en/index.htm

National Commission for Enterprises in the Unorganised Sector (NCEUS). (2015). *Report on conditions of work and promotion of livelihoods in the unorganised sector.* Ministry of Micro, Small and Medium Enterprises, Government of India. https://msme.gov.in/national-commission-enterprises-un-organised-sectornceus

National Crimes Record Bureau (NCRB). (2018). *Chapter 2A: Farmers' Suicides in India.* Government of India. https://ncrb.gov.in

National Rural Employment Guarantee Act. (2005). nrega.nic.in

National Rural Livelihood Mission (NRLM). (2017). *Manual for District 2017 National Rural Livelihood Mission manual for district-level functionaries.* https://darpg.gov.in/sites/default/files/National%20Rural%20Livilihood%20Mission.pdf

Pachauri, S. (2018). *Defeminisation of Indian agriculture.* Down to Earth. www.downtoearth.org.in/news/agriculture/defeminisation-of-indian-agriculture-59834

Patel, V. (1994). Women and structural adjustment in India. *Social Scientist, 22*(3/4), 16–34. www.jstor.org/stable/3517621

Patel, V. (2004, January 20). *Impact of economic globalization on women.* Presented at World Social Forum Seminar on 'Women for Just, Sustainable and Caring Trade', Mumbai.

Patel, V. (2020). Introduction: Changing contours of paid and unpaid work of women. *Social Change, 50*(1),7–11. https://journals.sagepub.com/doi/10.1177/0049085719901049

Patel, V. (2021). Gendered experiences of Covid-19: Women, labour and informal sector. *Economic and Political Weekly Engage, 56*(11). https://www.epw.in/engage/article/gendered-experiences-covid-19-women-labour-and

Patel, V., & Karne, M. (2006). *Macro-economic policies and the millennium development goals.* Gyan Publications.

Prevention of Sexual Harassment at Workplace Act. (2013). Ministry of Law and Justice. https://legislative.gov.in

PRS Legislative Research. (2020). *National family health survey 5 (NFHS-5).* International Institute of Population Sciences. https://prsindia.org/policy/vital-stats/national-family-health-survey-5#:~:text=TFRper cent2oisper cent2otheper cent2oaverageper cent2onumber,i.e.per cent2Cper cent2opopulationper cent2oreplacesper cent2oitself

Raman, S., & Rizvi, S. (2021, January 12). *India: As women's employment shifts to digital marketplace, gender pay gap and occupational segregation follows.* Business and Human Rights Resource Centre. www.business-humanrights.org/en/latest-news/india-as-womens-employment-shifts-to-digital-marketplace-gender-pay-gap-and-occupational-segregation-has-followed

Ratho, A. (2020, March). Promoting female participation in India's urban labour force. *Observer Research Foundation, Issue Brief, 348,* 2.

Reddy, A. A. (2018, July 24). *Here's why 40% of India's farmers want to quit.* Down to Earth. www.downtoearth.org.in/news/agriculture/here-s-why-40-of-india-s-farmers-want-to-quit-61177

Reserve Bank of India (RBI). (2019). *Report of the internal working group to review agricultural credit.*

Rukmini, S. (2019, June 10). *India's workforce is masculinising rapidly.* LIVEMINT. www.livemint.com/news/india/india-s-workforce-is-masculinising-rapidly-1560150389726.html

Sengupta, R. (2020, September 3). *Every day, 28 people dependent on farming die by suicide in India.* Down to Earth. www.downtoearth.org.in/news/agriculture/every-day-28-people-dependent-on-farming-die-by-suicide-in-india-73194

Shekhar, D. (2020). Women hold 17% of board positions in corporate India, but only 11% leadership roles. *Forbes India.* www.forbesindia.com/blog/missrepresent-women-gender-sexuality/women-hold-17-of-board-positions-in-corporate-india-but-only-11-leadership-roles

Shiva, V. (2005). *Earth democracy: Justice, sustainability, and peace.* South End Press.

Taylor, M. (2016). The British royal family and the colonial empire from the Georgians to Prince George. In R. Aldrish & C. McCreery (Eds.), *Crowns and colonies: European monarchies and overseas empires* (pp. 38–39). Manchester University Press.

Thakur, A. (2019, July 22). India enters 37-year period of demographic dividend. *Economic Times.* https://economictimes.indiatimes.com/news/economy/indicators/india-enters-37-year-period-of-demographic-dividend/articleshow/70324782.cms?from=md

Tongia, R. (2019, September 30). India's biggest challenge: The future of farming. *The India Forum*. www.theindiaforum.in/article/india-s-biggest-challenge-future-farming

Transgender Persons (Protection of Rights) Act. (2019). www.indiacode.nic.in

UN Women. (1995). *Fourth world conference on women. Action for equality, development and peace.*

UN Population Fund (UNFPA). (2020). *State of the world population 2020*. www.drishtiias.com/daily-updates/daily-news-analysis/state-of-the-world-population-2020-unfpa

Uniyal, M. (2019, April 3). For more gender equity in India's workforce, more women must get online. *Stanford Social Innovation Review*. https://ssir.org/articles/entry/for_more_gender_equity_in_indias_workforce_more_women_must_get_online

Velayudhan, M. (2020). The labour side of the story: Informalisation and new forms of mobilisation of Kerala's women workers. *Social Change, 50*(1), 109–20.

Vyas, M. (2022, January 18). Some unemployment puzzles: Why are so many young boys and girls keen to work but are not actively looking for work?. *Business Standard*. www.business-standard.com/article/opinion/some-unemployment-puzzles-122011701322_1.html

Wheebox. (2021). *India skills report 2020: Reimagining India's talent landscape for a $5T economy*. https://cse.azimpremjiuniversity.edu.in/state-of-working-india/swi-2021

Workmen's Compensation Act. (1923). Ministry of Labour and Employment. https://labour.gov.in

World Bank. (2020a). *Labour force participation rate, female (% of female population aged 15+) (modelled ILO estimate) — India*. www.catalyst.org/research/women-in-the-workforce-india

World Bank. (2020b). *Labour force participation rate, male (% of male population age 15+) (modelled ILO estimate) — India*. www.catalyst.org/research/women-in-the-workforce-india

World Bank. (2020c). *Labour force, female (per cent of total labour force) India*. https://data.worldbank.org/indicator/SL.TLF.TOTL.FE.ZS?locations=IN

World Bank. (2020d). *Women, business and the law*. https://openknowledge.worldbank.org/bitstream/handle/10986/32639/9781464815324.pdf?sequence=10

World Factbook. (2020). *India, people and society*. Central Intelligence Agency.

India in focus: Women, technology and the future of work

Bardhan, K. (1985). Women's work, welfare and status: Forces of tradition and change in India. *Economic and Political Weekly, 20*(50), 2207–20.

Basole, A., Abraham, R., Lahoti, R., Kesar, S., Jha, M., Nath, P., Kapoor, R., Mandela, S., Shrivastava, A., Dasgupta, Z., Gupta, G., & Narayanan, R. (2021). *State of working India 2021: One year of Covid-19.* Centre for Sustainable Employment. Karnataka: Azim Premji University, https://cse.azimpremjiuniversity.edu.in/wp-content/uploads/2021/08/SWI2021_August_WEB.pdf

Basole, A., Idiculla, M., Narayanan, R., Nagendra, H., & Mundoli, S. (2019). *State of working India 2019: Strengthening towns through sustainable employment: A job guarantee programme for urban India.* Centre for Sustainable Employment, Karanataka: Azim Premji University. https://cse.azimpremjiuniversity.edu.in/wp-content/uploads/2019/04/SWI2019_Urban_Job_Guarantee.pdf

Berg, J., Furrer, M., Harmon, E., Rani, U. and Silberman, M. (2018). Digital labour platforms and the future of work. In *Towards decent work in the online world. Rapport de l'OIT.* ILO.

Bhatt, V., Grover, S., & Sharma, A. (2020). *Mumbai working papers 2020–2023.* Indira Gandhi Institute of Development Research, Mumbai, India.

Chauhan, P. (2021). Gendering COVID-19: Impact of the pandemic on women's burden of unpaid work in India. *Gender Issues, 38,* 395–419.

Deshpande, A. (2020). *The Covid-19 pandemic and lockdown: First order effects on gender gaps in employment and domestic time use in India.* GLO Discussion Paper Series No. 607. Global Labour Organization, Essen.

Deshpande, A., & Kabeer, N. (2019). *(In)visibility, care and cultural barriers: The size and shape of women's work in India.* Discussion Paper No. 04/19. Department of Economics, Ashoka University.

Dewan, S., & Ernst, E. (2020). *Rethinking the world of work.* International Monetary Fund. www.imf.org/en/Publications/fandd/issues/2020/12/rethinking-the-world-of-work-dewan

Esteve-Volart, B. (2004). *Gender discrimination and growth: Theory and evidence from India.* LSE STICERD Research Paper No. DEDPS42. London School of Economics and Political Science.

Fletcher, E., Pande, R., & Moore, C. (2017). *Women and work in India: Descriptive evidence and a review of potential policies.* CID Working Papers (339). Harvard University, Cambridge, MA.

GSM Association. (2022). *The mobile gender gap Report 2022.* www.gsma.com/r/wp-content/uploads/2022/06/The-Mobile-Gender-Gap-Report-2022.pdf?utm_source=website&utm_medium=download-button&utm_campaign=gender-gap-2022

Hill, E., Baird, M., Vromen, A., Cooper, R., Meers, Z., & Probyn, E. (2019). Young women and men: Imagined futures of work and family formation in Australia. *Journal of Sociology, 55*(4), 778–98.

International Labour Organization (ILO). (2018). *Emerging technologies and the future of work in India.* ILO Asia Pacific working paper series. Decent Work Team for South Asia and Country Office for India.

Jayachandran, S. (2021). Social norms as a barrier to women's employment in developing countries. *IMF Economic Review, 69*(3), 576–95.

Kumar, S. (2021, August 3). India's female labour participation rate falls to 16.1% as pandemic hits jobs. *Reuters.* www.reuters.com/world/india/indias-female-labour-participation-rate-falls-161-pandemic-hits-jobs-2021-08-03

Kumar, S., & Preet, P. (2020). Manual scavenging: Women face double discrimination as caste and gender converge. *Economic and Political Weekly — Engage, 55*(26–27). www.epw.in/engage/article/manual-scavenging-women-face-double-discrimination-caste-gender

Madgavkar, A., Manyika, J., Krishnan, M., Ellingrud, K., Yee, L., Woetzel, J., Chui, M., Hunt, V., & Balakrishnan, S. (2019). *The future of women at work: Transitions in the age of automation.* McKinsey Global Institute 4.

Mehta, B., & Awasthi, I. (2019). Industry 4.0 and future of work in India. *FIIB Business Review, 8*(1), 9–16.

Mehta, B., Awasthi, I., & Mehta, N. (2021). Women's employment and digital technology: A regional analysis in India. *Indian Journal of Human Development, 15*(3), 427–42.

Ministry of Statistics and Program Implementation (MoSPI). (2021). *Periodic labour force surveys.* Government of India. http://mospi.nic.in/Periodic-Labour-Surveys

Mongey, S., Pilossoph, L., & Weinberg, A. (2020). *Which workers bear the burden of social distancing?* Working Paper No. 27085. National Bureau of Economic Research.

Nair, M., Shah, K., & Sivaraman, A. (2020). *Will women be a part of India's future workforce? A quest for inclusive and sustainable growth in India.* Occasional Paper Series 61. Southern Voice.

Nathan, D., & Ahmed, N. (2018). Technological change and employment: Creative destruction. *The Indian Journal of Labour Economics, 61,* 281–98. https://doi.org/10.1007/s41027-018-0137-0

National Statistical Office and Ministry of Statistics and Program Implementation. (2019). *Time use survey.* Government of India. http://mospi.nic.in/time-use-survey-0

Nayana, T., & Kumar, S. (2019). The contribution of vocational education and training in skilling India. In D. Guile and L. Unwin (Eds.), *The Wiley handbook of vocational education and training.* https://doi.org/10.1002/9781119098713.ch24

Nikore, M., & Ishita, U. (2021, August 22). *India's gendered digital divide: How the absence of digital access is leaving women behind.* Observer Research Foundation. www.orfonline.org/expert-speak/indias-gendered-digital-divide

Nirmala, A., & Parthasarathy, G. (1999). Marginalisation hypothesis and post Green Revolution period. In A. Sharma and T. Papola (Eds.), *Gender and employment in India.* Indian Society of Labour Economics, Vikas Publishing House.

7. WORKING WOMEN IN SRI LANKA

Abeywickrama, L. M., Sandika, A. L., Sooriyaarachchi, P., & Vidanapathirana, I. (2017). *Impacts of banning glyphosate on agriculture sector in Sri Lanka: A field evaluation.* Faculty of Agriculture, University of Ruhuna. www.croplifeasia.org/wp-content/uploads/2018/11/Impacts-of-Banning-Glyphosate-on-Agriculture-Sector-in-Sri-Lanka-A-Field-Evaluation.pdf

Amnesty International. (2021, April 15). *Saudi Arabia: Dozens of Sri Lankan women wrongfully detained for months due to abusive kafala system.* www.amnesty.org/en/latest/news/2021/04/saudi-arabia-dozens-of-sri-lankan-women-wrongfully-detained-for-months-due-to-abusive-kafala-system

Aoun, R. (2020). *COVID-19 impact on female migrant domestic workers in the Middle East.* GBV AoR Helpdesk, 2020–2005.

Arunatillake, N. (2017, July 27). *Women in the Sri Lankan workforce: Dissecting education and female labour force participation.* Talking Economics. www.ips.lk/talkingeconomics/2017/07/27/women-in-the-sri-lankan-workforce-dissecting-education-and-female-labour-force-participation

Asian Development Bank (ADB) and International Labour Organization (ILO). (2017). *Sri Lanka: Fostering workforce skills through education: Employment diagnostic study.* www.adb.org/sites/default/files/publication/382296/sri-lanka-employment-diagnostic.pdf

Athukorala, P. C. (2012). *Sri Lanka's trade policy: Reverting to dirigisme?* Working papers in trade and development, Australia National University. https://acde.crawford.anu.edu.au/sites/default/files/publication/acde_crawford_anu_edu_au/2016-10/wp_econ_2012_14_athukorala.pdf

Bandaranayake, R., Iqbal, T., Galpaya, H., Senanayake, L., & Perampalam, S. (2020). *'Now we are independent': Female online freelancers in India and Sri Lanka.* Paper presented at the International Conference on Gender Research.

Central Bank of Sri Lanka. (2022). *CCPI based headline inflation recorded at 54.6% on year-on-year basis in June 2022.* https://www.cbsl.gov.lk/sites/default/files/cbslweb_documents/press/pr/press_20220630_inflation_in_june_2022_ccpi_e.pdf

Dabindu Collective. (2021, April 28). *The voice of working people should not be silenced by the pandemic — Da Bindu Collective.* www.dabinducollective.org/the-voice-of-working-people-should-not-be-silenced-by-the-pandemic-da-bindu-collective/

Daily Financial Times. (2020, July 6). SL's descent to lower middle income: Strategise to move up to high-income level. www.ft.lk/Columnists/SL-s-descent-to-lower-middle-income-Strategise-to-move-up-to-high-income-level/4-702627

Daily Financial Times. (2020, October 27). Trade unions, civil society groups say manpower workers in self-quarantine face crisis. www.ft.lk/news/Trade-unions-civil-society-groups-say-manpower-workers-in-self-quarantine-face-crisis/56-708107

Department of Census and Statistics (DCS). (2017). *Sri Lanka time use survey — Final report 2017.* www.statistics.gov.lk/Resource/PressReleases/TUS_FinalReport_2017.pdf

Department of Census and Statistics (DCS). (2019a). *Population in Sri Lanka by census year and sex.* www.statistics.gov.lk/GenderStatistics/StaticalInformation/Population/PopulationSriLankaCensusYearSex

Department of Census and Statistics (DCS). (2019b). *Sri Lanka labour force survey: Annual report 2019.* www.statistics.gov.lk/LabourForce/StaticalInformation/AnnualReports/2019

Department of Census and Statistics (DCS). (2020). *Sri Lanka labour force statistics quarterly bulletin: Sri Lanka labour force survey 1st quarter — 2020.* www.statistics.gov.lk/Resource/en/LabourForce/Bulletins/LFS_Q1_Bulletin_2020

Department of Census and Statistics (DCS). (2021). *Sri Lanka annual GDP at current prices and GDP shares.* www.statistics.gov.lk

Department of Labour (n.d.). *Labour code of Sri Lanka.* www.labourdept.gov.lk/index.php?option=com_content&id=65&Itemid=59&lang=en

Dissanayaka, N., & Hussain A. (2013). *Impact of worklife balance on employees performance: An empirical study on seven apparel organizations in Sri Lanka.* Conference: 3rd international symposium at South Eastern University of Sri Lanka, Oluvil, Sri Lanka.

Dissanayake, K. (2017). *Teleworking as a mode of working for women in Sri Lanka: Concept, challenges and prospects.* Institute of Developing Economies, Japan External Trade Organization (JETRO).

Economynext. (2021, January 28). *Sri Lanka tenth best country in handling Covid pandemic.* https://economynext.com/sri-lanka-tenth-best-country-in-handling-covid-pandemic-78313

Forum-Asia. (2021, June 14). *[Joint Statement] Sri Lanka: Protect Free Trade Zone workers and abide by treaty obligations.* www.forum-asia.org/?p=35060

Galpaya, H., Perampalam, S., & Senanayake, L. (2018). Investigating the potential for micro-work and online-freelancing in Sri Lanka. In L. Pupillo, E. Noam, & L. Waverman (Eds.), *Digitized labor.* Springer.

Global Forest Watch. (n.d.). *Sri Lanka (Dashboard).* www.globalforestwatch.org/dashboards/country/LKA

Halton, M. (2018, March 8). Climate change 'impacts women more than men'. *BBC.* www.bbc.com/news/science-environment-43294221

Hansson, H., Mozelius, P., Gaiani, S., & Meegammana, N. (2010). *Women empowerment in rural areas through the usage of telecentres — a Sri Lankan case study.* Paper presented at the 2010 International Conference on Advances in ICT for Emerging Regions (ICTer).

Human Rights Watch. (2007). *Exported and exposed: Abuses against Sri Lankan domestic workers in Saudi Arabia, Kuwait, Lebanon, and the United Arab Emirates. Human Rights Watch 19(16 C).* www.hrw.org/reports/2007/srilanka1107/index.htm

International Finance Corporation (IFC). (2019). *Realizing sustainability through diversity: The case for gender diversity among Sri Lanka's business leadership.* www.ifc.org/wps/wcm/connect/c6cbb7b1-54e5-44f1-893f-6deae41440dd/The_Case_Gender_Diversity_Among_Sri_Lanka_Business_Leadership.pdf?MOD=AJPERES

International Labour Organization (ILO). (2016). *Factors affecting women's labour force participation in Sri Lanka.* ILO Country Office for Sri Lanka and the Maldives.

International Labour Organization (ILO). (2019). *Future of work in Sri Lanka: Shaping technology transitions for a brighter future.* www.ilo.org/wcmsp5/groups/public/---asia/---ro-bangkok/---ilo-colombo/documents/meetingdocument/wcms_677979.pdf

International Labour Organization (ILO). (2020a). *Domestic workers and decent work in Sri Lanka.* ILO Country Office for Sri Lanka and the Maldives. www.ilo.org/wcmsp5/groups/public/---asia/---ro-bangkok/---ilo-colombo/documents/publication/wcms_768671.pdf

International Labour Organization (ILO). (2020b). *Green jobs in Sri Lanka: Linkages between environmental sustainability and decent work.* www.ilo.org/wcmsp5/groups/public/---asia/---ro-bangkok/documents/publication/wcms_755006.pdf

International Labour Organization (ILO). (n.d.). *Ratifications for Sri Lanka.* www.ilo.org/dyn/normlex/en/f?p=NORMLEXPUB:11200:0::NO::P11200_COUNTRY_ID:103172

Karunaratne, H. D. (2012). *International labour migration, remittances and income inequality in a developing country: The case of Sri Lanka.* www.researchgate.net/publication/32051449_International_Labour_Migration_Remittances_and_Income_Inequality_in_a_Developing_Country_The_Case_of_Sri_Lanka

Kotikula, A., & Solotaroff, J. (2006). *Gender analysis of labor in Sri Lanka's estate sector.* World Bank. https://paa2007.princeton.edu/papers/71572

Kottegoda, S., Perera, S., & Emmanuel, S. (2012). *CITIGEN policy brief: ICT access for women from the margins: Lessons from Sri Lanka.* CITIGEN Asia Research Programme 2010–2012.

Kumara, S. K., & Weerakkody, P. R. (2011). *Changing role of women in rural agrarian communities.* Hector Kobbekaduwa Agrarian Research and Training Institute.

Liyanage, P., & Ekanayake, E. A. (2021). *Identification of the factor structure affecting work from home during Covid-19 outbreak in Sri Lankan context.* University of Kelaniya.

Madurawala, S. (2017). The dwindling stitching hands: Labour shortages in the apparel industry in Sri Lanka. *Talking Economics.*

Marambe, B., & Herath, S. (2020). Banning of herbicides and the impact on agriculture: The case of glyphosate in Sri Lanka. *Weed Science, 68*(3), 246–52.

McKinsey Global Institute. (2018). *The power of parity: Advancing women's equality in Asia Pacific.* www.mckinsey.com/featured-insights/gender-equality/the-power-of-parity-advancing-womens-equality-in-asia-pacific

Meegaswatta, T. N. K. (2021). The balancing act: Employed women navigating the COVID-19 lockdown in Sri Lanka. *South Asian Survey, 28*(1), 157–71.

Otobe, N. (2013). *Globalization, employment and gender in the open economy of Sri Lanka.* ILO.

Padmasiri, B. (2020). Rural women, agrarian capitalism and the environment in Monaragala. *Polity, 8*(1 & 2), 29–34.

Rajapaksa, G. (2019). *Vistas of prosperity and splendour.* https://gota.lk/sri-lanka-podujana-peramuna-manifesto-english.pdf

Rajapaksa, M. (2010). *Mahinda Chintana: Vision for the future.* www.preventionweb.net/files/mahinda_chintana_vision_for_the_future_eng%5B1%5D.pdf

Ridley, M. (2022, July 14). Eco-extremism has brought Sri Lanka to its knees. *The Telegraph.* www.telegraph.co.uk/news/2022/07/14/eco-extremism-has-brought-sri-lanka-knees

Robinson, J., & Kengatharan, N. (2020). Exploring the effect of Covid-19 on small and medium enterprises: Early evidence from Sri Lanka. *Journal of Applied Economics and Business Research, 10*(2), 115–25.

Roser, M. (2014). *Fertility rate.* OurWorldInData. https://ourworldindata.org/fertility-rate

Semasinghe, W. M. (2017). Women's labor force participation in Sri Lanka: An inquiry into the factors influencing women's participation in the labor market. *International Journal of Social Science and Humanity, 7*(3), 184–87.

Sirisena, W. M. (1986). Invisible labour: A study of women's contribution to agriculture in two traditional villages in the dry zone of Sri Lanka. *Modern Sri Lankan Studies, 1*(2), 115–38.

Solotaroff, J. L., Joseph, G., & Kuriakose, A. T. (2017). *Getting to work: Unlocking women's potential in Sri Lanka's labor force*. World Bank.

Sri Lanka Bureau of Foreign Employment. (2016). *Annual statistical report of foreign employment 2016*. www.slbfe.lk/file.php?FID=334

Sri Lanka Bureau of Foreign Employment. (2018). *Annual statistics of foreign employment — 2018*. www.slbfe.lk/page.php?LID=1&MID=232

Tidball, S. (2011). *Migration of Sri Lankan women as housemaids to the Middle East*. Third Annual Interdisciplinary Conference on Human Trafficking. University of Nebraska.

UN Development Program (UNDP). (2020). *Country profile: Sri Lanka*. http://hdr.undp.org/sites/default/files/Country-Profiles/LKA.pdf

UN News. (2022, June 9). *Sri Lanka: UN appeals for $47 million for life-saving aid to 1.7 million people*. https://news.un.org/en/story/2022/06/1120032

University Grants Commission. (2019). *University admission*. https://ugc.ac.lk/downloads/statistics/stat_2019/Chapter2.pdf

Weeraratne, B. (2019). *The gender dimension of remittances to Sri Lanka: Who remits more?* Talking Economics. www.ips.lk/talkingeconomics/2019/12/18/the-gender-dimension-of-remittances-to-sri-lanka-who-remits-more

Weeraratne, B. (2020). *Sri Lankan migrants abroad: Results from a Rapid Online Survey during the Spread of CoVID-19*. Policy Discussion Brief, Institute of Policy Studies of Sri Lanka. www.ips.lk/wp-content/uploads/2020/04/Results-from-a-Rapid-Online-Survey-during-the-Spread-of-COVID19_4.pdf

Withers, M., Henderson, S., & Shivakoti, R. (2021, January). International migration, remittances and Covid-19: Economic implications and policy options for South Asia. *Journal of Asian Public Policy*, 1–16.

World Bank. (2012). *Sri Lanka — demographic transition: Facing the challenges of an aging population with few resources*. http://documents.worldbank.org/curated/en/441601468102549492/Sri-Lanka-Demographic-transition-facing-the-challenges-of-an-aging-population-with-few-resources

World Bank. (2016, February 16). *Sri Lanka: A systematic country diagnostic*. www.worldbank.org/en/news/feature/2016/02/15/sri-lanka-a-systematic-country-diagnostic

World Bank. (2021a). *Sri Lanka: Overview*. www.worldbank.org/en/country/srilanka/

overview#:~:text=Amid%20the%20COVID%2D19%20pandemic,many%20
countries%20fighting%20the%20pandemic

World Bank. (2021b). *World development indicators.* https://databank.worldbank.org/
source/world-development-indicators

World Economic Forum. (2021). *Global gender gap report 2021.* www.weforum.org/docs/
WEF_GGGR_2021.pdf

8. WORKING WOMEN IN FIJI

Aipira, C., Kidd, A., & Morioka, K. (2017). Climate change adaptation in Pacific countries:
Fostering resilience through gender equality. In W. L. Filho, *Climate change
adaptation in Pacific countries: Fostering resilience and improving the quality of life*
(pp. 225–39). Springer.

Asian Development Bank (ADB). (2018). *Women and business in the Pacific.* http://dx.doi.
org/10.22617/BKK178655-2

Asian Development Bank (ADB). (2020). *Tackling the COVID-19 youth employment crisis in
Asia and the Pacific.* www.adb.org/publications/covid-19-youth-employment-crisis-
asia-pacific

Bennett, K., Neef, A., & Varea, R. (2020). Embodying resilience: Narrating gendered
experiences of disasters in Fiji. In A. Neef & N. Pauli (Eds.), *Climate-induced
disasters in the Asia-Pacific region: Response, recovery, adaptation.* Emerald
Publishing Limited. www.emerald.com/insight/publication/doi/10.1108/S2040-
7262202022

Boccuzzi, E. (2021). *The future of work for women in the Pacific Islands.* The Asia Foundation.

Boege, V., & Shibata, R. (2020). *Climate change, relocation and peacebuilding in Fiji:
Challenges, debates, and ways forward.* Toda Peace Institute.

Carswell, S. (2003). A family business: Women, children and smallholder sugar cane
farming in Fiji. *Asia Pacific Viewpoint, 44*(2), 131–48.

Chand, G. (2000). Labour market deregulation in Fiji. In A. Haroon Akram-Lodhi (Ed.),
Confronting Fiji futures (pp. 153–77). Australian National University.

Chand, N. V., Zheng, H., Bi, J., & Kumar, A. (2020). Women farmer participation and its determinants in agricultural training programmes, for Central Division Fiji. *Journal of Culture, Society and Development, 57.*

Chattier, P. (2013). Does schooling and work empower women in Fiji? Or have gender inequalities persisted and why? *Global Change, Peace and Security, 25*(1), 61–76.

Cliffe, E. (2020). A feminist future for the Pacific. *The Humanitarian Leader,* Paper-009.

Connell, J. (2021). COVID-19 and tourism in Pacific SIDS: Lessons from Fiji, Vanuatu and Samoa? *The Round Table, 110*(1), 149–58.

Dahal, S., & Wagle, S. (2020). Rapid policy appraisal on employment, MSMEs and the informal sector in Fiji in the time of Covid-19. Institute for Integrated Development Studies. https://think-asia.org/handle/11540/12207

DataReportal. (2021, 11 February). *Digital 2021: Fiji.* https://datareportal.com/reports/digital-2021-fiji

Dodd, R., Shanthosh, J., Lung, T., Robaigau, A., Perman, M. L., Rafai, E., Poulos, R., Zwi, A. B., John, R., & Palagyi, A. (2021). Gender, health and ageing in Fiji: A mixed methods analysis. *International Journal for Equity in Health, 20*(205). https://doi.org/10.1186/s12939-021-01529-9

Employment Relations (Amendment) Act. (2020). www.ilo.org/dyn/natlex/natlex4.detail?p_lang=en&p_isn=76385

Employment Relations Promulgation. (2007). www.ilo.org/dyn/travail/docs/820/Employment%20Relations%20Promulgation%202007.pdf

Fagaiava-Muller, M. (2021). Division over NZ's RSE worker boost, Pacific reacts. *Radio New Zealand.* www.rnz.co.nz/international/pacific-news/442623/division-over-nz-s-rse-worker-boost-pacific-reacts

Farran, S. (2020). Balancing livelihoods with environmental protection: A case study from Fiji. *Environmental Law Review, 22*(4), 266–79.

Farrell, P., Thow, A. M., Wate, J. T., Nonga, N., Vatucawaqa, P., Brewer, T., Sharp, M. K., Farmery, A., Trevena, H., Reeve, E., Eriksson, H., Gonzalez, I., Mulcahy, G., Eurich, J. G., & Andrew, N. L. (2020). COVID-19 and Pacific food system resilience: Opportunities to build a robust response. *Food Security, 12*(4), 783–91.

Fiji Bureau of Statistics. (2018). *Statement on ethnicity: Statement from the Government Statistician.* www.statsfiji.gov.fj/census-2017/census.html

Fijian Government. (2020). *Fiji Country Gender Assessment.* www.fiji.gov.fj/Media-Centre/

News/FIJI-COUNTRY-GENDER-ASSESSMENT%E2%80%AC

Fiji Trades Union Congress (FTUC). (2020). *Impact of COVID-19 on employment and business: In-crisis rapid assessment: 13 May–19 June 2020 (Volume 1).* www.ilo.org/suva/publications/WCMS_754703/lang--en/index.htm

Fiji Women's Rights Movement (FWRM). (2018). *Decent work for Fijian women — a stagnant reality.* www.fwrm.org.fj/images/fwrm2017/balance/Balance-Dec-2018-PRINT-1.pdf

Fiji Women's Rights Movement (FWRM). (n.d.). *Our vision and mission.* www.fwrm.org.fj/about

Finau, G., & Scobie, M. (2021, May). Old ways and new means: Indigenous accountings during and beyond the pandemic. *Accounting, Auditing and Accountability Journal.*

Fleming, F., Josephine, A., Lotawa, J., Manley, M., Maraivalu, S., Mudaliar, D., Ranadi, E., & Reddy, M. (2019). *Promising practices from Fiji in empowering women economically — learnings from Talanoa Treks, Ra Naari Parishad, Rise Beyond the Reef and the Fiji Women's Fund.* https://search.issuelab.org/resource/promising-practices-from-fiji-in-empowering-women-economically-learnings-from-talanoa-treks-ra-naari-parishad-rise-beyond-the-reef-and-the-fiji-women-s-fund.html

Gerasimova, E. (2020). COVID-19 and labour law: Pacific island countries and Fiji. *Italian Labour Law e-Journal, 13*(1S).

Gounder, N. (2020). Fiji economic survey: Low growth the new normal? *Asia and the Pacific Policy Studies, 7*(2), 145–57.

Gounder, R. (2020). Economic vulnerabilities and livelihoods: Impact of COVID-19 in Fiji and Vanuatu. *Oceania, 90,* 107–13.

Herr, R. (2020). The new in the 'new normal' for the post-COVID Pacific Islands. *Asia-Pacific Bulletin, 510.*

International Labour Organization (ILO). (2006). *National Labour Law profile: Fiji.* www.ilo.org/ifpdial/information-resources/national-labour-law-profiles/WCMS_158895/lang--en/index.htm

International Labour Organization (ILO). (2017). *A study on the future of work in the Pacific.* www.ilo.org/wcmsp5/groups/public/---asia/---ro-bangkok/---ilo-suva/documents/publication/wcms_553880.pdf

International Labour Organization (ILO). (2020). *Pacific labour market review 2020: Pre-COVID-19 baseline labour market information for post-disaster recovery.* www.ilo.

org/suva/publications/WCMS_754824/lang--en/index.htm

International Labour Organization (ILO). (2021a). *Informal sectors of Fiji, Palau, Tonga and Vanuatu key to COVID-19 economic recovery*. https://www.ilo.org/suva/public-information/press-releases/WCMS_774071/lang--en/index.htm

International Labour Organization (ILO). (2021b). *Progress in organizing the informal economy in the Pacific*. www.ilo.org/suva/public-information/WCMS_798422/lang--en/index.htm

International Labour Organization (ILO) & Asian Development Bank (ADB). (2015). *Fiji: Creating quality jobs — employment diagnostic study*. www.adb.org/publications/fiji-creating-quality-jobs-employment-diagnostic-study

International Trade Union Confederation (ITUC). (2019). *ITUC condemns arrests of Fiji trade unionists*. www.ituc-csi.org/Fiji-trade-union-arrests

Kabutaulaka, T. (2020). COVID-19 and re-storying economic development in Oceania. *Oceania, 90*, 47–52.

Kaur, M., & Prasad, S. (2020). Fijian women — key providers to sustainable development goals (a case study of the University of Fiji). *Contemporary Research in Education and English Language Teaching, 2*(1), 1–15.

Khosla, V., & Pillay, P. (2020). COVID-19 in the South Pacific: Science communication, Facebook and 'coconut wireless'. *Journal of Science Communication, 19*(5), A07.

Kline, A. (2021). Highlighting women's voices in a climate change and livelihood narrative: A case study in a rural Fiji community. *Deep Blue Documents*. https://dx.doi.org/10.7302/968

Kopf, A., Fink, M., & Weber, E. (2020). In S. Amin, D. Watson, & C. Girard (Eds.), *Mapping Security in the Pacific* (pp. 119–32). Routledge.

Leal Filho, W., Lütz, J. M., Sattler, D. N., & Nunn, P. D. (2020). Coronavirus: COVID-19 transmission in Pacific small island developing states. *International Journal of Environmental Research and Public Health, 17*(15), 5409.

Leckie, J. (2000). Women in post-coup Fiji: Negotiating work through old and new realities. In A. Haroon Akram-Lodhi (Ed.), *Confronting Fiji futures* (pp. 178–201). Australian National University.

Leweniqila, I., & Vunibola, S. (2020). Food security in COVID-19: Insights from Indigenous Fijian communities. *Oceania, 90*(1), 81–88.

Loumoli, H., & Bhati, J. P. (2015). Quantifying role of seaweed (*Caulerpa racemosa*) harvesting in livelihood system of some coastal communities in Fiji. *The South Pacific Journal of Natural and Applied Sciences, 33*(2), 13–17.

Macrotrends. (2021). *Fiji population growth rate 1950–2021.* www.macrotrends.net/countries/FJI/fiji/population-growth-rate

Malo, M. Á. (2017). *Labour market institutions in small Pacific island countries: Main guidelines for labour market reforms.* https://mpra.ub.uni-muenchen.de/79988/

Market Development Facility. (2020). *Women at work: A comparative analysis of the absorption and retention of women in Fiji's workforce.* https://beamexchange.org/uploads/filer_public/5e/b9/5eb9f3e9-81de-42b8-bd48-1884953a778e/women-at-work_fiji__v6_spreads_compressed.pdf

McKinnon, K., Carnegie, M., Gibson, K., & Rowland, C. (2016). Gender equality and economic empowerment in the Solomon Islands and Fiji: A place-based approach. *Gender, Place and Culture, 23*(10), 1376–91.

McMichael, C., & Powell, T. (2021). Planned relocation and health: A case study from Fiji. *International Journal of Environmental Research and Public Health, 18*(8), 4355.

Michalena, E., Straza, T. R. A., Singh, P., Morris, C. W., & Hills, J. M. (2020). Promoting sustainable and inclusive oceans management in Pacific islands through women and science. *Marine Pollution Bulletin, 150,* 110711. https://doi.org/10.1016/j.marpolbul.2019.110711

Ministry for Social Welfare, Women and Poverty Alleviation. (2014). *Fiji national gender policy.* www.fiji.gov.fj/getattachment/db294b55-f2ca-4d44-bc81-f832e73cab6c/NATIONAL-GENDER-POLICY-AWARENESS.aspx

Movono, A., & Hughes, E. (2020). Tourism partnerships: Localizing the SDG agenda in Fiji. *Journal of Sustainable Tourism,* 1–15.

Naidu, S. (2016). Does human development influence women's labour force participation rate? Evidences from the Fiji Islands. *Social Indicators Research, 127*(3), 1067–84.

Narsey, W. (2007). *Gender issues in employment, underemployment and incomes in Fiji.* Fiji Islands Bureau of Statistics.

New Zealand Government. (2022). *Travel with the Pacific Islands.* https://covid19.govt.nz/international-travel/how-to-enter-new-zealand/travel-with-the-pacific-islands

Novaczek, I., & Stuart, E. K. (2006). The contribution of women entrepreneurs to the local economy in small islands: Seaplant-based micro-enterprise in Fiji and Vanuatu. *Journal of Small Business and Entrepreneurship, 19*(4), 367–79.

OECD. (2020, 1 April). *Women at the core of the fight against COVID-19 crisis.* www.oecd.org/coronavirus/policy-responses/women-at-the-core-of-the-fight-against-covid-19-crisis-553a8269

One News. (2021, 30 March). WorkSafe concerned following rapid rise in fruit picking injuries. www.tvnz.co.nz/one-news/new-zealand/worksafe-concerned-following-rapid-rise-in-fruit-picking-injuries

Pacific Women. (2020). *Pacific women shaping Pacific development.* https://pacificwomen.org/wp-content/uploads/2019/01/Fiji-Country-Plan-Summary_Overview-of-all-activities_Aug-2020.pdf

Parker, J., & Arrowsmith, J. (2014). Collective regulation and working women in New Zealand and Fiji. *Relations Industrielles/Industrial Relations, 69*(2), 388–416.

Parker, J., Nemani, T., Arrowsmith, J., Douglas, J., with Cooper, R., & McDonnell, N. (2011). *Comparative study on social dialogue and gender equality in New Zealand, Australia and Fiji.* Industrial and Employment Relations Department, International Labour Office. www.ilo.org/wcmsp5/groups/public/---ed_dialogue/---dialogue/documents/publication/wcms_175007.pdf

Parliament of the Republic of Fiji. (2019). *Members of Parliament.* www.parliament.gov.fj/members-of-parliament

Rahman, M. H., & Naz, R. (2006). Digital divide within society: An account of poverty, community and e-governance in Fiji. *E-Learning and Digital Media, 3*(3), 325–43.

Scheyvens, R., Movono, A., Strickland, D., Bibi, P., Tasere, A., Hills, G., Rihai, N., & Teama, F. (2020). *Development in a world of disorder: Tourism, COVID-19 and the adaptivity of South Pacific people.* Institute of Development Studies, Massey University. https://mro.massey.ac.nz/handle/10179/15742

Singh, P. (2020). *The role of women in community resilience to climate change: A case study of Votua village, Fiji.* www.pimrisregional.library.usp.ac.fj/gsdl/collect/usplibr1/index/assoc/HASH0167/966d1970.dir/doc.pdf

United Nations (UN). (2020). *Women's human rights in the changing world of work: Report of the Working Group on Discrimination Against Women and Girls.* Working Group on Discrimination Against Women and Girls. www.ohchr.org/en/documents/thematic-reports/ahrc4451-womens-human-rights-changing-world-work-report-working-group

UN Development Programme (UNDP). (2020). *Human development indicators: Fiji.* http://hdr.undp.org/en/countries/profiles/FJI

UN Population Fund (UNFPA). (2020). Impact of the COVID-19 pandemic on family planning and ending gender-based violence, female genital mutilation and child marriage. *Interim Tech Note 7.* www.unfpa.org/resources/impact-covid-19-pandemic-family-planning-and-ending-gender-based-violence-female-genital

UN Women. (2021). *Why women should be at the forefront of world's sustainable Covid-19 recovery.* https://asiapacific.unwomen.org/en/news-and-events/stories/2021/06/why-women-should-be-at-the-forefront-of-worlds-sustainable-covid-19-recovery

Van Deursen, A., Helsper, E., Eynon, R., & Van Dijk, J. (2017). The compoundness and sequentiality of digital inequality. *International Journal of Communication, 11,* 452–73.

Vunisea, A. (2016). The participation of women in fishing activities in Fiji. *SPC Women in Fisheries Information Bulletin, 27,* 19–28.

Waring, M. (2020). *Unpaid contributions are excluded from the primary data used to make public policy.* https://women.govt.nz/node/1460/marilyn-waring

World Bank. (2020). *World development indicators.* https://databank.worldbank.org/source/world-development-indicators

World Economic Forum. (2020). *Our recovery from the coronavirus crisis must have gender empowerment at its heart.* www.weforum.org/agenda/2020/05/industries-gender-women-coronavirus-covid19-economic

World Economic Forum. (2021). *Global gender gap report 2021.* www.weforum.org/reports/global-gender-gap-report-2021

World Health Organization (WHO). (2021). *Health and climate change: Country profile 2021: Fiji.* https://apps.who.int/iris/handle/10665/339493

9. WORKING WOMEN IN PAKISTAN

Accordini, M., Giuliani, C., & Gennari, M. (2018). Migration as a challenge to couple relationships: The point of view of Muslim women. *Societies, 8*(4), 1–22.

Ács, Z. J., Szerb, L., Autio, E., & Lloyd, A. (2018). *The global entrepreneurship index 2018.* The Global Entrepreneurship and Development Institute, 72–88.

Afshan, G., Shahid, S., & Tunio, M. N. (2021). Learning experiences of women entrepreneurs amidst COVID-19. *International Journal of Gender and Entrepreneurship, 13*(2), 162–86. https://doi.org/10.1108/IJGE-09-2020-0153

Ali, M. (2018). The China-Pakistan economic corridor: Tapping potential to achieve the 2030 agenda in Pakistan. *China Quarterly of International Strategic Studies, 4*(2), 301–25.

Amir, M. (2020, September 16). In Pakistan, rape culture is not only systemic, it is reinforced at every level. *Dawn News.* www.dawn.com/news/1580011

Amir, S., & Pande, R. (2018, September 11). *Are Pakistan's urban professional women immune to sexual harassment?* World Bank. https://blogs.worldbank.org/endpovertyinsouthasia/are-pakistan-s-urban-professional-women-immune-sexual-harassment

Arora, S., Straiton, M., Rechel, B., Bergland, A., & Debesay, J. (2019). Ethnic boundary-making in health care: Experiences of older Pakistani immigrant women in Norway. *Social Science and Medicine, 239*(112555), 1–8.

Asghar, H. (2020). *UN Women, NCSW launch Young Women in Pakistan: Status report 2020.* UN Women. https://asiapacific.unwomen.org/en/news-and-events/stories/2020/07/un-women-ncsw-launch-young-women-in-pakistan

Asian Development Bank (ADB). (2016). *ADB briefs: Policy brief on female labor force participation in Pakistan.* www.adb.org/sites/default/files/publication/209661/female-labor-force-participation-pakistan.pdf

Baker, J. (2019). *How Asia's female entrepreneurs are reshaping tech for good.* Reuters Events, Sustainable Business. www.reutersevents.com/sustainability/how-asias-female-entrepreneurs-are-reshaping-tech-good

Bakhtyar, M. (2019). *Voluntary National Review of progress towards the Sustainable Development Goals: Pakistan.* United Nations Susatinable Development.https://sustainabledevelopment.un.org/content/documents/233812019_06_15_VNR_2019_Pakistan_latest_version.pdf

Bari, F. (2020, September 18). Women in the informal sector. *Dawn News.* https://www.dawn.com/news/1580309/women-in-the-informal-sector

BBC. (2014, October 26). Who are the 100 Women 2014? www.bbc.com/news/world-29758792

BBC. (2019). Pakistan profile — Timeline. www.bbc.com/news/world-south-asia-12966786

BBC. (2021). BBC 100 Women 2021: Who is on the list this year? www.bbc.com/news/world-59514598

Bhattacharya, S. (2014). Status of women in Pakistan. *Journal of the Research Society of Pakistan, 51*(1), 179–211.

Business Insider. (2021). Pakistan's Islamic Council halts legislation on Domestic Violence Bill. www.business-standard.com/article/international/pakistan-s-islamic-council-halts-legislation-on-domestic-violence-bill-121071000094_1.html

ClimateLaunchPad. (2020). *Why women rock Pakistan's cleantech sector.* https://climatelaunchpad.org/why-women-rock-pakistans-cleantech-sector

Dutta, S., & Lanvin, B. (Eds.). (2020). *The Network Readiness Index 2020: Fostering digital transformation in a post-COVID global economy.* Portulans Institute.

Ebrahim, T. Z. (2020). Pakistan's younger women riding a digital wave in drive for better jobs. *Reuters.* www.reuters.com/article/us-pakistan-women-technology-feature-idUSKCN22A0AL

Eckstein, D., Künzel, V., Schäfer, L., & Winges, M. (2020). *Global Climate Risk Index 2020: Who suffers most from extreme weather events? Weather-related loss events in 2018 and 1999–2018.* Germanwatch.

Empower Foundation. (2018). *Circle Pakistan.* www.empower-foundation.org/circle-pakistan

Farooq, S., Gul, S., & Khan, M. Z. (2018). Role of trained women workforce in China-Pakistan Economic Corridor (CPEC): A gender gap analysis. *Putaj Humanities and Social Sciences, 25*(1), 49–58.

FitzGerald, J. (2021, May 21). The women fighting for digital equality. *BBC.* www.bbc.com/news/technology-57193791

Ghani, S. (2020). *20 powerful business ladies of Pakistan.* Pakistan Tour and Travel. https://pakistantourntravel.com/2020/10/09/20-powerful-business-ladies-of-pakistan

Global Climate Risk Index. (2020). www.germanwatch.org/sites/germanwatch.org/files/20-2-01e%20Global%20Climate%20Risk%20Index%202020_13.pdf

Government of Pakistan. (2012). *The Constitution of the Islamic Republic of Pakistan.* https://na.gov.pk/uploads/documents/1333523681_951.pdf

Giuliani, C., Olivari, M. G., & Alfieri, S. (2017). Being a 'good' son and a 'good' daughter: Voices of Muslim immigrant adolescents. *Social Sciences, 6*(4), 142, 1–20.

Hafeez, A., Shamsuddin, A., Nazeer, S., & Saeed, B. (2018). *Barriers and challenges for technology transfer in ecosystem of ICT sector of Pakistan.* International Conference on Technology Management, Business and Entrepreneurship, 1–9.

Haq, R. (2020, August 23). Pakistan gig economy: Women freelancers earning 10% more than men. *South Asia Investor Review.* www.southasiainvestor.com/2020/08/pakistan-gig-economy-women-freelancers.html

Hasan, N. Z. (2015). *Unscripting piety: Muslim women, Pakistani nationalism, and Islamic feminism.* PhD dissertation, York University, Toronto. https://yorkspace.library.yorku.ca/xmlui/bitstream/handle/10315/32188/Hasan_Nadia_Z_2015_PHD.pdf?sequence=2

Human Rights Watch. (2021). *Pakistan: Events of 2020.* www.hrw.org/world-report/2021/country-chapters/pakistan

Ijaz, S. (2019). *No room to bargain: Unfair and abusive labor practices in Pakistan.* Human Rights Watch. www.hrw.org/report/2019/01/24/no-room-bargain/unfair-and-abusive-labor-practices-pakistan

Institute for Economics and Peace. (2020). *Global Terrorism Index 2020: Measuring the impact of terrorism.*https://visionofhumanity.org/wp content/uploads/2020/11/GTI-2020-web-1.pdf

International Labour Organization (ILO). (2018). *Global wage report 2018/19: What lies behind gender pay gap.* www.ilo.org/islamabad/info/public/pr/WCMS_651658/lang--en/index.htm

International Labour Organization (ILO). (2020a). *MIGRANT: Female labour migration from Pakistan: A situation analysis.*

International Labour Organization (ILO). (2020b). *National labour law profiles: Pakistan.* www.ilo.org/ifpdial/information-resources/national-labour-law-profiles/lang--en/index.htm

Jamal, S. (2021, March 8). Women's Day: 10 Pakistani women inspiring the country. *Gulf News.* https://gulfnews.com/world/asia/pakistan/womens-day-10-pakistani-women-inspiring-the-country-1.77696239

Jatoi, B. (2020, May 5). The impact of Covid-19 on women and girls. *The Express Tribune.* https://tribune.com.pk/story/2214105/6-impact-covid-19-women-girls

Junaid, F. A., Haar, J., & Parker, J. (2018). Local employees working in a terrorist region: HR managers' perceptions. *Labour and Industry: A Journal of the Social and Economic Relations of Work, 28*(4), 279–302.

Kalsoom, Q. (2021). Covid-19: Experiences of teaching-mothers in Pakistan. *Journal of Gender Studies, 31*(3), 390–402.

Khalil, Z. K. (2018). *A profile of trade unionism and industrial relations in Pakistan.* ILO.

Khan, J., Yousaf, M., & Mufti, M. (2020). *This is how Pakistan is closing its skills gap.* World Economic Forum Agenda. www.weforum.org/agenda/2020/11/this-is-how-pakistan-is-closing-its-skills-gap

Kiani, K. (2017). Sustainable development: How far has Pakistan come and how far do we have to go? *Dawn.* www.dawn.com/news/1360165

Klugman, J., Gaye, A., Dahl, M., Dale, K., & Ortiz, E. (2019). *Women, peace, and security index 2019/20.* Report, Georgetown Institute for Women, Peace and Security and Peace Research Institute, Oslo.

Malik, A. A. (2019). On the margins: Women workers and the future of work, narratives in Pakistan. *Friedrich Ebert Stifung.* http://library.fes.de/pdf-files/bueros/pakistan/15670.pdf

Malik, M. (2021, July 7). Punjab raises workers' minimum wage to Rs20,000. *Dawn.* www.dawn.com/news/1621558

Malik, M., Basit, A., & Qazi, A. (2011). Unions and management: A case study of Pakistan Telecommunication Corporation. *Pakistan Journal of Social Sciences, 31*(1), 185–99.

Mohiuddin, I., Kamran, M. A., Jalilov, S. M., Ahmad, M. U. D., Adil, S. A., Ullah, R., & Khaliq, T. (2020). Scale and drivers of female agricultural labor: Evidence from Pakistan. *Sustainability, 12*(16), 1–15.

Mohyuddin, A., & Begum, N. (2013). Changing role of women due to technology at household level: A case study of village Chontra, district Rawalpindi, Pakistan. *Journal of Asian Development Studies, 2*(3), 98–108.

Mustafa, M., Mazhar, N., Asghar, A., Usmani, M. Z., Razaq, L., & Anderson, R. (2019). *Digital financial needs of micro-entrepreneur women in Pakistan: Is mobile money the answer?* CHI Conference on Human Factors in Computing Systems Proceedings (CHI 2019), May 4–9, 2019, Glasgow, Scotland.

Mustafa, F., Khursheed, A., Fatima, M., & Rao, M. (2021). Exploring the impact of COVID-19 pandemic on women entrepreneurs in Pakistan. *International Journal of Gender and Entrepreneurship, 13*(2), 187–203.

Naz, L. (2020, May 17). Women at work and the pandemic. *News on Sunday.* www.thenews.com.pk/tns/detail/659186-women-at-work-and-the-pandemic

Pakistan Bureau of Statistics (PBS). (2018). *Population and household survey of Pakistan 2017.* www.pbs.gov.pk/sites/default/files//press_releases/2017/Population_Census_2017_Results.pdf

Pakistan Bureau of Statistics (PBS). (2019). *Labour force survey.* www.pbs.gov.pk/publication/labour-force-survey-2018-19-annual-report

Pakistan Business Council (PBC). (2017). *Gender diversity in business sector of Pakistan: Baseline survey of Pakistan Business Council member companies.* www.pbc.org.pk/wp-content/uploads/Baseline-Survey-on-Gender-Diversity-in-Business-Sector-of-Pakistan.pdf

Pakistani Women in Computing (PWiC). (2021). *About PWiC.* https://pwic.org

Palmer, T., & Ajadi, S. (2020). *Sehat Kahani: Improving women's healthcare experience in Pakistan.* GSMA. www.gsma.com/mobilefordevelopment/wp-content/uploads/2020/04/sehat_kahani_improving_womens_healthcare_experience_in_pakistan.pdf

Payoneer. (2020). *The global gig-economy index: Cross-border freelancing trends that defined Q2 2019.* https://pubs.payoneer.com/images/q2_global_freelancing_index.pdf

Peters, A., & Saeed, J. (2017). *Promoting inclusive policy frameworks for countering violent extremism — bridging theory and practice: A Pakistani policewomen case study.* Georgetown Institute for Women, Peace and Security. www.inclusivesecurity.org/wp-content/uploads/2018/01/Pakistan-CVE.pdf

Pofeldt, E. (2019, August 18). The top 10 fastest growing freelance markets in the world. *Forbes.* www.forbes.com/sites/elainepofeldt/2019/08/18/the-top-10-fastest-growing-freelance-markets-in-the-world/?sh=20af6b19733b

Protection Against Harassment of Women at the Workplace Act. (2010). https://na.gov.pk/uploads/documents/1399368475_218.pdf

Quresh, U. (2020). *Women and girls must be at the center of Pakistan's Covid-19 recovery.* World Bank. https://blogs.worldbank.org/endpovertyinsouthasia/women-and-girls-must-be-center-pakistans-covid-19-recovery

Qureshi, R., & Hameed, N. (2019, November 5). *Inspiring a new generation of Pakistani women leaders in STEM*. World Bank. https://blogs.worldbank.org/endpovertyinsouthasia/inspiring-new-generation-pakistani-women-leaders-stem

Rana, I. A., Bhatti, S. S., Aslam, A. B., Jamshed, A., Ahmad, J., & Shah, A. A. (2021). COVID-19 risk perception and coping mechanisms: Does gender make a difference? *International Journal of Disaster Risk Reduction, 55*, 102096. https://doi.org/10.1016/j.ijdrr.2021.102096

Redaelli, S., & Rahman, N. (2021). *In Pakistan, women's representation in the workforce remains low*. World Bank. https://blogs.worldbank.org/endpovertyinsouthasia/pakistan-womens-representation-workforce-remains-low

Reuters. (2018). Factbox: Which are the world's 10 most dangerous countries for women? www.reuters.com/article/us-women-dangerous-poll-factbox-idUSKBN1JM01Z

Sadaquat, M. B., & Sheikh, Q. A. (2011). Employment situation of women in Pakistan. *International Journal of Social Economics, (38)*2, 98–113.

Safdar, M., & Yasmin, M. (2020). COVID-19: A threat to educated Muslim women's negotiated identity in Pakistan. *Gender, Work and Organization, 27*(5), 683–94.

Salam, S., Zeng, J., Pathan, Z. H., Latif, Z., & Shaheen, A. (2018). Impediments to the integration of ICT in public schools of contemporary societies: A review of literature. *Journal of Information Processing Systems, 14*(1), 252–69.

Sarfaraz, S. (2020, December 6). 12.7 percent in other countries: Women hold 1.8 percent of CFOs positions in Pakistan: SECP. *Business Recorder*. www.brecorder.com/news/40037845/127-percent-in-other-countries-women-hold-18-percent-of-cfos-positions-in-pakistan-secp

Sarwar, A., & Jadoon, A. K. (2020). Is globalization empowering women? A case study of District Lahore, Pakistan. *Pakistan Journal of Social and Clinical Psychology, 18*(1), 16–27.

Sehat Kahani. (2021). *Sehat Kahani — about us*. https://sehatkahani.com

Seigmann, K. A. (2010). Strengthening whom? The role of international migration for women and men in Northwest Pakistan. *Progress in Development Studies, 10*(4), 345–61.

Shabbar, S. (2022). Innovation deficiency in Pakistan. *Express Tribune*. https://tribune.com.pk/story/2335751/innovation-deficiency-in-pakistan

Shaikh, H. (2021). *Has Covid-19 exacerbated gender inequalities in Pakistan?* International Growth Centre. www.theigc.org/blog/has-covid-19-exacerbated-gender-inequalities-in-pakistan

Tanaka, S., & Muzones. M. (2016). *Female labor force participation in Asia: Key trends, constraints, and opportunities.* Asian Development Bank (ADB). www.adb.org/sites/default/files/publication/209661/female-labor-force-participation-pakistan.pdf

Tanwir, M., & Khemka, N. (2018). Breaking the silicon ceiling: Gender equality and information technology in Pakistan. *Gender, Technology and Development, 22*(2), 109–29.

Tanwir, M., & Sidebottom, R. (2019). The trade and gender nexus in Pakistan. *Journal of International Women's Studies, 20*(2), 129–50.

Tariq, F., & Bibler, S. (2020). *Gender impact of COVID-19 in Pakistan: Contextual analysis and the way forward.* International Foundation for Electoral Systems. www.ifes.org/sites/default/files/gender_impact_of_covid-19_in_pakistan_contextual_analysis_and_the_way_forward_may_2020.pdf

Toppa, S. (2018). Pakistan's gig economy helps smash obstacles to women working. *HuffPost.* www.huffpost.com/entry/gig-economy-pakistan_n_5ad9e8ffe4b03c426dadba73

United Nations (UN). (2020). *One UN Pakistan: Annual report 2020.* https://unsdg.un.org/sites/default/files/2021-04/UN-ResultsReport-2020-Pakistan.pdf

UN Climate Change. (2021). *Pakistani women sustainable entrepreneurs — Pakistan.* https://unfccc.int/climate-action/momentum-for-change/activity-database/momentum-for-change-pakistani-women-sustainable-entrepreneurs

UN Development Programme (UNDP). (2021, March 12). *Womenomics: Women powering the economy of Pakistan.* www.pk.undp.org/content/pakistan/en/home/library/development_policy/dap-special-edition-womenomics-march2021.html

UN Women Asia Pacific. (2021). *UN Women Pakistan.* https://asiapacific.unwomen.org/en/countries/pakistan

Viqar, F. (2019, October 26). Tech revolution: Are Pakistani women being left behind? *Express Tribune.* https://tribune.com.pk/story/2087194/tech-revolution-pakistani-women-left-behind

Women Development Department. (2020). *Women rights.* Government of Punjab. https://wdd.punjab.gov.pk/women_rights

World Bank. (2020). *Girls learn women earn: December 01, 2019–March 10, 2020.* www.worldbank.org/en/events/2019/12/01/girls-learn-women-earn

World Economic Forum. (2020). *Global gender gap report 2020.* www3.weforum.org/docs/WEF_GGGR_2020.pdf

Zafar, Z. (2017, August 21). How to stop female doctors from dropping out in Pakistan. *BBC.* www.bbc.com/news/av/magazine-41003627

Zahra-Malik, M. (2016). Pakistan parliament passes legislation against 'honor killings'. *Reuters.* www.reuters.com/article/us-pakistan-honourkillings-idUSKCN1261OK

Zakariya, S. (2019, November 3). Pushed to the margins. *News on Sunday.* www.thenews.com.pk/tns/detail/568797-big-break

10. WORKING WOMEN IN THE PHILIPPINES

Arago, D. (2021). *Underwriting economic exploitation, unpaid labour and social reproduction.* Paper presented at UNCTAD 15 Gender and Development Forum, Barbados, September.

Asian Development Bank (ADB). (2021, December 21). *COVID-19 and labor markets in Southeast Asia — impacts on Indonesia, Malaysia, the Philippines, Thailand, and Vietnam.* www.adb.org/sites/default/files/publication/758611/covid-19-labor-markets-southeast-asia.pdf

Asian Development Bank (ADB) and International Labour Organization (ILO). (2011). *Women and labour markets in Asia: Rebalancing towards gender equality in labour markets in Asia.* www.ilo.org/wcmsp5/groups/public/---asia/---ro-bangkok/documents/publication/wcms_154846.pdf

Australian Broadcasting Corporation (ABC). (2019, January 1). Philippines President Rodrigo Duterte says he sexually assaulted a sleeping maid. www.abc.net.au/news/2019-01-01/rodrigo-duterte-says-he-sexually-assaulted-a-maid/10677124

Buan, L. (2020). PH again lands on global top 10 worst countries for workers. *Rappler News Service.* www.rappler.com/nation/264355-philippines-ranked-top-10-worst-countries-workers-ituc-2020

Calleja, P. J. (2020, October 9). Domestic violence all the rage in Philippine lockdown.

UCA News. www.ucanews.com/news/domestic-violence-all-the-rage-in-philippine-lockdown/89821#

Center for Trade Union and Human Rights (CTUHR). (2020). *Trade Union Rights Report,* 2020.

Center for Women's Resources (CWR). (2021a, March 1). *CWR opens Women's Month 2021 with report of Filipino Women situation during pandemic.* https://centerforwomensresources.org/blog/2021/03/01/cwr-opens-womens-month-2021-with-report-of-filipino-women-situation-during-pandemic

Center for Women's Resources (CWR). (2021b). *Women from different sectors celebrate International Working Women's Month by collectively fighting for their right to health, livelihood and emancipation.* https://centerforwomensresources.org/blog/2021/03/08/women-from-different-sectors-celebrate-international-working-womens-month-by-collectively-fighting-for-their-right-to-health-livelihood-and-emancipation

CNN Philippines. (2020, August 18). Human rights activist gunned down in Bacolod. www.cnnphilippines.com/news/2020/8/18/Bacolod-human-rights-activist-Zara-Alvarez-killed.html

Commission on Human Rights (CHR) Philippines. (2020, April 5). *Statement of CHR Spokesperson, Atty. Jacqueline Ann de Guia, on rising incidences of domestic violence during COVID-19 lockdown.* https://chr.gov.ph/statement-of-chr-spokesperson-atty-jacqueline-ann-de-guia-on-rising-incidences-of-domestic-violence-during-covid-19-lockdown

Concepcion, D. V. P. A. (2021). *Health on hold: The hidden injuries of call centre work.* PhD thesis, La Trobe University, Victoria. https://opal.latrobe.edu.au/articles/thesis/Health_on_Hold_The_Hidden_Injuries_of_Call_Centre_Work/16934608

Cotter, K. (2021, September 8). *Answering your customer support calls in our own backyard.* Telstra (Australia). https://exchange.telstra.com.au/answering-your-customer-support-calls-in-our-own-backyard

Dela Cruz, E. (2021, April 15). Philippines lifts nine-year ban on new mines to boost revenues. *Reuters.* www.reuters.com/business/energy/philippines-lifts-nine-year-old-ban-new-mines-boost-revenues-2021-04-15

Department of Foreign Affairs. (2020). *Distribution on Filipinos overseas.* Government of the Philippines. https://dfa.gov.ph/distribution-of-filipinos-overseas

Department of Labor and Employment (DOLE). (2020, April). Work displacement breaches

1M mark — no work with pay pushed. *Philippine Labor, XXVIII*(4). www.dole.gov.ph/php_assets/uploads/2020/08/April.pdf

Ecumenical Institute for Labor Education and Research (EILER). (2012). Philippine BPO industry facts and figures. *EILER.* https://eiler.ph/wp-content/uploads/2017/02/BPO-briefer.pdf

Ellao, J. A. J. (2021, March 2). Nearly 20M Filipino women now 'economically insecure' — research group. *Bulatlat.* www.bulatlat.com/2021/03/02/nearly-20m-filipino-women-now-economically-insecure-research-group

Eviota, E. U. (1992). *The political economy of gender: Women and the sexual division of labour in the Philippines.* Zed Books.

Frianeza, M. P. (2003). Women in the informal sector in the Philippines: A situationer. *Review of Women's Studies, 13*(2), 179–85. https://drive.google.com/drive/folders/1lwDhLNcc9YaTUpjNuZqkxw3tkqQxX6jR

GABRIELA. (1998). Philippines women bearing the cross of globalization. *Women's International Network News, 24*(4), 62. https://anthkb.sitehost.iu.edu/a104/philippines/globalizationwomen1.htm

Gonzales, C. (2021, March 26). COVID-19 hits over 15,000 health workers — DOH. *Philippine Daily Inquirer.* https://newsinfo.inquirer.net/1411707/covid-19-hits-over-15000-health-workers-doh

Ibañez, J. P. (2021, December 17). Women, young people in PHL most affected by job cuts during pandemic, ADB says. *Business World.* www.bworldonline.com/top-stories/2021/12/17/418152/women-young-people-in-phl-most-affected-by-job-cuts-during-pandemic-adb-says

International Labour Organization (ILO) & Women in Informal Employment: Globalizing and Organizing (WIEGO). (2013). *Women and men in the informal economy: A statistical picture,* 2nd ed. www.ilo.org/wcmsp5/groups/public/---dgreports/---stat/documents/publication/wcms_234413.pdf

International Labour Organization (ILO). (2020). *COVID-19 labour market impact in the Philippines: Assessment and national policy responses.* www.ilo.org/wcmsp5/groups/public/---asia/---ro-bangkok/---ilo-manila/documents/publication/wcms_762209.pdf

International Trade Union Confederation (ITUC). (2019). *2019 Philippine Workers' and Trade Union Report on the UN Sustainable Development Goals (SDGs).* https://

www.ituc-csi.org/IMG/pdf/philippines_labour_assessment_on_national_sdg_
implementation.pdf

Karapatan. (2017, March 28). *Karapatan to PNP: Extrajudicial killings continue in PH.* [Press release].

Karapatan. (2020, January 30). *Creation of JIPCO: Institutionalizing massive workers' rights violations & re-affirming state's policy vs militant unionism.* www.karapatan. org/Creation+of+JIPCO%3A+Institutionalizing+Massive+Workers%E2%80%99+Ri ghts+Violations+%2526+Re-Affirming+State%E2%80%99s+Policy+vs+Militant+Un ionism

Lazo, L. (2015). *Challenges in the economic participation of women as entrepreneurs.* Policy Notes No 2015-03, PIDS (Philippine Institute for Development Studies). https:// pidswebs.pids.gov.ph/CDN/PUBLICATIONS/pidspn1503_rev.pdf

Leyesa, D., & Obanil, C. F. (2021, September 13). *SHE-cession: Struggles of Filipinas amidst the COVID-19 pandemic.* Heinrich Boll Stiftung Southeast Asia. https://th.boell.org/ en/2021/09/13/she-cession

Malig, J. A. (2020, January 23). Central Luzon police set up at eco-zones to prevent union organizing. *Rappler News Service.* www.rappler.com/nation/250037-central-luzon-police-set-up-economic-zones-prevent-union-organizing

Mohyuddin, S. I. (2017). Female migrant labor in the Philippines: The institutionalization of traditional gender roles in the name of economic development. *Pursuit — The Journal of Undergraduate Research at The University of Tennessee, 8*(1), Article 10.

Ocampo, S. C. (2015, October 30). Big plantations create big problems in Mindanao. *Philippine Star.* https://www.philstar.com/opinion/2015/10/30/1516822/big-plantations-create-big-problems-mindanao

OECD/Scalabrini Migration Center. (2017). *Interrelations between public policies, migration and development in the Philippines, OECD development pathways.* OECD Publishing. www.oecd-ilibrary.org/development/interrelations-between-public-policies-migration-and-development-in-the-philippines/migration-and-the-labour-market-in-the-philippines_9789264272286-8-en

Ortiguero, R. R. (2018, May 16). BPO sector: An economic pillar. *BusinessWorld.* www. bworldonline.com/features/2018/05/16/158392/bpo-sector-an-economic-pillar

Parreñas, R. S. (2000). Migrant Filipina domestic workers and the international division of reproductive labor. *Gender and Society, 14*(4), 560–580. www.jstor.org/stable/190302

Philippine Commission on Women (PCW). (2019a). *Monitoring and evaluation of gender equality and women's empowerment in the Philippines: A compendium of indicators, volume 1.* https://library.pcw.gov.ph/wp-content/uploads/2020/12/PCW-Monitoring-and-Evaluation-of-Gender-Equality-and-Womens-Empowerment-in-the-Philippines-A-Compendium-of-Indicators-Volume-I-March-2019.pdf

Philippine Commission on Women (PCW). (2019b). *Policy Brief No. 8, Magna Carta for Workers in the Informal Economy.* https://pcw.gov.ph/magna-carta-of-workers-in-the-informal-economy-2

Philippine Commission on Women (PCW). (2019c). *Philippines drops 8 places in gender equality, remains top in Asia.* www.weforum.org/reports/gender-gap-2020-report-100-years-pay-equality

Philippine Statistics Authority (PSA). (2009). *Women in Business Process Outsourcing industries.* https://psa.gov.ph/content/women-business-process-outsourcing-industries

Philippine Statistics Authority (PSA). (2018a). *2018 Annual labor and employment status.* https://psa.gov.ph/content/2018-annual-labor-and-employment-status

Philippine Statistics Authority (PSA). (2018b). *2018 gender statistics on labor and employment (GSLE).* https://psa.gov.ph/sites/default/files/2018%20Gender%20Statistics%20on%20Labor%20and%20Employment.pdf

Philippine Statistics Authority (PSA). (2020a). *Employment situation in July 2020.* https://psa.gov.ph/statistics/survey/labor-and-employment/labor-force-survey/title/Employment%20Situation%20in%20July%202020

Philippine Statistics Authority (PSA). (2020b). *Total number of OFWs estimated at 2.2 million.* https://psa.gov.ph/content/total-number-ofws-estimated-22-million

Philippine Statistics Authority (PSA). (2021a). *Unemployment rate in July 2021 is estimated at 6.9 percent.* https://psa.gov.ph/statistics/survey/labor-and-employment/labor-force-survey/title/Unemployment%20Rate%20in%20July%202021%20is%20Estimated%20at%206.9%20percent

Philippine Statistics Authority (PSA). (2021b). *National QuickStats, November 2021.* https://psa.gov.ph/sites/default/files/attachments/ird/quickstat/National-Quickstat-November2021_As%20of%20Nov29.xls

Philippine Statistics Authority (PSA). (2022). *Unemployment rate in January 2022 is estimated at 6.4 percent.* https://psa.gov.ph/content/unemployment-rate-january-2022-estimated-64-percent

Porras, R., & Maningat, J. C. (2015). *Action research on the multi-dimensional vulnerabilities of women workers in the informal sector.* Ecumenical Institute for Labor Education and Research. https://amrc.org.hk/sites/default/files/EILER-PH-Vulnerabilities%20of%20Women%20Workers%20in%20Urban%20Poor%20communities.pdf

Putzel, J. (1992). *Captive land: The politics of agrarian reform in the Philippines.* Catholic Institute for International Relations (CIIR).

Ranada, P. (2021, January 14). Sexist Duterte says Philippine presidency not a job for women. *Rappler.* www.rappler.com/nation/sexist-duterte-says-philippine-presidency-not-a-job-for-women

Regencia, T. (2018, February 12). Duterte: Shoot female rebels in their genitals. *Al Jazeera.* www.aljazeera.com/news/2018/2/12/duterte-shoot-female-rebels-in-their-genitals

Sainato, M. (2018, November 21). 'No other way to fight back': Philippines call center workers battle unfair quotas. *The Guardian.* www.theguardian.com/business/2018/nov/21/no-other-way-to-fight-back-philippines-call-center-workers-battle-unfair-quotas

Statista. (2022a). *Number of mobile phone users in the Philippines from 2017 to 2025 (in millions).* www.statista.com/forecasts/558756/number-of-mobile-internet-user-in-the-philippines

Statista. (2022b). *Telecommunications industry in the Philippines — statistics & facts.* www.statista.com/topics/5678/telecommunication-industry-in-the-philippines/#dossierKeyfigures

Tomacruz, S. (2020, July 24). Female frontliners who cope during this coronavirus pandemic. *Rappler.* www.rappler.com/newsbreak/in-depth/female-frontliners-cope-coronavirus-pandemic

UN Office of the High Commissioner for Human Rights (UNOHCHR). (2022). *UN treaty bodies database.* https://tbinternet.ohchr.org/_layouts/15/TreatyBodyExternal/Treaty.aspx?CountryID=137&Lang=EN

UN Women. (2017). *Policy brief 1: Women's labour migration — an overview from Mexico, Moldova and the Philippines.* www.unwomen.org/sites/default/files/Headquarters/

Attachments/Sections/Library/Publications/2017/Policy-brief-An-overview-of-pilot-countries-en.pdf

UN Women Asia Pacific. (2020a). *Gender snapshot: COVID-19 in the Philippines.* https://asiapacific.unwomen.org/sites/default/files/Field%20Office%20ESEAsia/Docs/Publications/2020/04/PHL-COVID%20Gender%20Snapshot%20April%202020.pdf

UN Women Asia Pacific. (2020b). *Gendered dimensions of COVID-19 in the Philippines.* https://asiapacific.unwomen.org/sites/default/files/Field%20Office%20ESEAsia/Docs/Publications/2020/06/FINAL-Gender%20Snapshot%202-PHL.pdf

Unson, J. (2018, September 25). Human rights volunteer ambushed in Maguindanao. *Philippine Star.* www.philstar.com/nation/2018/09/25/1854570/human-rights-volunteer-ambushed-maguindanao

Venzon, C. (2021, February 15). Philippines 'modern-day heroes' sent record remittances last year. *Nikkei Asia.* https://asia.nikkei.com/Economy/Philippines-modern-day-heroes-sent-record-remittances-last-year

Venzon, C. (2022, March 22). Philippines allows foreigners to own telcos, airlines and railways. *Nikkei Asia.* https://asia.nikkei.com/Economy/Philippines-allows-foreigners-to-own-telcos-airlines-and-railways

Women WISE3 (Women Workers in Struggle for Employment, Empowerment and Emancipation). (n.d.). *Research design for Feminist Participatory Action Research (FPAR).*

World Bank. (2019). *Population, female (% of total population) — Philippines.* https://data.worldbank.org/indicator/SP.POP.TOTL.FE.ZS?locations=PH

World Economic Forum. (2019). *The Philippines looks for ways to boost the number of women in jobs.* www.weforum.org/agenda/2019/10/philippines-women-work

The Philippines in focus: Breaking-in — union women and young leaders

ASEAN Trade Union Council (ATUC). (2018, September 5). *ASEAN unions form youth and women committee within ATUC.* http://aseantuc.org/2018/09/asean-unions-form-youth-and-women-committee-within-atuc-prepare-its-work-plan

Bagtas, C. (2019). *Briefing on the [project] baseline survey analysis.* PowerPoint slides, unpublished.

International Trade Union Confederation — Asia Pacific (ITUC-AP).
(2019). *4th Regional Conference: Action Programme 2019–2023,*
Conference Thematic Paper, Tokyo, Japan. https://uploads-ssl.webflow.
com/6177a47207bd8b3a8f4b6de9/61832bd5330ac81bdf24ac2e_ITUC-AP%20
Action%20Programme%202019%20-%202023.pdf

International Trade Union Confederation — Asia Pacific (ITUC-AP) & DGB Bildungswerk
(BW) & Asean Trade Union Congress (ATUC). (2020a, February 12). Non-verbatim
notes on ITUC-AP and ATUC leaders' conversation on women and youth participation
in trade unions at the Project Assembly and Launching, 25–26 July 2019, Bangkok,
Thailand. *NEWYs2GO, 2.* http://aseantuc.org/wp-content/uploads/2020/05/
NEWYs2Go-Newsletter_Issue-02.pdf

International Trade Union Confederation — Asia Pacific (ITUC-AP) & DGB Bildungswerk
(BW) & Asean Trade Union Congress (ATUC). (2020b, January 13). Strengthening
women and youth leadership within the trade union movement for decent
work in Southeast Asia (2019–2021) *NEWYs2GO, 1.* https://uploads-ssl.webflow.
com/6177a47207bd8b3a8f4b6de9/61832bd5330ac81bdf24ac2e_ITUC-AP%20
Action%20Programme%202019%20-%202023.pdf

National Trade Union Center (Philippines) (NTUC Phl). (2019a). *DGB-BW Project NTUC*
Phl Proposal. Unpublished.

National Trade Union Center (Philippines) (NTUC Phl). (2019b). *Who we are.* https://
ntucphl.org/2019/09/about-us

About the contributors

Daisy Arago is a long-time activist in the Philippines with more than 20 years' engagement in the labour movement. She is the executive director of the Center for Trade Union and Human Rights (CTUHR) in the Philippines, a focal member of the labour programme for the Thailand-based Asia Pacific Forum on Women, Law and Development (APWLD), and a member of the Board of Trustees of the Amsterdam-based Electronics Watch.

Cedric Bagtas has been the honorary general secretary of the National Trade Union Center since 2018, and is the deputy general secretary of the ASEAN Trade Union Council. He has held governing body positions in national centres and national unions, as well as tripartite posts, representing labour. Cedric was formerly an assistant professor and economist at the Center for Research and Communication and a professorial lecturer at the University of the Philippines' School of Labor and Industrial Relations. He holds a bachelor's in chemistry and master's in industrial economics.

Dr Marian Baird AO, FASSA is a professor of gender and employment relations, head of the Discipline of Work and Organisation Studies, and co-director of the Women and Work Research Group at the University of Sydney Business School in Australia. She is an internationally recognised scholar in the fields of industrial relations and women and work over the life cycle. Her research has a policy focus, and she has contributed to the development of government and company policies on maternity and parental leaves, flexibility, discrimination, and the ageing workforce.

Jane Brock has been a community activist since martial law was imposed in the Philippines in 1972 by the dictator Ferdinand Marcos. Together with her husband and young son, Jane moved to Geneva, Switzerland, where she became involved in sowing the seeds of a local chapter of Migrante, a Filipino migrant workers' organisation. She is a member of the International Coordinating Committee of the International League of Peoples' Struggle (ILPS). Jane works with the Sydney-based Immigrant Women's Speakout Association (IWSA) as an executive officer. Her work at IWSA includes advocacy for migrant women workers' rights.

Peter Brock is a lawyer and human rights activist in Sydney, Australia. He worked in the Philippines from 1986 to 1989 as a human rights researcher and has been active in solidarity for the Philippine people since 1983.

Elizabeth Broderick AO is an Australian lawyer. She was the Australian Sex Discrimination Commissioner from 2007 to 2015 and has been a United Nations special rapporteur for discrimination against women and girls since 2017. She was formerly a partner and head of legal technology at Ashurst Australia (then Blake Dawson Waldron), a global commercial law firm. Elizabeth is a board member of the International Service for Human Rights and a member of the Global Institute for Women's Leadership Advisory Council, Kings College London. She is an adjunct professor at the University of Sydney, and holds honorary doctorates of law from the University of Sydney, University of New South Wales and the University of Technology, and honorary doctorates from Deakin, Edith Cowan and Griffith universities.

Rae Cooper AO is a professor of gender, work and employment relations at the University of Sydney Business School and is an Australian Research Council future fellow. She is director of the University of Sydney Gender Equality in Working Life (GEWL) Research Initiative. Rae is president elect of the International Labour and Employment Relations Association

ABOUT THE CONTRIBUTORS 349

(ILERA) and is an executive member of several Australian industrial relations bodies. She has published widely in relation to work, industrial relations policy and women's working lives. Rae is known for her collaboration with labour market stakeholders, having collaborated on research projects with key organisations, including industry groups and businesses, governments at the state and national levels, and with unions and union peak councils. Rae has significant experience as a member and chair of government and community sector boards and committees.

Daniel Dinale completed his PhD thesis in the discipline of work and organisational studies at the University of Sydney Business School. He is affiliated as a researcher to the Centre of Excellence in Population Ageing Research (CEPAR). His research focuses on cross-national patterns of female labour force participation, fertility, and public policy regarding the reconciliation of employment and family. His publications include an article in the *International Journal of Care and Caring* on the effects of care strain on work withdrawal among Australian workers (2022), and he has contributed to *The Conversation* on how English-speaking countries have influenced the trade-off between having children and working.

Dr Noelle Donnelly is a senior lecturer at Victoria University of Wellington Te Herenga Waka, where she researches gender and workplace issues including pay inequity, flexible work, job quality and employee voice. She is a lead researcher with the Centre for Labour, Employment and Work (CLEW), co-editor in chief of *Labour and Industry: A Journal of the Social and Economic Relations of Work* and an editorial board member of the *International Journal of Human Resource Management*. Noelle is the current president of the Association of Industrial Relations Academics in Australia and New Zealand (AIRAANZ). She holds a PhD in industrial relations from the University of Warwick.

Dr Natalia D'Souza has research expertise in the management of workplace psychosocial hazards, with a specific focus on gendered outcomes. Her previous background in academia, most recently as a senior lecturer at Massey University, means she has taught, supervised and collaborated on projects related to healthy and decent work. She was also a named investigator on a NZ$1.2 million Health Research Council/Worksafe-funded intervention project aimed at improving wellbeing in small and medium enterprises in Aotearoa New Zealand. Natalia's publications include articles in the *Journal of Health Organization and Management, Personnel Review, Journal of Management and Organization* and *Safety Science*. Natalia is currently a social investment and strategic consultant at Habilis New Zealand, and is also on the board of directors at Netsafe, an independent non-profit online safety agency.

Professor Michele Ford is director of the Sydney Southeast Asia Centre at the University of Sydney, Australia, where she researches labour activism in Southeast Asia. Michele's work has been supported by Australian Research Council grants, including a Future Fellowship on trade union aid in Indonesia, Malaysia and Timor-Leste. She leads ARC Discovery projects on Myanmar's garment industry and Indonesia's commercial fishing industry, and a Linkage project on gender-based violence in Cambodia's construction industry. Her latest book is *Labor and Politics in Indonesia* (Cambridge, 2020, with Teri Caraway). Michele is also the editor of *Social Activism in Southeast Asia* (Routledge, 2013) and the co-editor of several volumes, including *Women, Work and Care in the Asia-Pacific* (Routledge, 2017).

Shingou Ikeda is a senior researcher at the Japan Institute for Labour Policy and Training (JILPT) and holds a Master of Arts from the Tokyo Institute of Technology. He has published in *Japan Labour Issues* and *Japan Labour Review* on workplace issues, including reduced working hours and eldercare; women's employment status and family responsibilities in Japan; and company size and childcare leave. Shingou has also authored numerous JILPT research reports over the past two decades, including a study on the consequences of post-industrialisation and increase in unmarried workers in Japan (2021). He is a member of the Japan Sociological Society and the Japan Society of Human Resource Management.

Dr Fatima Junaid is a senior lecturer at Massey University's School of Management, Palmerston North. Her research focuses on employee wellbeing, looking at the influence of psychosocial risks, trauma and organisational support. Fatima has taught management and organisational behaviour in New Zealand and Pakistan. She has been a consultant for large and small public and private organisations, and has delivered training for public sector employees. She coordinates the Women and Work Special Interest Group in Massey's School of Management, and has delivered online talks on women's stress and mental health. She holds a PhD in organisational behaviour from Massey University.

Thilini Meegaswatta is a lecturer in the Department of Language Studies at the Open University of Sri Lanka. She is engaged in doctoral research in Germany on gender and conflict in South Asia. Thilini's postgraduate research on gender in the context of Sri Lanka's war has resulted in a number of publications in the *Journal of International Women's Studies*, *South Asia: Journal of South Asian Studies*, and *Contemporary South Asia*. Her recent research has focused on the impact of Covid-19 on women, and her work has been published in the *South Asian Survey*. Thilini holds a master's in English studies from the University of Colombo.

Professor Jane Parker specialises in employment relations and human resource management. She is an associate fellow of the Industrial Relations Research Unit (University of Warwick), a member of the International Labour and Employment Relations Association (ILERA) Executive

Committee, and co-directs Massey University's People, Organisation, Work and Employment (MPOWER) Group. Jane has led many national and cross-national projects and consultancies, including for the International Labour Organization, Pacific Islands Forum Secretariat, UK ESRC and Eurofound. She is a co-editor in chief of *Labour and Industry*, an editorial board member of *Human Relations* and *Employee Relations*, and an associate editor of the *Journal of Organizational Effectiveness: People and Performance*. She holds a PhD (Industrial Relations) from the University of Warwick.

Vibhuti Patel retired as a professor from the Advanced Centre for Women's Studies in the School of Development Studies at the Tata Institute of Social Sciences, Mumbai, at the end of June 2020. She retired as a professor and head of the Economics Department at the SNDT Women's University in Mumbai in mid-2017, where she was the director of Postgraduate Studies and Research from 2006 to 2012. Vibhuti received her doctorate in economics from the University of Mumbai and was awarded a post-doctoral fellowship from the Association of Commonwealth Universities in 1992 to conduct research at the London School of Economics and Political Science in the UK. Vibhuti is the Chair of the Ethics Committee (IRB) of International Institute of Population Sciences (IIPS) in Mumbai. Over the past four decades, her work has focused on issues at the intersection of gender, development and social justice.

Kazufumi Sakai is a research associate at the Japan Institute for Labour Policy and Training (JILPT), which contributes to the planning of labour policies and their effective implementation, promotes the livelihood of workers, and develops the economy through comprehensive research projects on labour issues and policies. His publications include studies of the work–childcare balance of male workers in Japan for *Japan Labour Review*; JILPT research reports on work–life balance at small to medium-sized enterprises; and child and family care and the pursuit of vocational careers. Kazufumi holds a master's in sociology.

ABOUT THE CONTRIBUTORS

Dr Afia Saleem is a lecturer at the Institute of Management Sciences in Peshawar, Pakistan. She has taught human resource management and organisational behaviour for over a decade, and supervises research projects within her areas of specialisation using quantitative methods. Her research focus is on stress and employee outcomes. Afia holds a PhD in management from the above institute.

Dr Binitha V. Thampi is an associate professor at the Department of Humanities and Social Sciences at the Indian Institute of Technology Madras (IITM) in Chennai. She holds a PhD in development studies, and her research interests lie in the broad domain of gender and development. She has published several articles in international journals, including the *Journal of Marriage and Family* and the *Indian Journal of Gender Studies*. Binitha has also co-authored (with J. Devika) *New Lamps for Old: Gender: Paradoxes of Political Decentralization in Kerala* (Zubaan, 2011).

Dr Kristy Ward is a post-doctoral researcher in the Sydney Southeast Asia Centre at the University of Sydney. She researches labour movements in Southeast Asia, with a particular focus on their gendered and political dimensions. Kristy's research encompasses broader questions about politics of representation in civil society organisations, and the role of labour as a political actor. Her current projects examine gender-based violence at work in Cambodia's construction sector, and worker resilience and recovery in Cambodia's tourism sector. She has undertaken a wide variety of consultancies for international development and labour union organisations and received funding for her research from the Australian Research Council and the Asia Foundation.

Dr Kasuni Weerasinghe is a lecturer in the School of Management at Massey University, Auckland. She has a background in information systems and her research focuses on technology management, business-IT alignment, social media management and health information systems. Her work has appeared in journals, including the *Australasian Journal of Information Systems* and *Technology Forecasting and Social Change*. Kasuni's research has been presented at conferences, including the Australasian Conference on Information Systems and Pacific Asia Conference on Information Systems. She is a member of Massey University's Management Analytics and Decision-making research group in the School of Management, and she holds a PhD in management from Massey.

Huiping Xian is an associate professor in the School of Business at the University of Leicester. Her research interests include women's careers, qualitative research methods, cross-cultural research methods and language/translation issues in international research. Huiping's publications include articles in *Human Resource Management*, *International Journal of Human Resource Management* and *International Small Business Journal*. She is an associate editor of *International Journal of Organisation Theory and Behaviour* and co-chair of the Research Methodology and Research Practice Strategic Interests Group at the European Academy of Management. Huiping holds a PhD in human resource management from Manchester Metropolitan University.

Acknowledgements

We would like to thank the many people who have contributed to this book. The work by Elizabeth Broderick (former chair and current independent expert of the United Nations Human Rights Council's Working Group on Discrimination Against Women and Girls, as well as adjunct professor at the University of Sydney), and her team inspired its rationale: to explore key challenges and opportunities for working women around globalisation, technological development, sustainability and demographic shifts in countries of the Asia Pacific region. We appreciate their expertise, ability to listen well to advocates for change, and their conversion of dialogue into informative and motivational resources.

We also value the efforts of our country and shorter-item contributors in providing much-needed and insightful commentaries on a diverse range of nations in the Asia Pacific region. A special mention is due to Daniel Dinale (Researcher at the University of Sydney's Business School) who willingly constructed statistical datasets that helped to inform a number of the chapter analyses.

We would also like to thank those who helped us to coordinate authors for some of the chapter contributions, particularly Ana Tuvera (Gender Specialist at the International Trade Union Confederation — Asia Pacific), Professor Fang Lee Cooke (Professor of Human Resource Management and Asia Studies at Monash University in Australia), Professor Yanfei Zhou (Japan Institute for Labour Policy and Training [JILPT]), and the late Lina Cabaero (who established Asian Women at Work, a community-based organisation seeking to empower Asian women workers in Australia).

We were very fortunate to work with Tracey Borgfeldt and Anna Bowbyes at Massey University Press, who deftly shepherded us through the book publishing process.

We are also indebted to the Massey People, Organisation, Work and Employment Research (MPOWER) Group and Massey University Business School for providing financial assistance for this endeavour.

Jane, Marian, Noelle and Rae

INDEX

A

administrative and support services 53, 79, 122, 136, 228, 248
aged care *see* eldercare
ageing population 16–19
  Aotearoa New Zealand 18, 19, 52
  Australia 18, 70, 71–72, 82
  China 124, 126, 130
  Fiji 18, 210
  Japan 18, 19, 86, 88, 91, 92, 98, 99, 111, 113
  Sri Lanka 187, 188–89
agricultural sector 20, 35
  see also land degradation
  Aotearoa New Zealand 41
  Australia 78, 79
  Cambodia 134, 136, 139, 143
  Fiji 210, 214, 215
  India 150, 153, 154, 155, 159, 161–62, 164, 165, 168, 169, 173
  Japan 98, 99
  organic production 198–99
  Pakistan 223, 226, 234
  Philippines 26, 237, 238, 240, 245–46, 256–57
  Sri Lanka 183–84, 188, 196, 197, 198–99
algorithms 30, 73, 165
Alibaba platform 120–21, 122
Aotearoa New Zealand
  see also under individual topics, e.g. employment regulation; sustainability
  Caritas Aotearoa New Zealand 57
  legislation 41, 46–47, 49, 55, 58, 60
  New Zealand's Plan of Action

Against Forced Labour, People Trafficking and Slavery (2021) 57
  overview 40–41
  Wellbeing Budget (2021) 56, 58
  Women's Employment Action Plan (2022) 47, 55
apparel manufacturing *see* garment manufacturing
artificial intelligence (AI) 55, 150, 165, 172, 175
ASEAN Trade Union Council (ATUC) 260–61, 263
Australia
  see also under individual topics, e.g. employment regulation; sustainability
  Fair Work Commission 68
  legislation 68–70
  overview 61–63
automation 29, 53–54, 162, 163, 172, 176, 177, 213–14, 228, 256

B

Beijing Declaration and Platform for Action 243
birth rate 26
  Aotearoa New Zealand 16, 52
  China 23, 125, 130, 131
  India 154
  Japan 91, 92, 93, 98, 99, 106, 109
'brain drain' 25, 194, 208
breastfeeding 116, 242
bushfires 78, 80
business counselling 34, 122, 131
business process outsourcing *see* outsourcing services

C

call centres 162, 240, 257–58
Cambodia
  see also under individual topics, e.g. employment regulation; sustainability
  Arbitration Council 137–38
  IDPoor 146
  legacies of conflict and totalitarian rule 142
  legislation 136–37
  overview 133–34
care work 32, 33
  see also eldercare; family responsibilities; parenthood; and under men
  Aotearoa New Zealand 44, 45–46, 49, 56, 57
  Australia 26, 64, 65, 72–73, 81, 83
  Cambodia 141, 148
  China 128
  Fiji 211, 216
  India 156–57, 159, 172, 178, 181
  Japan 26, 102, 105, 109–13
  Pakistan 233
  Philippines 239, 241, 242
  Sri Lanka 184, 188, 191, 201
career development 30, 33, 34, 35, 75, 82, 93, 109, 125, 130, 147, 148, 157, 170, 199, 211
casual work 25–26, 153, 159, 177
  Aotearoa New Zealand 44, 49
  Australia 65
child labour 22, 24, 56, 57, 136, 137, 146, 252, 259
childcare services 32
  see also parenthood

Aotearoa New Zealand 46, 54
Australia 17, 71, 77, 82
Cambodia 139, 141
China 119, 126, 130
Japan 17, 91, 92–93, 105, 109
Philippines 242, 246, 259
Sri Lanka 186, 188, 190, 200
China
  see also under individual
    topics, e.g. employment
    regulation; sustainability
  legislation 115–16, 117, 119
  overview 114–15
Circle (Pakistani skills training
  initiative) 229
citizenship rights 34, 234
climate change 20, 21, 33, 34,
  197–98
  Aotearoa New Zealand 55–56
  Australia 78–80, 82–83
  Fiji 20, 214–16, 218, 219
  India 166–67, 171
  Pakistan 232
Climate Launchpad 232
collectivism 129, 223
community networks and
  services 34, 46, 77, 81, 104,
  215, 218, 251
Confucian traditions 120,
  124–25, 126
construction industry 44, 65,
  67, 98, 133, 135, 139–40, 141,
  146, 147–48
contract work 44, 90, 153, 168,
  239, 242
cost of living 79, 80, 82, 126
Covid-19 pandemic 13, 23–24,
  26, 27–28, 36, 37, 39
  Aotearoa New Zealand 42,
    43–44, 46, 47, 50–51,
    52–53, 54, 58, 59–60
  Australia 19, 64, 70–71,
    74–75, 76, 78, 81–82
  Cambodia 133, 141, 142, 143,
    144–46, 147
  China 114, 118–19, 127–29,
    130–32
  cross-national

recommendations 31–32
Fiji 204, 206, 207–09,
  211–13, 217, 219–20
India 150, 155, 160, 166,
  167–69, 171, 172, 173–75,
  178–79
Japan 88–89, 96–97, 99–100,
  104–05, 106, 107, 110–11
masculinisation of
  workforce 27, 42, 43, 59,
  64, 104, 128–29, 155, 167,
  178, 233, 238, 249–51
Pakistan 225, 229, 233,
  235, 236
Philippines 237–38, 246–52,
  253, 257, 258, 259, 262,
  268, 272
Sri Lanka 182–83, 184–85, 187,
  191, 193, 195–96, 201, 202
and technological
  change 29, 30–31, 35, 36,
  54, 81, 114, 150, 173–75,
  193, 213, 229, 233, 245, 257
cultural values and norms 216,
  218, 219, 230, 258
cyber bullying 228
cyber coolies 30, 165

D

data collection and
  monitoring 38–39, 70, 134,
  204–05, 212–13, 238, 254,
  255, 259
decision-making 38, 102, 142,
  153, 160, 171, 172, 185–86,
  223, 265
  climate change and disaster
    responses 34, 79, 81, 83,
    103, 167, 171, 215
  Fiji 204, 205, 212, 215, 216,
    218, 219
de-feminisation of the
  workforce 29, 159, 164, 169,
  213–14
  see also under Covid-19
    pandemic —
    masculinisation of the
    workforce

demography 14, 16–19
  Aotearoa New Zealand 16,
    18, 19, 51–53, 60
  Australia 16, 17, 18, 19, 70–73
  Cambodia 16, 18, 134, 139,
    142–43
  China 16, 17, 18, 114–15, 120,
    122, 123–25, 130
  cross-national
    recommendations 32–33
  Fiji 16, 18, 150, 209–12, 219
  India 16, 18, 154–60, 173
  Japan 16, 17, 19, 92–95, 109
  Pakistan 16, 17, 225–27
  Philippines 16, 246–47, 258
  Sri Lanka 16, 187–91
deregulation of labour
  markets 27, 46, 48, 245
Deutscher Gewerkschaftsbund
  Bildungswerk (DBG
  BW) 260
  project on women and youth
    participation in unions
    and elsewhere 263, 264
digital divide
  gendered 174, 175, 212, 229,
    235
  rural and urban areas 29,
    36, 212
digital literacy 145, 147, 193,
  213, 214, 229, 234–35
disability care and support
  services 30, 64, 69, 73, 81
  see also women living with a
    disability
disasters see natural disasters
discrimination 36, 37–38,
  57–58, 74, 151, 153, 188, 200,
  219
  see also positive
    discrimination
  Aotearoa New Zealand 57–
    58
  China 23, 114, 116, 117,
    118, 119–20, 122–23, 125,
    126–27, 130, 131
  Japan 17, 84, 86, 90, 91, 93,
    107, 109

Pakistan 223, 228
Philippines 239, 258–59
division of labour 20, 32
  Cambodia 148
  Fiji 204, 205, 211, 215, 216
  India 155, 157–58, 163, 178
  Japan 86, 102
  Philippines 244–45
domestic violence 24, 34
  Aotearoa New Zealand 57, 58, 60
  Australia 61, 69, 80–81, 82
  China 129
  Fiji 211–12
  India 168
  Pakistan 224, 225
  Philippines 252, 262
domestic work 14, 27, 38
  Aotearoa New Zealand 44, 58
  Cambodia 137, 146
  China 119, 128
  Fiji 204, 211
  India 156, 157, 159, 161, 165, 167, 168, 175, 180, 181
  Japan 85, 86, 93–95, 97
  Pakistan 234
  Philippines 239, 241, 242, 247
  Sri Lanka 185, 186, 188, 190, 201
double-income couples 89, 119

E
e-commerce 121, 150, 213
Economic Partnership Agreements (EPAs) 99
economy 16–17, 33
  Aotearoa New Zealand 41, 46, 48, 50, 53
  Australia 63, 78
  Cambodia 22, 134–35, 139, 148
  China 115, 119, 124, 127
  Fiji 213
  India 151, 161, 163, 167, 171
  Japan 85, 86, 89, 92
  Pakistan 22, 225, 226, 229, 231

Philippines 242, 245, 246, 254
Sri Lanka 182–84, 196–97, 200–01, 202
education 22–23, 24, 25, 35–36
  see also students, international; training
  Aotearoa New Zealand 44, 47, 48, 56
  Australia 61, 65, 67, 77
  Cambodia 143, 145–46
  China 118–19, 121, 125, 127, 128
  Fiji 210, 212, 213
  home schooling 128, 133, 150, 167, 178–79, 247, 248, 262
  India 149–50, 151, 153, 155, 156–57, 158–59, 160, 161, 167, 169, 171, 173, 178–79
  Japan 86, 98
  overseas education 98, 118–19
  Pakistan 227, 228, 230, 231, 233, 236
  Philippines 237, 247, 255, 262
  Sri Lanka 182, 189–91, 196, 200, 201
eldercare
  Aotearoa New Zealand 18
  Australia 18, 64, 72, 77, 78, 81, 82
  China 18, 122, 124–25, 126, 127, 130
  India 157, 163, 165, 167, 171, 180
  Japan 18, 94–95, 96, 111–12, 113
  Philippines 247, 259
  Sri Lanka 188–89, 190, 201
electricity sector 80, 82
electronics industry 85, 98, 162, 240, 250–51, 256
employment regulation 11
  Aotearoa New Zealand 41
  Australia 67–70, 79, 82
  Cambodia 133, 136–39

China 115–17
Fiji 204, 205–07
India 150–54
Japan 89–92, 107–08
Pakistan 222–23
Philippines 243–45, 259
Sri Lanka 185–87
entertainment workers 144, 146
  see also sex workers
entrepreneurship 34–35
  see also micro-businesses
  Aotearoa New Zealand 44
  China 114, 120–22, 123, 131
  Fiji 217, 218
  India 160, 164, 167, 170, 171–72
  Pakistan 231, 235
  Sri Lanka 186, 200
environmental management 20, 79
  see also sustainability
  India 166–67
  Philippines 257
  Sri Lanka 196–99
equal employment opportunities 38, 84, 109, 222, 258
equal pay 47, 116, 136, 151–53, 185
  see also gender pay gap (GPG)
ethnic pay gap (EPG) 44–45, 47
exploitive practices 20, 27, 29–30, 34
  Aotearoa New Zealand 50, 57
  Australia 78
  China 120, 122, 129
  India 161, 162
  Japan 101
  Pakistan 235
  Philippines 246, 259
  Sri Lanka 184–85, 187, 193, 195, 197, 198
extremism 232

F

fair pay agreements 60
families
  China 23, 114–15, 120,
    122–26, 129, 130, 131
  Fiji 211
  Japan 103, 111, 112
  Pakistan 223–24, 228, 234
family responsibilities 32, 36
  see also care work; eldercare;
    grandparental care;
    parenthood; unpaid work;
    work–life balance; and
    under men
  Aotearoa New Zealand 46,
    56
  Australia 64, 81
  Cambodia 139, 141
  China 123–25, 126–27
  Fiji 206
  India 156–57, 161, 166–67,
    178, 180
  Japan 90, 102, 109–13
  Philippines 238, 239, 242
  Sri Lanka 188, 191, 201
family violence *see* domestic
  violence
female-headed households 18,
  141, 142–43
fertility 16
  Aotearoa New
    Zealand 51, 52
  Australia 17, 19, 61, 70–71,
    73, 82
  China 17, 23, 124, 126
  India 18, 150, 173
  Japan 17
  Pakistan 17
  Sri Lanka 187, 188, 196
Fiji
  see also under individual
    topics, e.g. employment
    regulation; sustainability
  Bill of Rights 214
  Employment Relations
    Promulgation (2007) 205
  legislation 206
  overview 203–05

political coups 205–06
Fiji National Gender Policy
  (2014) 207
Fiji Women's Rights Movement
  (FWRM) 206
financial advice 34
financial literacy and
  management 52, 164–65,
  217
fisheries 35, 79, 98, 136, 210,
  211, 214, 215, 218
fixed-term work 44, 49, 85, 88,
  92, 93, 94, 105–06, 108, 239
flexibilisation of labour
  markets 27–28, 36, 48,
  60, 162
flexible working arrangements
  (FWA) 27–28, 32, 33, 155, 181
  Aotearoa New Zealand 47,
    48–49, 59
  Australia 68–69, 74
  Philippines 239, 251, 258
  Sri Lanka 189, 191, 193, 200
food industry and services 44,
  86, 98–99, 119, 135, 157, 159,
  162, 169, 171, 192, 235, 243,
  250, 251
food security 20, 80, 123, 141,
  163, 164, 169, 171, 173, 183,
  197, 211, 214, 216, 218
foreign direct investment
  (FDI) 25, 48, 118, 127, 139,
  147–48
foreign workers *see* labour
  migration
forests and forestry 79, 136,
  197
foundational economy 30
framework of the book 14, 15
free trade 28, 41, 76
free trade agreements 41, 48
future of work
  Aotearoa New Zealand
    54–55
  Australia 73, 81
  India 165, 173, 175–81

G

garment manufacturing
  Cambodia 25, 133, 134–35,
    137, 138, 139, 140–41, 142,
    143, 147–48
  India 157
  Philippines 240, 242, 243,
    246, 255
  Sri Lanka 25, 185, 187, 193,
    196–97
gender-based violence 20, 21,
  22, 47, 58, 60, 138, 147, 171,
  211–12, 216, 219, 224, 225,
  244, 246, 262
gender equity 11–12, 32, 39,
  172, 177, 203
  see also individual topics
  Aotearoa New Zealand 42,
    43, 46–47, 54, 55, 57–58,
    59–60
  Australia 61, 64–66, 68,
    73–74, 75, 76–77, 79–83
  ethical gender
    equality 89, 90
Gender Inequality Index 224
gender pay gap (GPG) 33
  Aotearoa New Zealand
    44–46, 47, 49, 52, 57, 59
  Australia 64, 68, 80
  Cambodia 144, 147
  China 119
  Fiji 211
  India 155, 165
  Japan 84, 89
  Pakistan 226, 235
  Philippines 239, 245, 254, 258
  Sri Lanka 184
gender roles and norms 20–21,
  25, 37, 83, 162
  see also paid and unpaid
    work combined; unpaid
    work
  Cambodia 139
  China 23, 120, 122, 124–25
  Fiji 203, 204, 211, 215, 216, 219
  India 157, 158, 165, 172,
    174, 177
  Japan 84, 85–86, 89, 90,

93–94, 97, 102–03, 105, 109–13

Pakistan 223–25

Philippines 239, 241, 246, 258

Sri Lanka 188, 199, 201–02

Generation Equality Forum, Paris, 2021 171

gig work 28, 30, 33, 44, 73, 149, 159, 165, 170, 172, 180, 192

see also platform labour market

Pakistan 227–28

Global Agenda for Sustainable Development 243

Global Entrepreneurship Index 231

Global Gender Gap Index 203, 226, 244

Global North 29–30, 140

Global South 29–30, 76, 162, 176

Global Terrorism Index 21

globalisation 24–28

Aotearoa New Zealand 25, 48–51, 60

Australia 25, 75–78

Cambodia 139–41

China 118–20

cross-national recommendations 36

Fiji 207–09, 219

India 149, 161–62, 172

Japan 25, 97–102

Pakistan 229–31

Philippines 245–46

Sri Lanka 193–96

grandparental care 73, 93, 126, 189

Green Revolution

India 164, 173

Philippines 256–57

H

harassment 74, 138, 147, 224, 267, 270

see also sexual harassment

healthcare sector 30

see also occupational safety and health

Aotearoa New Zealand 43–44, 56

Australia 63, 65, 67, 77, 79

Fiji 210, 216, 217

India 150, 153, 159–60, 161, 171, 172, 175

Japan 86, 88, 98, 104, 105, 106

Pakistan 231, 232

Philippines 246, 250, 255

Sri Lanka 184, 192

homeworking *see* working from home

honoraria 159–60

horticulture 171–72, 208

hospitality workforce 26, 43, 44, 57, 64, 78, 86, 88, 104, 106, 119, 128, 159, 167, 193, 246, 250

hours of work 73

men 65–66, 97, 110, 235

women 42, 43, 59, 65–66, 82, 97, 235

housing 47, 70–71, 80, 126, 171, 244

human resource management (HRM) 25, 91, 118, 227

see also recruitment practices

human rights 12, 26, 99–100, 102, 154, 171, 172, 223, 224, 231, 243, 252–54

Human Rights Watch 233

human trafficking 22, 56, 57, 58, 246

I

income security 206, 217

income supplementation and subsidies

Aotearoa New Zealand 43, 58

Cambodia 141

China 128

Fiji 207–08

India 169

Philippines 428

India

see also under individual topics, e.g. employment regulation; sustainability

Constitution of India 1950 151–52

Industrial Training Institutes (ITIs) 158–59, 163, 169, 170

legislation 151–54, 160, 179

National Urban Employment Guarantee Scheme proposal 180–81

overview 149–51

Rural Livelihood Missions 159, 170

Rural Women Banks 164–65

The State of Working India Report 2021 174–75

Towards Equality Report 155–56

Women Empowerment Policy 153

industrial training

foreign trainees in Japan 99–101, 106

India 158–59, 163–64, 169, 170

industries

see also construction; electronics industry; food industry and services; forests and forestry; manufacturing; mining; services sector

Aotearoa New Zealand 43–44

Australia 63, 65, 67, 79

Cambodia 134–35

Fiji 207

India 156–58, 159, 162–63, 169, 170

Japan 85, 86, 98–99

Philippines 238, 240, 249–50

Sri Lanka 183, 196–97

informal sector 11, 14, 21, 24, 26, 31, 33, 36, 39, 162

Aotearoa New Zealand 50, 57

Cambodia 21, 137, 139, 146, 147, 148

China 21, 122, 128, 129

Fiji 205, 206, 207, 217, 220
India 18, 21, 150, 157, 168, 169, 172, 176–77, 179, 180–81
Pakistan 21, 222–23, 226, 228, 231
Philippines 21, 242–43, 244, 249, 251, 254, 259
Sri Lanka 21, 185, 186, 189
information and communication technologies (ICT) 23, 28, 36, 95, 97, 106, 146, 149, 162, 170, 191–92, 212–13, 228, 229, 230
see also telecommunications services
insecure work 21, 22, 26, 32–33, 36
see also casual work; contract work; fixed-term work; gig work; informal sector; piece-rate labour; seasonal labour; sweatshops
Aotearoa New Zealand 42, 48–49, 59
Australia 70, 73
Cambodia 134, 139–40, 141, 146, 148
China 131–32
Fiji 204
India 153, 157–59, 165
Pakistan 226
Philippines 239, 245, 254, 257–58
Sri Lanka 184–85, 197
internal migration
Australia 62, 71
Cambodia 141
China 116, 127
India 161, 168
Pakistan 230
Philippines 246
International Labour Organization (ILO) 136, 222
Better Factories Cambodia Programme 137
Domestic Workers

Convention (2011) 186
Employment Relationship Recommendation (2006) 33, 170
Freedom of Association Convention (1948) 222
Home Work Convention (1996) 186
Maternity Protection Convention 2000 (2017) 152
Right to Organise and Collective Bargaining Convention (1949) 222
Violence and Harassment Convention (2019) 154, 186, 267, 270
Workers with Family Responsibilities Convention (1981) 186
International Trade Union Confederation — Asia Pacific (ITUC-AP) 260, 261
project on women and youth participation in unions and elsewhere 263, 264
internet 24, 114, 120–21, 145, 164, 174, 192, 212, 228, 229, 233, 250, 257, 272
intimate partner violence (IPV) 58
Islamic finance 235

J

Japan
see also under individual topics, e.g. employment regulation; sustainability
foreign technical worker intern trainee system 27, 99–101, 106
legislation 84–85, 86, 90–91, 92, 109, 110, 111, 113
overview 85–86
Specified Skilled Workers visa system 98–99
job displacement 27, 31, 35
job satisfaction 23–24, 105

K

kafala (sponsorship) system, Middle East 195
killings
honour killings 34, 223–24, 233
Philippines rights defenders 251, 252–53

L

labour force participation (LFP) rate for mature-aged workers 72, 88
labour force participation (LFP) rate for men
Aotearoa New Zealand 41–43
Australia 63–64
Cambodia 135
Fiji 209
India 149, 155, 156
Japan 87, 88
Philippines 238, 239, 242
Sri Lanka 184
labour force participation (LFP) rate for women 11, 25, 28, 33, 38
Aotearoa New Zealand 41–43, 48
Australia 63–64, 65, 71
Cambodia 133, 134, 135–36, 139, 146
China 114, 119, 126
Fiji 204, 209, 211, 217, 219
globalisation impacts
India 18, 149, 154–55, 156, 162, 173, 177, 179–80
Japan 85–86, 87, 88, 92, 105–06
Pakistan 17, 225, 226, 227, 234
Philippines 238, 239, 241
Sri Lanka 184, 186, 188, 189–91, 192, 196, 198, 200–01
labour force shortages 19, 26, 27, 33, 53, 78, 91, 92, 98, 99, 101, 105–06, 163, 208

see also skill shortages
labour-intensive industries 26, 155
labour markets
  see also deregulation of labour markets; employment regulation; flexibilisation of labour markets
  Aotearoa New Zealand 26, 44, 46–47, 48–49, 53
  Australia 26, 63–67
  Cambodia 139, 141, 147
  China 118
  Fiji 204
  Japan 84–85
  Pakistan 222–23
  Philippines 237, 238–39, 246
labour migration 21–22, 24, 26–27, 36, 38, 179
  Aotearoa New Zealand 28, 51, 57, 208
  Australia 76–77
  Cambodians working abroad 21–22, 147
  China 116
  Fijians working abroad 27, 208
  Filipinos working abroad 237, 240–41, 246, 259
  Indian women 179
  Japan 26, 98–102, 106
  Pakistanis working abroad 27, 229–30
  Sri Lankans working abroad 27, 187, 195–96
Laging, Precy 248–49
land degradation 70, 161, 197, 198
land tenure 35
  Philippines 237, 256
language skills 25, 98
leadership positions *see* managerial and leadership positions
leave entitlements 65, 130, 172
  see also parental leave

life expectancy 85, 187, 196
  Aotearoa New Zealand 16, 51–52
living standards 26–27, 194, 203
loans 35, 141, 142, 172, 217, 244, 257
  see also micro-credit finance
long-term care leave 86, 90, 109, 111, 112–13
low-paid work 25–26, 27, 30, 32, 140
  Aotearoa New Zealand 28, 29, 44, 45, 49, 50, 58, 60
  Australia 26, 78
  Cambodia 133, 134, 135, 139, 143
  China 119, 122, 131
  India 159, 161, 165, 177, 180
  Japan 26, 88, 99–100, 104, 111
  Pakistan 231
  Philippines 239, 243, 244, 245, 248, 251, 254, 256
low-skilled work 27
  see also unskilled labour
  Aotearoa New Zealand 28, 29, 49, 54, 60
  Cambodia 133, 134, 135, 136, 147
  China 119, 128, 129, 131
  Fiji 211
  India 157, 177
  Pakistan 228
  Philippines 241
  Sri Lanka 185, 192

M

managerial and leadership positions 30, 38
  Aotearoa New Zealand 30, 44, 45, 47, 58, 59
  Australia 30, 61, 64, 65
  Cambodia 135, 136
  China 116, 119, 122
  Fiji 211
  India 160, 166, 167
  Japan 84, 86, 90

  Pakistan 225, 227, 234
  Philippines 260–72
  Sri Lanka 184
  in unions 260–72
manual scavenging 179
manufacturing 63, 79, 95
  see also garment manufacturing
  Cambodia 134, 139, 144
  China 115, 119, 128
  India 150, 157, 158, 163, 165, 177, 180
  Philippines 239, 240, 242, 245, 255
Māori women, Aotearoa New Zealand 22, 28, 43, 44–45, 46, 47, 49, 52, 57, 58, 59, 60
married women 17, 84, 85, 92–93, 95, 96, 108, 120, 127, 142, 175, 189, 234
maternity leave *see* parental leave
men
  see also labour force participation (LFP) rate for men
  breadwinner model 65, 89, 94, 111, 112–13, 239
  care work 18, 94–95, 109–13, 130, 148, 156, 172, 188–89
  domestic work 93–94, 97, 106, 156
  family responsibilities 69–70, 94–95, 109–13, 130, 200
  hours of work 65–66, 97
mentoring 34, 131, 229, 232, 233, 235, 262
micro-businesses 24, 34, 131, 143, 160, 192, 207, 217, 218, 229, 233
micro-credit finance 34, 131, 162, 186, 235
migration
  see also internal migration; labour migration; nurses, migrant; students, international

Aotearoa New Zealand 19,
43, 45, 48–50, 51, 52–53, 59
Australia 19, 75–78
Cambodia 147
China 119
Fiji 208
India 163, 168
Japan 19, 97–102, 106
Pakistan 229–30
Philippines 51, 259
Sri Lanka 195–96
mining 26, 44, 63, 65, 67, 79,
116, 159, 214, 245
mobile technologies
Cambodia 143–44
China 114, 120–21
India 164, 174
Pakistan 228, 229
motherhood *see* parenthood
multinational corporations 25,
49, 118, 199, 227, 256
multiple job holding 44, 49

N
National Trade Union Centre
of the Philippines (NTUC
Phl) project 262, 263–72
natural disaster recovery and
relocation 20, 21, 24, 34,
80, 81
Fiji 215, 216
Japan 102–04, 107
natural disasters 20–21, 167,
197–98
Australia 78–79, 80–81, 82
Fiji 214, 215, 218
Japan 20–21, 102–03,
106–07
Sri Lanka 197
natural resources
Australia 63
Fiji 214–15
Sri Lanka 197–98
neoliberal ideology 25, 41, 76,
120, 161, 199, 245, 258
nurses, migrant 50, 77, 98, 99

O
occupational safety and
health 21, 34, 57, 144, 208
India 153, 154, 165, 166, 181
Philippines 244, 246, 250,
257, 259
Sri Lanka 185, 197, 199
occupations
Aotearoa New Zealand 44,
45, 53–54
Australia 73–74, 77
Cambodia 135–36
Fiji 211
India 178, 179
Japan 86
Pakistan 226–27, 228–29,
231
Philippines 239–40, 242–43,
254
one-child policy, China 17, 23,
120, 122–25, 126, 131
online freelancing 192,
227–28, 235
see also gig work; platform
labour market
online retailing 120–21, 129,
130–31, 175
outsourcing services 213, 240
see also call centres

P
Pacific Women (2020)
strategy 219
Pacific women, Aotearoa New
Zealand 28, 44–45, 47, 49,
50, 52, 57, 58, 59, 60
paid and unpaid work
combined 11, 19, 22, 31, 33
see also gender roles and
norms; unpaid work
Aotearoa New Zealand 46,
56, 57, 59
Australia 83
Cambodia 134, 135, 141
Fiji 204, 211
India 149, 150, 164, 168,
172, 178
Japan 86, 95, 97

Philippines 242
Sri Lanka 189, 191, 199–200,
201
Pak-China Economic
Corridor 235
Pakistan
see also under individual
topics, e.g. employment
regulation; sustainability
Agenda 2030 231
constitution 221, 222
legislation 222, 224
military coups and
dictatorships 221–22
overview 221–25
social media support groups
women's technology
initiatives
Pakistani Women in
Computing (PWiC) 229
parental leave 32
Australia 17, 65, 69–70,
71, 82
Cambodia 136, 138
China 127, 130
Fiji 206
India 152, 172
Japan 86, 90, 93, 109–10
Philippines 246
Sri Lanka 187, 188, 200
parenthood
see also care work;
family responsibilities;
grandparental care;
pregnancy and childbirth;
single parents; unpaid
work
Aotearoa New Zealand 42,
45–46, 49
Australia 64, 69–70, 71,
72–73, 81, 82
China 120, 122, 126–27
Fiji 211
India 157, 165, 178–79, 180
Japan 85, 88, 93–94, 95, 106
Philippines 247, 258–59
Sri Lanka 186, 188, 200, 201
part-time work 27, 168, 189

Aotearoa New Zealand 42, 43, 44, 45, 49
Australia 65, 72
India 149, 168
Japan 20, 85, 88, 89, 92, 93, 101, 103, 104, 105–06, 108
Sri Lanka 189
PassApp ride-hailing mobile technology 143–44
pay *see* fair pay agreements; gender pay gap (GPG); low-paid work
Philippines
  see also under individual topics, e.g. employment regulation; sustainability
  Anti-Terrorism Law (ATL) 251, 259
  Center for Trade Union and Human Rights (CTUHR) 240, 253
  Center for Women's Resources (CWR) 247, 253
  Commission on Human Rights (CHR) 252
  Gender Equality and Women's Empowerment (GEWE) Plan 2019–2025 243–44
  Joint Industrial Peace and Concern Office (JIPCO) 253
  killing of rights defenders 251, 252–53
  legislation 243, 251, 257
  Magna Carta of Women 243
  Magna Carta of Workers in the Informal Economy 244
  mail-order brides 51
  National Task Force to End Local Communist Armed Conflict (NTF-ELCAC) 251, 259
  National Trade Union Centre of the Philippines (NTUC Phl) project 262, 263–72
  overview 237–38

special economic zones (SEZs) 240, 242, 245, 251, 256
piece-rate labour 153, 163, 164
platform labour market 30, 33, 73, 149, 159, 170, 177–78, 180, 192
  see also gig work
positive discrimination 151, 235
poverty 16, 21, 24, 28, 33
  Aotearoa New Zealand 43, 52, 56, 57, 59
  Australia 18
  Cambodia 140, 143, 145, 148
  Fiji 18, 210, 212
  India 151, 161, 170, 171
  Japan 89, 106, 111
  Pakistan 226, 233
  Philippines 237, 242, 247, 252, 254
  Sri Lanka 196
precarious work *see* insecure work
pregnancy and childbirth 90, 100, 107, 109, 116, 126–27, 186, 212, 258–59
public sector
  Aotearoa New Zealand 45, 47, 59, 60
  China 119–20
  Fiji 206

R

recruitment practices 91, 116, 120, 122–23, 127, 131, 200, 239
regionalisation 24, 62
remittances
  from migrant workers 24, 27, 147, 195–96, 208, 229–30, 241, 246
  to rural households 141, 143, 146, 147
remote working 30–31, 36
  Aotearoa New Zealand 30, 54
  Australia 30, 69, 74–75, 82
  Fiji 213, 214

India 162
Japan 30, 95, 96, 97, 106, 110–11
Sri Lanka 191, 193
retail work 43, 44, 53, 57, 64, 101, 105, 128, 134
  see also online retailing
retirement 43, 52, 72, 90, 116–17, 254, 258
robotics 150, 162, 165, 172, 175
rural women 21, 29, 34, 38, 96, 121, 122, 145
  Fiji 18, 29, 210–11, 212, 215, 218
  India 155, 156, 161, 163, 164, 167, 169–70, 171–72, 175
  Philippines 257, 259
  Sri Lanka 186, 192
Rural Women Banks, India 164–65

S

safety in the workplace *see* occupational safety and health
seasonal labour 49, 208
self employment
  see also entrepreneurship
  Aotearoa New Zealand 44
  China 114, 123, 129, 131
  India 159, 168, 170, 171, 177
  Pakistan 233, 234
  Philippines 238, 242, 244
  Sri Lanka 185
self-help groups 164–65, 172
services sector 28
  see also social services
  Aotearoa New Zealand 41, 43, 45, 49, 53
  Australia 63
  Cambodia 136
  India 159, 177
  Japan 86, 104
  Pakistan 223
  Philippines 238, 239–40, 242, 243, 245, 246
  Sri Lanka 183
sex workers 144, 167, 169, 246

sexual harassment 34, 102, 107, 116, 120, 152, 160, 165, 186, 224, 239, 243, 259
sexual violence 21, 34, 57, 102, 147, 211–12, 225, 233, 252
single parents 20, 42, 80, 95
single women 17, 20, 85, 86, 89, 94, 95, 103, 111, 113, 142, 143, 169, 225
skill shortages 26, 228
  see also unskilled labour
skills training 31, 35, 36, 78, 106, 122, 131, 144–45, 148, 193, 200, 218, 229, 234, 236
  India 162, 169, 170, 171, 180–81
slavery 22, 56, 57
small businesses 34, 145, 207, 217, 232, 235, 242
social media 160, 213
  support groups 232–33
social services 44
  see also care work; childcare; community networks and services; disability care and support services; eldercare; healthcare sector
  Australia 63, 65, 67, 68, 77, 79
  Japan 86, 88, 99, 104, 111, 112
  mobile phone apps 143
social welfare 21, 28, 32–33, 76
  Aotearoa New Zealand 44, 52, 56
  China 23, 124, 126
  India 152, 153, 154, 163, 172, 180–81
Sri Lanka
  see also under individual topics, e.g. employment regulation; sustainability
  Free Trade Zones (FTZ) 187
  legislation 185–87
  overview 182–84
  telecentres (NenaSala) 193
STEMM (science, technology, engineering, mathematics and medicine) fields 30, 35, 54, 59, 73–74, 81, 82, 170, 189, 234

stereotypes 25, 37, 120, 158, 169, 239, 258
  see also gender roles and norms
street vending 146, 159
students, international 25–26, 76, 77–78, 101, 106, 119
superannuation 64, 72
supply chains
  disruptions 80, 214
  technology 144, 145, 162
  unequal distribution of benefits 140
sustainability 16, 19–24
  see also environmental management
  Aotearoa New Zealand 20, 21, 55–58, 60
  Australia 20, 21, 78–81, 82–83
  Cambodia 21–22, 145–47
  China 21, 23, 125–27
  cross-national recommendations 33–35
  Fiji 20, 214–16, 219, 220
  India 21, 166–67, 171
  Japan 20–21, 102–05, 106–07
  Pakistan 20, 21, 231–33
  Philippines 21, 252–55, 259
  Sri Lanka 20, 21, 196–99, 201
sweatshops 163

T

taxation 32, 130
tea production 198
technology 24, 28–31
  see also future of work; information and communication technologies (ICT)
  Aotearoa New Zealand 29, 30, 53–55, 56, 60
  Australia 30, 73–75, 82
  Cambodia 29, 133, 143–45
  China 29, 30, 120–23, 130–31
  cross-national recommendations 35–36

Fiji 29, 212–14, 218, 219, 220
Global South 29–30, 176
India 29, 30, 150, 162–65, 170–71, 173–81
Japan 29, 95–97, 106
Pakistan 29, 30, 225, 227–29, 231, 234–35
Philippines 255–58, 259
Sri Lanka 29, 191–93
telecommunications
  services 95, 96, 192, 257
  see also information and communication technologies (ICT)
teleworking see remote working
terrorism 21, 232, 249, 254
Te Tiriti o Waitangi (Treaty of Waitangi) 40
tourism 26, 104, 128, 159, 167, 189, 196
  Aotearoa New Zealand 41, 43, 208
  Cambodia 133, 135, 139, 141
  Fiji 207, 208, 209, 214
trade 24, 26, 28, 36
  see also free trade; free trade agreements
  Aotearoa New Zealand 41, 48, 51
  China 115, 128
  India 163, 173
  Pakistan 231
  Philippines 237
  Sri Lanka 25, 183, 184, 198
trade unions see unions
training 34, 144–45, 170
  see also industrial training; skills training
  Aotearoa New Zealand 44, 56
  Australia 78
  union participation and leadership, Philippines 268–69
transgender persons 153, 167, 169
'triple burden of work' (productive, reproductive and community roles) 211

INDEX 367

two-child policy, China 17, 23, 122, 125, 126, 130, 131

U

UN Climate Change 232
under-employment 23
  Aotearoa New Zealand 42–43, 44, 58, 59
  Australia 64
  India 164, 180
  Philippines 237, 238, 239, 245, 258
unemployment 34
  Aotearoa New Zealand 41, 42–43, 44, 53
  Australia 64
  Cambodia 135
  China 128, 129, 131
  Fiji 209, 218
  India 155, 157, 164, 167, 174–75, 180
  Japan 87, 103, 104
  Philippines 237–38, 245
  Sri Lanka 189, 190–91
unions 38
  Aotearoa New Zealand 41
  Australia 67–68
  Cambodia 134, 137–38
  Fiji 206
  India 154, 169, 172
  Japan 84
  Pakistan 222, 223, 226
  Philippines 245, 251, 252, 253, 254, 256, 257, 259, 260–72
United Nations
  2030 Agenda for Sustainable Development 32
  Committee on Economic, Social and Cultural Rights 258
  Convention on the Elimination of All Forms of Discrimination Against Women (CEDAW) 58, 90, 153, 205, 243, 258
  Gender Inequality Index (2020) 224

Human Development Index 85
Human Rights Council 12
Security Council Resolutions on Women, Peace and Security 243
Sustainable Development Goals (SDGs) 20, 21, 33–34, 56, 107, 203, 222, 224, 231–32, 252, 254, 255
Women Policy Briefs 241
Working Group on Discrimination Against Women and Girls 12
United Nations Conference on Trade and Development (UNCTAD), FDI attractiveness index 48
unpaid work 11, 19, 20, 21, 22, 31, 32, 33
  see also eldercare; family responsibilities; parenthood
  Aotearoa New Zealand 45–46, 47, 56, 57, 58, 59
  Australia 64, 73, 75, 81, 83
  Cambodia 134, 135, 139, 148
  China 128
  Fiji 204, 205, 211
  India 149, 150, 156–57, 158, 161, 165, 168, 172, 175, 180
  Japan 86
  Pakistan 231
  Philippines 238, 242, 247, 257, 259
  Sri Lanka 184, 188, 198
unskilled labour 45, 101, 157
  see also low-skilled work; skill shortages
urbanisation 95–96, 168, 173, 211, 216, 237
urban–rural divide 161, 175, 212, 257

V

violence 154, 186, 251, 252–53, 267, 270
  see also domestic violence;

gender-based violence; intimate partner violence (IPV); sexual violence
volunteer work 81, 103–04, 106, 158, 160

W

wage theft 21, 146, 147
waste collection and processing 159, 166
WhatsApp groups 165
women living with a disability 38, 49, 59, 259
  see also disability care and support services
Women, Peace and Security Index
WomenWise3, Philippines 239, 249, 250
working conditions 91, 99, 137, 138, 152, 153, 154, 206, 226
working from home 31
  Aotearoa New Zealand 48, 54
  Australia 64, 74–75, 81
  China 128
  India 150, 157, 158, 163, 164, 168, 178
  Japan 88, 96–97, 106, 110
  Pakistan 223, 229, 231, 234, 235
  Philippines 242–43, 244, 250, 262
  Sri Lanka 191, 193, 201
work–life balance 23, 36, 96, 109, 125, 127, 130, 189, 192, 199–200, 201
  see also care work; domestic work; family responsibilities; parenthood
World Bank 160, 183, 200, 229

Y

youth leadership 260–72

Z

zero-hour contracts 49

First published in 2023 by Massey University Press
Private Bag 102904, North Shore Mail Centre
Auckland 0745, New Zealand
www.masseypress.ac.nz

Text copyright © individual contributors, 2023

Design by Megan van Staden
Cover photographs by iStock

The moral right of the authors has been asserted

All rights reserved. Except as provided by the Copyright Act 1994, no part of this book may be reproduced, stored in or introduced into a retrieval system or transmitted in any form or by any means (electronic, mechanical, photocopying, recording or otherwise) without the prior written permission of both the copyright owner(s) and the publisher.

A catalogue record for this book is available from the National Library of New Zealand

Printed and bound in New Zealand by Ligare

ISBN: 978-1-99-101603-4
eISBN: 978-1-99-101632-4

The publisher is grateful for the support of MPOWER and Massey Business School